8.55

6P6-21-72

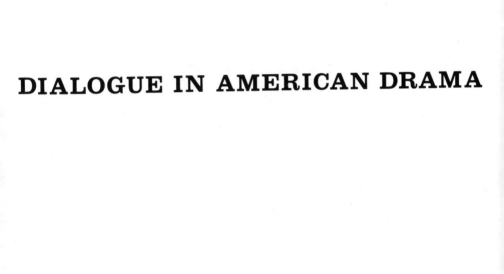

DIALOGUE IN AMERICAN DRAMA

DIALOGUE IN

Ruby Cohn

AMERICAN DRAMA

Indiana University Press

BLOOMINGTON / LONDON

TO EDMUND WILSON

WHO PROVOKED THIS BOOK

FOR THEIR HELP, I THANK
  Lester Beaurline
  Dolora Cunningham
  Donald Doub
  Bernard Dukore
  Daniel Gerould
  Neil Guiney
  Leon Katz
  Walter Meserve
  Kathleen Omura
  Linda Ramey

For permission to revise and reprint previously published material, I thank the editors of *Comparative Drama, Modern Drama,* University of Minnesota Press, and *Yale French Studies*

Contents

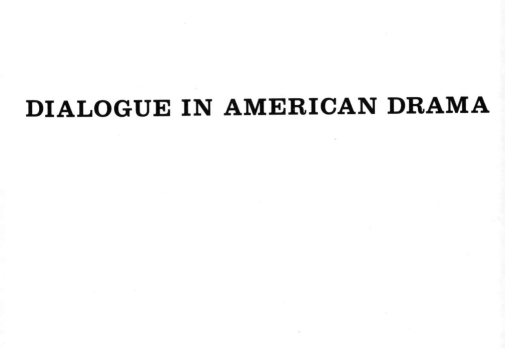

DIALOGUE IN AMERICAN DRAMA

1 / Artaud versus Aristotle

in America

ARISTOTLE AND ARTAUD ARE POLES APART. THE ONE IS AN ACCU-
rate critic, the other an erratic prophet; the one has been a
respectable power from his time to ours, the other a marginal
madman whose impact is recent. However we may comprehend
catharsis, the Aristotelian dramatist moves us through the rational intelligence; we follow a plot through meaningful words.
Aristotle's six parts of tragedy divide neatly in half: three belong
to dramaturgy (plot, character, and thought), and three to performance (spectacle, song, and diction). But Aristotle himself
focuses on plot, and he assumes that plot is conveyed mainly
through words—the dialogue of the drama.

However we may comprehend Artaud's cruelty, it entails
shock reaction. Artaud scorns the three parts of Aristotelian
dramaturgy, and most particularly thought in its garb of words.
His "Letters on Language" in *The Theatre and its Double* militate
against language. In the first letter, Artaud states his position
unequivocally: "In order to revive or simply to live, it is incum-
bent upon theater, an independent and autonomous art, to
emphasize what differentiates it from text, pure speech, literature, and all other fixed and written means." And in the last
letter: "Rhythmic repetitions of syllables and particular modu-
lations of the voice cloaking the precise sense of words, will
evoke great numbers of images in the brain by means of a more
or less hallucinatory state, and will impose upon the sensibility
and mind a kind of organic alteration which will help strip from
written poetry the gratuitousness that commonly characterizes

3

it. And it is around this gratuitousness that the whole problem of theater is centered."[1]

Artaud does not bar dialogue from the theater, but he refuses it the primacy that it has enjoyed in Western theater, as is evident from medieval papyri of Greek plays through carelessly printed Renaissance playscripts; from strict neoclassical rhythms through the dialects of realism. Even absurdist drama abounds in words, which are pregnant with intelligible meaning in context. But post-absurdist drama seeks a *Gestalt* in myth, ritual, incantation. Full circle to the putative genesis of Western drama, though Artaud drew inspiration from a half-invented East. After centuries of Aristotelian dramaturgy, Artaud is the vatic force of today's young theater.

Though theater dialogue continues to be written, it is today fading into the background in performance of what we may loosely call the New Theater. Theater innovators have become self-conscious about the whole of theater experience. In 1964 Samuel Beckett wrote a play called *Play*, and in 1966 Witold Gombrowicz wrote an operetta called *Operetta*. By 1970 the several theater productions of Grotowski, Barba, the Becks, and Chaikin—Artaud students all—can be called *Theater*. Their actors no longer flesh out a script with Aristotelian beginning, middle, and end. Instead, actors, director, playwright, and sometimes audience improvise and experiment toward a unique theatrical event. Afterwards, a script may be recorded, though that does not insure its inviolability.[2]

By 1970, often under the aegis of Artaud, theater events have taken place in many countries, but most numerously in the United States, and these events have tended to overlook linguistic distinction, or even distinctness. McLuhan reënforces Artaud in this anti-Aristotelian tendency: American theater people discovered Artaud at a time of visual assault by film and television, at a time of linguistic deterioration into pat phrases and routine rhetoric. So that pervasive mistrust of language nourishes the self-conscious theatricalism of today's theater.

It is from this terminus that I look back on some half-century of dialogue in American drama, which I take to begin with O'Neill. The hundred odd years of American performance that precede his work may be theater, or sociology, or preaching, or posing. But American drama—a written text that can be taken seriously for stage and page—begins with O'Neill. From this point of departure, I go on to examine the dialogue of what may appear to be an arbitrary selection of playwrights. But in setting the boundaries for a book, a critic depends upon his experience and sensibility. Mine prompted me not to waste formal analysis on the vast majority of Broadway plays. Instead, I limit my study to the few American playwrights who seem to me to have written original and distinctive dramatic dialogue, and to the many American writers who achieved distinction in fiction or poetry, but who also tried dramatic form.

In preparing the reader for the contents of this book, I find myself forced to begin with conclusions. Having read through (and often seen) plays of Maxwell Anderson, Philip Barry, S. N. Behrman, Lillian Hellman, Sidney Howard, Sidney Kingsley, even Clifford Odets, Elmer Rice, Robert Sherwood, I concluded that their language does not deserve extensive analysis. In spite of a plethora of words on stage—and a few atypical plays such as Hellman's *Little Foxes*, Kingsley's *Dead End*, Odets' *Awake and Sing!*, Rice's *Adding Machine*—most twentieth century American dramatists followed their predecessors in writing genteel, anonymous English. In the twentieth century, as in the nineteenth century, comic relief often entered in the form of dialect. Today we forget that O'Neill was celebrated and castigated for his raw language. But O'Neill fathered realistic American dialogue as he fathered serious American drama—especially in his efforts to render uneducated speech.

In this Arthur Miller is his heir. Lacking O'Neill's diversity, Miller has a truer ear for his own limited register. Though his plays have various settings, they are often expressed in simple language with a Jewish syntax. Employing repetition more discreetly than O'Neill, Miller appreciates the dramatic force of questions, hesitations, and inflections.

Almost an exact contemporary of Miller, Tennessee Williams brought to the stage the langorous rhythms and lyrical images of Southern speech, which caused him to be dubbed a dramatic poet. Unlike the flaccid blank verse and limping language of Maxwell Anderson, however, Williams' poetic prose can function dramatically, rather than decoratively.

5

Poetry is as poetry does, and dramatic poetry must further an action in Aristotelian dramaturgy. While doing just that, the dialogue of Edward Albee has drawn upon O'Neill's repetitions, Miller's inflections, and Williams' atmospheric imagery. But the idiomatic pungency and studied rhythms are his own.

A fleeting survey is probably unwarranted at this point, but I hope the book will substantiate it. Members of my generation tend to look back nostalgically at American drama, and they do not seem to hear the monotony of its language. Allergic to monotony, I deal only with those dramatists—four—whose dialogue achieves a recognizable style.

In contrast to dramatists, twentieth century American poets have often carved distinctive styles, and a surprising quantity of American poets have turned sporadically to drama. But the quantity was rarely productive of quality. Similarly, American novelists have strayed into dramatic form, with differently poor results. But novelists and poets had a negligible effect upon the mainstream of American drama, which has been channeled narrowly on to Broadway. Only after Broadway production have regional theaters and school texts come to most American plays, but I have nevertheless thought it useful to examine plays of novelists and poets in a kind of might-have-been spirit. If they had written dialogue of the quality of their fiction or verse, what a drama we might have had.

As is, the mainstream of American drama has coursed freely, but it seems to be slowing down to a trickle. More than eighty per cent of Broadway productions are no longer dramas but musicals; off Broadway the spirit of Artaud hovers over the Living Theater (no longer living in America, in 1970), the Open Theater, Judson Memorial and St. Marc-in-the-Bowerie Churches, Cafes la Mama and (the now defunct) Cino. That is to say, scripted dialogue is being replaced by incantation, improvisation, laboratory, participation, life style. How that may affect future drama—if there is a future drama—remains an open question.

For the present, I propose to examine American dramatic dialogue of the past. The premise of such drama is Aristotelian —that dialogue furthers plot and reveals character, and I shall examine fulfillment of that premise in the plays of O'Neill,

Miller, Williams, Albee, the only Americans to write consistently distinctive dialogue. Poets and novelists give freer play to fancy, and because they are craftsmen of language, I will examine that play in their dialogue. Perhaps this backward glance will illuminate the present and future of American drama. Or perhaps a backward glance may justify itself.

2 / The Wet Sponge of

EUGENE O'NEILL

O'NEILL'S DIALOGUE HAS BEEN THE SUBJECT OF CONTROVERSY from his earliest reviews to the present, and critical evaluation of O'Neill as a playwright very often depends upon one's view of the dialogue. In 1922 Isaac Goldberg wrote: "The dialogue as often as not is a string of *clichés.*"[1] In 1930 Francis Fergusson called O'Neill's dialogue "a language of childish superlatives which are always trying to imply more than they succeed in stating."[2] In 1961 George Steiner found O'Neill "committed, in a somber and rather moving way, to the practice of bad writing."[3]

But over a span of fifty years, O'Neill criticism swings the balance heavily toward his defenders. As early as 1920 Alexander Woollcott wrote: "O'Neill's aptitude for sketching in a figure in a few telling speeches has been apparent from the first of his plays."[4] Well known is Joseph Wood Krutch's left-handed praise in his introduction to the 1932 collection of O'Neill's plays: "But no modern is capable of language really worthy of O'Neill's play [*Mourning Becomes Electra*], and the lack of that one thing is the penalty we must pay for living in an age which is not equal to more than prose."[5] In 1959 playwright S. N. Behrman wrote: "Eugene O'Neill had a tin ear for the sonorities of the English language, and it did him no harm whatever in the theater."[6]

In general, O'Neill critics write in generalities, but Edmund Wilson early—1922—tried to analyze O'Neill's dialogue specifically: "When [O'Neill] is writing the more or less grammatical dialogue of the middle-class characters of his plays, his prose is heavy and indigestible even beyond the needs of naturalism. People say the same things to one another over and over again and never succeed in saying them any more effectively than the first time; long speeches shuffle dragging feet, marking time without progressing, for pages. But as soon as Mr. O'Neill gets a character who can only talk some kind of vernacular, he begins to write like a poet."[7] Significant is Wilson's recognition of O'Neill's techniques of repetition and monologue, techniques that he was to use throughout his career. But O'Neill's vernacular is *not* free of the very repetition and monologue which Wilson finds so distasteful in his own middle class. Over forty years later John Henry Raleigh also finds O'Neill's strength in his rendering of the vernacular: "He detached dramatic dialogue from the stilted conventionality of the average American play of the early twentieth century and attached it to the living, spoken language."[8]

Today O'Neill detractors would be willing to grant his superiority to "the average American play of the early twentieth century," but his defenders have always reached for loftier comparisons—Ibsen, Strindberg, Chekhov. Though the cross-section of quotations has been limited to Americans, O'Neill has always had his European enthusiasts. One of his earliest critics was European poet and playwright Hugo von Hofmannsthal, whose 1923 "Reflections on O'Neill" is truly reflective.[9] Though Hofmannsthal wrote on the basis of reading, without seeing, four O'Neill plays, he read them in English. His essay is extremely acute on the whole question of dialogue in the long European tradition of Aristotelian dramaturgy. Ready to admit that "[O'Neill's] dialogue is powerful, often direct, and frequently endowed with a brutal though picturesque lyricism," Hofmannsthal compares him to Ibsen, Strindberg, and Shakespeare. "Measured by this high ideal, the characters in Mr. O'Neill's plays seem to me a little too direct; they utter the precise words demanded of them by the logic of the situation; they seem to stand rooted in the situation where for the time being they happen to be placed; they are not sufficiently drenched in the atmosphere of their own individual past." In other words, O'Neill's dialogue delineates character too clearly; almost two decades would pass before O'Neill learned to drench his characters in the past. But in 1923 Hofmannsthal concludes his essay by a comparison of Hauptmann and O'Neill, both contemporary realists. He finds that the former begins his plays weakly but ends in strength, whereas the converse is true of the latter: "The close of *The Hairy Ape*, as well as that of *The Emperor Jones*, seems to me to be too direct, too simple, too expected; it is a little disappointing to a European with his complex background, to see the arrow strike the target towards which he has watched it speeding all the while. . . . The reason for this general weakness is, I think, that the dramatist, unable to make his dialogue a complete expression of human motives, is forced at the end simply to squeeze it out like a wet sponge."

Hofmannsthal based his essay on the reading of four O'Neill plays that were fortuitously representative of O'Neill's early work. *The First Man* is the last of O'Neill's melodramatic shockers about forbidden subjects—the dominant genre of his earliest plays; seething passions are couched in stilted rhetoric. *Anna Christie* is the last of O'Neill's sea plays—the realistic genre that brought him critical attention; ungrammatical repetitions attempt to drench us in the marine atmosphere. *The Emperor Jones* and *The Hairy Ape* are frequently paired as O'Neill's Expressionist plays; each of the protagonists expresses himself in a seeming inarticulacy that was new to the American stage.

Though it is unlikely that O'Neill read Hofmannsthal's analysis, he defended his dramatic dialogue in a letter to Professor Arthur H. Quinn, in which he mentions these last two plays: "But where I feel myself most neglected is just where I set most store by myself—as a bit of a poet, who has labored with the spoken word to evolve original rhythms of beauty, where beauty apparently isn't—*Jones, Ape, God's Chillun, Desire*, etc.— and to see the transfiguring nobility of tragedy, in as near the Greek sense as one can grasp it, in seemingly the most ignoble, debased lives."[10] Significant is O'Neill's own coupling of tragedy and poetic dialogue. He claims "rhythms of beauty" for at least the four plays named, two containing Negro dialect, one that of New England, and one a medley of several dialects with Brooklynese predominating. *All God's Chillun* and *Desire Under the Elms* attempt fidelity to real speech; *Emperor Jones* and *The Hairy Ape* abound in the passionate monologues of Expressionist drama, punctuated with ellipses, series, and antitheses.

Emperor Jones (1920) is O'Neill's first frankly experimental play.[11] Like the Expressionists, O'Neill exploits sound and light effects, and like them he uses staccato exclamations. Phonically, the dialogue of *Emperor Jones* resembles the unlettered speech of his earlier realistic plays. Though there are minor differences in the three versions of the published text, dialect is ubiquitous: the Island Negroes speak pidgin English, the English trader Smithers talks like a stage Cockney, and, most importantly, Brutus Jones uses conventional stage Negroese (as do the Negroes of O'Neill's 1918 *Dreamy Kid*)—substituting *d* for *th*, *b* for *v*, and short *i* for *e*, slurring *l* and *r*, and dropping consonants.[12] In spite of its stageworn familiarity, however, the dialect of Brutus Jones does establish a rhythm through O'Neill's almost incantatory use of repetition.

Incantation rarely invites close textual examination. Just before the play-long tom-tom beat begins, Jones boasts to Smithers: "I kin outguess, outrun, outfight, an' outplay de whole lot o' dem [natives] all ovah de board any time o' de day er night!" The repeated "out"s are rhythmically strong, but "outplay" is irrelevant in context, and it is anticlimactic after the other three verbs, which bear directly on Jones' conflict with the natives. "Ovah de board" carries incongruous connotations of games and flatness; the colloquial "o' de day" is weighted down by "er night." This inflation is unimportant in itself, in spite of the strategic position of the line, but it is indicative of the wet sponge tendency that Hofmannsthal observed.

In *Emperor Jones* this is no more than a tendency, for O'Neill shows restraint in building the play's tension. Like classical tragedy, the drama begins close to the catastrophe, which is a foregone conclusion; suspense lies in the progress towards that conclusion. The realistic opening and closing scenes are, respectively, expository and choral; scenes two through seven—the body of the play—constitute an Expressionist quest, terminated by death. During that quest, which leads Brutus Jones through actual and racial memories, O'Neill creates tension in several ways: the tom-tom starts at normal pulse-beat and steadily increases in frequency; Jones first appears in full military dress but gradually strips down to his naked self; as Jones penetrates

11

more deeply into dark memory, the scenes are lighted more and more brightly—from the scarcely visible Formless Fears to the brilliant river into which the crocodile sinks, with Jones' silver bullet.[13] The bullets, too, build tension, since we know that there are six, and we count as Jones shoots at the phantoms of his memory.

But dialogue remains O'Neill's major theatrical instrument. During the six Expressionist scenes Jones delivers a monologue that grows more feverish as time passes. Jones has all the language on stage, as opposed to the "ha'nts"—mechanical Jeff, the automaton chain gang, the "marionettish" 1850 planters. As Jones retreats further into his past, his bursts of speech grow shorter; by Scene 7 he echoes the chant of the Witch Doctor *"without articulate word division."* The American Negro is finally absorbed by a pre-verbal magic of his racial inheritance; nothing remains of the rational robber-emperor. In the final scene West Indian Lem tolls a verbal knell for Jones with four repetitions of "We cotch him."

The "cotch" itself is staged awkwardly, lacking resolution. Since the silver of the bullets is not visible, O'Neill uses reported action for Jones' death. But reported action requires an expressive reporter, and Lem is barely articulate. When Lem's soldiers carry Jones' body on stage, it is impossible to see what inspires Smithers' exclamation: "Silver bullets! Gawd blimey, but yer died in the 'eighth o' style, any'ow!" Smithers' admiration clashes, moreover, with his first reaction to Jones' death: "Dead as a 'erring!" Herrings, dead or alive, lack the height of style that Jones deserves and that most of the staging accords him. Hofmannsthal's disappointment with the end has been quoted, and Heywood Broun wrote of the first production: "We cannot understand just why [O'Neill] has allowed the Emperor to die to the sound of off-stage shots. It is our idea that he should come crawling to the very spot where he meets his death and that the natives should be molding silver bullets there and waiting without so much as stretching out a finger for him."[14] Broun understood that the progressive deverbalization should end in climactic silence.

Often described as a study of fear, O'Neill's play dramatizes socio-anthropology rather than psychology, and it does so with theatrical flare, despite its occasional verbal lapses. Since Jones is an emperor, he is not the Everyman questing hero of Expressionist drama. But he is not a classical hero either, since he is Brutus Jones, Pullman porter. Suffering the passion of his race, and venting his violence at injustice and oppression, Brutus has betrayed his people by ruling them like a white emperor. Lacking the self-recognition of Aimé Césaire's King Christophe, O'Neill's Emperor Jones (which made use of the life of Henri Christophe of Haiti)¹⁵ is entirely selfseeking. He is defeated less by fear than by the racial identity he implicitly denied. The play is a chronicle of Brutus Jones' progress from a false white surface to his authentic black roots—a progress of high contemporary relevance. *Et tu Brute* Jones does not atone for treason to his race, and he dies at the hands of Blacks who are closer than he to an indigenous culture and the forces of nature. "Ignoble and debased" as Jones is in a white power structure, he has set the scene for his "high style" death. Because of the intensity of Jones' imagination, expressed with inhabitual verbal restraint on O'Neill's part, *Emperor Jones* evokes the "transfiguring nobility of tragedy" that O'Neill claimed.

HE CLAIMED THIS, TOO, FOR *The Hairy Ape*, WRITTEN swiftly the following year, 1921 (as a dramatization of a lost short story). The two plays have been coupled from the period of composition on. In a letter to Charles Kennedy, a director, O'Neill described his play in progress: "It's going to be strong stuff with a kick in each mit—and stuff done in a new way, along the lines of *Emperor Jones* in construction but even more so."¹⁶ After *The Hairy Ape* was completed, O'Neill told Barrett Clark: "*The Hairy Ape* is a direct descendant of *Jones*, written long before I had ever heard of Expressionism, and its form needs no explanation but this."¹⁷ But his own subsequent statements belie the remark.

Unlike *Emperor Jones*, but like many Expressionist dramas, *The Hairy Ape* is an Everyman quest play—the quest of Yank Smith to belong. Yank appears in seven of the play's eight scenes, and he talks his way through much of his quest. Though he is a representative of instinctual man, Yank is very loquacious.

13

"Dragged up" on the Brooklyn waterfront, Yank speaks in comic-book Brooklynese—*oi* for *ir*, *d* for *th*, dropped initial *h*, *ain't* for negatives of the verb *to be*, *youse* and *yuh* for *you*, and flagrant anti-grammar. O'Neill tries to poeticize Yank's language through alliteration, repetition of the short *u* sound, original oaths, and ubiquitous slang. At the time of its first production, Walter Pritchard Eaton called O'Neill's slang "a sort of wild organ music,"[18] and Alexander Woollcott defied a middle-class audience to disapprove of it: "Squirm as you may, he holds you while you listen to the rumble of [the stokers'] discontent, and while you listen, also, to speech more squalid than an American audience heard before in an American theatre; it is true talk, all of it, and only those who have been so softly bred that they have never really heard the vulgate spoken in all its richness would venture to suggest that he has exaggerated it by so much as a syllable in order to agitate the refined."[19] But of course Woollcott is fascinated by a rich vulgate precisely because *he* has been softly bred, for Yank's speech is so systematic and repetitious that it is far more mechanical than musical, more repetitive than rich.

Perhaps because Yank talks so compulsively, O'Neill makes errors in diction for a Brooklyn waterfront character; the italicized words are too literary for him: "Youse *needn't* put me trou de toid degree. . . . Wait a *moment.* . . . I'll *fling* her in de furnace!" Occasionally, too, O'Neill inflates colloquial clichés: "She was like some *dead* ting de cat brung in." Or he misuses slang: "All dis is too clean and quiet and dolled-up"; only people, not places, are dolled up.

Though it may be carping to ask for naturalistic veracity in a play which O'Neill specified as "by no means . . . naturalistic," such errors suggest that O'Neill is forcing his idiom, rather than exploring through it. Most inadequate, most like a squeezed wet sponge, is the dialogue of the play's provocative confrontation —Yank and Mildred, dissimilar human products of a steel civilization. Unaware that Mildred is watching him, Yank reacts to the engineer's insistent whistle: "Toin off dat whistle! Come down outa dere, yuh yellow, brass-buttoned, Belfast bum, yuh! Come down and I'll knock yer brains out! Yuh lousy, stinkin', yellow mut of a Catholic-moiderin' bastard! Come down and I'll moider yuh! Pullin' dat whistle on me, huh? I'll show yuh! I'll crash yer skull in! I'll drive yer teet' down yer troat! I'll slam yer nose trou de back of yer head! I'll cut yer guts out for a nickel, yuh lousy boob, yuh dirty, crummy, muck-eatin' son of a . . ."

In spite of strong trochaic rhythm, Yank's speech teeters at the edge of comedy because the dialogue is squeezed out sloppily, rather than built up for tension. The three series of names beginning with "yuh" are haphazardly ordered; Protestantism, dirt, and cowardice are irrelevant to Yank's indignation, which is aroused by exploitation of the stokers. Of Yank's several threats, the teeth and nose oaths are comic (and only used with comic intention in colloquial speech); O'Neill undermines Yank's strength through the comic suggestion, and Yank's threats do not reënforce one another.

Compare Yank's threats with those of Mick in Pinter's comedy of menace, *The Caretaker:*

> You're stinking the place out. You're an old robber, there's no getting away from it. You're an old skate. You don't belong in a nice place like this. You're an old barbarian. Honest. You got no business wandering about in an unfurnished flat. I could charge seven quid a week for this if I wanted to. Get a taker tomorrow. Three hundred and fifty a year exclusive. No argument. I mean, if that sort of money's in your range don't be afraid to say so. Here you are. Furniture and fittings, I'll take four hundred or the nearest offer. Rateable value ninety quid for the annum. You can reckon water, heating and lighting at close on fifty. That'll cost you eight hundred and ninety if you're all that keen. Say the word and I'll have my solicitors draft you out a contract. Otherwise I've got the van outside, I can run you to the police station in five minutes, have you in for trespassing, loitering with intent, daylight robbery, filching, thieving and stinking the place out.

Here, too, the idiom is comic and colloquial, but it intensifies Mick's menace against the whimpering Davies. Mick's cumulative and sardonic arithmetic implies more than it says about Davies' bankruptcy, and the repetition of "stinking the place out" converts Davies' fault into a condition.

Though Mildred calls Yank a "filthy beast," and faints at his verbal torrent, Yank's words scarcely warrant her reaction. On stage, Mildred is confronted by an Inferno—*"terrific light and*

15

heat. " *"The grating, teeth-gritting grind of steel against steel, of crunching coal"*—peopled with sooty demons. A celestial figure in white, Mildred faints in this black Hell. But the immediacy of effect is delayed and diluted by Yank's words. Before fainting, Mildred utters phrases lifted from popular melodrama: "Take me away! Oh, the filthy beast!"

Warranted or not, Mildred's reaction sets Yank thinking. Thought is the instrument of Yank's quest, undertaken when the play is almost half over. Yank Smith, the most natural of men, nevertheless feels himself at one with steel, the basis of industrialization. Shaken in this feeling, Yank Smith, the most animal of men, tries to think, and he verbalizes his thoughts expansively. He weaves several leitmotifs through the play; Mildred is a "skoit" and a "tart," like all the women he mentions, and yet the play is curiously asexual. Yank denigrates opinions as "tripe" and people as "stiffs," but he himself is neither coherent nor galvanic. Most important is Yank's hammered insistence on the abstract verb *belong*—we belong, it belongs, I belong, she'll belong, yuh don't belong, I'll show her who belongs, I tought I belonged, and, finally, Even him didn't tink I belonged.

Though *thinking* and *belonging* may seem comparably abstract, O'Neill tries to theatricalize the former through repetitive and mocking use of Rodin's "Thinker" pose (even the gorilla takes "The Thinker" position). But in spite of this semi-comic insistence on thinking, O'Neill's Yank is a *feeler* rather than a *thinker*, and his ambivalent feeling about belonging is verbalized over thirty times, without theatricalization. The climax occurs when Yank confronts the ape: "Yuh don't belong wit 'em and yuh know it. But me, I belong wit 'em—but I don't, see? . . . Yuh can't tink, can yuh? Yuh can't talk neider. But I kin make a bluff at talkin' and tinkin'—a'most git away wit it." As the most urgent word of the play is *belong*, so it is the final word, in a stage direction: *"And, perhaps the Hairy Ape at last belongs."* O'Neill's own use of the verb is as vague as that of Yank; perhaps O'Neill means that death restores Yank Smith to nature, from which modern industrial civilization had estranged him. O'Neill's own explanation of the play is not incompatible with this: *"The Hairy Ape* was propaganda in the sense that it was a symbol of man, who has lost his old harmony with nature, the harmony which he used to have as an animal and has not yet acquired in a spiritual way. . . . The subject here is the same ancient one that always was and always will be the one subject for drama, and that is man and his struggle with his own fate. The struggle used to be with the gods, but is now with himself, his own past, his attempt 'to belong.' "[20] O'Neill's comment suggests a tragic subject, and yet he subtitles the play "A *Comedy* of Ancient and Modern Life." (my italics) O'Neill's protagonist meets frustration and death, but perhaps the ironic genre designation *comedy* means that Yank is incongruously out of his element—ancient natural man in a modern industrial setting.

Yank Smith, as his name suggests, is an American Everyman. In his strength, he has accepted steel as his symbol, and the ship's stokehole as his habitat. But Mildred's horror of him disturbs this security, and he begins to ponder upon his position in the world. His verbalized thoughts are as ridiculous as his brute strength was impressive. Unable to return to *un*thinking acceptance, foiled in his rage to inflict physical damage, Yank is finally embraced by a real animal. Caged like that animal, human Yank thinks and talks his way to death, mocking himself as a freak-show.

In claiming that "the whole play is expressionistic," in emphasizing that "Yank is really yourself, and myself. He is *every* human being.",[21] O'Neill underlines his metaphysical intention: to dramatize man's ambiguous position in the modern world. Twenty years before the French Existentialists, contemporary with Kafka, O'Neill was attracted by their theme, but he lacked their vocabulary. Kafka's ape breaks into language only when he is drunk, but O'Neill's Yank is drunk with volubility. Camus' Caligula is traumatized by death, Sartre's Orestes by Jupiter's magic—into questioning man's position in the cosmos; O'Neill's Yank is shocked by the reaction of steel heiress Mildred Douglas, but his subsequent conduct does not grow out of his trauma. Though it is difficult today to understand how contemporary reviewers misinterpreted the play as pro-labor propaganda, one can sympathize with their confusion about its meaning.

As Stark Young saw, the play is an expansion of its ironic title: Man is the Hairy Ape. (O'Neill had already used the phrase in his 1917 *Moon of the Caribbees,* but surely Hairless Ape would have been more accurate?) O'Neill labors the ape-symbol so diffusely that it loses meaning: all the stokers are apelike; a Fifth Avenue shop displays monkey-fur; the Senator's speech condemns the I.W.W. by which "man, God's masterpiece, would soon degenerate back to the ape!"; Yank takes a monkey-position to bend the bars of his prison; Yank, suffering and questioning, is "like an ape gibbering at the moon." And, finally, Yank is crushed by a real gorilla. Unlike the ape, however, Yank is compulsively verbal. The ape is an apt enough symbol for natural man, who is destroyed by industrial society, but O'Neill hammers the animal-symbol so that it almost buries his human protagonist, who is unnaturally prodigal with words.

Despite his disclaimers, O'Neill learned about quest drama from the Expressionists.[22] However, he failed to understand how firmly he had to ground the quest in the protagonist. Other characters can be no more than markers on the hero's way, but O'Neill loiters over local color, which he renders through expansive dialogue—the wet sponge again. Before Yank is provoked to thought, while he still feels he belongs, he rejects two different ways of life—that of Paddy and that of Long. Fellow stokers of Yank, they should be foils to one another—Irish clipper-sailor and Cockney social rebel, esthetic man vs. social man.

To Paddy, O'Neill gives Syngian rhythms and images: "the sky'd be blazing and winking wid stars."[23] It is Paddy who first enunciates the sustained metaphor of the play: "caged in by steel from a sight of the sky like bloody apes in the Zoo!" It is Paddy who coins the title phrase: "Sure, 'twas as if she'd seen a great hairy ape." Paddy offers Yank a romantic vision of man's preindustrial past: " 'Twas them days a ship was part of the sea, and man was part of a ship, and the sea joined all together and made it one." Paddy's speech indicts industrialization, and yet Yank's final address to the ape indicts himself: "I got it aw right —what Paddy said about dat bein' de right dope—on'y I couldn't get *in* it, see? I couldn't belong in dat. It was over my head." Over one's head implies a lack of understanding, and yet Yank says he *did* "get it." At the end of Scene 1 Yank rejects Paddy's clipper-ships, and in Scene 7 he rejects the sunrise associated with Paddy, but there has been no dramatic progress; the repeated rejection is as arbitrary as the idiom.

Yank's rejection of Long is similarly static. Before he starts to think, Yank brushes off Long's class-conscious rhetoric. He mocks Long's words (which are also mocked by a metallic Chorus: "Law, Governments, God.") In Scene 4 Yank uses Long as a guide in his search for Mildred. Yank wants *personal* vengeance against Mildred, but Long wants *class* vengeance. Afraid that Yank's violence may bring the police, Long leaves Yank and the play. But his spirit is present in the seventh scene, where Yank's personal desire for violence again clashes with the class orientation of the I.W.W. Before and after he starts to think, Yank rejects a class interpretation of his problem: "Dis ting's in your inside, but it ain't your belly." Again, there has been no dramatic progress. On Fifth Avenue, in jail, and at the I.W.W. office, Yank tries clumsily to understand the social structure, but soon turns to violence. In each of the three scenes, he is frustrated by the limitations of his mind and his muscle. But the limitations are neither progressive nor cumulative; like the language, they simply repeat his sense of non-belonging.

O'Neill's major error of proportion is Mildred, played by Carlotta Monterey in the original production. Though her only dramatic importance lies in her effect on Yank, O'Neill wastes a whole scene in which she converses with her aunt. This stilted conversation gives no insight into Yank's quest, and it gives too explicit an insight into Mildred—over and above her meaning to Yank. Like a realistic heredity-environment product, she intones: "I'm afraid I have neither the vitality nor integrity. All that was burnt out in our stock before I was born. Grandfather's blast furnaces, flaming to the sky, melting steel, making millions —then father keeping those home fires burning, making more millions—and little me at the tail-end of it all. I'm a waste product in the Bessemer process—like the millions. Or rather, I inherit the acquired trait of the by-product, wealth, but none of the energy, none of the strength of the steel that made it. I am sired by gold and damned by it, as they say at the race track —damned in more ways than one." In spite of the unintentional comedy of her "tail-end," and the intentional pun in "sired and damned," Mildred's unsolicited confession is out of place. She should be seen only briefly, in white silence, for Yank to attain

19

his self-recognition when he gazes at the gorilla: "So yuh're what she seen when she looked at me, de white-faced tart!" Here again, O'Neill blurs the point by laboring too explicitly—his wet sponge tendency: "I was you to her, get me? On'y outa de cage—broke out—free to moider her, see? Sure! Dat's what she tought. She wasn't wise dat I was in a cage, too—worser'n yours —sure—a damn sight—'cause you got some chanct to bust loose —but me—" and on and on until Yank is literally in the cage, with no chance to "bust loose" from death.

Incapable of distinction in any single idiom, O'Neill reached out ambitiously for several in *The Hairy Ape*—Yank's stage Brooklynese, Paddy's Syngian Irish, Long's Cockney labor jargon, Mildred's mannered boredom, Senator Queen's sanctimonious rhetoric, and a disunited Europe in the chorus of ship stokers. Only in farce could such cacophany be effective, and the contemporary taste for tragic farce might make theatrical profit on the very inadequacy of O'Neill's dialogue.

O'Neill mocks Yank Smith as a thinker, but a meaningful production might also mock him as a talker. As the Old Man of Ionesco's *Chairs* undermines his message by clichés, so Yank undermines his quest by pose and intransigence in a play that O'Neill labelled as comedy but described as tragedy. If a production were to focus on Yank's quest as absurd, on his inability to cope with being-in-the-world—any world—O'Neill's ineptitude could be converted to Yank's inefficacy; Yank's confusion of the social and the metaphysical would be apparent *as* confusion; his repeated rejections of Paddy and Long would appear as ape-headed stubbornness; the bravado of his laborious slang would be the dialogue of a poseur. By the time Yank offers his hand to the ape, we might find the irony heavyhanded, but Yank might nevertheless arouse our affection because of the ridiculous persistence with which he resists forces so much larger than himself. We might therefore sympathize more fully with the final petulant whimper of the Yank who tried to bang his way to self-definition.

In his claim for "original rhythms of beauty, where beauty apparently isn't," O'Neill names four plays writ-

20

ten between 1920 and 1924—*Emperor Jones, The Hairy Ape, All God's Chillun Got Wings,* and *Desire Under the Elms.* The first two are clearly symbolic; the second two concentrate their symbolism in the setting, while presenting a fairly realistic action and dialogue. Though all four plays caused something of a sensation when first produced, the latter two cut more directly into contemporary hypocrisy, evoking racist reaction in the one case and prurient outrage on the other. And yet, *All God's Chillun* is so inadequate in its exploration of a black-white relationship that few people cherish it today. In contrast, almost all O'Neill admirers praise *Desire.* In language, the former combines two idioms that O'Neill had used for earlier plays—stage Negroese, and correct middle-class diction. *Desire Under the Elms* picks up the New England dialect that O'Neill had also used earlier, in such plays as *Ile, Gold,* and *Diff'rent;* as never before, however, he uses repetition in an effort to enlarge his play to a tragic dimension.

O'Neill thought all four plays sought "the transfiguring nobility of tragedy, in as near the Greek sense as one can grasp it, in seemingly the most ignoble, debased lives," but *Desire Under the Elms* shows his fascination with Greek tragedy most openly, for the plot contains echoes of the incestuous loves of *Oedipus* and *Hippolytus,* of the infanticide of *Medea.* In trying to elevate his characters to Greek mythic stature, O'Neill relies heavily on his setting, on biblical names, and on the rhythmic repetitions of his dialect-dialogue.

While working on *Desire,* O'Neill wrote a program note for the Provincetown Playhouse production of Strindberg's *Spook Sonata,* in which he observed:

[Naturalism] represents our Fathers' daring aspiration toward self-recognition by holding the family kodak up to ill-nature. But to us their old audacity is blague; we have taken too many snap-shots of each other in every graceless position; we have endured too much from the banality of surfaces. We are ashamed of having peeked through so many keyholes, squinting always at heavy, uninspired bodies—the fat facts—with not a nude spirit among them; we have been sick with appearances and are convalescing; we 'wipe out and pass on' to some as yet unrealized region where our souls, maddened by loneliness and the ignoble inarticulateness of flesh, are slowly evolving their new language of kinship. . . . Hence, *The Spook Sonata* at our Playhouse. One of the most difficult of Strindberg's 'behind-life' (if I may coin the term) plays to interpret with insight and distinction.[24]

Instead of peeking through a keyhole with the family kodak, O'Neill followed Strindberg in his "behind-life" staging of *Desire Under the Elms*. Like Strindberg in *Spook Sonata*, O'Neill moves from exterior to interior, both literally on the set and spiritually in his characters. Even in translation, Strindberg's work gathers intensity as it moves relentlessly inward, until room, girl, and hyacinth are one. O'Neill, in contrast, moves his characters in *and out* of the exterior-interior set, and he relies on the elms to establish atmosphere:

> Two enormous elms are on each side of the house. They bend their trailing branches down over the roof. They appear to protect and at the same time subdue. There is a sinister maternity in their aspect, a crushing, jealous absorption. They have developed from their intimate contact with the life of man in the house an appalling humaneness. They brood oppressively over the house. They are like exhausted women resting their sagging breasts and hands and hair on its roof, and when it rains their tears trickle down montonously and rot the shingles.

Unlike Strindberg's hyacinth, whose physical form and Buddhist symbolism reënforce the meaning of the dialogue, O'Neill's elms are arbitrary symbols without traditional associations. They suggest neither the poor soil of Ephraim Cabot's farm nor the illicit desire in his house. Since there is no rain in the play, their leaf-tears are not only pathetic fallacy but gratuitous sentimentality. The elms' "sinister maternity" and "jealous absorption" foreshadow Abbie's actions, and yet nothing in the play relates Abbie to the elms. Perhaps O'Neill used trees to suggest a mythic quality of accursed maternity—Jocasta, Clytemnestra, Phaedra, Medea—but that theme emerges only at the end of the play. The elms are visually striking in most productions, and they serve to dwarf the farmhouse and the humans within it. Significantly, Ephraim Cabot is rarely seen inside, but tends to loom lonely on the horizon.

To convey loneliness and inarticulateness, O'Neill relies in large part on laconic New England dialect. Curbing his wet sponge tendency toward monologue, he nevertheless situates an important monologue in each of the three acts, which he calls Parts possibly to suggest the three parts of the Greek tragic trilogy. At the end of Part I, when Abbie and Eben first meet, she analyzes her past, climaxing the effusion with phallic imagery; in Part II Ephraim explains his loneliness to Abbie; and in Part III Ephraim yearns at some length for the gold of California.

The play's opening scene announces the theme of gold vs. stones, and this theme is conveyed in both dialogue and setting. In the original production of *Desire Under the Elms* Robert Edmond Jones, the designer, built a wall of actual stone on stage, to theatricalize the contrast specified by the dialogue. While Ephraim is mysteriously absent from the farm, his son Peter muses: "Gold in the sky—in the West—Golden Gate—California!—Golden West!—fields o' gold!" Peter then comments on reality: "Here—it's stones atop o' the ground—stones atop o' stones—makin' stone walls—year atop o' year—him 'n' yew 'n' me 'n' then Eben—makin' stone walls for him to fence us in!" Eben echoes Peter: "An' makin' walls—stone atop o' stone—makin' walls till yer heart's a stone ye heft up out o' the way o' growth onto a stone wall t' wall in yer heart!" The power behind the stones (and the most interesting character in the play) is Ephraim Cabot, who glories in the hardwon victory over his rocky land: "God's in the stones! build my church on a rock—out o' stones an' I'll be in them! That's what he meant to Peter!" Later, when Ephraim learns of Abbie's sin, he admonishes himself: "I got to be—like a stone—a rock o' jedgment!"

Monolithic, O'Neill's nineteenth-century New Englanders are almost monosyllabic, but they dispense their monosyllables liberally and repetitively. Yet the most frequent repetition of the play is the disyllable "purty": Sunset and sky are purty; Minnie the prostitute, Eben's dead mother, and Abbie are purty; the house and the farm are purty; his sin is purty to Eben; love and heaven are purty to Abbie; and, above all, the baby is purty. After the infanticide, Eben decides to share Abbie's guilt with her, and Ephraim praises him climactically: "Purty good —fur yew!" The play's last "purty" comes from Eben, as he gazes at the sunrise with Abbie, *"looking up raptly in attitudes strangely aloof and devout."* O'Neill might well have heeded his own remark in an interview: "I don't love life because it's pretty. Prettiness is only clothes-deep."[25] And dialect does not deepen it.

Bathed in dawnlight, the end of *Desire Under the Elms* is just barely rescued from maudlin romanticism by the sheriff's curtain-line, which resonates with irony: "It's a jim-dandy farm, no denyin'. Wished I owned it!" But if the last line saves the play from the rosy dawn, it trivializes the action. Tragic action must have wide resonance; action centered on farm ownership is limited to realism or melodrama. In Tolstoi's *Power of Darkness* peasant greed leads to the murder of an old man and a baby. But the sinners feel neither "aloof" nor "devout" after their heinous deeds; the Abbie-figure, Anisia, is haunted by the husband she killed, and the Eben-figure, Nikita, is driven to public confession by the physical horror of his infanticide. Nikita keeps repeating, "Ah, the way he squealed! . . . The way they cracked under me, his little bones." Abbie, in contrast, almost denies her murder: "I left the piller over his little face. *Then he killed himself.* He stopped breathin'." (my italics)

Russian Orthodox peasants and Puritan New Englanders need not behave similarly even on stage, but they must behave appropriately to their dramatic genre. Only the formality of tragedy can justify aloofness. Stones and gold might figure in tragedy, but a "jim-dandy farm" demands realism. Tragic figures might "look up raptly" even after infanticide, but they cannot admire the "purty" sunrise. Colloquialism can intensify tragicomedy, but it can only undercut tragedy.

Desire Under the Elms lacks tragic depth not because the characters are lonely and inarticulate, but because O'Neill tries too hard to articulate their loneliness—his old wet sponge tendency. O'Neill accords Simeon and Peter (whose names mean *stone*) too much speech and playing time. The Abbie-Eben love scenes are ludicrous through dialect, and the couple's sudden final grandeur is incredible.

Brushing by the lovers, many critics have seen Ephraim Cabot as the play's tragic hero, and he certainly commands more respect. Yet his name recalls the *comic* rhyme about Boston,

"Where the Lowells speak only to Cabots / And the Cabots speak only to God." O'Neill's Ephraim Cabot speaks to and of God, but he speaks to everyone else as well—even his cows. Ephraim's patriarchal solitude is especially dissipated in the crowd party, though O'Neill retrieves his laconic isolation after the infanticide.

Most awkwardly articulate are the dialogue references to the infanticide; Abbie, Ephraim, and Eben talk about the death of the baby, but it is no wonder that they forget so easily, for their words convey no sense at all of the monstrous concreteness of a smothered infant. Ephraim tries to redeem himself by reaching toward his lonely God in his final extended speech, while Abbie and Eben retreat into platitudes about love.

In the opening scenic direction, O'Neill claims that the elms learned from *"the life of man in the house an appalling humaneness."* Whether he actually meant *humaneness* or merely *humanity,* none of the play's characters is capable of teaching either one— even to an elm.

Desire Under the Elms COMPLETED, O'NEILL TURNED away from "seemingly the most ignoble, debased lives" to lives that loomed large. In succession, he embarked on seven ambitious plays: *Marco Millions, The Great God Brown, Lazarus Laughed, Strange Interlude, Dynamo, Mourning Becomes Electra,* and *Days Without End.* In these plays that range from biblical to modern times, O'Neill uses the middle-class American speech which embraces most of his plays from *A Wife for a Life* to *Long Day's Journey Into Night.*[26] Influenced by literature and philosophy, these plays show O'Neill's resolute search for theatrical variety. Thus, *Marco Millions,* a satire on American commercialism, and *Lazarus Laughed,* an apocalyptic celebration, exploit lavish spectacle. *The Great God Brown,* which translates Nietzsche into a contemporary American context, *Strange Interlude,* which places Freud in a contemporary American context, and *Days Without End,* which insists on the contemporaneity of Christ, use masks and asides. *Dynamo* injects mysticism into the industrial age, and *Mourning Becomes Electra* injects Greek tragedy into Civil War New England, both liberally dosed with Freudian attitudes.

These are the plays that Eric Bentley deprecated in his well-known essay, "Trying to Like O'Neill," and he summarized: "The more he attempts, the less he succeeds."[27]

"More" is both quantitative and qualitative. *Marco Millions* and *Lazarus Laughed* take over three hours of playing time; *Strange Interlude* takes five hours, and *Mourning Becomes Electra* nearly six. When first presented, the latter two plays allowed for dinner during an intermission. The prolixity is perhaps explained by the prophetic reach; through symbol, staging, and especially loquaciousness, they strive toward myth. And when they fail, it is mainly because O'Neill's mythic figures utter words that are naively explicit and exceedingly flat—what Hofmannsthal early saw as his wet sponge failing. At worst, O'Neill's dialogue strains toward poetic prose. In *Marco Millions* Kublai Khan's wisdom is steeped in abstraction, climaxed by a pathetic fallacy that is more comic than pathetic: "Girl whom we call dead, whose beauty is even in death more living than we, smile with infinite silence upon our speech, smile with infinite forbearance upon our wisdom, smile with infinite remoteness upon our sorrow, *smile as a star smiles!*" (my italics)

More extended pseudo-lyricism occurs at the end of Act I of *The Great God Brown*. After evoking his dead parents, Dion Anthony, artist, *describes* thought and emotion instead of *dramatizing* them: "So I shrank away, back into life, with naked nerves jumping like fleas, and in due course of nature another girl called me her boy in the moon and married me and became three mothers in one person, while I got paint on my paws in an endeavor to see God! *(He laughs wildly—claps on his mask.)* But that Ancient Humorist had given me weak eyes, so now I'll have to forswear my quest for Him and go in for the Omnipresent Successful Serious One, the Great God Mr. Brown, instead!" Though Dion's contrast between Dionysian vigor and Babbittian abstraction is important, O'Neill obscures that contrast with his unselective wet sponge monologues, comic through strain.

A pretentious declaration of *The Great God Brown* leads thematically to *Lazarus Laughed:* "Only he that has wept can laugh! The laughter of Heaven sows earth with a rain of tears, and out of Earth's transfigured birth-pain the laughter of Man

26

returns to bless and play again in innumerable dancing gales of flame upon the knees of God! *(He dies.)" Lazarus Laughed* is a quarter again as long as *The Great God Brown;* its extravagance runs to spectacle and rhapsody. The play makes unparallelled use of masks and crowd scenes, and the dialogue makes unparallelled use of "O"s and exclamation marks. Otherwise, O'Neill does not experiment with the dialogue as he does with the staging, but such experiment made for the notoriety of his next play, *Strange Interlude.*

In the realistic theater of O'Neill's America, a return to past dramatic techniques seemed experimental. Given O'Neill's penchant for tragedy, it was inevitable that he borrow from the two great tragic theaters, Greek and Elizabethan. From the former he took myth and mask for *The Great God Brown* and *Lazarus Laughed.* From the latter (and from melodrama) he took soliloquy and aside for *Strange Interlude, Dynamo,* and *Days Without End.* Since economy was always foreign to O'Neill, he scattered these devices more liberally than did the originators. His variety of masks differs markedly from the few types of the Greek theater, and, similarly, his profusion of soliloquies and asides differs from that of Elizabethan convention. Over half the dialogue of *Strange Interlude* is composed of unspoken thoughts.[28]

The Elizabethans used asides to establish an entente between a character and the audience. More versatile, the soliloquy might take the form of direct address to the audience, of a character talking to himself, or of a character thinking aloud; the second and third forms overlap, and tragedy accommodates them. Though any character may utter an aside, Elizabethan soliloquies are usually reserved for central characters. In melodrama, however, soliloquies and especially asides are used indiscriminately to conceal dramaturgical ineptitude, telling the audience what it needs to know in order to understand the plot. Like melodramatists, O'Neill makes no qualitative distinction between his asides and soliloquies, which are both meant to reveal the characters' unspoken thoughts.   ·

Though O'Neill revived these devices of older *drama,* he seems to have sought the textural density of the interior monologue *novel.* Joyce's *Ulysses* (1922) and Woolf's *Mrs. Dalloway* (1925) were published before O'Neill began to work on *Strange Inter-*

lude. O'Neill's friend, the drama critic George Jean Nathan, described O'Neill's technique as "a combination of the method of the novel and that of the drama."²⁹ O'Neill himself declared that his work (then in progress) was about "the life of a woman without the padding of a novel."³⁰ And yet, the very use of the word *novel* suggests that he had an eye on that form. Perhaps the seemingly free form of the interior monologue novel aggravated O'Neill's wet sponge affliction that labored the abstract and the overly explicit, instead of relying on association, like Joyce, or on cumulative imagery, like Woolf. But then Shakespeare's soliloquies had already shown the way.

In a parody of Hamlet's soliloquy à la O'Neill, the designer Lee Simonson has caught O'Neill's weakness—the discussion rather than the dramatization of emotion:

> Damn my stepfather; lecherous old bastard. If I could only kill him. But I'm a snivelling introvert. All I can do is complain. I can't do anything. . . . Mother—Mother's nothing but a whore. No! I shouldn't have said that. Forgive me, mother. . . . But it drives me almost mad to think of it. God! if I could only kill myself—get away from it all. There's nothing to live for. *(He hunches more deeply into his coat collar.)* I'm afraid! Afraid to do anything. Afraid of death. *(He shivers.)* Spooks. What they told me when I was a kid. Just afraid of the dark—but it sticks. It gets me. *(Looking at the snow man.)* I'm just so much mush—mush like you. *(He breaks into bitter laughter, takes off the battered derby from the snow man's head and salutes him elaborately.)* If I could only thaw with you tomorrow—thaw, just dissolve, trickle into the earth—run off into the sewer, etc., etc.³¹

Passages of *Strange Interlude* sound like this parody.

Divided into two parts, *Strange Interlude* spans nine acts and over a quarter of a century, ending at a time posterior to the date of composition. Of the eight characters, four are present over the entire period—Nina Leeds and the three men of her adult life. Nina is at the center of the play, as O'Neill intended, referring to his work in progress as "my woman play." Her very name is a punning affirmation of feminine dominance: Nina or nine—the period of human gestation matched by the number of acts in the play; and Leeds or leads. Nina Leeds is an archetypal woman who commands the devotion of her trinity of men. As Shaw's women unconsciously serve the Life Force, so does Nina

Leeds, and that service is divided into two large periods, since the two parts of the play are separated by the birth of Nina's son, Gordon. Part I might be entitled "Prelude to Motherhood" and Part II "Motherhood Achieved."

Though Nina is at the center of *Strange Interlude*, all the characters verbalize their private thoughts. Each of the five acts of Part I begins with unspoken thoughts—Nina opens two acts, Charlie opens two, and Sam one. In Part II Acts 6 and 7 open with unspoken thoughts, and Acts 8 and 9 with direct theater dialogue. Starting with the thought asides of Charlie Marsden, the play closes on his unspoken thoughts. Aloud, Charlie early takes the stance of Nina's father (Act 2), and he concludes the play acting like a father toward Nina. But despite this suggestion of circularity in the interlude that is life, the body of the play stresses the relentless passing of time. Particularly near the beginning of each act, O'Neill uses unspoken thoughts to convey the lapse of time, by informing the audience of what has happened between the acts—as in melodrama. More often, however, O'Neill assigns to unspoken thoughts what the characters do not dare tell each other, and yet their revelations are rarely surprising.

The plot nucleus of *Strange Interlude* is the old romantic love triangle, updated to the 1920's. By focussing unspoken thoughts on the subject of sex, O'Neill provided some credible rationale for his technique, since sex in the American 1920's remained an unspoken subject. In Act 1 Nina Leeds is a reluctant virgin because her father will not permit her to marry a man going to war, and because her fiancé Gordon will not "dishonor" her before marriage. But after Gordon's death, Nina sheds her virginity with alacrity, and for seven of the nine acts she is married to Sam but loves Ned. We are thus witness to passionate reiterations of the Nina-Ned magnetism, to irritation of Nina with Sam, to insecurity of Sam with Nina, to guilt of Ned vis à vis Sam. Further, O'Neill enlarges the conventional triangle by the addition of an asexual novelist-raisonneur, Charlie Marsden, who is at once a participant in the plot and a spectator of the plot, commenting on it in his thought asides. Charlie drives Nina into a marriage with Sam, Charlie suspects Nina's relationship with Ned, Charlie acts as uncle to young Gordon, and

Charlie finally becomes a kind of father to Nina. As novelist, he is fascinated by the vigorous life that his novels cannot capture: "My novels . . . not of cosmic importance, hardly." And yet, it is mainly through Charlie that O'Neill attempts to inject "cosmic importance" into his own play of American middle-class characters. With some frequency (and perilous imagery) Charlie moves from the specifics of the plot to generalizations: "What son can ever understand?" "Thoughts . . . damn pests! . . . mosquitoes of the soul." "No woman likes to lose a man even when she no longer loves him." "Even our new God has His price!" "Oh, russet-golden afternoon, you are a mellow fruit of happiness ripely falling!" Charlie twice mentions the titular *interlude:* In his opening thoughts Charlie refers to their New England university town as "the interlude that gently questions." Toward the end of the play, Charlie watches the growing love of Nina's son, Gordon, for his Madeleine, and he comments: "Age's terms of peace, after the long interlude of war with life, have still to be concluded."

But it is Nina who twice uses the full title, *strange interlude,* infusing it with her passionate evocation of a feminine transcendence. After finding no comfort in sexual promiscuity, unexpectedly distressed at the death of her father, Nina early speaks (aloud) of a female God: "We should have imagined life as created in the birth-pain of God the Mother." When she herself is pregnant, Nina affirms: "God is a mother." A mother herself, Nina prays to a Mother God that she may some day reveal the truth of Gordon's fatherhood. When her son Gordon is grown and in love, Nina prays to her Mother God for complete possession of him. But her three men conspire to deprive her of her son, and she is compelled to acknowledge the power of male transcendence: "My old lover . . . how well and young he looks . . . now we can no longer love each other at all . . . our account with God the Father is settled . . . afternoons of happiness paid for with years of pain . . . love, passion, ecstasy . . . in what a far-off life were they alive! . . . the only living life is in the past and future . . . the present is an interlude . . . strange interlude in which we call on past and future to bear witness we are living!" In this abstract terminology, O'Neill (through Nina) seems to suggest that man (and especially woman) is a plaything in the hands of God the Father, that human passion is an insubstantial interlude whose reality depends upon memory or hope —past or future. This sense of evanescence is particularly poignant in drama, pre-eminently the art of the present, and Nina's statement pulls against the slow length of the play's quarter century.

In Nina's words at the end of the play—spoken aloud to Charlie—O'Neill tries again to establish a cosmic context: "Strange interlude! Yes, our lives are merely strange dark interludes in the electrical display of God the Father!" Even archetypal matriarchy becomes a pitiful human hubris reduced to its small dark scale; in a masculine God's universe of dazzling abstraction, human life is no more than a momentary short circuit. The image is difficult but forceful, and it gains force by restriction to the single sentence. In the printed text of the play, however, Nina's line has been preceded by O'Neill's fifty-odd repetitions of the word *strange*, mainly in scenic directions. By persistent "strangification" O'Neill tries to enlarge middle-class life to cosmic scope.

Though O'Neill's reach is unmistakably long—especially in the lines of Nina and Charlie—his grasp falls short, stunted by inadequate language. With the exception of a few slang phrases by Sam, all the characters speak alike, neither subtle nor concrete. The characters tell us at length *about* their feelings, but their words do not express those feelings. At a climactic juncture of the play—when Nina enunciates the pattern of her life —she speaks in prosaic monosyllables, without an image to fix the pattern in our view. And the unspoken words of the three men are similarly diagrammatic:

NED: My experiment with guinea pigs has been a success.
SAM: She's a wonderful wife and Mother.
CHARLIE: Her child is the child of our three loves for her.

O'Neill's individualization of the men does not enter their idiom.

Nor does O'Neill differentiate dialogue rhythm from thought rhythm. Despite the three-dot punctuation with which O'Neill peppers the text of the meditations, the phrases are coherent and conceptually complete. They move in logical sequence; never, as in Proust's *petite madeleine*, is there a triggering of thought by sensual association; lacking are the esthetic-emotional associations of Woolf; or the sonic-sensuous-mythic associations of Joyce; or anything distinctive of O'Neill—except repetition. As one of the first reviewers saw: "The turbulent stream of consciousness Joyce photographs so perfectly finds itself, in 'Strange Interlude,' confined to neat concrete containers which are far more like summaries of the momentary situation as Mr. O'Neill wishes one to understand it than like what the characters are actually thinking at the time."[32] This is not to reproach O'Neill for not being a novelist, or even for seeking fictional texture in the drama; but his wet sponge sloppiness cannot wash away the poverty of his insights. Hamlet's soliloquies are riddled with questions; the imagery of disease marks the asides of Thersites. O'Neill does not explore through his technique; his rhythms are based on short phrases and repetition, and his imagery is sparse or incongruous. His characters are too lucid about themselves, and he is too lucid about them.

Philip Moeller, director of the first production of *Strange Interlude*, evolved an "arrested motion" method of playing the unspoken thoughts: "The actual physical action and usual dialogue of the play was to be momentarily arrested. There was to be a space of physical quiet in which the unheard thoughts could, so to speak, be heard."[33] By the time of the 1964 Actor's Studio revival, the whole process was laboriously old-fashioned. But even in the original production, Lynn Fontanne as Nina feared audience laughter when the unheard thoughts merely echoed or paraphrased normal dialogue: "For instance, I would have to say an aside something like, 'Ned has the bluest eyes I ever saw; I must tell him so.' Then I would go to Ned and tell him he had the bluest eyes I ever saw. I felt it was unnecessary to say this twice. I told O'Neill I thought it would be better if I looked at Ned's eyes with admiration the first time, silently, instead of saying the line as an aside. I asked him if I could cut the line. He said, 'No, you can't. Play it as I wrote it.' But the play was so long that I felt O'Neill wouldn't realize it if I cut a line here and there, so, with fear and trembling, I cut a few of those horse-laugh lines. O'Neill never knew about this sly business of mine."[34] The printed text, however, remains uncut, and the middle-class mediocrity of its dialogue borders on unintentional comedy, as Lynn Fontanne realized.

In seeking to reveal a mythic dimension beneath modern everyday life, O'Neill was trapped by his modern everyday dialogue, and one cannot say, as one can of *The Hairy Ape,* that inadequate idiom is part of the tragedy. Though O'Neill tried to achieve scope through Charlie's generalizations and Nina's transcendent vision, such attempts constitute no more than a small fraction of the five-hour play. Thought asides and symbolism undercut the dramatic drive, so that O'Neill's *Interlude* is more tedious than strange.

BETWEEN *Strange Interlude* AND *Mourning Becomes Electra* O'Neill wrote *Dynamo,* replete with symbol, thought aside, murder, suicide, and a hint of plans for continuation into a trilogy. Though he was enthusiastic about it, *Dynamo* was harmed by O'Neill's personal difficulties at that time. Coldly received in the theater, its failure was eventually admitted by O'Neill. Since *Dynamo* has no defenders today, it is needless to analyze its ponderous rhetoric of love and religion, its screaming symbolism of maternity and electricity. But Robert Benchley's review points out that typical O'Neill weaknesses emerge in this bad play: "Nobody who could write *Dynamo* is above being kidded. And *Dynamo* gives the tip-off on *Strange Interlude* and *The Great God Brown.* They *were* just as bad as we thought they were."[35] "Just as bad" because similarly pretentious and loquacious—the soaked sponge.

Chastened by diappointment in *Dynamo,* O'Neill turned with unparallelled diligence to what his working notes call "Greek tragedy plot idea."[36] Two years in the writing, *Mourning Becomes Electra* is O'Neill's most painstaking and ambitious dramatic effort before he conceived the idea of dramatic cycles. He subsequently published his notes on the work in progress, and they reveal his search for a dialogue that would match the ambitious subject and form. While working on his tragic trilogy, O'Neill wrote to critic Joseph Wood Krutch: "Oh, for a language to write drama in! For a speech that is dramatic and isn't just conversation! I'm so strait-jacketed by writing in terms of talk!

33

I'm so fed up with the dodge-question of dialect! But where to find that language?"[37]

O'Neill wanted to write "modern psychological approxima-tion of Greek sense of fate," since fate had haunted him from the period of his earliest melodramas. Casting about among Greek tragedies, he found "story of Electra and family psychologically most interesting." A few months later, he chose New England and a post-Civil War setting—some fifteen years later than that of *Desire Under the Elms*, and several rungs higher on the social ladder. In adapting Greek names, he seems not to have seen any connection between Mannon and Mammon; nor an implied negative of Man in Mannon. The name Lavinia was patterned on a lesser-known name of Electra, Laodicea, but O'Neill kept Electra in his title: *"Mourning Becomes Electra*—that is, in old sense of word—it befits—it becomes Electra to mourn—it is her fate—also, in usual sense (made ironical here), mourning (black) is becoming to her—it is the only color that becomes her destiny —" Before actually writing, he chose titles for the three plays of his tragic trilogy: The Homecoming, The Hunted, The Haunted. He decided on "comparatively straight realism" for the first draft, "then lay aside for period and later decide how to go to final version—whether to use masks, soliloquies, asides, etc.—" Nearly a year later, when he had finished his first draft, O'Neill was dissatisfied and decided on a "second draft using half masks and an *Interlude* technique (combination *Lazarus* and *Interlude*)." From these, he hoped to attain "more sense of the unreal behind what we call reality which is the real reality!"

In three more months of concentrated work, O'Neill com-pleted this second draft, and was even more disappointed: "Chief thing, thought asides now seem entirely unnecessary—don't reveal anything about the characters I can't bring out quite naturally in their talk or their soliloquies when alone—simply get in the way of the play's drive, make the line waver, cause action to halt and limp—must be deleted in toto—Warn-ing!—always hereafter regard with suspicion hangover inclina-tions to use "Interlude" technique regardless—that was what principally hurt "Dynamo" . . . "Interlude" aside technique is special expression for special type of modern neurotic, disinte-grated soul—when dealing with simple direct folk or characters of strong will and intense passions, it is superfluous show-shop 'business.' " Still unable to see how the technique had harmed *Strange Interlude*, O'Neill nevertheless seems to have heeded his own warning; of the extant plays, only *Days Without End* and *More Stately Mansions* suffer from his "hangover inclinations to use 'Interlude' technique."

Even though he ruled out thought asides, however, O'Neill found it difficult to limit himself to realistic dialogue for his Neo-Greek trilogy. He took about two months to rewrite again, introducing stylized soliloquies whose rhythm was "monotonous, simple words driving insistence—tom tom from 'Jones' in thought repetition—" When this version was completed, O'Neill found the soliloquies as distasteful as the thought asides of the second version. He again decided to write "in straight dialogue—as simple and direct and dynamic as possible—with as few words." O'Neill finished this fourth version, and though "fairly well satisfied," worked at some unspecified "new ideas," which he subsequently rejected, to revert essentially to the fourth version. Reading galleys of the play in August, 1931, O'Neill was pleased: "has power and drive and the strange quality of unreal reality I wanted—main purpose seems to me soundly achieved—there is a feeling of fate in it, or I am a fool —a psychological modern approximation of the fate in the Greek tragedies on this theme—attained without benefit of supernatural."

As his working notes suggest, however, O'Neill was striving not so much for "modern approximation of . . . fate" as for a mythic dimension in the action. Thus, his title deliberately recalls Greek Electra, though the play's heroine is named Lavinia; his script parallels the plot of the *Oresteia* even though specific events may differ: the poisoning of Ezra by Christine Mannon corresponds to the murder of Agamemnon by Clytemnestra; Christine's suicide corresponds to the murder of Clytemnestra by Orestes; Orin's suicide differs from the relatively happy ending for Aeschylus' Orestes, but Lavinia's final masochistic incarceration is without Aeschylean parallel. Though O'Neill prided himself that "each play [is a] complete episode completely realized," the parts are less independent than those of the *Oresteia*, and yet the American play inevitably recalls the Greek trilogy.[38]

In the three parts of his trilogy, O'Neill emphasizes the resemblance of the Mannon faces to masks; he even specifies that the Mannon mansion has a mask-like exterior. His three plays move from the exterior to the interior of the Mannon mansion —a technique that O'Neill had already used in *Beyond the Horizon* and *Desire Under the Elms*. His three plays open on a chorus whose remarks prepare the entrance of the main characters.

More than any other O'Neill play, the pattern of *Mourning* is based on repetition: Ezra and Brand replace Abraham and David Mannon; exotic Christine replaces French-Canadian Marie. By the end of the trilogy, Orin resembles Ezra and Lavinia Christine. These character repetitions are emphasized by verbal repetitions: near the end of the trilogy, Lavinia threatens Orin as her mother had threatened her near the beginning: "Take care. . . . You'll be responsible if—!" For the first time, O'Neill threads such textural repetition through a structural symmetry; the five-act middle play is balanced by a four-acter before and after. Into this balance O'Neill seeks to weave his sense of tragic fate, or a psychological approximation thereof. Thus, the dots of *Strange Interlude* are replaced by comparable dashes, evidently meant to convey the psychological fragmentation of the characters. Like dots and thought asides, however, dash-pauses are difficult to enact and on stage the actors seem to suffer from memory lapses.

O'Neill's working notes affirm that he wanted to write "straight dialogue—as simple and direct and dynamic as possible—with as few words." He achieved much simplicity and some directness, but dynamism eluded him because of his predilection for abstract nouns rather than concrete verbs. And his resolution to use "few words" was incompatible with his wet sponge habit.

The thematic words, *love* and *death*, are repeated so often that their meaning is blunted. Back from the Civil War, Ezra and Orin Mannon speak obsessively about death, as in Ezra's lines: "It was seeing death all the time in this war got me to thinking these things. Death was so common it didn't mean anything. That freed me to think of life. Queer; isn't it? Death made me think of life. Before that life had only made me think of death!"

36

Compare this abstract polarity with the concrete imagery of Didi in *Waiting for Godot:* "Astride of a grave and a difficult birth. Down in the hole, lingeringly, the grave-digger puts on the forceps." O'Neill's passage exhausts itself; that of Beckett is significantly resonant.

Love is not so much an emotion as a subject for rhetoric in the duologues of Christine and Brant, Christine and Ezra, Lavinia and Ezra, Lavinia and Peter, Orin and Hazel, Orin and Lavinia. Except for Brant, who compares women to sailing ships, the words of love are bare of imagery. O'Neill's repetition of the word *love* is frequently found in polar opposition to *hate*. The polarity, if not the vocabulary, shows the influence of Strindberg. As in Strindberg's *Dance of Death*, O'Neill's Christine deliberately converts her speech into a lethal weapon; Strindberg's Alice attacks the Captain with his daughter's broken engagement; O'Neill's Christine attacks the General with a confession of her infidelity. Knowing that Ezra has a weak heart, Christine torments him with praise of her lover: "He's gentle and tender, he's everything you've never been. He's what I've longed for all these years with you—a lover! I love him! So now you know the truth!" Her soap-opera confession evokes an epithet that would not have been permitted in soap opera: "You— you whore—I'll kill you!" But it is Ezra who is killed; felled by a heart attack, he takes the poison which Christine administers instead of medicine. This first death of the tragic trilogy tops the others in its melodramatic aspect.[39]

Throughout the trilogy, violent Mannon temperaments express themselves in static abstractions. Brant alone has a different idiom, sailor that he is. Not only does he sprinkle his conversation with "Aye"s and "Belay"s, but he introduces imagery. His description of the unpuritan Blessed Isles differs from the matter-of-fact accounts in O'Neill's *Diff'rent* (1922), where sensual natives were also contrasted to sex-starved New Englanders. To suggest the sensual quality of the islands, O'Neill borrows gerunds, open vowels, imagery, and rhythms from Synge's *Playboy*, as he had done for Paddy's speech in *The Hairy Ape:* "The clouds like down on the mountain tops, the sun drowsing in your blood, and always the surf on the barrier reef singing a croon in your ears like a lullaby!" But O'Neill is not

Synge, who would have built such phrases climactically or cumulatively.

Before Orin shoots Brant, the latter again evokes the Blessed Isles for Christine: "The warm earth in the moonlight, the trade winds rustling the coco palms, the surf on the barrier reef singing a croon in your ears like a lullabye!" This time the incongruous background of sleep is ironically counterpointed against the anxiety of the characters. And Brant's final series of abstractions predicts his death: "There's peace, and forgetfulness for us there."

By the time Lavinia evokes the Blessed Isles, she has actually visited the South Seas, and yet her details repeat those she heard from Brant: "There was something there mysterious and beautiful—a good spirit—of love—coming out of the land and sea. It made me forget death. There was no hereafter. There was only this world—the warm earth in the moonlight—the trade wind in the coco palms—the surf on the reef—the fires at night and the drum throbbing in my heart—the natives dancing naked and innocent—without knowledge of sin!" Lacking Synge's sweep and humor, the passage is nevertheless meaningful, until O'Neill shatters the mood with the unintentionally comic: "But what in the world! I'm gabbing on like a regular chatterbox. You must think I've become awfully scatter-brained!"

In the final play of the trilogy, such idiomatic incongruity is particularly unfortunate, after O'Neill has been explicit and repetitious about the chatterbox role of the Chorus. Intended seriously, *"a chorus of types representing the town as a human background for the drama of the Mannons"* usually functions more as comic relief. In Part I the chorus delivers the exposition and announces the "strange" atmosphere, which O'Neill's text subsequently emphasizes by some fifty repetitions of the word *strange* and some thirty of *queer*, usually in scenic directions. In Part II the Chorus belongs to a slightly higher stratum of society; still folksy and colloquial but no longer speaking dialect, they seem to enjoy the Mannon disasters and are quite thrilled by the sexual undercurrent. Part III returns us to the New England dialect of Part I, introducing "The Haunted" on the grotesque humor of a satyr-play. Seth, the Chorypheus-caretaker of the Mannon mansion, plays a practical joke on

Abner Small, who has scoffed at ghosts. Though Seth leads the townspeople in their laughter at Small's fright, he hammers the point of the joke: "Between you 'n' me 'n' the lamp-post, it ain't all sech a joke as it sounds—that about the hauntin', I mean."

An omnicomprehensive raisonneur, Seth knows more of the Mannon scandals than he utters in his laconic dialect. At the last, his themesong "Shenandoah" is woven into the tragedy of Lavinia, the last of the Mannons: *"Picking up the words of the chanty [I'm bound away] with a grim writhen smile,"* she declares: "I'm not bound away—not now, Seth. I'm bound here—to the Mannon dead!" Then she expands upon her indenture to the Mannon dead. In the last words and gestures, however, O'Neill manages economy. Lavinia orders Seth: "And tell Hannah to throw out all the flowers." Repeating his habitual "Ayeh," Seth *"goes past her up the steps into the house. She ascends to the portico— and then turns and stands for a while, stiff and square-shouldered, staring into the sunlight with frozen eyes. Seth leans out of the window at the right of the door and pulls the shutters closed with a decisive bang. As if this were a word of command, Lavinia pivots sharply on her heel and marches woodenly into the house, closing the door behind her."* Not a *strange* or a *queer*, not an exclamation point or an abstraction sentimentalizes the specificity of the final direction.

Mourning Becomes Electra won O'Neill immediate and widespread acclaim, but O'Neill himself was aware of its central weakness, about which he wrote to Professor Arthur H. Quinn: "[*Mourning*] needed great language. . . . I haven't got that. And, by way of self-consolation, I don't think, from the evidence of all that is being written today, that great language is possible for anyone living in the discordant, broken, faithless rhythm of our time. The best one can do is to be pathetically eloquent by one's moving, dramatic inarticulations!"[40] It may have been O'Neill's self-justification that inspired the often-quoted opinion of Joseph Wood Krutch: "But no modern is capable of language really worthy of O'Neill's play [*Mourning*], and the lack of that one thing is the penalty we must pay for living in an age which is not equal to more than prose."[41] One would not suppose that Yeats, Valéry, Benn, or Lorca were O'Neill's contemporaries; or that prose could carry the eloquence of Joyce and Faulkner.

Moreover, dramatists like O'Casey, Eliot, and Gertrude Stein sought rather than avoided "the discordant, broken, faithless rhythm of our time."

AFTER *Mourning Becomes Electra*, DELIBERATELY PATterned on the *Oresteia*, O'Neill returned to his desire to dramatize an *American* myth. Continuing the theme of *Dynamo*—an American Adam's search for God—O'Neill began *Days Without End*, which was originally to be followed by a third play. That third play was never written, and O'Neill's most fervent admirers do not defend the two existing plays of the truncated trilogy.

While struggling with *Days Without End*, O'Neill shifted for comic relief to *Ah, Wilderness!*. Far from mere "nostalgia for a youth [he] never had,"[42] *Ah, Wilderness!* conceals smug acceptance of a double standard, hypocrisy of American family life, and unfocused boredom of July 4th, America's national holiday. As Clifford Leech observed: "There is a mild irony in Richard Miller's rebelliousness showing itself on the day nominally celebrating a rebellion, actually hallowing an establishment."[43]

The play's title comes from a favorite poem of both O'Neill and the play's protagonist, Richard Miller—Fitzgerald's translation of the *Rubaiyat*: "A Book of Verses underneath the Bough,/ A Jug of Wine, A Loaf of Bread—and Thou/ Beside me singing in the Wilderness./ Ah—wilderness were Paradise enow." O'Neill changes wine to whiskey and gin; bread to bluefish and lobster; and he sets several singers in the wilderness of a small New England town at the turn of the century. As noted by one of the characters, "We seem to be completely surrounded by love." The love is explicitly verbalized and unconvincingly dramatized—as in O'Neill plays that aim at tragedy rather than comedy.

Though *Ah, Wilderness!* centers on a New England family, dialect is limited to the Irish brogue of Norah, the maid. The Miller family occasionally uses folksy phrases, and the children —age eleven to fifty-odd—burst into "Aw"s, "Gee"s, and "Darn"s. Despite an effort at casualness, the dialogue is laborious, insisting upon Richard's rebellious sensitivity, his father's benign tolerance, his mother's fussy concern, his old maid aunt's prim generosity, his drunken uncle's good intentions, and the purity of love—stock reactions of stock characters, who had long been worth their weight in Broadway gold.

O'Neill apparently made a grim effort to be funny—in puns, two drunk scenes, and a pseudo-seduction. Mrs. Miller, whom Edwin Engel aptly calls a "Mother's Day Mother," clucks at her brother: "Sid, you're a caution. You turn everything into a joke." But Sid's jokes are as heavy as his pouring hand. Like uncle, like nephew. Thus, Richard, *"with a tragic sneer,"* declares, "Life is a joke!" Later, miraculously free of hangover in spite of a night of drinking, Richard punctuates a soliloquy with four "Gee"s, four "Aw"s, and a climactic "Gosh." Earnestly, he confesses to his Muriel that his father had given him hell. When she admonishes him for swearing, he claims: "Hell is the only word that can describe it. And on top of that, to torture me more, he gave me your letter. After I'd read that, I didn't want to live any more. Life seemed like a tragic farce."

Unlike Ionesco, however, who means us to cringe in self-recognition at his tragic farce, O'Neill means us to smile a superior smile at Richard's exaggerations. But the adolescent self-dramatization is dully undramatic, as the appreciative stage laughter is dully non-contagious. Richard's hell is simply silly, but less than a decade later O'Neill was to explore hell in an American family—*Long Day's Journey Into Night.* The language is similarly simple in the two plays; but the earlier play wallows in smug, middle-class sentimentality whereas the later play does not shrink from cruelty, suffering, and the human impurity of love. Were O'Neill not the author of *Ah, Wilderness!*, it would have faded into the oblivion it deserves.

SHORTLY AFTER COMPLETING *Days Without End* IN 1934, O'Neill began work on a cycle of plays about several generations of an American family. By 1941, he noted in his Work Diary: "Idea was first 5 plays, then 7, then 8, then 9, now 11!—will never live to do it—but what price anything but a dream these days!"[44] Preyed upon by a debilitating disease and by the horrors of World War II, O'Neill nevertheless completed rough drafts of the first two double-length plays (and scenarios of plays 7 to II), but he destroyed the first four plays in 1944. In 1936 he completed a draft of what was to be the fifth play, *A Touch of the Poet*, and in 1938 he abandoned revision of the sixth play, *More Stately Mansions*, to work on *The Iceman Cometh* (completed 1939), *Long Day's Journey Into Night* (completed 1940), *Hughie* (completed 1941—the first of a projected cycle of eight one-act plays, *By Way of Obit*), and *A Moon for the Misbegotten* (completed 1942). These non-cycle last plays are similar in their lack of pretentiousness; returning to surface realism, the plays are distinguished by temporal and spatial concentration, and by simple, concrete dialogue.

A Touch of the Poet, the only cycle play whose production O'Neill permitted, seems to have occupied him intermittently from 1935 to 1946, but the play, unlike *More Stately Mansions*, has continuity and coherence. It foreshadows the subdued action of the late non-cycle plays, for love-making, fighting, and shooting take place off stage, while stage action concerns the repetitive pattern of a woman's devotion to the man she loves—Nora to Con Melody, Sara to Simon Harford, who never appears on stage.

The play opens with a clumsy exposition about this Irish immigrant family on the eve of Andrew Jackson's presidency. Often as O'Neill had used Irish brogue in his earlier plays, it functions in the plot for the first time in *A Touch of the Poet*. Con Melody, the Irish protagonist in love with his past as an English Major, speaks like an English gentleman even in soliloquy, breaking into brogue only once, when he is very drunk. He spends his time drinking at his inn with Irish hangers-on, who fawn upon him in brogue. Con's wife Nora, who shares name and station with the maid in *Ah, Wilderness!*, has a soft voice, *"with a rich brogue."* Sara, the daughter of Con and Nora, can shift in and out of brogue.

Doris Alexander has documented the dependence of O'Neill's brogue on the dialogue of the Irish novelist, Charles Lever: "One important aspect of *A Touch of the Poet* certainly derives from *Charles O'Malley* [by Charles Lever]: the language. Eugene O'Neill recreates Irish speech in 1828 largely by use of a few exclamations, a few endearments, and a handful of dialect phrases and pronunciations."[45] Among these are "faith," "Arrah," "troth," "mursha," "sure," "begorra," and "och." Moreover, "The Irish endearments O'Neill uses in *A Touch of the Poet,* such as 'acushla,' 'allanah,' and 'darlin' are all in *Charles O'Malley* and so are all the Irish words with which O'Neill peppers his dialogue: 'dew' (meaning whiskey), 'shebeen,' 'shindy.' . . . Sara, putting on the brogue to annoy her father, says, 'I'll have your plate, av ye plaze.' In Lever, it's 'av ye plase.' Both O'Neill and Lever use 'are you hurted?' Both use 'devil a one,' and 'devil a' in a variety of other ways; O'Neill in such phrases as 'divil a penny,' 'divil a care,' and Lever in 'devil a bit,' 'devil a doubt,' and so on."

The play opens on a brogue that suggests Dublin rather than Boston. After an over-obvious exposition, Sara addresses the barflies in King's English, but she breaks into brogue when her mother defends her father. Through both brogue and formal English thread the words *pride* and *shame*—the polar reactions of each member of this Irish family that has known better days. Father and daughter diverge sharply because the daughter seeks a future in marriage to Simon Harford, whereas the father keeps reliving his past as an English Major. The love story of the fine lord and a poor Irish girl smacks of the melodramas of Dion Boucicault, but the progressive deterioration of Con Melody is pure O'Neill.

"By the Eternal" is Con Melody's favorite oath, and it proves to be ironic, since he undergoes a dramatic change that the dialogue captures. When he is beaten by *servants* of the Mr. Harford he meant to challenge to a duel, Con comes to realize that he is an Irish immigrant and not an English nobleman. Symbolically, he kills his beloved thoroughbred mare, the single reminder of his aristocratic life. After that act, Con begins to speak *"in the broadest brogue, his voice coarse and harsh."* He sneers at himself in the third person, lapsing into pure English only for a brief tribute to his mare. Con himself classifies English as a language of illusion, of the poet Byron whom he has quoted and emulated. Denying his past, Con assumes a new role: "It was the Major played a game all his life, the crazy auld loon, and cheated only himself. But I'll be content to stay meself in the proper station I was born to, from this day on."

In his new humility, Con Melody uses the titular "touch of a poet" about himself, for the first and only time. Earlier, both Con and Nora had applied the phrase to young Simon Harford. (Only Sara claims "there's a true poet in Simon.") But Con twists the titular phrase to condemn his own illusions; leering into the mirror, he burlesques his former poses, exclaiming: "Be Jaysus, if it ain't the mirror the auld loon was always admirin' his mug in while he spouted Byron to pretend himself was a lord wid a touch av the poet—" Young Simon Harford, scion of an old New England family, can afford the luxury of poetic illusion, but Con Melody is beaten to an acceptance of his Irish penury. However, he assumes that new reality with the panache of his old role.

THE MARRIAGE OF SIMON AND SARA IS THE SUBJECT OF *More Stately Mansions*, which spans the decade from 1832 to 1841. Intending to destroy this play, O'Neill did not revise it. According to its editor, the published text constitutes less than half of O'Neill's typescript. Close examination of the dialogue is therefore unwarranted, and yet it is instructive to see how O'Neill grafted the dialogue technique of *Strange Interlude* upon the residual brogue of *Touch of the Poet*.

As Nina is at the center of the several minds of *Strange Interlude*, Simon Harford is at the center of the minds of *More Stately Mansions*. Emerging from his invisibility in *A Touch of the Poet*, Simon sets his wife and mother against one another. While he amasses a fortune, he converts his wife into his mistress and his mother into a French courtesan. Together, the two women people his fantasy life—erotic with Sara, exotic with Deborah. Influenced by poetry, gifted with a touch of the poet, Simon applies the Oliver Wendell Holmes title to their respective lives. He tells Sara: "You must have that engraved over the entrance [of your estate]. And Mother should put it over the magic door to her summerhouse. And I, on the ceiling of this Company's offices—in letters of gold." All three characters build more stately mansions to "shut [them] from heaven."

In the shifting alliances of the three characters, each has at least two languages. Simon uses abstractions in both business and meditation, but he also utters broken sentences of anguished feeling. More schizophrenically, Deborah alternates between her Napoleonic fantasy and a "normal" matronly role. Sara ranges from Irish servant to capable housekeeper to femme fatale to cruel businesswoman, though her speech changes in substance rather than rhythm. At times of stress, she breaks into brogue.

The play opens with soliloquy—that of Deborah. In Act II Simon mutters a thought aside: "Yes, Mother and Sara, henceforth I must demand that each of you takes upon herself her full responsibility for what I have become." After Simon has wooed each woman in turn—in direct dialogue—O'Neill revives the *Strange Interlude* device. The three characters of this love-hate triangle voice their unspoken thoughts, and stylized tableaux anchor the words. Yet the thoughts are often less strange than the spoken dialogue—as in *Strange Interlude.* Having sowed mutual mistrust, Simon leaves the two women alone:

DEBORAH
(Thinking).
Then my beloved son will have no one but me!
SARA
(Thinking).
Then my darling will have only me!

In Act III it is Sara's turn to soliloquize—into a mirror that reflects the expensive whore Simon has desired. The ensuing husband-wife dialogue of passion is naive, full of the verb *want* and the noun *kiss.* In public, Sara imitates Simon's business abstractions, as she had earlier imitated Deborah's elegant phrases.

In the final scene, Deborah, on the brink of insanity, soliloquizes in fragments that contrast with her opening soliloquy ten years earlier. Weary of their "duel to death," Deborah and Sara unite temporarily to mother Simon, who once again contrives to set Sara against Deborah. In a long, clumsily written scene Deborah crosses the border into the insanity of her imperial fantasy, from which she now bars Simon permanently. With Simon lying unconscious in her arms, Sara breaks into a brogue soliloquy, resolving to ruin the Company financially so that

Simon can revert to "the dreamer with a touch of the poet in his soul, and the heart of a boy!" Early in the play, the old phrase was a description of Simon, but as the years passed, Simon came to be called a Napoleon of finance, trade, affairs, facts, and he actually becomes Napoleon in his mother's delusion. It is in the tension between these two words, Napoleon and poet, that the drama lies. The Possessor is Self-Dispossessed as Napoleon defeats the poet in O'Neill's unfinished play of an unfinished cycle, *A Tale of Possessors Self-Dispossessed.*

INTERRUPTING THE CYCLE TO WHICH HE HAD DECIDED to dedicate the rest of his life, O'Neill produced his masterpieces. Inner compulsion proved stronger than elaborate plans, and dramatic literature is the richer for it. In spite of its length, *The Iceman Cometh* was written swiftly between June 8 and November 26, 1939. Using his characteristic repetitions and monologues more insistently than ever before, O'Neill for the first time was able to reach without strain for a theme of wide significance that could not be reduced simply to Fate.

Very near the beginning of the play, its theme is stated by Larry Slade: "The lie of a pipe dream is what gives life to the whole misbegotten mad lot of us, drunk or sober." Through the four acts and forty odd repetitions of "pipe-dream," it is life that sustains the play. In connection with the 1946 production of *The Iceman*—the last production whose rehearsals O'Neill attended —he said at a press conference: "I think I'm aware of comedy more than I ever was before; a big kind of comedy that doesn't stay funny very long. I've made some use of it in *The Iceman*. The first act is hilarious comedy, *I think*, but then some people may not even laugh. At any rate, the comedy breaks up and the tragedy comes on."[46]

The comedy is particularly consistent in the first act, which is about half the length of the play, and though "the tragedy comes on," the comedy never quite disappears. Much of that comedy lies in the shared affection of the down-and-outs, who josh each other good-humoredly in a booze-soaked Utopia. To some extent, the drinking scenes of *A Touch of the Poet* are rough sketches for *The Iceman*, but in the cycle play drinking leads to quarrels and hangovers; in the symbolism of *The Iceman* drinking thaws the ice of death.

O'Neill's combination of the comic and the tragic is present even in the title, *The Iceman Cometh*, as explained by his friend, Dudley Nichols: "The iceman of the title is, of course, death. I don't think O'Neill ever explained, publicly, what he meant by the use of the archaic word, 'cometh,' but he told me at the time he was writing the play that he meant a combination of the poetic and biblical 'Death cometh'—that is, cometh to all the living—and the old bawdy story, a typical Hickey story, of the man who calls upstairs, 'Has the iceman come yet?' and his wife calls back, 'No, but he's breathin' hard.' . . . It is a strange and poetic intermingling of the exalted and the vulgar, that title."[47] Less strange today, the intermingling of the exalted and the vulgar suggests the range of the play—from the Christian "The Bridegroom cometh" to a well-worn dirty joke.

More evidence of the range, and also contributing to the humor, is the variety of idioms and dialects—a wider orchestration than in *The Hairy Ape*, written nearly two decades earlier. Willie Oban, the Harvard Law School graduate, is educated and rhetorical; James Cameron, the journalist, is educated and pointed. Larry Slade, the Foolosopher, casts his metaphysics in a slight Irish brogue; Harry Hope combines New York slang with his Irish brogue, as do Mosher and McGloin. Joe Mott's Negro dialect is more subdued than that of earlier O'Neill Negroes. General Wetjoen has a pronounced Boer accent, and Captain Lewis speaks like an English officer. Hugo Kalmar has a heavy if indeterminate accent of central Europe. Don Parritt talks like a middle-class adolescent, in spite of his Anarchist mother. The bartenders and tarts use stage New Yorkese. Most of these dialects have been heard in earlier O'Neill plays, so that he manipulates them with the ease of familiarity. New to his repertory is the salesman lingo of Hickey—a combination of evangelism and the hard sell; absorbing the vocabulary of pulpit and saloon, Hickey can talk to anyone. Shortly after he arrives on scene, Hickey begins a sermon that he belittles *as* a sermon. In his long final confession, the saloon audience undercuts the theater audience by expressions of boredom and indifference. The dialogue thus mocks itself in all earnestness.

O'Neill uses his dialogue for dramatic comparison and contrast. Almost all the characters contribute to the forty-odd repetitions of "pipe dream" and the twenty odd "tomorrow"s. The tarts and bartenders talk alike, in Damon Runyonese. The onetime enemies in the Boer War speak similar words in different accents, and the onetime Anarchists, Larry and Hugo, speak different words in different accents. Hickey and Parritt, so different in personality, speak identical words at climactic points in their lives.

Not only are pipe dreams differentiated by idiom, but the minor pipe dreams float on semantics. Joe Mott, a black, insists that he is white, and it is ambiguous whether he means color or character. Rocky Pioggi, the night bartender, resents the word *pimp*, though he does send "his" girls to walk the streets. Similarly, Pearl and Margie, called "street walkers" in the cast of characters, resent the word *whore*. Chuck and Cora, their social equals, project a future which is rendered and ridiculed through their language; pimp and whore of the urban ghetto, they chant clichés about marriage and bucolic bliss. They are the only characters to evoke pipe dreams of the future.

Except for Willie Oban, the regulars at Harry Hope's saloon are in their 50's and 60's, so that their pipe dreams are anchored in their past—to return to what they imagine they were. The first of the many repetitions in the play are the eight "onetime"s in the cast of characters. Thus, Ed Mosher, the one-time circus man, dreams of returning to the circus; Pat McGloin to the police force; Joe Mott to ownership of a gambling house; Piet Wetjoen and Cecil Lewis to their respective countries; Jimmy Tomorrow to a journalism job, Hugo Kalmar to revolutionary leadership, Harry Hope to petty politics. Only Larry Slade dreams of *reacting against* rather than *returning to;* against life by sitting on the sidelines till death claims him.

Not only do these pipe dreams show a range of desires, but collectively these drink-nurtured hopes represent what Robert Brustein calls "the total content of human illusion"—political, racial, domestic, psychological, intellectual, philosophical, and religious.[48] But these categories are not tight compartments: Hugo's illusion is both psychological and political, that of Chuck and Cora more romantic than domestic. All the characters possess status illusion, for Harry Hope's saloon offers hope in its bad booze—enough hope for "the whole misbegotten mad lot" of them to retain dignity. When Hickey espouses truth, he assaults the dignity born of illusion.

No admirer of O'Neill, Eric Bentley has affirmed: "In a way the truth-illusion theme is a red herring, and . . . the author's real interest is in the love-hate theme."[49] But, *pace* Bentley, O'Neill relates the two themes organically; the truth-illusion theme is central to the play, and love is the most insidious of all illusions. Harry Hope, Hickey, and Jimmy Tomorrow think they loved their wives, as Don Parritt thinks he loved his mother.[50] Larry Slade thinks he is free of love and pity, for the opposite of love is not hate but indifference, and it is this last that is Larry's illusion. Each of these characters thus languishes in emotional illusion, and they are played against one another in the carefully modulated action that rests solidly on the dialogue.

Though the play seems to end where it began, there is significant change. In Act I Hickey arrives; in Act II he reveals that his wife is dead, in Act III that she has been murdered, and much of Act IV is taken up with his confession of murder. With the exception of Parritt, the Hope saloon has the same human complement at beginning and end, but the sameness has been threatened by Hickey, selling his *hard* ware, the truth in which death is frozen. It is no surprise that the denizens of "No Chance Saloon" cannot sober up to truth; if there is any surprise, it is that they are finally able to relax back into illusion, after brushing so close to the truth which is death.

Though each of the first three acts ends with Hickey's word "happy," O'Neill sinks Hickey's sixteen non-disciples more and more deeply in gloom. In Act I the verbal good will thrives on whiskey; each one teases his neighbor but is tolerant of his illusion. By Act II, Pearl and Cora *"fly at each other,"* Rocky slaps Margie and Pearl, Lewis and Wetjoen have to be pulled apart, McGloin and Mosher make fists at each other. Even more vicious than this physical violence is the verbal spite. In his birthday speech, host Harry Hope insults his guests. Animosity deepens in Act III; Chuck fights with Rocky, and both turn upon Joe; knife and gun replace fists. Worse than the weapons is the scrubbed sobriety with which each denizen gives up his room-key at Hope's saloon, in order to brave the bright, pitiless morning. Climactically, Harry Hope goes forth into daylight, only to flee back from the danger of an imaginary automobile. Funny as this is, it also signals the resurrection of collective illusion in Hope's saloon.

In tracing the progression from illusion to near-truth to illusion, O'Neill uses language functionally if repetitively. Each pipe dream is differently phrased, and the collection is composed of several idioms. The frequent repetition is cumulative in meaning, as the thirteenth "We're waiting for Godot" is far more poignant than the first. Cumulative repetition can, of course, reach a point of no returns, and there will never be agreement as to whether O'Neill passed this point in *The Iceman*. What must be agreed upon, however, is the lack of strain, the concrete consistency, and the comic unpretentiousness of these repetitions—as contrasted with *Strange Interlude* or *Mourning Becomes Electra*.

Each act of *The Iceman* opens on some combination of bartender or Larry, the characters closest to reality. Then we move from pipe dream to pipe dream, until the entrance of Hickey, the biggest pipe dreamer of all, because he espouses reality; that is his pipe dream. Hickey almost converts Larry to truth when Larry breaks out in ironic imagery that mocks him: "I'm afraid to live, am I?—and even more afraid to die! So I sit here, with my pride drowned on the bottom of a bottle, keeping drunk so I won't see myself shaking in my britches with fright, or hear myself whining and praying: Beloved Christ, let me live a little longer at any price! If it's only for a few days more, or a few hours even, have mercy, Almighty God, and let me still clutch greedily to my yellow heart this sweet treasure, this jewel beyond price, the dirty, stinking bit of withered old flesh which is my beautiful little life!" Larry's admission is both voluptuous and ridiculous before he returns to his Stoic pose. And all the other characters, beginning with Harry Hope, return to illusion after being injured by their exposure to truth.

Climactic are the parallel revelations of Hickey and Parritt, which begin by *not* revealing the truth about themselves. Parritt's brief exclamations echo fragments of Hickey's lengthy confession:

HICKEY: I loved Evelyn. Even as a kid.
PARRITT: I loved Mother, Larry! No matter what she did.

HICKEY: I always carry her picture. No, I'm forgetting. I tore it up.
PARRITT: I burnt up Mother's picture, Larry.

Before either of them comes to emotional truth, Jimmy Tomorrow, with "lifeless" voice and "embalmed" face, confesses that he never loved his wife. But Hickey's unacknowledged hatred of his wife resembles Parritt's unacknowledged hatred of his mother:

HICKEY: There was love in my heart, not hate.
PARRITT: You're a liar! I don't hate her! I couldn't.

Then, within moments of one another, they obliquely confess their hatred:

HICKEY: "Well, you know what you can do with your pipe dream
    now, you damned bitch!"
PARRITT: Yes, that's it! Her and the damned old Movement pipe
    dream!

Suitably, Parritt's name is the homonym of parrot. Hickey and his parrot are absolved similarly by Larry, the "weary old priest"; of Hickey he says, "May the Chair bring him peace at last, the poor tortured bastard!" And, sending Parritt to suicide: "Go, for the love of Christ, you mad tortured bastard, for your own sake!"

Parritt alone faces his pipe dream, finally, and O'Neill uses repetition to emphasize his courage. Hugo has begged Parritt to buy him a drink, and with "dramatic bravado" Parritt answers: "Sure, I will, Hugo! Tomorrow! Beneath the willow trees." Parritt then goes upstairs to jump out of the window *today*, here and now. At the final curtain, the whole company *shout in enthusiastic jeering chorus:* "Tis cool beneath thy willow trees!' " They do not know that eighteen-year old Don Parritt is dead, but we know it as we hear them echo his final sporting words.

Much has been said about O'Neill's repetitions in the play, and they are all too evident. But something should be said too about his variety—dialect, pipe dream, character, groups of three or four; and the comedy that functions not for relief but for grave meaning. Thus, Joe Mott uses an old Socialist-Anarchist joke against the stage anarchists, Harry Hope pretends deafness to his thirsty boarders, Lewis twice repeats the stale witticism about recognizing a Boer from a baboon by the latter's blue behind, Mosher lives to bury the doctor who recommended bad whiskey and no work. Several of the names comment on the situations of their bearers, and the play ends on a cacaphonous chorus of different songs, each suited to the singer.

No longer straining for "great language" in this play of the lower depths, O'Neill sustains two main threads of imagery —animals and death. Their conflict is not polar but subtle, for animals are of course vulnerable to death. In the play, however, animal imagery suggests life, which is synonymous with illusion. In Act I, the happy drunks talk about "a line of bull"; they admire Hickey who can "make a cat laugh," and they laugh at his "water-wagon bull." Rocky affectionately refers to the whores as "pigs." Chuck and Cora dream of a farm with cows. Whiskey is referred to as "bug juice" or "rat poison." The tarts call Larry a goat or a fox, who is "full of bull." In the moments before Hickey confesses that his wife is dead, Lewis says that he has the horns of an antelope, Wetjoen of a water buffalo. When Hickey claims that he is crazy—the excuse that will enable hope to be reborn among his victims—Moran calls him "foxy" and the others "rats." After Harry Hope hears Hickey plead that he was crazy, *"he begins to bristle"* and then *"cackles insultingly,"* as his companions *"growl assent."* With such animal vigor, illusion is revived and death delayed by drink.

But before that revival, linguistic death knells sound in *The Iceman*, realizing the symbolism of the title. Even before Hickey's arrival on stage, respects are paid to Willie Oban's dead father, to Harry Hope's dead wife. Colloquialisms involving death are sprinkled through the lines: "You'd steal the pennies off your dead mother's eyes!" "He's killed a half-pint." "The cops got them all dead to rights." "This dump is like a morgue." "It's a dead cinch." "It's as harmless as a graveyard." And many others.

When Willie Oban sings a well-known song of sexual suggestion, the drunks slowly wake: "He rapped and rapped, and tapped and tapped/ Enough to wake the dead." Just before bursting into song, Willie has linked Hickey to death: "Would that Hickey or Death would come!" Once Hickey arrives, death references thicken—both harmless colloquialisms and explicit mention of poison, guillotine, hanging, blowing up the world, graves, corpses, funerals. In Act II, Hickey calls Larry "Old Cemetery, the Barker for the Big Sleep," and in Act III, Larry declares: "Death was the Iceman Hickey called to his home!" Hickey, who constantly invokes the Iceman, has thus gradually emerged as the disciple of Death—not allegorically imposed but concretely constructed through the chilly words on stage. By Act IV, the suggestion of death grows out of the commonest prop, the Chair, for this is where Larry envisages Hickey. Near the end, Hickey, who is virtually condemned to death for murder, accuses the barflies of "acting like a lot of stiffs cheating the undertaker." Not until Hickey moves toward his death in the chair do they come to life.

Hickey confesses his murder in one of the longest speeches ever heard on the American stage—some fifteen minutes of playing time. Hickey's story is chronological, and it leads to death: boyhood, youth, professional life, marriage, profligacy, venereal disease, self-hatred, murder. Early in his life story Hickey cites the colloquial phrase: "Ministers' sons are sons of guns." to explain his wild oats. But we know that Hickey has shot his wife, and the colloquialism, sexually suggestive, is also grotesquely literal; Hickey has become the son of his gun. Threaded through Hickey's confession are snatches of a love duet between himself and his wife Evelyn, which sound like the abstract love duologues of O'Neill's early plays. But in Hickey's mouth, love *is* abstract, having turned to murderous hate. In the written text of the play, Hickey's "So I killed her." is followed by *"dead silence."*

After Hickey's arrest, Hope's boarders eagerly persuade themselves that the salesman was insane, so that they can ease back to their own illusions, and a zest for the liquor of their life. Only Larry, Parritt's executioner and lone witness of his death, pays homage to Hickey's power: "Be God, I'm the only real convert to death Hickey made here." But in spite of Larry's reiterated wish to die, it is Parritt alone who has the courage to commit suicide. In Act II, Hickey had told Larry: "Hell, if you really wanted to die, you'd just take a hop off your fire escape, wouldn't you?" Parritt finally parrots Hickey in suicidal deed as well as confessional word. Hickey, freed by murder, preached a gospel of new life, which proved to be death through truth; Larry, enslaved by his cowardice, resumes his old life at the edge of illusion, into which the others slowly wade.

Their wading is a triumph. In contrast to Gorki's *Lower Depths*, to which *The Iceman* has often been compared, O'Neill's play contains general kindness among the down-and-outs. Old jokes and stale slang are the currency of mutual compassion. Only the two outsiders, Hickey and Parritt, stare at truth's Medusa head; when one is dead and the other soon to be condemned, the company reaches its high point of cheer. Oblivious to tragedy, they have nevertheless tried to prevent tragedy by welcoming the two outsiders into their liquor-soaked ethos. As the Chorus of classical tragedy finally reaffirms a moral order, the Chorus of O'Neill's tragedy reaffirms an affectional order, based on human illusion.[51] That is itself a dark view of the human condition, as O'Neill appreciated when he refused to have the play produced during World War II. But there are gleams through that dark vision in the dim stage light and in the cumulative repetitions of phrase, group, and act. Realistic and symbolic, the play's dialogue reflects the melting-pot of America in 1912, and the planet's inhabitants always.

A FEW MONTHS AFTER COMPLETING *The Iceman Cometh*, while war raged in Europe, O'Neill wrote to Theater Guild Producer Lawrence Langner: "I'm working again on something—not the Cycle—after a lapse of several months spent with an ear glued to the radio for war news. You can't keep a hop head off his dope for long!"[52] The dope is probably a reference to *Long Day's Journey into Night*, which was begun even before *The Iceman* was completed.

Like *The Iceman*, the latter play is set in 1912, the year in which O'Neill attempted suicide and later entered a tuberculosis sanatorium. Like the characters in *The Iceman*, those of *Long Day's Journey* evoke the past. In other respects, though, the two plays are different: *The Iceman*, in O'Neill's words, "flowed right along, page after page," whereas he suffered deeply during the two years he worked on *Long Day's Journey*. A lower-depths saloon is the setting of the one and an upper middle-class country home of the other. The nineteen characters are replaced by five, the many different dialects by middle-class American speech and the brogue of an Irish maid. The geometric breadth of *The Iceman* contrasts with the focused depth of *Long Day's Journey*. *The Iceman Cometh* drags through the blinding day into the soft night of illusion. *Long Day's Journey into Night*, on the other hand, dramatizes the process by which each member of a family travels into his particular night. (Despite the ever-ready Edmund Tyrone-Eugene O'Neill equation, there is at least the possibility that the play's Edmund may die young.) *Day* and *journey* are traditional metaphors for man's life. As opposed to the many references to the titular iceman in the earlier play, there is only one oblique titular recollection in the latter—Mary Tyrone's "It's getting dark already. It will soon be night, thank goodness." But though this is the one verbal reference, the approach of night is audible, visible, and almost palpable through lighting and dialogue, which are carefully blended.

Without leaning on dialect O'Neill nevertheless differentiated the idiom of the four members of the Tyrone family: James' Irish Catholic clichés, Mary's genteel euphemisms, Edmund's quotations and lyricism, and Jamie's quotations and New Yorkese that his father calls "Broadway loafer's lingo." Though each character has an illusion, these differ from those in *The Iceman*, where most characters are reduced to their illusions. In *Long Day's Journey*, the characters are larger than their illusions, and they are all subliminally aware of the truth—Mary her dope, James his miserliness, Jamie his need to destroy, and Edmund his tuberculosis. Not pipe dreams for a vague tomorrow, their lies are today's efforts to escape the reality of yesterday. In the most integrated dialogue that O'Neill ever wrote, each of them interrupts the other's accusative truth. Lonely as each one may be, their dialogue creates a family.

In *Long Day's Journey*, truth is not the polar opposite of illusion. Instead, truth is complex and variable, lying partly within illusion. Less obsessively than either Pirandello or Genet, O'Neill also finds truth deceptive and evanescent in this play.

"Here's how" is Edmund's toast, offered four times during the play, and the interrogative adverb questions all of life's journey; *here* is always a *how*, and can only be captured momentarily, refracted through a particular vision.

Though *Long Day's Journey* is a long play, its repetitions are more subtle than in *The Iceman*. The "pipe dream" of the latter becomes a shifting "lie." All four characters use forms of the verb "to lie," more in self-defense than in attack. James replies to accusations of avarice with "lie," Jamie shouts "lie" to accusations of his responsibility for Edmund's tuberculosis; Edmund calls the diagnosing doctor a liar, and he pleads "lie" to Jamie's insinuation that their mother is back on dope. Sinking into a dope-induced calm, Mary declares: "The past is the present, isn't it? It's the future, too. We all try to lie out of that but life won't let us." And a little later: "I've become such a liar. I never lied about anything once upon a time. Now I have to lie, especially to myself." In soliloquy, Mary sneers at herself: "You expect the Blessed Virgin to be fooled by a lying dope fiend reciting words!" In their last semi-drunken exchange, Edmund and his father fling "lie" in one another's faces until they are liberated of reciprocal resentment. The repetition is muted by syntactical variety and by the everyday normalcy of the word "lie."

Only a little more unusual, the word "blame" is on everyone's tongue; but "lie" and "blame," unlike "love" and "death" in *Mourning Becomes Electra*, are concretized by accumulation of excruciating detail. Mary blames her husband for his penury in robbing her of a home, for committing her to the care of cheap doctors who introduced her to morphine; she blames Jamie for his wasted life and for his suspicion of her; she blames Edmund because his birth ruined her health so that she resorted to morphine to alleviate pain, and she blames him for the cold that worries her into using the drug again. James blames his family for driving him toward the poor-house, he blames Jamie for not bringing credit to the name of Tyrone, and he blames Edmund for following in his brother's footsteps. Jamie blames Edmund for writing better than he did. Both sons blame their father for seeking bargains at the cost of health, and all three men blame Mary for returning to dope. Though the play is remarkably self-enclosed in the tight family circle, all its members are worried about their status in the world, and this too becomes a source of blame: James performs before any passing neighbor while Mary is painfully conscious that their home is not the equal of that of their New England neighbors, and Jamie feels like a hired man when he works on the grounds. Even Edmund, who blames the others for caring about public opinion, worries about it, accusing his father: "But to think when it's a question of your son having consumption, you can show yourself up before the whole town as such a stinking old tightwad!" Like the characters in Chekhov's plays, the members of the Tyrone family are free with expressions of condemnation, and yet such expression does not begin to exhaust the emotional complexity of word and deed.

Early in the play, O'Neill uses repetition to undermine the visual image of middle-aged felicity; Mary declares: "I'm not upset. There's nothing to be upset about. What makes you think I'm upset?" Jamie realizes that his mother "watches us watching her." As Mary succumbs to the drug, she intones that her hands have grown ugly, her eyesight poor, her hair untidy. But Mary's addiction is variously described; skirting mention of the drug, Mary speaks of her "pain"; James, in contrast, refers to the "poison" within her (and he later warns Edmund not to let Jamie "poison" his life.) "Pain" and "poison" oppose each other in an exchange at the end of Act III:

MARY: My hands pain me dreadfully. I think the best thing for me is to go to bed and rest. Good night, dear.
TYRONE: Up to take more of that God-damned poison, is that it? You'll be like a mad ghost before the night's over!

By Act IV, Mary is indeed a mad ghost—a word that has already haunted this play immured in the past. Earlier references to Mary's addiction—her own "lying dope fiend," Edmund's "a dope fiend for a mother," and Jamie's "hophead" are so spare that we are all the more shocked at the final scene, in which we see her as mad ghost. O'Neill has learned to play his repetitions against scenic images. Though the whole play is classically intense in its relentless drive to catastrophe, Act IV is merciless in its tragic thrust. The three men bare themselves in virtual monologues, and Mary finally enters in the full horror of her mental absence.

For most of Act IV, James and Edmund are alone on stage; each has been drinking throughout the evening, and they continue to drink together in an effort to forget the noises from Mary upstairs. They are highly verbal drinkers, and their dialogue only gradually accumulates intensity. When Edmund first returns home, father and son bicker about the lights, and the actor James Tyrone indulges in "dramatic self-pity" as he flamboyantly turns lights on. Edmund laughs, commending the performance: "That's a grand curtain." Later on, they fight bitterly about a sanatorium, and again James reacts extravagantly: "You can choose any place you like! Never mind what it costs! Any place I can afford. Any place you like—within reason." The repetitions are unstrained, and "within reason" at once undercuts and climaxes the repetitions.

Unable to avoid the subjects of dope and consumption, father and son desultorily play cards until Jamie returns. The conversation rambles, but it never stops, and it always functions dramatically. As the two men pick at their cards, James reveals his most profound disappointment in life—"that God-damned play I bought for a song and made such a great success in," ruining his creativity as an actor. Looking back at his cards after the long reminiscence of Booth's admiration for him, James queries ambiguously: "My play, isn't it?" Which play is his— Shakespeare whom he loved, or the melodrama he bought, or the prop card-game on stage? This poignant, understated ambiguity is the antithesis of O'Neill's wet sponge habit.

Even in Edmund's lyric monologue, that habit disappears. No longer so obvious in character delineation, O'Neill has learned to make his dialogue further the action (a journey into night), reveal Edmund, and resonate symbolically through imagery. Edmund rambles, but O'Neill is purposeful in his deployment of fog, sea, and the sense of man's mortality.

Edmund's stammering rhapsody contrasts with Jamie's patchwork of quotations, as Edmund's untutored responses contrast with Jamie's cynical pose. At the same time, the dialogue of Jamie-poseur-quoter prepares for and contrasts with his own climactic, drunken confession. After the maudlin self-pitying quotation, Jamie confesses without using the pronoun "I." Early in Act I, Mary speaks of her reaction to dope in the second grammatical person; late in Act IV, Jamie, too, is ashamed to say "I."

Wearied by drink, talk, and recollection, the three men have almost dozed off when Mary enters theatrically, with lights, music, costume (carried), and Jamie's cynical announcement: "The Mad Scene. Enter Ophelia!" Mary does not recognize them; as Jamie retreats into a Swinburne lament, she mumbles about something she has lost—another meaningful contrast of quotation and hesitation. Again, Edmund's direct dialogue contrasts with Jamie's pose as the younger son tries to reach his mother with the news of his tuberculosis. Mary's final words are especially moving because she has been absent through most of the act. She evokes the certainty of her faith and the memory of her happiness in love, but the dialogue of the play has made us doubt her view of the past. Was there ever faith or love before the journey so deep into the night?

In this "play of old sorrow"[53] O'Neill plays—both dramatically and theatrically—upon various meanings of the word "touch." James Tyrone, in his avarice, is sure that his sons are plotting to touch him for money; Mary complains that Edmund doesn't touch his lunch, and she rejects the suggestion that his illness is a touch of something else than a cold. Jamie is touchy, and Mary is touched that Tyrone has bought a car for her. The Irish maid says primly to Edmund: "I'd never suggest a man or a woman touch drink." in this play of cumulative drinking. In James' first reaction to the knowledge that Mary is back on dope, he is careful not to touch her, and this must be evident visually. Mary laments that she hasn't touched a piano in years. As she sinks into her night, Mary uses the word more ambiguously; speaking of the fog both literally and metaphorically, she claims: "No one can find or touch you any more." Of her wedding dress, Mary declares that the dressmaker "refused to touch it any more or she might spoil it." Edmund, the would-be poet, realizes that he cannot touch what he wants to say, but merely stammers. And when Edmund makes a last plea for his mother's concern, she protests: "you must not try to touch me."—a tragic multivalent pun.

At the last, the three men, who have been drinking throughout the play, put their glasses on the table. Touched so deeply by Mary's escape into a past, they cease physically to touch the alcoholic source of their own escape; word and deed of touch are absent in the final moments. But the playlong insistence upon the word "touch" makes us aware of its absence at the end, as the three Tyrone men, each an actor, are silent spectators of a performance by a woman who "never had the slightest desire to be an actress."

Long Day's Journey represents O'Neill's most dramatic use of dialogue. Edmund's fog-people passage is sometimes cited as proof that O'Neill finally came to terms with his own verbal limitations: "I couldn't touch what I tried to tell you just now. I just stammered. That's the best I'll ever do I mean, if I live. Well, it will be faithful realism, at least. Stammering is the native eloquence of us fog people." Ironically, though, Edmund precedes this apology with a vividly lyric description, where every detail is named precisely and tenderly, and where the sea of mortality relates to the journey of the play's title. If Edmund's passage indeed does reflect O'Neill's evaluation of his own late dialogue, it indicates a new modesty for his new mastery.

Comparable mastery was to be displayed once again, briefly, in *Hughie*, the only play preserved from the projected cycle of one-actors, *By Way of Obit*. When O'Neill realized that he would not be able to write his cycles, he came to think of his last four long plays as a group: *The Iceman Cometh*, *A Moon for the Misbegotten*, *A Touch of the Poet*, and *Long Day's Journey into Night*. But *Hughie*, also completed during that period, remains a play apart.

O'Neill's first one-act play in over two decades, *Hughie* shows the continued variety of his dramaturgy. Unlike his earlier one-acters, *Hughie* is a static semi-soliloquy. And unlike those early one-actors, the realistic surface of *Hughie* is merely its surface, but its depths join those of Absurdist drama. Like Beckett, O'Neill of *Hughie* strips drama to its skeletal components— actors and minimal set. Like Beckett, too, O'Neill attains extraordinary inclusiveness through such stripping, which causes us to focus on the human condition.

The cast of characters reads: " 'Erie' Smith, a teller of tales," and "a night clerk." During his playwriting career, O'Neill used the name Smith in the *Glencairn* plays and in *The Hairy Ape*. Of Yank Smith, the hairy ape, O'Neill said that he was "really yourself and myself." So is Erie Smith, a teller of tales about himself. Like yourself and myself, Erie Smith is mortal. Facing a Night Clerk, Erie Smith faces his own mortality. In *Hughie* O'Neill dramatizes the prototypical Absurdist situation—man's confrontation with mortality—as do Sartre, Camus, Beckett, Ionesco, Genet. Like the characters of French Absurdists, O'Neill's Erie Smith has been shocked by death into an awareness of metaphysical Absurdity. As Camus' Caligula disappears for a few days after the death of his sister-mistress, O'Neill's Erie has been drunk for a few days after the death of Hughie, a hotel Night Clerk. Hughie's death has jinxed Erie, causing him to disbelieve in his own luck. Hung over with doubt, Erie Smith confronts Hughie II, the replacement Night Clerk of the "third class dump" in which he lives. Erie demands of Hughie II: "Key"—a meaningful word.

Shared by two Night Clerks, the name Hughie, nickname for Hughes, belongs to one man who is dead and to another whose thoughts dwell on death. Into the stream of consciousness of Hughie II enter heaven, obsequies of the night, shootouts, ambulance-hopping, fire engines, an ace of spades—all redolent of death. And Erie, too, is haunted by death: *"His face is set in the prescribed pattern of gamblers' dead pan."* Erie tries to philosophize: "When a guy's dead, he's dead. He don't give a damn so why should anybody else?" Though Erie doesn't like to talk about death, he makes such Freudian slips as "tickled to death," "made a big killing," "dead dump," "homey as the Morgue," "dead wrong G's." And these slips make *us* aware of man's mortality.

O'Neill builds his drama on two central symbols, night and gambling. Night is a traditional metaphor for death. The play takes place at night, opening *"between 3 and 4 a.m.,"* when Erie enters the seedy hotel lobby. Both Erie and the Night Clerk have a *"night-life complexion,"* and *"the night vaguely reminds* [Hughie] *of death."* The Night Clerk, who wonders *"what anything has to do with anything,"* muses, toward the end of the play, that he can use Erie *"to help* [him] *live through the night."* As Erie and Hughie

6 1

I used to use each other, each bearing witness to the other's living reality.

Like Genet's maids, Beckett's tramps, or Ionesco's Old Couple, Erie and Hughie contain the human race. Only the Other can testify to the reality of the Self, but the identity of that Other is unimportant. Thus, the two night clerks have the same name —Hughes—the same age, the same job, the same family situation. They both trust Erie with dice (bones); Erie calls them both "dope" and "pal." Interchangeable, they are necessary to Erie because they are not Erie. As Erie tells Hughie II about Hughie I: "I'd get to seein' myself like he seen me."

Gambler and clerk, playboy and husband, separated in their thoughts, Erie and Hughie make "some sort of contact" through repetition of a well-worn gambling colloquialism.

ERIE: But Hughie's better off, at that, being dead. He's got all the luck. He needn't do no worryin' now. He's out of the racket. I mean, the whole *goddamned racket*. I mean life.
NIGHT CLERK: Yes, it is a *goddamned racket* when you stop to think, isn't it? [my italics]

Life as a racket, with man the eternal sucker, is a cliché concept and phrase. But O'Neill deepens the cliché into a symbol for the Absurdity of being-in-the-world. Like the heroes of Sartre and Camus, Erie Smith is aware of Absurdity, and like the heroes of Sartre and Camus, he rebels against Absurdity. He rebels by gambling and tales of gambling. He uses his own money to gamble with both Hughies, but it is real gambling for all that: "We gotta use real jack or it don't look real." Against all odds, Erie Smith banks on both Hughies for confidence, so that life may seem less eerie. Unlike O'Neill's Hickey, who tries to convert men to icy death, Erie Smith persuades them to believe in, to gamble on life, even though it is an absurd racket. Converting himself through conversion of Hughie, Erie energetically tells Hughie II his gambling tales. As the night ebbs, Wise Guy and Sucker are shooting dice. Who is to say which is which?

In *Hughie* O'Neill uses a well-worn stage dialect—that of the New York wise guy, as popularized by Damon Runyon—a dialect that Jamie Tyrone liked to assume. Though Erie Smith grew up in Erie, Pa., he chose Big City life, including its language. *"Consciously a Broadway sport and a Wise Guy,"* Erie flaunts his stereotyped jargon, which is part of the gamble; stance and style defined the game, that long day's gamble against the night.

More original than the Damon Runyonese of Erie Smith's speech is the modified stream-of-consciousness technique for the thoughts of the Night Clerk. In the first New York production (which took place in 1964, eleven years after O'Neill's death) the Night Clerk was overshadowed by an agressive, comic Erie, thus missing the play's resonance.[54] The play is focused not on a small-time gambler, but on the Gambler who is Man, that "teller of tales." Erie and Hughie, an eternal couple threatened by the night, learn to kill the time of their lives by gambling *together*, and their game is a parable of humanity seeking the courage to live through reality. Erie Smith is Everyman in quest of that courage, and Hughie, which contains *you*, is Other. Only by engaging the other in play can we bet on our own reality. By the end of *Hughie* the protagonist and the eponymous antagonist have given one another a tenuous confidence in the luck of the living.

THE OBVERSE OF ERIE SMITH IN *Hughie* IS JIM TYRONE in *A Moon for the Misbegotten*, O'Neill's last play. Ten years older than in *Long Day's Journey*, Jim Tyrone has survived that night, and *Moon* dramatizes his deeper descent toward death. *Moon* not only continues *Long Day's Journey*, it repeats the ice-pond incident. A lesser work than *Iceman, Journey*, or *Hughie, Moon* closes O'Neill's dramatic career not in triumph but in a joshing sadness that borders on sentimentality.

In *The Dramatic Event* Eric Bentley aptly called the play "Eugene O'Neill's Pietà," with a happy middle to substitute for a happy ending.[55] As in *A Touch of the Poet*, the play opens on a clumsy exposition in comic Irish brogue—the exchange of Josie and her brother. As in *Anna Christie*, the tough whore-heroine (actually a virgin in *Moon*)) has a warm heart. As in *Desire Under the Elms*, the unattractive family members leave the farm. Though her brother Mike charges that Josie has "a tongue as dirty as the Old Man's," her idiom is too determinedly hard-boiled to be shocking, as in the following exchange between father and daughter:

HOGAN: Haven't you a tongue in your head, you great slut you?

JOSIE (*With provoking calm*): Don't be calling me names, you bad-tempered old hornet, or maybe I'll lose my temper, too.

HOGAN: To hell with your temper, you overgrown cow!

JOSIE: I'd rather be a cow than an ugly little buck goat. You'd better sit down and cool off. Old men shouldn't run around raging in the noon sun. You'll get sunstroke.

In O'Neill's other late plays, he uses his own verbal limitations functionally—the stale slang of *The Iceman*, the fin-de-siècle quotations of Jamie in *Long Day's Journey*, the Damon Runyonese of Erie in *Hughie*. In *Moon*, however, there is too conscious an effort at drunken Irish charm, at soft hearts beating beneath tough talk, at an old-fashioned love story behind drinking and promiscuity. Though the play is a love story, it sags badly in the love scenes—its happy middle—and O'Neill tries valiantly to invigorate the dialogue through comedy. His scenic directions for the Hogan-Harder confrontation reveal the rapier thrusts he intended:

> It would be hard to find anyone more ill-equipped for combat with the HOGANS. [Harder] has never come in contact with anyone like them. To make matters easier for them he is deliberate in his speech, slow on the uptake, and has no sense of humor. The experienced strategy of the HOGANS in verbal battle is to take the offensive at once and never let an opponent get set to hit back. Also, they use a beautifully co-ordinated, bewildering change of pace, switching suddenly from jarring shouts to low, confidential vituperation. And they exaggerate their Irish brogue to confuse an enemy still further.

O'Neill's actual words, however, do not function as weapons for this attack; instead, the exchange merely expands the brothers' ice-pond anecdote at the beginning of *Long Day's Journey*, and expansion never improves an anecdote.

Though the incident is laboriously described, it is significantly related to the other main event of the play—which does not take place on stage either. The image of *pigs* links the invasion of Mr. Harder's ice pond to Jim Tyrone's cross-country train trip with his mother's body. In the play's movement from comedy to pathos, these off-stage events are crucial.

Hogan, the victor of the ice-pond battle, has eyelashes and eyebrows that *"remind one of a white pig's,"* and his name contains the word *hog*. He paints his pigs as avatars of himself—thirsty Irish animals victimized by Yankee Mr. Harder. In Jim Tyrone's confession to Josie, however,the pig is a blonde whore in whose arms he had drunkenly sought asylum from the reality of his mother's death. Only liquor leads Jim to unburden himself to Josie, and, ex-actor that he is, Jim makes a scene of it. But even in this play of his past, he is conscous of playing; reënacting his grief at his mother's coffin, he accuses himself: "You lousy ham! You Goddamned lousy ham!" In his very choice of words, Jim is tainted in his own eyes; a ham is part of a pig. Thus, the frail farcical animal of the ice-pond anecdote becomes the symbol of a man's tragic dissolution in his own eyes. But the last reference to *pig* comes from Hogan. When he learns of the chaste night of the misbegotten lovers, he protests to his daughter: "I'm not a pig that has no other thought but eating!" This return to the everyday use of the image is also a return from the mythopoetic Pietà to everyday rough-and-tumble on the farm.

In harmony with the farm setting, O'Neill lards the Hogan conversation with other animals beside pigs—cows, goats, horses, skunk, fox, snake—and such imagery contributes to the effect of comic vigor. On the other hand, Jim too uses animal imagery, but more obliquely—"old poetic bull," "slap in the puss," "hair of the dog." Of the blonde whore, Jim describes "a come-on smile as cold as a polar bear's feet." Less elegant and cutting than the Jamie of *Long Day's Journey*, *Moon's* Jim quotes the same poets and uses the same idiom that Josie calls "rotten Broadway blather," as James Tyrone had called it "Broadway loafer's lingo." But the sustained idiom of each character of *Moon* is less intense and functional than in *Long Day's Journey*; only a few duologues energize the play more successfully than the plots and counterplots under the full moon. O'Neill's own less certain hand may be heard in the frequent recurrence of "strange" and especially "queer" on all lips.

Lacking the mastery of the other late plays, *A Moon for the Misbegotten* is rarely seen because of the physical demands for

the heroine, a *tellus mater*. As O'Neill's last play, it has nevertheless received critical attention, and Eric Bentley has indicated
that it tends to be viewed as symbolic of the whole canon:

> *A Moon for the Misbegotten* will change no one's opinion of Eugene
> O'Neill. It is neither his worst work nor his best. . . . I think its
> central image'—that of a giant virgin holding in her arms a dip-
> somaniac lecher with a heart of gold—may stand in all minds as
> O'Neill's monument; for admirers will find it characteristic in gran-
> deur and poetry, while others will find in it, clinically speaking,
> neurotic fantasy indulged rather than exploited and, critically
> speaking, poetry strained after rather than achieved.[56]

What is ironic is the clinical and critical lapse after the superbly
functional achievements of the unstrained poetry of *The Iceman*,
Long Day's Journey, and *Hughie*.

EUGENE O'NEILL'S PLAYWRITING CAREER RESEMBLES
a saint's legend. Having committed himself to drama at the age
of twenty-four, by beginning to write plays while in a tuberculosis sanatorium, he never swerved—"an artist or nothing."
Neither money nor fame seduced him; he neglected family and
friends for his work; he allowed neither alcohol nor illness to
prevent him from writing. He persevered monomaniacally,
seeking to create great American tragedy. His strongest expression of disapproval was "easy."[57] He never wooed Broadway, he
suffered no play-doctors, and he rarely accepted suggestions
from actors or directors. He received the Nobel Prize at ap-
proximately the time he was struck by a debilitating illness, but
he kept on writing. Crippled beyond the possibility of creation,
O'Neill had the courage to destroy all but one of the plays of the
Cycle to which he had decided to dedicate his life. Astound-
ingly, he made these sacrifices though he lacked that basic gift
of a major playwright—the ability to write dialogue that was
both functional and distinctive.

O'Neill's early plays oscillate between the stilted rhetoric of
melodrama and the ungrammatical colloquialism (including dialect) of the realistic novel. He was to continue using these two
main idioms until his last plays. In both idioms O'Neill early

began to use two techniques that have become synonymous with his name—verbal repetition and extended monologue (however often the latter might be interrupted by scenic directions). Moving from a realistic surface to his two Expressionist plays, *Emperor Jones* and *The Hairy Ape*, O'Neill combined these techniques—in different dialects—more effectively than in any of the pretentious and messianic plays of the following decade. Between 1924 and 1934 O'Neill wrote dramas based on black-white polarities: literally black and white in *All God's Chillun*, metaphorized into stones vs. gold in *Desire Under the Elms*, theatricalized into opposing masks in *The Great God Brown*, experimentalized into normal speech vs. thought asides in *Strange Interlude*, abstracted into love vs. death in *Mourning Becomes Electra*. In spite of extravagant staging, these dramas revolve about a few simple ideas which are repeated in refrains, rather than translated into acton and character by means of dialogue.

After this decade of verbal stretch and strain, O'Neill is often said to have "returned" to realism, but we have too little evidence to be sure, since he destroyed so many manuscripts. *More Stately Mansions*, which he meant to destroy, bursts and languishes in the feverish idiom of the plays of the extravagant decade. And in spite of the new control, humor, and concreteness of the language of the "Irish" plays, *A Touch of the Poet* and *A Moon for the Misbegotten*, they are not major works. Finally, there are three masterpieces among O'Neill's forty-six published plays: *Hughie*, *The Iceman Cometh*, *Long Day's Journey into Night*. And even these last two have traces of what Hofmannsthal early designated as O'Neill's wet sponge tendency. Hofmannsthal also criticized O'Neill's characters as "not sufficiently fixed in the present because they are not sufficiently fixed in the past." Only at the end of his creative life was O'Neill able to fix his characters indelibly in our present by making them resonate through his own past. Though he was just past fifty when he wrote his great works, the world's ills and his own had aged him and wisened him.What is miraculous is that he should have been able, exceptionally and extraordinarily, to express his new wisdom through the anxieties of his characters' credible speech.

But then saints' legends traditionally end in miracle.

3 / The Articulate Victims of

ARTHUR MILLER

Though it is clear to us today that O'Neill dominated American drama of two decades, this was not clear in the theater of the time. A box-office success in the 1920's, O'Neill lapsed into obscurity after the failure of *Days Without End* in January, 1934. Toward the end of the 1930's, two different kinds of drama were popular—the verse plays of Maxwell Anderson and the indignant pleas of Clifford Odets. Anderson's language was neither modern nor period nor recognizably his, falling into imperfect pentameters. Odets, on the other hand, coined a ringing urban idiom. His longtime friend and coworker, Harold Clurman, describes Odets' dialogue: "It was a compound of lofty moral feeling, anger, and the feverish argot of the big city. It bespoke a warm heart, an outraged spirit, and a rough tongue."[1] Moreover, the warm heart and outraged spirit were dramatized only because of the rough tongue.

"Rough" is a highly relative adjective, and today we smile at the idea of a shock reaction to the dialogue of either O'Neill or Odets. In phonographic fidelity to colloquial speech, Odets moved a step onward from O'Neill by recording urban Jewish-American—both syntax and vocabulary. Where O'Neill had gone to books, Odets went to voices.[2] O'Neill had lived through his sea voyages and bar periods before he began to write; Odets began to write because of his immerson in the "hangdog, ratty, and low."[3] With success and celebrity, however, Odets lost his ear for this idiom. But Arthur Miller, also a product of a Jewish urban environment, responded to Odets' *Awake and Sing!* just as he was beginning to write. As Odets took from John Howard Lawson a blend of lofty morality and city slang, so Miller took them from Odets. And made them distinctively his own.

In the Introduction to his *Collected Plays*, Miller tells of the genesis of each play. Though Miller had earlier written several plays, *All My Sons* (1947) was the first to be published. Conceived and partially written during World War II, the play was intended to be untheatrical, but traditional theatricalism is certainly present in two war-hero brothers in love with the same girl, two businessmen involved in the same crime, the hidden-letter trick of the well-made play, son and father who commit suicide to teach a moral lesson, and final union of hero and heroine. In the fashion, too, of certain well-made plays, Miller's theatricalism focuses on a contemporary subject—war profits. But contrary to the fashion of well-made plays, Miller's villain inspires pity rather than hisses, because his villain looks, thinks, and talks like a member of the Broadway audience. Many in that audience thought that Miller was blaming the system rather than the man, Joe Keller.

Just before villain-protagonist Joe Keller shoots himself in atonement for his social sin—illicit war profits—he refers us to Miller's title, *All My Sons:* "Sure, [Larry] was my son. But I think to him they were all my sons. And I guess they were, I guess they were." And one shouldn't profit by the death of one's sons. Joe's final recognition is prepared by his expressions of affection for his son, Chris, and, to a lesser extent, by his easy cameraderie with the neighborhood children.

Though the play is based on an incident that took place in the Middle West, and though Miller sets the play "in the outskirts of an American *town*, " (my italics) the drama is heightened by Joe's Jewish rhythms and vivid if familiar idiom: "You look at a page like this you realize how ignorant you are." "You can talk yourself blue in the face, but there's no body and there's no grave, so where are you?" "It's a tragedy: you stand on the street today and spit, you're gonna hit a college man." "A little man makes a mistake and they hang him by the thumbs; the big ones become ambassadors." "I'm his father and he's my son, and if there's something bigger than that I'll put a bullet in my head!" In each of these sentences, rhythm reenforces sentiment—respect for learning, cynicism about civic duty, emphasis on family feeling. It is loyalty to these familiar American qualities, expressed in Jewish syntax, that turns Joe Keller, family-man, into a killer of G. I. Joe's, all of whom should be as sons to him.

Father and son, Joe and Chris, are moral antagonists, and Miller gives them different idioms. Particularly in moments of crisis, Joe cries out in expletives whereas Chris pontificates in abstractions. This tends to arouse greater sympathy for Joe, so that he becomes more victim than villain, weakening the moral intent of the play. Further weakening that intent are the questions that thread through the dialogue, since no one is actually seeking answers. Chris has his prim moral stance, and Joe has his pragmatic stance—both unshakable through the body of the play. The two women want peace and happiness, which might be disturbed by questions. Nevertheless, the four characters ask questions, which contribute vivacity to the play's dialogue. Questions are absent from the climax, however, for dead Larry's letter is frank in its statement, though it pleads inability to state: "It is impossible to put down the things I feel. . . . I can't express myself. I can't tell you how I feel. . . . I don't know how to tell you what I feel. . . ." The verbal hesitations of dead Larry are spoken on stage by live Chris;—thus the two sons judge their father.

BOTH *All My Sons* AND MILLER'S BEST-KNOWN PLAY, *Death of A Salesman*, (1949) presumably dramatize Wasp families, since Miller does not specify racial or religious origins. Mary McCarthy has scolded Miller for concealing the Jewishness of the Loman family,[4] and Leslie Fiedler has claimed that Miller creates "crypto-Jewish characters . . . who are presented as something else." Miller has countered that "Jewishing" the families would undercut their all-American typicality, and Miller views the drive toward success as all-American.[5] In *Death of A Salesman* Miller uses an appropriately informal syntax and many casual repetitions to suggest an all-American quality. It is hardly relevant to claim, as does George Steiner, that "The brute snobbish fact is that men who die speaking as does Macbeth are more tragic than those who sputter platitudes in the style of Willy Loman.''[6] *Macbeth* today can be food for farce, not tragedy, as illustrated by the success of *McBird* and the failure of *Makbeth*. And platitudes can be meaningful if the total play rises above them.

Whatever Miller may have written afterwards, *The Death of A Salesman* is larger than Willy Loman, and a variety of dialogue contrasts with his platitudes. Leonard Moss mentions a hundred odd repetitions of the word "man," about a hundred of "boy" and "kid" (with its easy, undiscriminating bisexual affection), about fifty variants of the verb "to make."[7] But this flatness is relieved by Charley's cynical urban idiom, Uncle Ben's rugged phrases, Linda's sentableious or sentimental outbursts, Happy's wise guy banter, Biff's lyricism about Nature, and, most important of all, the range of Willy Loman's clichés.

Like Buechner's Woyzeck, Willy's feelings overflow his language. But Woyzeck is sparing of words, and Willy is lavish. He himself admits: "I talk too much. . . . I joke too much!" And Miller dramatizes the "too much" in comparison with the dialogue of the other characters. As in *Woyzeck*, there is no raisonneur or norm character; there are only different inadequacies expressed through different idioms. Unlike Buechner, Miller does not use folk songs and the Bible to cement his modern Tower of Babel. And yet, the moral logic of the play reveals the bankruptcy of Willy's language.

The original title of *Death of A Salesman* was *The Inside of His Head*, and Miller's dramatic achievement has been the skillful manipulation of Willy's last hours to reveal what goes on inside his head. In Act I four extended memory scenes are climaxed by Biff's discovery of the woman in his father's hotel room. Near the end of Act II Willy has a fantasy of asking his dead brother Ben for advice about his own suicide. Through blocking, lighting, and music, Miller sets off these verbal excursions into Willy's memory and fantasy, so that we never confuse them with the suspenseful present.

We are able to shuttle between past and present because of the "partially transparent" Loman house. Jo Mielziner's set for the original New York production of *Salesman* is a descendant of Strindberg's set for *Ghost Sonata*. Perhaps under Strindberg's influence, O'Neill built similarly in *Desire Under the Elms*; Williams continued the mode in *Glass Menagerie* and *Streetcar Named Desire*. And *Salesman* is the last of the series.

The English critic Dennis Welland has summarized the thematic importance of these transparent settings: "The cataclysms that cause the fall of the frontage of the houses of Eugene O'Neill's Ephraim Cabot and Ezra Mannon, of Tennessee Williams's Amanda Wingfield and Stanley Kowalski, and of Miller's Willy Loman, are psychological rather than meteorological. . . . The 'exploded' house set is integral to the impression at which all these plays aim, for not only does it mirror the family combustion that has come more and more to dominate the American theatre, but it is peculiarly suited to their dramatic idiom."[8] Particularly astute is Welland's recognition that the exploded house is background for an exploding idiom. *Desire*, *Salesman*, and *Menagerie* abound in expletives and sentence fragments. Without the blatant subjectivism of expressionist drama, these plays nevertheless seek to make a similarly general statement, transcending realism. Miller has called attention to his "expressionistic elements . . . to create a subjective truth" in *Death of A Salesman*.[9] And the father of such elements is Strindberg in his *Dream Play*.

Miller has often acknowledged his debt to Ibsen rather than Strindberg, and yet *The Dream Play* is the ancestor of *Death of A Salesman*, where dream is theme, refrain, and technique. Rather than a tragedy of failure, as the play is often described, *Death of A Salesman* dramatizes the failure of a *dream*. The intrusion of Willy's past and fantasy into his present resembles a dream, and the word "dream" recurs, from the early scenic direction: "*An air of the dream clings to the place, a dream rising out of reality.*" through the introduction of Willy's sons: "[Biff's] *dreams are stronger and less acceptable than Happy's.*" to the triple evocation in the Requiem:

BIFF: He had the wrong dreams.
HAPPY: He had a good dream.
CHARLEY: A salesman is got to dream, boy. It comes with the territory.

Miller's play is as much about the salesman's dreams as about his death, but death lies immanent in Willy's dreams.

Though Willy is prey to the American dream of success, and to the tribal dream of success through heirs, the dream itself is vague in detail. Only obliquely does Willy's success dream come "with the territory," through salesmanship; rather, Willy feels that success will come in some undefined way, through the most insistent phrase in the play—being "well liked."[10] The phrase is Willy's, but it is echoed by Linda, Biff, and Happy. Only Charley challenges this central aspect of Willy's dream, and he does so with a pithy Jewish inflection: "Why must everybody like you? Who liked J. P. Morgan? Was he impressive? In a Turkish bath he'd look like a butcher. But with his pockets on he was very well liked." While Willy tries to win friends and influence people, Charley insists that money talks; each of them voices a different aspect of the success dream.

Willy is sufficiently sure of his dream to reject Charley—advice and money. But at the same time he is so insecure in his dream that he carries on a lifelong debate with his brother Ben. Both Charley and Ben—a small businessman and a ruthless adventurer—are foils for Willy, and their respective idioms contrast with his simple clichés of success through popularity. Charley's salty prose has been quoted, and Ben speaks in active epigrams: "Never fight fair with a stranger, boy." But monosyllabically and boisterously, Willy preaches popularity more loudly than he is able to practice it. Though Willy sometimes claims to be well liked, he confides to Linda that people laugh at him instead of liking him. Even his infidelity is the result of making a woman laugh. Certainly he often makes *us* laugh—in large part by the juxtaposition of his ephemeral dream against the irritating concreteness of his Chevvy, Studebaker, and Hastings refrigerator. We may not know what Willy sells, but we know what he buys: "The refrigerator consumes belts like a goddam maniac." The death of the salesman is foreshadowed in the comic deaths of his installment-plan purchases, which we witness only through dialogue.

A sequence of shiny, treacherous machines is suggested through the play's abrupt opening and Willy's first memory scene. In these two important early scenes, Biff's boyhood popularity is contrasted with Willy's laughableness. The memory scene begins when Willy praises Biff for polishing his car, but he soon gives advice about the girls with whom Biff is "makin' a hit." At the end of Willy's recollection of Biff's day of success, Willy boasts and complains in typical self-contradiction: "Oh, I'll knock 'em dead next week. I'll go to Hartford. I'm very well liked in Hartford. You know, the trouble is, Linda, people don't seem to take to me." As he describes how people laugh at him, a woman's laugh is heard, introducing Willy's memory within a memory. Unlike the girls who pay for Biff, Willy's Woman has to be bought with silk stockings, while Linda mends her stockings at home. When Willy returns to his first memory, all is soured—Biff is failing math, he steals, the mothers complain that he is too rough with the girls. The emotional shift—conveyed entirely by dialogue—foreshadows the play's climactic confrontation between Willy and Biff.

The opening scenes of Act II not only develop the precarious quality of Willy's dream; they also set up father-son foils to Willy-Biff. Old man Wagner's son Howard is successful by inheritance, and his idiom reflects his security. Charley's son Bernard is successful by hard work, and his idiom reflects his studiousness. Both sons succeed within the framework of American capitalism. Yet Biff is a failure because he remained a slave to his father's "phoney dream" even after he has rejected his father as a "phoney fake." His idiom reflects his immaturity; even his name is a boy's nickname.

In the swift sequence of scenes in Howard's office, Charley's office, Frank's chop-house, Miller skillfully disintegrates Willy's dream for us (though not for him). The scene in Howard's office offers a paradigm for the whole play: Howard is no more faithful to his father's memory than Willy is to the memory of his father's flutes; Howard is as blind and provincial about his children as Willy is about his; Howard speaks inconsiderately to his wife, as Willy does to Linda. The tape-recorder is a symbol of both Howard and Willy, with ready-made phrases uttered mechanically. Howard and Willy show two sides of American progress: one is failure and the other success, with little to choose between them.

In Howard's office Willy evokes the memory of the great salesman, Dave Singleman, whose name denies "a dime a dozen." Singleman is singular, unique. He achieved the popularity to which Willy aspired; it is his death, narrated by Willy, that evokes the play's title: "When he died—and by the way he died the death of a salesman, in his green velvet slippers in the smoker of the New York, New Haven and Hartford, going into Boston—when he died, hundreds of salesmen and buyers were at his funeral." And that is the kind of funeral Willy envisions for himself. After leaving Biff his insurance, Willy addresses the fantasy figure of his dead brother Ben: "Ben, that funeral will be massive! They'll come from Maine, Massachusetts, Vermont, New Hampshire! All the old-timers with the strange license plates—that boy will be thunderstruck, Ben, because he never realized—I am known! Rhode Island, New York, New Jersey—I am known, Ben, and he'll see it with his eyes once and for all." Geography and repetition sound lyric notes for Willy, but the old-timers with the strange license plates are dead, if they ever existed; only the family and faithful Charley come to Willy's actual funeral.

The imaginary funeral underlines the poverty of Willy's imagination. Compare his listing of states with the vision of Genet's Solange for the funeral of a maid: "The funeral will unfold its pomp. It's beautiful; isn't it? First come the butlers, in full livery, but without silk lining. They're wearing their crowns. Then come the footmen, the lackeys in knee breeches and white stockings. They're wearing their crowns. Then come the valets, and the chambermaids wearing our colors. Then the porters. And then come the delegations from heaven." (Frechtman translation) Pomp and circumstance create a mythology, so that servitude bursts its bonds to achieve royalty—in the imagination of a maid.

Willy's linguistic poverty, by contrast, reflects both the poverty of his world and the poverty of his dream. Henry Popkin has described Willy's world as "full of aspirin, arch supports, saccharine (all the wrong cures for what ails Willy), Studebakers, Chevrolets, shaving lotion, refrigerators, silk stockings, washing machines."[11] But the first three items are (perhaps) remedies, and most of the others break down. Willy's life embodies the contradiction between these concrete trivialities and his grandiose verbal projections. In past, present, and fantasy, Willy usually expresses himself through repetition and cliché, a formulaic chant which is unaffected by the stubbornness of things. *"An air of the dream"* may *"ris[e] out of reality,"* but Willy's vague dream is at odds with concrete reality. He has achieved neither popularity nor success as a salesman, and he has failed as gardener, carpenter, and father.

Willy's opening words suggest his immaturity: "Oh, boy, oh, boy." To the figure of Ben he confesses that he feels "kind of temporary" about himself. His repetitions of "The woods are burning" indicate some perception of the Inferno in which he lives, but his perception is limited. Willy's Hell may be paved with good intentions, but even they appear to be rationalizations after the fact; Willy dreams of success for Biff because he himself is a failure. Willy refuses Charley's charity because he himself cannot accept the truth of his failure. Though he has been toying with the idea of suicide, Willy actually kills himself only when he can disguise his death as a gift to Biff.

Miller and others have written many pages about Willy Loman, the low man. Consistently conceived, Willy does not speak out of character.[12] But Miller disturbs his own thematic consistency by his climactic scene—Willy's memory of Biff's discovery of a woman in his Boston hotel room. Willy's dream, vague in detail, is the American dream of success. Though Willy dies without recognizing the triviality of his dream, the play makes *us* aware of that triviality. Before the climax, Miller dramatizes Biff's recognition of the impossibility, if not the insubstantiality, of Willy's dream. We see Willy rejected by Howard, and we hear of Biff's parallel rejection by Oliver.

The scene of Biff's self-recognition is a recognition of the phoniness of his father's dream. Rhythmically colloquial—"He thinks I've been spiting him all these years and it's eating him up."—pointedly economical—"We've been talking in a dream for fifteen years."—the dialogue is nervous with questions, interruptions, and muted repetitions.

WILLY: What happened? He took you into his office and what?
BIFF: Well—I talked. And—and he listened, see.
WILLY: Famous for the way he listens, y'know. What was his answer?

BIFF: His answer was—*(He breaks off, suddenly angry)*. Dad, you're
    not letting me tell you what I want to tell you!
WILLY, *(accusing, angered)*: You didn't see him, did you?
BIFF: I did see him!
WILLY: What'd you insult him or something? You insulted him,
    didn't you?
BIFF: Listen, will you let me out of it, will you just let me out of it!
HAPPY: What the hell!
WILLY: Tell me what happened!
BIFF, *(to Happy)*: I can't talk to him!

The repetitions of "listen" stress Willy's inability to listen to
any contradiction of his dream. Uttered without strain, Biff's "I
can't talk to him." summarizes the scene and Biff's whole life.

Biff's recognition scene dovetails neatly with Willy's next
memory scene, but the two are not related thematically. A
phoney dream of success should be exploded by a scene about
the phoniness of success, and not about illicit sex. The final
tableau of the scene leaves us with a strong impression of Willy's
self-contradiction—begging on his knees as he threatens Biff
with a beating. But there are flaws in the woman's dialogue—
she insists that Willy open the door and she pointlessly questions Biff: "Are you football or baseball?"

As the climax violates the thematic drive of the play, so the
Requiem violates its form. *Death of A Salesman* is not rigidly
contained by Willy's mind, but the Requiem is jarringly and
flagrantly outside his mind. More important, the Epilogue provides us with few new insights, and those are confusing. We
have already heard the divergence of Willy's sons in their judgment of their father; Happy remains subject to Willy's dream
while Biff attains self-recognition in Oliver's office; this bifurca-
tion scarcely needs to be spelled out again. Charley, on the other
hand, changes surprisingly; having repeatedly urged Willy to
give up his phoney dream as a traveling salesman, Charley is
suddenly sentimental about that dream. Earlier, he had said to
Willy: "The only thing you got in this world is what you can
sell," but by the Requiem the "what" gives way to a shine and
a smile—an utterly incongruous coupling on the sharp tongue
of the cynical businessman.

It is Linda, however, whose words in the Requiem are most confusing. We have witnessed her devotion to her husband, and we can sympathize with her grief. However, it is difficult to understand her lack of understanding. When Linda found the rubber pipe near the gas jet, she worried, but she did not wonder *why* Willy wanted to kill himself, discouraged and exhausted as he was. Desperate (and deluded) by the end of the play, Willy finally carries out his threat. Her bereavement evokes our pity, but her astonishment is astonishing. Like Charley's final speech, hers sentimentalizes the tragedy in its flagrant bid for tears.

Though Miller's stage directions specify that Linda *"lacks the temperament to utter"* the longings she shares with Willy, she is quite articulate—too articulate for her final lack of understanding. Willy treats her badly, but she defends him eloquently. Far from the Jewish Mother who has been detected beneath Linda's syntax, Willy's wife is a tear-making tool for Miller, from her "Attention must be paid" speech, through her remonstrances with her sons, to the final ironic chant: "We're free. We're free . . . We're free . . ." Bound to Willy's dream, she defends it against the temptation represented by Ben. She claims attention for Willy as a "human being," but she magnifies Willy's importance through her use of generalizations, passive constructions, resonant "that man"'s, and her pretentious or sentimental epigrams: "Life is a casting off." "A man is not a bird, to come and go with the springtime." "He's only a little boat looking for a harbor." At such lines, one can sympathize with Willy's efforts to shut her up; and yet she is, more perniciously than Willy realizes, his "foundation and . . . support."

Near the beginning of the play, Willy grumbles: "Figure it out. Work a lifetime to pay off a house. You finally own it, and there's nobody to live in it." Linda almost echoes him at the end: "I made the last payment on the house today. Today, dear. And there'll be nobody home." What neither of them learns is that a house is not a home when clichés boomerang transparently. Ironically, however, much of the play's strength lies in the carefully rhythmed poverty of Willy's language. His mass-produced phrases belie his claim to special attention. His sentimental fantasies are inevitably punctured by concrete reality. But rather than risk complete deflation, he risks—and loses—his life.

Somewhat superfluously, Miller told an interviewer that he was not Willy Loman but a writer; "Willy Loman is there because I could see beyond him."[13] And it may well be that Willy's durable stage thereness rests on the fact that all of us see, and especially hear, beyond him. Willy's vocabulary is totally familiar—endearingly so because it is so limited. Willy's questions seem totally familiar—again endearing because limited. It is easy to pity and even love Willy, who is our father, brother, cousin, friend. But never *me*.

Compared to O'Neill's Hickey, Willy is bankrupt of words. Hickey begins by being well liked and successful; he has the gift of gab, and he spends it lavishly. Willy is not frugal of words, but he has so few of them that he keeps repeating his small stock. Hickey's relentless flow of words finally turns us against him, but we remain attached to Willy because we can talk and think rings around him. *Death of A Salesman* triumphs because Willy falls short of us, but within touching distance.

AFTER *Death of A Salesman* MILLER BECAME A SPEcialist of the protagonist-victim whom he sought to elevate to tragic stature. In Miller's following play, *The Crucible* (1953) the hero-victim preserves integrity by sacrificing his life. Thus, in Miller's first three published plays we move from villain-victim to protagonist-victim to hero-victim; all these are extremely verbal while producing an effect of inarticulacy.

Since *The Crucible* is set in colonial New England, Miller invents a language that vaguely recalls colonial English; its main features are using *be* as a main verb and *do* as an auxiliary verb, juggling with tense and number of verbs, and voicing *you* in the frequent imperatives. This unfamiliar language permits Miller to indulge in a more mannered rhetoric than in the colloquial dialogue of his first two plays. Willy Loman expressed his love of nature simply: "The trees are so thick, and the sun is warm." But John Proctor, a man who loves his land, can say unabashedly to his wife: "Lilacs have a purple smell. Lilac is the smell of nightfall, I think. Massachusetts is a beauty in the spring!"

Fortunately for Miller, his dramatic thrust is not toward a Rousseauistic past, but toward a punch-packed present. The play's title refers to high-temperature testing, and Miller raises the temperature in scenes of passion: a sick child inspires an orgy of hysteria in Act I; innocent Elizabeth Proctor is roughly imprisoned in Act II; hysteria mounts, and John Proctor is imprisoned in Act III; finally, in Act IV, John Proctor, after slight hesitation, goes to his martyrdom. In spite of John's adultery, there is never any doubt that he is admirable, and there is never any doubt that the persecuting witch-hunters (with the exception of Hale) are evil; their economic and political interests are propped up by the "evidence" of their fanatical faith. In the confrontations, the good victims speak in heroic phrases and the bad villains speak in sadistic phrases. The latter occasionally sound like Grand Guignol, as when Abigail threatens the other girls: "I will come to you in the black of some terrible night and I will bring a pointy reckoning that will shudder you. And you know I can do it; I saw Indians smash my dear parents' heads on the pillow next to mine, and I have seen some reddish work done at night, and I can make you wish you had never seen the sun go down!"

For all the hysterical histrionics of the play, the moral choices turn simply upon the word and concept of *name*. Abigail brazenly assures her uncle: "There be no blush about my name." Both to her uncle and to John Proctor, Abigail accuses Elizabeth Proctor of blackening her name in the village. (Nor does Miller seem to notice the irony of making this charge to John.) Her credibility depends upon her good name.

The importance of having a good name is insidiously shifted by the witch-hunters, into the naming of names. Giles Corey, foreshadowing John Proctor's final conduct, preserves his good name by refusing to name names. As John Proctor's perlious position is intensified, he expresses himself more and more angrily in more and more abstractions, which Miller anchors by repetitions and the word *name*. John tarnishes his name by confessing his adultery, in order to stain Abigail's name. When Elizabeth lies about John's adultery, he cries out: "She only thought to save my name!" Ready to sacrifice his name in exchange for his freedom, John is not willing to testify that any of his fellow-victims spoke to the Devil: "They think to go like saints. I like not to spoil their names."

After John signs his name to his confession, he refuses to relinquish the document: "God has seen my name on this! It is enough!" Guilty in the sight of his God, Proctor is not willing to have his neighbors know his guilt. His final plea to Mr. Danforth is: "I have given you my soul; leave me my name!" The play has made soul and name synonymous, and Proctor realizes this with melodramatic gestures: *"His breast heaving, his eyes staring, Proctor tears the paper and crumples it, and he is weeping in fury, but erect."* His last words are as heroically sanctimonious as the stock gestures: "You have made your magic now, for now I do think I see some shred of goodness in John Proctor. Not enough to weave a banner with, but white enough to keep it from such dogs. *Elizabeth, in a burst of terror, rushes to him and weeps against his hand.* Give them no tear! Tears pleasure them! Show honor now, show a stony heart and sink them with it!" In spite of the repetitive immediacy of "now," the shift from "name" to "honor" weakens these heroics by abstraction. The stale image of a "stony heart" is particularly infelicitous for the frigid Elizabeth. And the lack of a body of water for "sink"ing illustrates the effort with which Miller imposes imagery without organic context. Lack of language turns heroics into melodrama, which Miller was never again to risk to this degree.

TURNING HIS BACK ON BOTH HEROICS AND HISTRIONICS, Miller next wrote his own favorite among his plays, *A Memory of Two Mondays* (1955). As the title indicates, the play is presented as a nostalgic memory, and Miller attempts to invest it with poetry through use of free blank verse. The melting-pot of New York City speech is heard as prose, flavored by dialects of Slavic Gus and Irish Kenneth in the auto-parts warehouse where the characters work. Midway through the play's largely prose dialogue, college-bound Bert and lyrical Kenneth wash the grimy windows of the warehouse shipping-room, and they burst into verse at the sight of summer outside. Since the verse scarcely scans, and is almost barren of imagery, it goes unheard as verse in the theater, in spite of the five rough feet to the line:

> She's not giving me the heat I'm entitled to.
> Eleven dollars a week room and board,
> And all she puts in the bag is a lousy pork sandwich,
> The same every day and no surprises.

Much later in the play, before Bert leaves his warehouse job, he indulges in a rough tetrameter soliloquy, attempting through verse to invest his co-workers with significance:

> I know I'll remember them as long as I live,
> As long as I live they'll never die,
> And still I know that in a month or two
> They'll forget my name, and mix me up
> With another boy who worked here once,
> And went. Gee, it's a mystery!

"Gee," as Willy Loman noted, "is a boy's word." And the mystery of "it" is a boy's indefinite pronoun reference. Spoken by a boy, the broken lines give us no reason to remember these people "as long as I live." Undistinguished and undistinctive, Miller's "Pathetic comedy" is neither pathetic nor comic. Audiences have not shared Miller's preference for this verse play. Rather, they have responded to the more economical prose of his violent dramas with their protagonist-victims.

Also set in New York city, *A View from the Bridge* was originally performed on the same bill as *A Memory of Two Mondays* in 1955. Later, Miller expanded the play to two acts, occupying a whole theater evening. In *A View from the Bridge* the colorful colloquialisms of Eddie Carbone, the longshoreman protagonist, contrast with the rhetorical prose of Mr. Alfieri, the commentator-lawyer (much of the latter's dialogue is in free verse in the original one-act version.) Leonard Moss has succinctly described Alfieri's speech: "His sonorous periodic sentences (with repeated connectives, in the Biblical tradition), his dignified diction, elegant imagery, and legendary allusion are obviously far removed from the protagonist's lower-class Brooklynese, and succeed in fixing Eddie's tortured, inarticulate protests in a rational perspective."[14] Moss notices, too, that Alfieri's perspective slackens the dramatic tension, but Miller is willing to sacrifice tension to obtain resonance through the choric commentator. The play's title is "a view from the *bridge*," and Alfieri, an American attorney of Sicilian origin, is the bridge between two civilizations, the one founded on written law and the other on tribal loyalty.

Eddie Carbone, frustrated by his unacknowledged lust for his niece, seeks legal recourse against her marriage, but he thereby betrays tribal law. A man who thinks with his fists, Eddie endears himself to us mainly by his concrete speech, which is more pointed in the original one-act version of the play. Though Eddie tells his wife: "I can't talk about it," he talks about "it" and other things in colorful idiom, which occasionally has an incongruous Jewish rather than Sicilian syntax: "You're savin' their lives, what're you worryin' about the table cloth?" In general, however, his wisdom springs from urban experience, of no particular national origin. "Most people," he warns his niece Catherine, "ain't people." Or, warning her against the blonde Rudolpho, he claims: "That's a hit-and-run guy, baby; he's got bright lights in his head, Broadway." Or again: "Just remember, kid, you can quicker get back a million dollars that was stole than a word that you gave away." To his wife, Eddie complains: "It's a shootin' gallery in here and I'm the pigeon." Such vivid phrases contrast not only with the measured prose of Alfieri but with the formal foreignness of the "submarines."

Aware of the enormity of betraying the "submarines" to the Immigration Service, Eddie rationalizes his deed as protection of Catherine against a homosexual Rudolpho. And after his fatal telephone call to authority, he tries to retrieve the "word that [he] gave away." Eddie attempts to move the submarines before the arrival of the Immigration officers. When the brothers are apprehended, Marco spits in Eddie's face. Guilty though he is, Eddie obsessively demands respect for his good name. As Eddie and Marco square off for a physical battle, the former shouts: "Wipin' the neighborhood with my name like a dirty rag! I want my name, Marco!" But Eddie fights no more fairly in war than in love. Pulling a knife against Marco, he himself is stabbed to death. The two women, his wife and niece, "*call . . . his name again and again.*" (In the original version, they merely weep.) As in *The Crucible*, Miller invests the repetition of "name" with thematic significance.

Alfieri delivers a eulogy that is confusing—"not purely good, but himself purely, for he allowed himself to be wholly known." But Eddie did not know himself, and since we know him through Alfieri's "view from the bridge," is that whole knowledge? Alfieri's final sentence is also puzzling: "And so I mourn him—I admit it—with a certain . . . alarm." As usual when Miller resorts to abstraction—alarm—his meaning is fuzzy. What alarms Alfieri? His own mourning? Or Eddie's death? Or the whole sequence of events? In the original one-act version, Alfieri's choric finale is broken into verse lines that repeat phrases of the play's opening lines. Though the verse is commonplace, its meaning is clear, and it is clearly related to the titular bridge:

> Most of the time now we settle for half,
> And I like it better.
> And yet, when the tide is right
> And the green smell of the sea
> Floats in through my window,
> The waves of this bay
> And the waves against Siracuse
> And I see a face that suddenly seems carved;
> The eyes look like tunnels
> Leading back toward some ancestral beach
> Where all of us once lived.
> And I wonder at those times
> How much of all of us
> Really lives there yet,
> And when we have truly moved on,
> On and away from that dark place,
> That world that has fallen to stones.

In expanding *A View* from one act to two, and in converting the verse to prose, Miller leaves certain scenes intact, and he should have done this with Alfieri's opening and closing lines. Miller himself feels that "by the addition of significant psychological and behavioral detail the play became not only more human, warmer and less remote, but also a clearer statement."[15] But it is precisely "a clearer statement" that is lost in the revised version. In spite of Alfieri's self-conscious poetry in the one-act version, he does provide a bridge between instinctual man and codified law. In the revised version, "significant psychological and behavioral detail" is added dialogue—robbing Eddie and B of children, spelling out their lack of sexual relations, pointing to Catherine's specifically sexual fascination—which blunts the play's drive and the protagonist's passion. Eddie becomes a victim of circumstance, to whose fate choral commentary is incongruously irrelevant.

As Miller uses the narrator Alfieri to broaden the meaning of *A View from the Bridge*, he uses an unnamed Listener ("God or analyst") to broaden the meaning of *After the Fall* (1964). Though the opening scenic direction claims that *"The action takes place in the mind, thought, and memory of Quentin,"* the play is far less "mental" than *Death of a Salesman* because Quentin addresses himself *consciously and explicitly* to the Listener. For the Listener, Quentin summons scenes of his past, whereas Willy is at the mercy of his own random associations. Controlled and uncontrolled, however, neither confession leads to self-awareness: Willy dreams of success as a result of being well liked, and Quentin looks for innocence as though the Fall had not taken place. Each play insists upon the beguiling illusion of its protagonist—*well liked* and *innocent.*

Now that the biographical echoes have faded from *After the Fall*, the play resounds with rhetoric. The overt confessional form is more viable for fiction than for drama, which thereby becomes a virtual monologue.[16] Especially since Miller's Listener is invisible, inaudible, and unfathomable, his Quentin sounds humorlessly self-important. Not a "low man" but an attorney with "an important career," Quentin is at once prosecutor and defendent at his own trial. But his long plea for judgment is addressed to an imaginary Listener and the real theater audience. Like Baudelaire's personal address, implicating his *"hypocrite lecteur, mon semblable, mon frère,"* Miller's Quentin seeks to implicate his whole civilization.

The name *Quentin* evokes Faulknerian resonance of the last (and suicidal) American aristocrat, as well as associations with the words *quest* and *question*. (There is a mild play on words when Louise says: "Quentin, that's the question!") Miller's Quentin undertakes a quest in self-exploration, during the course of which he asks a good many rhetorical questions, but his own specific question—whether to marry for the third time—is trivial against the concentration camp background, always on stage. As the medieval Everyman made his personal decisions in the light of death and eternity, Miller seeks to present a modern Everyman who has to make his personal decision in the light of the concentration camp towers. Realizing that the modern Morality must be clothed in contemporary specifics, Miller tries to obtain general resonance from the specific details of Quentin's life, but the play's language is inadequate to both specifics and generalizations.

Quentin never leaves the stage, but he lacks *presence* because he talks so much and does so little. Detached from his life, Quentin dramatizes it chronologically. He seems to be an audience for rather than an actor in the scenes of his past. For all his explicit commentary, he learns little as spectator, and the play as a whole is no richer in texture because of Quentin's dual role—as, for example, Weiss' *Marat/Sade* is richer for Sade's dual role as director and spectator. Though we witness some dozen incidents of Quentin's past—as opposed to the four main events in Willy's past and fantasy—they are far less concrete. We don't know what Willy sells; but we not only don't know what kind of law Quentin practises; we don't know whether he can drive, we don't know where he lives, and we don't know his last name. Though his parents and friends are Jewish, Quentin's speech is almost free of Jewish inflection. Instead, his dialogue is burdened with abstractions and forced images.

In the long opening scenic direction, Miller specifies: *"The dialogue will make clear who is 'alive' at any moment and who is in abeyance."* And dialogue of minor characters is livelier than Quentin's monologue: Quentin's father speaks in salty Jewish cynicism, his mother is virulent in accusation, and Maggie is endearing through her repetitive use of "like," "whereas," " 'scuse me," "right?" "see?" We do not know what kind of law Quentin practices, but we know that his friend Lou has written a book in which he lied about Soviet law. We do not know whether Quentin can drive, but we know that his illiterate father used to buy *his* mother a new Packard every year. And we don't know Quentin's last name, but we know that Maggie takes the pseudonym of Sarah None, that puns on nun. So brief and fragmentary are the remarks of the secondary characters, however, that their concreteness cannot dominate Quentin's abstractions.

After the Fall begins with Quentin's extended address to the Listener, and in that first speech he runs through a catalogue of abstractions—decision, success, feeling, despair, way of life, hope. In addition to personal pronouns—you, I, and we—Quentin often generalizes with editorial we, one, whoever. Leonard Moss has counted one hundred repetitions of the word "love," and about fifty each of "death" and "truth" in the first published version of the play. Although some of these were deleted subsequently, they are still as abstract as the dozen odd repetitions of "innocence" and of "power."[17] Arguing with his first wife Louise, Quentin charges: "We are killing one another with abstractions." And it is true that Louise seems to learn abstraction from Quentin, but he alone is capable of the sententiousness of: "We conspired to violate the past, and the past is holy and its horrors are holiest of all!" Or his pretentiousness to Maggie, his second wife: "Darling, I'm happy to spend my time on you; my greatest pleasure is to know I've helped your work to grow!"

However, when Quentin shifts to images, there is no relief. His first memory gives way to his second through the image of a mirror. He attempts to be casual about Felice, the woman who admires him: "I feel like a mirror in which she somehow saw herself as glorious." And his dead mother causes him to generalize: "That whole cemetery—I saw it like a field of buried mirrors in which the living merely saw themselves." Rather than sensual perception, this is simply a clumsy transition from Quentin's mother to the human race.

Other images are strained, as in O'Neill's middle plays. Quentin leads up to his meeting with Maggie: "How few the days are that hold the mind in place; like a tapestry hung on four or five hooks. Especially the day you stop becoming; the day you merely are. I suppose it's when the principles dissolve, and instead of the general gray of what ought to be you begin to see what is. Even the bench by the park seems alive, having held so many actual men. The word 'now' is like a bomb through the window, and it ticks." There is no progression from tapestry to bomb; the concrete park bench is a prediction of Maggie, who will also seem alive for having held many men, but the connection does not emerge from the speech. The imageless second and third sentences are difficult for an actor to speak, and hollow when finally spoken. But perhaps the worst image in the whole play is spoken while Quentin listens to Maggie's suffocated breathing after a suicide attempt: "And her precious seconds squirming in my hand, *alive as bugs.*" (my italics)

Even repetition, normally one of Miller's most skillful techniques, is rendered ineffectual by the heaviness of his imagery: "It's that if there is love, it must be limitless; a love not even of persons but blind, blind to insult, blind to the spear in the flesh, like justice blind, like . . ." Love of persons can of course be blind, but only a rare conceit can embrace deafness and numbness within blindness. And the introduction of the abstraction, justice, undermines Quentin's point—that love should be limitless, therefore vaster than limited justice.

Whatever Miller's intention may be, Quentin's repetitions and images serve, like his abstractions, to reveal his self-obsession and his shallowness of understanding. Whatever Miller may have written discursively, Willy's clichés are exploded by the thematic drive of *Death of A Salesman.* In contrast, Quentin's limitations are at the center of the limitations of *After the Fall.* Lou, Mickey, and Louise echo Quentin's abstractions, and the two main images of the play are even less effective than Quentin's own forays—the word "idiot" and the concentration camp tower.

Though the tower is always on stage, it comes into focus after specific cruelties: Quentin's mother toward his father, Quentin's fight with Louise, Mickey's betrayal of Lou, Quentin's relief at Lou's suicide, the first evocation of Maggie, and Quentin's mother's apology to him. Finally, after the last appearance of Lou, Mickey, Father, Dan, Carrie, Felice, Louise, and Holga, "[Quentin] *turns toward the tower, moves toward it as toward a terrible God,*" and accuses himself even as he excuses himself: "Who can be innocent again on this mountain of skulls? I tell you what I know! My brothers died here—*He looks from the tower down at the fallen Maggie*—but my brothers built this place; our hearts have cut these stones!" Accepting his guilt abstractly, Quentin prepares for his third marriage in the most ambitious speech of the play: "Is the knowing all? To know, and even happily, that we meet unblessed; not in some garden of wax fruit and painted trees, that lie of Eden, but after, after the Fall, after many, many deaths. Is the knowing all? And the wish to kill is never killed, but with some gift of courage one may look into its face when it appears, and with a stroke of love—as to an idiot in the house—forgive it; again and again . . . forever?" The painted Eden is the one textural image among these Shakespearean echoes, and the passage joins the main verbal image, idiot, to the main visual image, concentration camp tower. But is the union credible or dramatically functional?

Early in the play, Holga, the prospective third wife, describes a dream in which her idiot child was her life; by an effort of will, she manages to kiss its horrible, broken face "finally tak[ing] one's life in one's arms." Through Holga, Miller mangles Shakespeare's image of life as a *tale* told by an idiot, and that mangling inspires the skew and sentimental metaphor of taking one's life in one's arms. So inept is this image that it undercuts the subsequent dramatic use of the word "idiot"—Quentin's mother to his father, Elsie about her husband Mickey, Louise about her husband Quentin, Maggie about her husband Quentin. The honest intimacy of these accusations is diluted by Quentin's abstractions about courage and love.

Though Quentin assures us that innocence is impossible, his final confession of guilt is a disguised self-justification: his mother left him alone, she nagged his father, Louise was cold in bed, his friend Lou lied about Communist law, his friend Mickey named names, his wife Maggie became a shrew and tried to destroy him. Thus, Quentin implicitly exonerates himself, and he compares himself to those who staffed the concentration camps (who also exonerated themselves): "My brothers died here . . . but my brothers built this place." Allowing for no difference in degree between the unspecified cruelties of the concentration camp and the drama's limited cruelties (signalled by the lighted tower), Quentin draws the monstrous conclusion that we are all equally guilty because no one is innocent.

Like Willy Loman, Quentin is self-contradictory: searching into himself, he is sure that self-knowledge is futile; attractive to women, he is a misogynist; confessing his guilt, he actually implies his innocence; dulled by abstraction, he seeks significance in the boyhood joy with which he wakens each morning; steeped in his personal particulars, he strains for universal significance. In spite of his "important career," "majestic quality," and "classic opinion," Quentin is, finally, like Willy, a "low man," a slave to his illusion about personal success—in paying lip service to guilt. Instead of suicide, however, Quentin goes blithely off to his third marriage, playing God with his final stage gesture.

After the Fall, written after an eight-year silence, must have been written at some personal cost to Miller, but perhaps that very cost hindered effective use of his main dramatic skill—to evoke pity through poignant scenes centering on a protagonist-victim who expresses himself in rhythmed colloquialisms. Miller himself declared: "Look, *After the Fall* would have been altogether different if by some means the hero was killed or shot himself. Then we would have been in business."[18] In his next play, *Incident at Vichy* (1964), Miller was back in business.

THE TITLE, *Incident at Vichy*, STATES ITS SPECIFIC SETting, and yet the drama emerges as a general Morality play with representative type characters. Even the names sometimes indicate this: a a painter named Lebeau (the Beautiful), a businessman named Marchand (Merchant), and two contrasting portraits of nobility, the Jewish psychoanalyst named Leduc (Duke) and the moral tower Von Berg (from the Mountain). After perfunctorily differentiating his characters—by profession and initial reaction to the summons by Nazi occupation authorities—Miller levels them through their fear.

Threatened by the Nazis, a bench of Jews soon becomes involved in the discussion that is characteristic of problem plays. The first words of the non-Jew pose the problem: "Have you all been arrested for being Jewish?" When there is no answer, he adds: "I'm terribly sorry. I had no idea." A little later he steadies an old Jew and asks him: "Are you all right, sir?" The question recalls bitter Jewish jokes about trivia in the face of holocaust, since the Jews are clearly marked for the extermination-ovens. On stage, however, only Lebeau's speech has any flavor of bitter Jewish wit. Though the stage Jews are anxious about their fate, they discuss it with the impersonal pronoun, one. And except for Lebeau, the characters actually seem detached from their plight—an effect that Miller surely did not intend. Relying on an audience's spontaneous reaction of horror to Nazi treatment of Jews, Miller barely individualizes his Jews, who remain representative.

Leduc, the psychiatrist, has the largest role, and he is difficult to understand. He studied in Vienna, had a safe hiding-place near Vichy, but it is not clear whether he himself made the political commitments to which he urges the others. Declaring that he no longer loves his wife, resenting the fact that he is caught while on an errand for her, he nevertheless seems too sadistic in using his probable death to torture her. Better educated than the other Jews, he enunciates what seems to be the message of the play, in a passage that recalls Sartre's *Anti-Semite and Jew:* "Until you know it is true of you you will destroy whatever truth can come of this atrocity. Part of knowing who we are is knowing we are not someone else. And Jew is only the name we give to that stranger, that agony we cannot feel, that death we look at like a cold abstraction. Each man has his Jew; it is the other. And the Jews have their Jews. And now, now above all, you must see that you have yours—the man whose death leaves you relieved that you are not him, despite your decency. And that is why there is nothing and will be nothing —until you face your own complicity with this . . . your own humanity." As in *After the Fall,* the emphasis of repetition is diluted by abstraction. Pontificating like Quentin, Leduc scarcely seems concerned about his life. In *Incident at Vichy,* this series of generalizations nevertheless seems to be the point of personal poignancy at which Von Berg resolves to lay down his own life for that of Leduc.

That climax has been prepared by two comparably abstract debates. The Communist Bayard and Prince Von Berg have argued class consciousness versus individual consciousness but only the latter will act upon his argument. Though Von Berg and the German major do not confront each other directly, the latter resembles the French Communist in denying the worth of the individual: "There are no persons any more, don't you see that? There will never be persons again." Collectivist and individualist, the major and the prince have similar contempt for the "racial anthropologist."

> MAJOR: Hands off, you civilian bastard.
> VON BERG: Hände weg!"

These are the last words of the prince before he gives his pass to Leduc, urging him to flee. The Major exclaims in annoyance, but Von Berg merits "Hands off" with his life.

It is Von Berg's heroic act that suddenly turns the problem play into melodrama. Melodrama although thousands of Von Bergs have actually laid down their lives for strangers; melodrama because Von Berg's act does not grow out of the play. In Miller's view, Von Berg is a hero because he believes the worst about men, and nevertheless acts like the best. Less simple than John Proctor, he becomes incomprehensible in his very complexity. He apologizes for human evil, and yet claims that the Nazi *putsch* drove him close to suicide. Vaguely homosexual— he has "no great . . . facility with women"—he imagines Hitler as a beautiful woman. And yet he emerges as the only brave man in the fearful stage group, who are symbolized by the white feathers of the old Jew.

Contradictions can be made credible through dialogue, as for example Kleist's *Prince of Hamburg,* but Miller lacks the language for subtleties. As heroic utterances simplify John Proctor, Von Berg's complexities undermine his martyrdom. His aristocratic disapproval of Nazism is trivial: "My housekeeper dreams of [Hitler] in her bed, she'd serve my breakfast like a god slept with her, in a dream slicing my toast!" An amateur musician, he uses an incongruous simile about the Nazis: "Their motives are musical, and people are merely sounds they play." Above all, in the description of how the Nazis seized a Jewish member of his orchestra, he speaks in cliché and strained images: "the heart stopped when he played certain tones. They came for him in the garden. They took him out of his chair. The instrument lay on the lawn like a dead bone."

In a new departure for Miller, he renders Von Berg's moral triumph silently, and the triumph was hardly noticeable in the original New York production. After Leduc's exit with Von Berg's pass, "*Von Berg turns and faces* [the Major]. *Then he gets to his feet. The moment lengthens, and lengthens yet. . . . They stand there, forever incomprehensible to one another, looking into each other's eyes . . .*" The two men—foils—end in silent opposition, after the many long discussions of the play itself. Like the homespun heroics of *The Crucible*, the many arguments of *Incident at Vichy* seek to explore moral depths. But Miller lacks the verbal instruments. Proctor's "You are pulling Heaven down and raising up a whore!" and Leduc's "It's not your guilt I want, it's your responsibility" get lost in their own generalization. The two plays may arouse pity through the final *frisson*, but they cannot bear the pitiless eye of criticism.

AFTER SUCH HEROICS—NOBLE SUICIDES ARTICULATING abstractions of nobility—Miller wrote his least ambitious play of a protagonist-victim, *The Price* (1968). The play seems to have grown from a character who hardly figures in the plot— Gregory Solomon, eighty-nine year old dealer in second-hand furniture.[19] In *The Price*, Victor Franz, policeman, has concealed from himself the motives that led him to interrupt his scientific education in order to support his father who was ruined by the 1929 stock market crash. His adult life is the price he paid for that self-concealment. More immediately, however, *The Price* has to do with a house full of furniture crammed into a single room; the furniture is up for sale since the building is to be torn down.

Although Miller has acknowledged his debt to Ibsen, *The Price* is his most extreme example of that playwright's technique of delayed exposition, since the exposition lasts virtually through the whole play. This technique makes large demands on dialogue. At first immersed in the chaos of old furniture, Victor Franz reminisces about a laughing record, fencing foils, homemade radio, and harp. When policeman Victor informs his wife that his surgeon brother Walter has not answered his long distance telephone calls, we learn that the two brothers have not seen each other for sixteen years. But as Victor is about to receive payment for the second-hand furniture (from Gregory Solomon), the missing Walter enters to close Act I. Act II brings revelations about the past: though Walter at first refused Victor a five-hundred dollar loan to complete his education, he had later changed his mind—a fact their father concealed from Victor. The father had accepted Victor's support, concealing a sum of four thousand dollars. Moreover, Walter charges that Victor was always aware of the spirit if not the letter of these truths, and that Victor had submerged them because he wanted to feel self-sacrificial: "It's a fantasy, Victor. Your father was penniless and your brother a son of a bitch, and you play no part at all. I said to ask him because you could see in front of your face that he had some money. You knew it then and you certainly know it now."

Miller, unlike Ibsen, allows his characters only a small stake in the present that emerges from the past. Victor and his wife, approaching the age of fifty, have to decide what to do with their lives, but there is no urgency to that decision. Walter arrives like Santa Claus, first refusing any share of the furniture price, then suggesting a way to manipulate tax forms so as to obtain a larger sum, and finally offering Victor a job for which he is not qualified.

The divided brothers is an old Romantic theme, and Miller has used aspects of this theme in several earlier plays—*All My Sons, Death of A Salesman* (twice), *A View from the Bridge, After the Fall.* For the first time, however, divided brotherhood is his central theme, and for the first time, one cannot distinguish the brothers by their speech—both loquacious while implying that they are not, both educated but careless of grammar, both ready to draw generalizations from the details of their lives. Though Walter stands for success, and Victor for family loyalty, each is temporarily seduced by the other's ideal. Walter notes: "It's almost as though . . . we're like two halves of the same guy."

The play is an unpretentious exploration into a family relationship, enlivened by the experiential wisdom of the appropriately named furniture-dealer, Gregory Solomon. His salty Jewish expressions provide both comic relief and a feeling of tragic endurance in a world of uncertain values and prices:"The price of used furniture is nothing but a viewpoint." "The only thing you can do today without a license is you'll go up the elevator and jump out the window." At the end, when the ironically named Victor realizes that nothing has come of his talk with his brother, Solomon comments on the price of human pain: "I had a daughter, should rest in peace, she took her own life . . . But if it was a miracle and she came to life, what would I say to her?" None of Miller's articulate victims attempts an answer.

IN SPITE OF PERSONAL DEDICATION AND PUBLIC OPTIMISM, Miller's plays are remarkably full of suicide. Larry Keller crashed his airplane, and Joe Keller shot himself. Willy Loman crashed his car and did not die his dream death of a salesman. John Proctor (and several lesser characters) of *The Crucible* went to death to assert their integrity, as Eddie Carbone met death in a vain effort to assert his integrity. Lou and Maggie killed themselves in despair in *After the Fall*. Prince Von Berg sacrificed his life to prove his faith in individual life, and Gregory Solomon lost his daughter by a suicide that is not particularized. For all these misfortunes, Miller seeks our pity, and pity is what he evokes when most adept. Though Miller is said to specialize in the inarticulate, all his victims are articulate; they talk. Incisive dialogue etches Miller's low men in our minds; Joe Keller, Willy Loman, Eddie Carbone, Gregory Solomon are vigorous with concrete colloquialisms, Jewish inflections, or rhythmic repetitions of everyday words. Often, however, Miller tries to convert his low man into Everyman, or—worse—into the Tragic Hero. Then Miller is betrayed by his weakness for sonorous abstraction or incongruous image. He finds it hard to accept that he is most true when most trivial.

The heir of O'Neill's realism—like most successful, serious Broadway writers—Miller nevertheless forged his own distinctive dialogue. Though he probably learned effective repetition from O'Neill, his effects are markedly different. Even at his best, O'Neill builds ponderously, connects clumsily, and hammers dully. At his best, Miller's dialogue vibrates with questions, interruptions, oral inflections. Though Miller borrowed Odets' blend of preaching and pithiness, he sometimes succeeds in muting the preaching. His victims are most moving when they are least exemplary. Like O'Neill, he achieves most when he attempts least, sparing us effort with a capital E.

It is meaningless to speak of "real" language on stage, since all language is real. But O'Neill was the first American playwright whose dialogue gave his audience a feeling of observed life rather than books read or formulae followed. Miller furthered such feeling. Rarely indulging in dialect, Miller also creates dignified uneducated characters who articulate functionally in dramatic context. If we can apply to the stage what Philip Rahv has called the Paleface versus the Redskin traditions in American literature, O'Neill finally achieved a competent Redskin *Iceman* and *Hughie*, and a Paleface *Journey*. Miller always places his Palefaces in a pulpit of abstraction, but his urbanized Redskins drive to disaster through simple vigorous dialogue.

4 / *The Garrulous Grotesques of*

TENNESSEE WILLIAMS

THE LAST PLAYS OF EUGENE O'NEILL WERE PRODUCED AFTER World War II; the first plays of Arthur Miller and Tennessee Williams were produced after World War II. Though Miller and Williams strain, like O'Neill, toward tragedy, each of them early settled into his own idiom, little tempted by O'Neill's restless experimentation. Since Miller and Williams dominated a decade of American theater, their names have often been coupled, if only for contrast. The British critic Kenneth Tynan wrote of them: "Miller's plays are hard, 'patrist,' athletic, concerned mostly with men. Williams's are soft, 'matrist,' sickly, concerned mostly with women. What links them is their love for the bruised individual soul and its life of 'quiet desperation.' "[1] What also links them is the dramaturgy whereby those souls are bruised; not at all quiet in their desperation, these victim-souls indulge in language to evoke our pity. The most effective dialogue of Miller often relies on his Jewish background, whereas that of Williams leans on his Southern background.

Always expansive, Williams has written many more plays than Miller, but they do not all deserve close attention. Williams often reuses the same materials—phrase, theme, scene, or character. Williams himself acknowledged: "My longer plays emerge out of earlier one-acters or short stories I may have written years before. I work over them again and again."[2] Consistently, Williams reworks by expansion, and comparison of the short works with the longer plays illuminates his focus on dialogue of pathos.

97

The Glass Menagerie, Williams' first popular play, emerged in several stages from a fifteen-page short story, written in the early 1940's but not published until 1948.[3] In dramatizing the story, Williams wrote four, perhaps five, versions. A one-act play may have preceded a movie scenario called *The Gentleman Caller,* which was submitted to MGM in 1943. Subsequently, Williams wrote a five-scene, sixty-page play, twenty-one pages of which were incorporated into a seven-scene, hundred-and-five page typescript (now in the University of Virginia library). This last manuscript became the so-called "reading version" of *The Glass Menagerie,* and it is better known than the final eight-scene revision, first staged in 1944.

The original short story, "Portrait of a Girl in Glass," contains four characters—the narrator Tom, his nameless mother, his sister Laura, and a red-headed Irishman named Jim Delaney. The first half of the story is largely expository, but the second half is the kernel of the Gentleman Caller scenes of the dramatic versions. In the story, Laura is not lame, but she has withdrawn so deeply into her private world that she is not quite sane. In the story, Laura and Jim share no high school past, but, because he has freckles, she equates him with the freckled, one-armed orphan in a novel by Gene Stratton Porter—as real to her as her St. Louis apartment. In "Portrait of a Girl in Glass," Laura "covered the walls with shelves of little glass articles," but the articles have no particular shape. As in Williams' subsequent dramas, Tom brings Jim to dinner, but Laura does not show him her glass collection. As in the dramatic versions, Laura and Jim dance after dinner, but they scarcely converse; Laura's entire dialogue is: "Oh—you have freckles! . . . Freckles? . . . What?"

The most sustained dialogue of the short story begins with the interruption of Laura's mother:

"Good heavens! Laura? Dancing?"
Her look was absurdly grateful as well as startled.
"But isn't she stepping all over you, Mr. Delaney?"
"What if she does?" said Jim, with bearish gallantry. "I'm not made of eggs!"
"Well, well, well!" said Mother, senselessly beaming.
"She's light as a feather!" said Jim. "With a little more practice she'd dance as good as Betty!"

There was a little pause of silence.

"Betty?" said Mother.

"The girl I go out with!" said Jim.

"Oh!" said Mother.

She set the pitcher of lemonade carefully down and with her back to the caller and her eyes on me, she asked him just how often he and the lucky young lady went out together.

"Steady!" said Jim.

Mother's look, remaining on my face, turned into a glare of fury. "Tom didn't mention that you went out with a girl!"

"Nope," said Jim. "I didn't mean to let the cat out of the bag. The boys at the warehouse'll kid me to death when Slim gives the news away."

He laughed heartily but his laughter dropped heavily and awkwardly away as even his dull senses were gradually penetrated by the unpleasant sensation the news of Betty had made.

"Are you thinking of getting married?" said Mother.

"First of next month!" he told her.

It took several moments to pull herself together. Then she said in a dismal tone, "How nice! If Tom had only told us we could have asked you *both!*"

The story's climactic revelation is softened in the play—Jim first reveals his engagement to Laura, and then, separately, to Amanda, so that we watch the effect on each of them. Laura is almost wordless as she gives Jim the broken glass unicorn—"A —souvenir." But Amanda nags Tom so vociferously that he leaves the family shortly afterwards. Williams has expanded the story to evoke our compassion for all four characters.

As Williams developed the Gentleman Caller incident from story to short play, and then again to full-length play, he had room to intensify the pathos. Except for a residual "Freckles" in the reading version, Laura no longer identifies Jim with the Gene Stratton Porter character; she no longer reads to escape from reality. No longer "foolish" as in the story, Laura appeals to us by her fragility—lameness, pleurosis, and pathological shyness. Though Amanda refuses to use the word "crippled," Laura faces that reality about herself. She talks to Jim about "clumping up the aisle with everyone watching" even as we have watched her clump around the stage. Because she is lame, the dancing scene is poignant. But Williams also bends her few sentences to evoke our pity, and he emphasizes the glass menagerie—both verbally and theatrically—to show Laura's pathos.

As far back as high school, sensitive Laura was attracted to worldly Jim. Neither a gentleman nor a caller on Laura, the "gentleman caller" mouths clichés of practicality and progress, but his actual career has been a constant retrogression from its high school pinnacle. At the warehouse, Jim evidently uses Tom to recall his high school glory, and in the apartment Jim audibly uses Laura to bolster his sagging self-confidence. Reduced to stale jokes, sports reports, and makeshift psychology, Jim boasts: "I'm not made of glass." (as opposed to the story's less pointed: "I'm not made of eggs!"). However, we can read his fragility through his veneer of psychology, electrodynamics, and public speaking. While dancing with Laura, Jim bumps into a table, breaking the horn of Laura's glass unicorn. As even Jim knows, unicorns are "extinct in the modern world." In the remainder of the scene, Jim virtually breaks Laura, a girl in glass, who lives on imagination and is therefore almost extinct in the modern world. After Jim pays attention to Laura with well-worn clichés —"I'm glad to see that you have a sense of humor." "Did anybody ever tell you that you were pretty?" "I'm talking to you sincerely."—after he kisses her, he reveals that he will not call again because he is engaged to Betty. By the time Amanda intrudes upon the intimacy of Laura and Jim, the brief romance is over. Vulnerable as Jim is in the wider world, he has been injurious to the world of the glass menagerie. The Gentleman Caller of the old South has been replaced by a pathetic shipping clerk of industrial St. Louis, and even he has other allegiances.

More complex than either Jim or Laura, Tom evolves considerably from the narrator of the short story. Designated as a poet in the final version of the play, Tom carries Williams' lyric flights, his verbal creation of atmosphere, and his ironic commentary upon the action. Unlike Wilder's State Manager, Tom remains a character in his own right—fond of his sister, ambiguous about his mother, and eager to follow in his father's escapist footsteps. As Laura is symbolized by her glass unicorn, Tom is symbolized by his movies, which we know only through dialogue. He explains movies to his mother as sublimated adventure, but by the time Jim comes to the house, Tom is tired of vicarious adventures: "People go to the *movies* instead of *moving.* . . . I'm tired of the movies and I'm about to move!" Tom's final speech tells us how far he has moved, and yet he has been unable to escape Proustian recollections of his sister, which are inevitably triggered by colored glass or music.

Though Narrator Tom closes *The Glass Menagerie* on our view of Laura blowing out her candles in a world lit by lightning, the stage viability of the play has always rested upon the character of Amanda. No longer the mere martinet of the short story, she possesses as many qualities "to love and pity . . . as to laugh at."[4] She speaks the most distinctive as well as the most extensive dialogue of the play. It is Amanda who names Laura's collection a "glass menagerie," in which animal drives are frozen into esthetic objects, and it is she who longs for gentleman callers in an ungentle world. At once nostalgic about her genteel past and minimally practical about the sordid present, she punctuates her drawling elegance with sharp questions and terse commands. She recalls every detail of the balls of her youth, and she goes into absurd physiological detail about the daily lives, and especially meals, of her children. In the final version of the play, Williams heightens the Southern quality of her speech, increases her use of "honey" to Laura, her nagging of Tom, and her repetitions. The cumulative effect of these final revisions (particularly the added opening lines about her rejection at church) is to endear her to us, and to evoke pity for the garrulous mother, as for the timid daughter.

After the Gentleman Caller leaves, near the end of the play, Amanda accuses Tom: "You live in a dream; you manufacture illusions!" But the play's pathos arises from the illusions manufactured by *all* the characters. Though the glass menagerie is most directly relevant to Laura, all four characters have sublimated their animal drives into esthetics. Laura has her glass animals, Tom his movies and poems, Amanda her jonquil-filled memories distorted into hopes, and Jim his baritone clichés of progress.

The Glass Menagerie has often been called Chekhovian in its atmospheric rendition of a dying aristocracy. As the last scene opens, a blackout pointedly occurs while Jim and Amanda toast ·

the Old South. What dies into darkness, however, is not a class but a frail feminine household, and we do not feel, as in Chekhov's plays, that the household represents a class. In subsequent plays, however, Williams dramatizes various aspects of the disintegration of the Old South. The cumulative effect embraces a dying civilization, which makes its impact through rhythm and imagery.[5]

THREE YEARS SEPARATE *The Glass Menagerie* FROM Williams next extended drama, *A Streetcar Named Desire* (1947). Two one-act plays written during that interval point toward the latter. *Streetcar*, like *The Glass Menagerie*, is a poignant portrait of a Southern gentlewoman who is "extinct in the modern world." Similarly, the pathetic protagonists of two 1945 one-acters take refuge from reality in a world of fantasy. Thirteen-year-old Willie in *This Property is Condemned* invents her own romanticized life in imitation of her prostitute sister, Alva, who is dead. Miss Lucretia Collins, a demented old maid in *Portrait of a Madonna*, imagines herself pregnant by a youthful lover; like Blanche Dubois in *Streetcar*, she is taken to an institution by a doctor and nurse.[6] Both Willie and Miss Lucretia are as garrulous as Amanda Wingfield. Lacking her energy, however, they exist only through their brave, bright words, which are contradicted by the sexless pathos of their visual stage reality— child and old maid. But Blanche Dubois is Williams' masterpiece of contradiction.

The very name Blanche Dubois suggests her duality. In the play, she herself translates it for Mitch as "white woods. Like an orchard in spring." But even her translation is a fantasy. Blanche is past her spring, and the purity of Blanche-white is undermined by the thicket of Dubois-woods. Anglicized, Blanche's name is Duboys, and under her chaste surface, Blanche lusts for boys. Comparably, her clothes reflect her divided nature—mothlike white for day and red satin robe for intimacy. More pointedly, the two streetcars—Desire and Cemeteries—suggest the opposing forces that claim Blanche. Her deeds—impulsive and reckless—give the lie to her words—consciously poetic and proper. Blanche never understands the deep division within her, as Williams understands that division in himself: "Roughly there was a combination of Puritan and Cavalier strains in my blood which may be accountable for the conflicting impulses I often represent in the people I write about."[7] The Dubois sisters seem to have only the one Puritan (French Huguenot) strain in *their* blood, but Blanche is nevertheless prey to "conflicting impulses." Preserving the veneer of an aristocratic belle of the Old South, criticizing her sister for an animal marriage, Blanche herself slips into vulgarisms. Though she claims to be "compiling a notebook of quaint little words and phrases" of the New Orleans milieu, she has, as Stanley charges, heard them all before.

Early in the play, Blanche sprays Stanley with her atomizer, so that he responds: "If I didn't know that you was my wife's sister I'd get ideas about you!" Later, Blanche tells Stella that the only way to live with Stanley "is to—go to bed with him." While waiting for Mitch, Blanche toys amorously with a newspaper boy who has just had a cherry soda. "Cherry!" Blanche teases, confessing, "You make my mouth water." Much later that night, Blanche mocks Mitch: *"Voulez-vous coucher avec moi ce soir?"* The question has wider currency than the French language, and Blanche takes a risk for her poor little joke—the risk of destroying her pure Southern Belle image in the opinion of Mitch. A few minutes later, *"she rolls her eyes"* when she mentions her "old-fashioned ideals" to Mitch. But that is the last time she shows any awareness of playing a role.

During most of the eleven scenes of the play, Blanche appears to believe in her role of proper Southern lady, and that way her madness lies. In Scene 1, Blanche plays the *grande dame* for her own sister, until her impassioned outburst about death at Belle Reve. In Scene 2, she plays a sex kitten for Stanley (which is compatible with the cliché portrait of a vivacious Southern lady); as she protects her love letters and delivers the Belle Reve papers to him, she explains that all the male Dubois "exchanged the land for their epic fornications." Only obliquely does she admit that the plantation is finally foreclosed to pay for her own fornications. The very name Belle Reve feminizes dreams since *rêve* is a masculine noun and *belle* a feminine adjective.

In Scene 3, Blanche plays the refined lady—her sustained pose with Mitch: "I can't stand a naked light bulb, any more than I can a rude remark or a vulgar action." In Scene 4, Blanche plays the outraged aristocrat, complaining of animal Stanley, and culminating in her plea to Stella: *Don't—don't hang back with the brutes!*" In Scene 5, Blanche acts superior to Stanley even when he hints at her past. In Scene 6, Blanche continues to play the refined lady for Mitch, but the memory of her marriage tears through that role. She is only momentarily present in Scene 7, but her aristocratic role is shattered in Scene 8, when Stanley gives her a bus ticket back to Laurel, an ironic name for the town of her humiliation. When Mitch arrives in Scene 9, Blanche attempts briefly to resume her refined lady role, then abruptly confesses and explains her promiscuities: "Death . . . The opposite is desire." Rather than suffer the desire of Mitch, however, Blanche cries out wildly: "Fire! Fire! Fire!" In the climactic tenth scene, both Blanche and Stanley have been drinking. We are not quite sure whether her story of Shep Huntleigh is an illusion or a brave front against Stanley, who scoffs at her pose of purity. Forcing Blanche to drop the broken bottle-top of self-defense, Stanley calls her "Tiger." Earlier, she had called Stanley an animal, but now the animal accusation is turned against her. In the final scene, Blanche is the victim of her own Southern-belle fantasy; the role has become her reality as she seems not to recognize the poker-playing men. Expecting Shep Huntleigh, Blanche responds to the Institution doctor, who is both her Hunter and her Shepherd. Her exit line, addressed to the doctor, intensifies her pathos: "Whoever you are—I have always depended on the kindness of strangers." But we know that Blanche has found no kindness among strangers, and we may recall her first use of the word "strangers," in her confession to Mitch: "After the death of Allan—intimacies with strangers was all I seemed able to fill my empty heart with."

To play her role in the two-room Kowalski apartment, Blanche has brought a trunk full of clothes; her stage business involves drinking, dimming lights, emerging from hot baths, and seeking compliments about her appearance. But it is mainly through her dialogue that Blanche underlines her manor-born superiority. She introduces cultural references into the French Quarter dwelling, which evokes an Edgar Allen Poe horror story for her. She recognizes that the lines on Mitch's cigarette case belong to a sonnet by Mrs. Browning; she has evidently taught American literature, since she mentions Poe, Hawthorne, and Whitman. She calls the newspaper boy a young Prince out of the Arabian nights, and Mitch her Rosenkavalier, Armand, and Samson. In the last scene, Blanche is blind to the reality of her situation, but she specifies that her jacket is Della Robbia blue: "the blue of the robe in the old Madonna pictures."

Blanche's speech is distinguished not only by her cultural references. She alone uses correct grammar and varied syntax. Her vocabulary contains such Latinisms as "heterogeneous," "absconding," "judicial," "transitory," and "recriminations." But when Blanche uses images, they are stale or incongruous. Defeated, she tells Mitch that she had viewed him as "a cleft in the rock of the world that I could hide in." A little later, she compares her past to "an old tin can [on] the tail of the kite." Of her soldier boy-friends, Blanche remarks: "The paddy-wagon would gather them up like daisies." Even her most moving speech—the story of her husband's suicide—closes with pretentious imagery: "And then the searchlight which had been turned on the world was turned off again and never for one moment since has there been any light that's stronger than this —kitchen—candle." Seemingly related but not functionally linked is her hope that Stella's baby will have eyes "like two blue candles lighted in a white cake."

When Blanche tries to be uplifting, her images are most inadequate. Seeking to inspire Stella, she becomes trite and abstract: poetry and music, new light, tender feelings, our flag. When Blanche insists upon her superiority to Stanley, she can summon only the cliché phrases of popular magazines: "But beauty of the mind and richness of the spirit and tenderness of the heart —and I have all of those things—aren't taken away, but grow!" Whatever Williams may have intended, Blanche Dubois is trapped by the poverty of her imagery which reflects the poverty of her dreams, like Miller's Willie Loman. But whereas Miller supplies Willy with weak foils, Blanche is challenged and destroyed by a strong antagonist, Stanley Kowalski, whom she correctly views as her executioner.

The hard consonants of Stanley Kowalski contrast with the open vowels of Blanche Dubois. As opposed to her mothlike whiteness, Stanley moves in a world of vivid color; Williams compares him to *"a richly feathered male bird."* Stanley wears a green bowling shirt or bright silk pyjamas. He and Stella make love under colored lights. His poker party resembles Van Gogh's *Night Cafe,* with its *"raw colors of childhood's spectrum."*

Visually and verbally, Williams opposes Stanley to Blanche. Each character is summarized by his opening lines:

> STANLEY: Hey, there! Stella, Baby! . . . . Catch! . . . Meat!
> BLANCHE: They told me to take a streetcar named Desire, and then transfer to one called Cemeteries and ride six blocks and get off at—Elysian Fields!

Stanley has trained his wife to catch his meat, in every sense. Blanche has come to the end of the line named Desire, and Williams' drama traces her ride to Cemeteries. Forcing her toward that destination is the implacable solidity of Stanley's speech: "Be comfortable is my motto." "You going to shack up here?" "To hold front position in this rat-race you've got to believe you are lucky." "You left nothing here but spilt talcum and old empty perfume bottles—unless it's the paper lantern you want to take with you."

On stage, Stanley's physicality contrasts with Blanche's ready verbalizations. His cruellest gesture in the play is to tear the paper lantern off the light bulb, in order to hand it to Blanche. His other rough acts are understandable—tossing the meat package to Stella, ruffling Blanche's rich clothes, throwing the radio out of the window, breaking plates when he is insulted, and handing Blanche a one-way ticket to Laurel. We do not see Stanley hit Stella, and we do not see him rape Blanche; the first deed is mitigated by his contrition, and the second by Blanche's provocation. In the last scene of the play, however, when Blanche is helpless and defeated, Stanley acts with the kind of cruelty that Blanche has called "unforgiveable," and of which she herself was guilty when she told her young husband: "You disgust me."

Blanche and Stanley are protagonist and antagonist in *Streetcar,* and yet, whatever Williams has said in commentary, his play is not a simple picture of victim and villain. Blanche is cruel to her husband, rude to Eunice, patronizing to Stella, and arrogant to Stanley. Though Stanley is finally cruel to Blanche, he is a faithful friend to Mitch and a satisfying husband to Stella. Especially as played by Marlon Brando, Stanley hides vulnerability beneath taunts and boasts; his cruelty defends his world.

Between Blanche and Stanley are Stella and Mitch, each part-victim and part-brute. Naturally kind, admittedly sensual, Stella is ironically named for a star. She remembers Belle Reve without nostalgia, and she lives contentedly in the Elysian Fields, acquiescing to Stanley's dominance as quietly as she evidently did to Blanche in their childhood. "Thrilled" by Stanley, she accepts all facets of his violence—except the truth of his rape of her sister.

Like Stella, Mitch is pulled between Stanley and Blanche. Responsive to women, Mitch willingly accedes to Blanche's instructions in gentility, and he suffers visibly at Stanley's revelations about her past. An Army buddy, fellow-worker, and poker pal of Stanley, Mitch shares Stanley's ethics— "Poker should not be played in a house with women." But he also shares Blanche's awareness of death. Mitch has a dead girl-friend as Blanche has a dead husband. As Blanche watched the members of her family die, Mitch is watching his mother die. Mitch's feeling for his dying mother elicits Blanche's confession of her husband's suicide. Death makes them realize their need of one another. But after Mitch learns about Blanche's past, a Mexican woman chants: "Flores. Flores. Flores para los muertos." It is not clear whether Blanche understands the Spanish, but she reminisces on the same theme: "Death—I used to sit here and she used to sit over there and death was as close as you are." Death of the mind is precisely as close to Blanche as is Mitch. By the next scene, even before the rape, Blanche panics into derangement.

The play's last scene so victimizes Blanche—sister, brother-in-law, poker players, nurse—that it borders on sentimentality, which is aggravated, in reading, by such pretentious stage directions as *"tragic radiance"* for Blanche, on whose face *"all human experience shows."* But Williams saves the scene by the very triviality of the dialogue—Blanche's preoccupation with her adornments, the men's preoccupation with their poker game. Both preoccupations have been repeated during the course of the play, so that they take on cumulative significance in this last scene. Other repeated motifs culminate in this scene—the Shep Huntleigh of Blanche's fantasy, her hot bath and search for compliments, her references to death, the distortion of the "Varsouviana" into jungle noises, Stanley's revelation of the naked light bulb. At the last, Blanche follows the doctor as blindly as she followed Stella during the first poker game. Once Blanche is gone, civilized discourse vanishes, Stanley and Stella relax into an almost wordless animal abandon as we hear the blue piano music and the final words of the play: "This game is seven-card stud," which summarizes life in the French Quarter.

Williams had intended at first to call his play *The Poker Game*, and the actual title may indicate his shift of focus from Stanley to Blanche. Elia Kazan's much-publicized Director's Notes center every scene on Blanche, whose role has been called an "actor-killer."[8] Though the psycho-pathology of Blanche has absorbed two decades of critics, directors like Kazan build from climax to climax of the play on the firm ground of Stanley's brute vigor. While Blanche's desire goes the way of Belle Reve, Stanley and his entourage raucously ride the streetcar named Desire. Like D. H. Lawrence, Williams presents desire as synonymous with life, and its opposite is Cemeteries. Before the play began, Blanche used desire to escape from death, but in the Elysian Fields, the world of seven-card stud, her past desires turn to present death, and Williams summons our pity with light, music, repetition, and her paste-images that she displays like diamonds.

THOUGH WILLIAMS WAS NEVER TO MATCH THE SHOCK effect of Scene 10 and the pathos of Scene 11 of *Streetcar*, he built his subsequent drama on this basic combination of shock and pathos. New on the stage, that mixture is central to the Southern grotesque tradition, which finds in deviates a warmth that is absent from normal members of society. Like other members of the Southern gothic tradition, Williams strives to establish the mythic importance of his grotesques. To do this, he introduces increasingly obvious symbols into his plays.

In 1948, Williams wrote two plays that show the determination of his symbolism (and a concommitant weakness of his dialogue)—*Ten Blocks on the Camino Real* and *Summer and Smoke*. The first of these was revised and expanded in 1953. Though the second was also revised to *The Eccentricities of a Nightingale*, it is usually played in the first version. The source of both plays is Williams' short story, "The Yellow Bird." In that story, a minister's daughter, Alma, rebels against her background. Following in the footsteps of an ancestor who was burned as a witch when she obeyed the injunctions of a yellow bird named Bobo, the twentieth-century Alma progresses from smoking to dying her hair, to "juking" with men. Happily ensconced in the old French Quarter of New Orleans, she bears an illegitimate child who presents her with "fists full of gold and jewels that smelled of the sea." When the child grows up, he goes off to sea, and when Alma dies, she is reclaimed by the child's father, who appears like Neptune with a cornucopia. Alma's son erects a monument to her memory—"three figures of indeterminate gender astride a leaping dolphin," whose name is Bobo, like the provocative yellow bird of Alma's ancestor.

Summer and Smoke seems to have imploded from this fanciful celebration of sexual freedom. Pushed back to the early years of the twentieth century, Alma's sexual rigidity recalls that of Emma in O'Neill's *Diff'rent*; in both plays, the sexually inhibited woman turns to perverse behavior. But Williams is even more lavish with the dialogue of his Southern characters than is O'Neill with his not so laconic New Englanders. And though O'Neill's play is schematic in its condemnation of the Puritanical "difference," it is less simplistic than that of Williams, which is a long *carpe diem*. Under the stone angel of Eternity, mere flesh should gather rosebuds while and where it may. Dr. John Buchanan gathers a literal Rosa Gonzales, when Alma provides nothing but soul. For several scenes, John and Alma engage in a virtual medieval debate between body and soul. After John's father dies, however, and he is offered a combination of attractive body and soul in Nellie Ewell, Alma and John change sides in the debate. "The tables have turned with a vengeance!" By the end of the play, John's wild oats sowed, he snuggles up to wife and career, while Alma sets about seducing a young traveling salesman, who will be the first of a series.

Containing more discussion than Williams' previous plays, *Summer and Smoke* also strives to shock through violence—John throws a wild party, John's father strikes Rosa's father, Rosa's father shoots John's father—but the violence is peripheral and recherché, since the eruptions do not arise out of the situations. Violence and discussion seem to belong in different plays. As characters, sexy John and soulful Alma often disappear into their debates. They are even less substantial than the titular Summer and Smoke, which imply the concreteness of heat and fire.

CONVERSELY, WILLIAMS' *Rose Tattoo* (1950) SUFFERS from too much concreteness, with obvious symbolic intention. Again the theme is *carpe diem*, but instead of gathering rosebuds, Williams gushes roses. The dead but ever-virile husband of the protagonist is named Rosario Delle Rose, his daughter Rosa Delle Rose. The Delle Rose home has rose-patterned wallpaper and rose-colored carpet. When first seen, protagonist Serafina wears a pale rose silk dress and a rose in her hair. Her husband's mistress has ordered him a rose silk shirt, and she lays a bunch of roses on his grave. Rosario Delle Rose had a rose tattooed on his chest, and that rose appeared on his wife's breast after she conceived. Only slightly less blatant, are the dialogue references to roses. Three years after the death of Rosario Delle Rose, his wife Serafina recalls her husband as "a rose of a man," and declares: "The memory of the rose in my heart is perfect!" But her would-be lover tries to dim that memory by applying rose oil in his own hair and having a rose tattooed on his own chest. After a night with her new lover, Serafina declares: "Just now I felt on my breast the burning again of the rose." By such hammering, Williams pounds the fertility symbol to the edge of farce. He probably intended *The Rose Tattoo* to be something of a saturnalia, a joyous celebration of sex, but (when we are not simply bored) we tend to laugh *at* rather than *with* the celebrants.

The dialogue of the play, like its roses, strains for celebration.

Larded with Italian phrases and locutions, the English is surprisingly grammatical, the vocabulary extensive, and the emotions self-consciously expressed. As in *Summer and Smoke,*
violence erupts almost gratuitously—Rosa tries to cut her
wrists, a traveling salesman digs his knee into Alvaro's groin,
Alvaro captures a rampaging goat, then pursues Serafina around
the room. Williams specifies: *"The chase is grotesquely violent and
comic."* But it is superfluous. As are Williams' directions that the
final scene *"should be played with the pantomimic lightness, almost
fantasy, of early Chaplin comedy."* This is abandoning dialogue for
mime, but even in this domain Williams insists upon a symbolism of which Chaplin is rarely guilty. In the last scene, a hill full
of women flourish the rose-colored shirt like a banner. Accompanied by music, the flag of sex *"moves in a zig-zag course through
the pampas grass to the very top of the embankment, like a streak of flame
shooting up a dry hill."* And after the flag runs Serafina, whose
name promises fine nights.

FIVE YEARS LATER, IN *Cat on a Hot Tin Roof* (1955),
Williams creates Maggie the Cat, who longs to offer such fine
nights. In *The Rose Tattoo*, the Delle Rose cottage is topped by
a tin roof, which sizzles in the Gulf Coast summer. In *Ten Blocks
on the Camino Real* (1948), a hotel proprietor remarks: "The girls
in the Panama clip-joints are drinking Blue Moons, the gobs and
the sea-going bell-hops are getting stewed, screwed and tattooed, and the S.P.s are busy as cats on a hot tin-roof!" Some
time between 1952, when Williams published "Three Players of
a Summer Game" and 1955, when *Cat on a Hot Tin Roof* was first
produced, Williams came to associate Margaret Pollitt with that
metaphor of monosyllables—cat on a hot tin roof.

Of the "three players of a summer game," none is Margaret
Pollitt. In the story she is never compared to a cat, and she is
never called Maggie. But Brick Pollitt, her husband, is trans-
planted almost intact from story to play. In both story and play,
Brick takes to drink for sexual reasons, but in the story it is
Margaret's parasitic masculinity that is responsible. "Margaret
Pollitt lost her pale, feminine prettiness and assumed in its place
something more impressive—a firm and rough-textured sort of

handsomeness." Margaret thrives on Brick's weakness, but a widow and her daughter play croquet with Brick, seeking to restore his self-respect. When the summer is over, widow and daughter leave town, and Brick returns to liquor and wife, who drives him in their Pierce-Arrow "as Caesar or Alexander the Great or Hannibal might have led in chains through a capital city the prince of a state newly conquered."

In *Cat on a Hot Tin Roof*, Williams reverses Brick's passion for his wife to hers for him, and he changes Margaret's masculinity to Brick's fear of his own homosexuality. The story's widow and daughter disappear, to be replaced by Big Daddy, Big Momma, and Gooper Pollitt's brood. But the most important change is reflected in the new title: "Three Players of a Summer Game" suggests the ephemeral nature of their activity, whereas *Cat on a Hot Tin Roof* couples animal and metal, two durables in uncomfortable contact.

The prevalence of animal imagery in *Cat* has been noted by Bernard Dukore:[9] the Negro servants pronounce the family name as "Polly;" Big Daddy eats like a horse; Big Momma charges like a rhino; Mae and Gooper jaw, jabber, and watch like hawks; their children are compared to county fair animals, monkeys, pigs, and no-neck monsters; the celebrants of Big Daddy's birthday sound "like a great aviary of chattering birds," and they are all deep in "catty talk." For no specified reason, Margaret has been nicknamed Maggie the Cat, and she makes three references to herself as a cat on a hot tin roof (in the original version). In reviewing her affair with Skipper, Maggie calls herself a mouse and says she "shot cock-robbin" Skipper. Brick alone is free of animal resonance, and Maggie even calls him "godlike." Only in his confession to Big Daddy does Brick liken his marriage to "two cats on a fence humping." But he refers to the past, before he sought refuge in alcohol.

Like the roses in *The Rose Tattoo* and desire in *Streetcar*, animality in *Cat* is synonymous with life. Grasping, screeching, devouring, the Pollitts are greedily alive, and the shadow of cancer on Big Daddy has made them all the more aggressive in their vigor. The Reverend Tooker announces sententiously that "the Stork and the Reaper are running neck and neck." In *Cat on a Hot Tin Roof*, Mae Pollitt is pregnant while Big Daddy is dying

112

of cancer. By the end of the play Maggie Pollitt lies that she is pregnant while Brick Pollitt may die of alcoholism. Fear of dying and zest for living distinguish the dialogue of *Cat*, and they dramatize Brick rather than Big Daddy as the moribund stranger in this vital family.

Like O'Neill's drinkers, Brick holds his liquor well. So courteous is he that it is difficult to believe that Big Momma and Big Daddy are his parents; so aloof, it is difficult to view acquisitive Gooper as his brother; so cool, it is difficult to imagine him with desire for either woman or man. The darling of father, mother, and wife, Brick repeats the word "disgust" almost as a leitmotif. When Maggie admires Big Daddy because he "drops his eyes to my boobs an' licks his old chops," Brick comments: "That kind of talk is disgusting." In the crucial scene between Brick and his father, Big Daddy asks: "Why do you drink? Why are you throwing your life away, boy, like somethin' disgusting you picked up on the street?" As if taking the word for a cue, Brick answers the question in one word: "DISGUST!" When Brick realizes that Big Daddy is not horrified that he and Skipper might have been lovers, he exclaims: "Don't you know how people *feel* about things like that? How, how *disgusted* they are by things like that?" The word "disgust" is repeated six times before Brick shifts to mendacity as his reason for drinking. Rejecting this excuse, Big Daddy concludes a long speech to Brick: "*I've* lived with mendacity!—Why can't *you* live with it? Hell, you *got* to live with it, there's nothing *else* to *live* with except mendacity, is there?" Though the words appear abstract out of context, they are a coda to the specific lies of Big Daddy's life, and the italicized words give rhythm and meaning to the coda, which declares that lies are life.

Cat on a Hot Tin Roof thrives on the life of its lies and animality, to all of which Brick reacts with the tall drinks of his disgust. Ironically, his liveliest reaction emerges from his disgust, and it serves death. When Big Daddy accuses Brick of drinking to kill his disgust with his own lie, Brick bares the truth of mortality to his father: "*How about these birthday congratulations, these many, many happy returns of the day, when ev'rybody but you knows there won't be any!*" At the end of the second act, Brick and Daddy enunciate the theme of the play, each in his own idiom:

BRICK: Mendacity is a system that we live in.
BIG DADDY: Yes, all liars, all liars, all lying dying liars! . . . Lying!
Dying! Liars!

The original version of the play stresses the contrast between Big Daddy's acceptance and Brick's rejection of the lies that are life. Big Daddy proclaims a sexual aversion to Big Momma, as Brick does to Maggie. As Brick voices his disgust, Big Daddy voices *his* disgust. But Brick will not touch his wife, and Big Daddy *"laid* [his]!—regular as a piston" and fathered his two sons. In the Act II birthday celebration, Big Momma tells Big Daddy: "I even loved your hate and your hardness, Big Daddy!" He muses: *"Wouldn't it be funny if that was true . . ."* In the original ending of the play, after Maggie has lied that she is pregnant, after she has locked Brick's liquor away, she turns out the lights and declares her love for Brick, who responds: "Wouldn't it be funny if that was true?" to close the play.

Williams supplied an alternate ending for *Cat*, at the suggestion of Broadway director Elia Kazan, who wanted 1) Big Daddy to reappear, 2) Brick to change, and 3) Maggie to be more sympathetic. The five new pages introduce slack into the already slack third act. Brick's declaration of life to Gooper, and of admiration to Maggie, is no more convincing than mere declaration ever is. And Maggie becomes more garrulous rather than more sympathetic. In the original version, the last scene highlights the ambiguous relationship of truth and lies; living is lying, but if one continues to live, even that lie can become truth. In that context, Brick's curtain line is a meaningful echo of Big Daddy: "Wouldn't it be funny if that was true?" In the Kazan-inspired ending, however, Williams confusingly introduces the titular metaphor. Maggie tritely links her love with Brick's life, then closes the play with the line: "I'm determined to do it—and nothing's more determined than a cat on a tin roof—is there? Is there, Baby?" The comparison is preposterous, for the whole play has equated the metaphor with nervousness and discomfort, not determination. On the other hand, if Williams *intends* the metaphor to be preposterous in order to win sympathy for Maggie's determination in the face of impossible odds, then Brick cannot acquiesce tacitly, undergoing the change that Ka-

zan requested. In either case, repetition of the metaphor emphasizes the more flaccid writing of the alternate version.[10]

In both *Streetcar* and *Cat*, the life of the dialogue lies in animal
vigor. But *Streetcar* is more dramatic because of the tension
between a genteel dream and that vigor, whereas catty energy
easily overwhelms aloofness in *Cat*. Kazan's directorial instinct
did not err in clinging to Big Daddy, who, without pretentiousness, looms like a god of life from his first word "Crap" to his
final furious cry. His speech embraces all the living kingdoms:
"The human machine is not so different from the animal machine or the fish machine or the bird machine or the reptile
machine or the insect machine!" For all the repetitions of the
word "machine," they are organic to him. He is tolerant of all
forms of sexuality except what is sold. Big Daddy is the richest
planter in the Delta—the man whose life and livelihood are
organically interrelated. And this man reacts to the news of his
death with rage. It is for Big Daddy that Williams precedes his
play by the Dylan Thomas line: "Rage, rage against the dying
of the light."

Like many colorful characters, Big Daddy manhandles his
creator, growing too big for his play. Thus, his reminiscences
about Europe, his generalizations about mendacity, and his ele-
phantine joke diffuse the dramatic drive. Unlike Maggie, he
never becomes maudlin. In spite of Big Daddy's digressions and
Maggie's unfeline sentimentality, however, *Cat* contains concrete and cohesive dramatic dialogue. All Williams' subsequent
plays, like most of his previous ones, are marred by pretentious
symbols that seek to inflate psychopathology into poetic myth.

Suddenly Last Summer (1957) IS THE QUINTESSENTIAL
example. Because Williams describes it as "a short morality
play," he complains that audiences understood it as "a literal
study of such things as cannibalism, madness and sexual devia-
tion."[11] And such suggestions are almost absent from the seed
of the play, Williams' 1945 one-actor *Auto-da-fé*. The early work,
like the later one, is plotted on an intense mother-son involve-
ment. In *Auto-da-fé* the son's name is Eloi, a Hebrew word for
the Lord, and his auto-da-fé or act of faith is to burn down the

house in which he has locked himself. Earlier, he has told his mother: "All through the Scriptures are cases of cities destroyed by the justice of fire when they got to be nests of foulness!"

In *Suddenly Last Summer* the Lord gives way to His saints—Sebastian and Catherine. These Christian names are those of martyrs, and Williams' characters are also martyrs. Catherine's family name, Holly, is associated with the Christmas season, and the word puns on "holy." Sebastian's family name, Venable, shares its root with the family name in *Auto-da-fé*—Duvenet—and that root suggests venery or fleshly gratification. The name is ironically applicable to both mothers in their prurience, but Eloi's denial of the flesh leads to his suicide, whereas Sebastian's gratification of his homosexuality leads to his murder. In both plays, Williams drives hard to a shocking conclusion, but in the decade between the writing of the two plays Williams learned how to increase shock effect through suspense. In *Suddenly Last Summer* exclamatory interruptions heighten two lines of suspense: What will happen to Catherine? What did happen to Sebastian?

In answering the second question, Williams makes meticulous preparation. Sebastian's "well-groomed" jungle, which hisses and screeches in the play's background, symbolizes both his world and himself. Even his grisly fate is foreshadowed in the *"massive tree-flowers that suggest organs of a body, torn out, still glistening with undried blood."* The only specifically named plant of the jungle, the Venus fly-trap, is a metaphor for Sebastian's life and death. The most sustained savage imagery is not of plants, but of birds. Carnivorous birds of the Encantadas devour newly hatched turtles. The stage jungle birds scream as Catherine is verbally attacked, first by her mother and brother, then by Mrs. Venable. Sebastian took notes for his poems in a Blue Jay notebook. Catherine as procurer, in her lisle bathing-suit, is a "scandal to the jay-birds," and Sebastian addresses her as "little bird." Most importantly, the cannibalistic children are associated with "plucked birds," "black plucked little birds," "featherless little black sparrows" who make gobbling noises, and who finally gobble up Sebastian.

In another passage, too, Williams prepares for cannibalism. Fastidious and abstemious in his own diet, Sebastian speaks of people as items on a menu, and Catherine explains this with unconscious lugubriousness: "I think because he was really nearly half-starved from living on pills and salads . . ." One might wonder why he should prove such a tempting morsel when he himself lived on a single cocktail before dinner, a single lean chop, and lime juice on a salad. But such frivolous questions arise only outside of the theater, after one recovers from the first shock of the play's final lines.

At that time, however, the questions do come. Granted that Catherine is telling what she thinks to be the truth, how can she *know* that Sebastian was eaten? Torn apart he may be—even though this horror is weakened by her image of "a big white-paper-wrapped bunch of red roses"—but *eaten?* We have only Catherine's word for it, and she did not see that grisly meal. Perhaps her own trauma has converted the unfortunate dark children of Cabeza da Lobo into ravening wolves. Or perhaps Williams does not mean us to take the cannibalism literally at all, but symbols must convince first at the literal level.

Literal or not, Williams adroitly mingles the cannibal story with our concern for Catherine's fate, all conveyed through suspenseful dialogue. As Benjamin Nelson has observed: "One woman is attempting to destroy another as surely as the Venus fly-trap destroys the insect, the birds destroy the newly-hatched turtles, and the pack of hungry children destroy the man."[12] Destruction emanates from Violet Venable, who is anything but a shrinking violet, and whose name also suggests violence. She strikes George with her cane, she tries to strike Catherine, and she orders Dr. Cukrowicz (after first bribing him) to perform a lobotomy on Catherine: "State asylum, cut this hideous story out of her brain!" Mrs. Venable is subtly implicated, too, in the death of her son, which occurs at five o'clock in the afternoon, the immutable time of her frozen diaquiri.

Joining the past horror of Sebastian Venable's world to the present horror of Violet Venable's world, Williams has written his most shocking play—a play that he has called "a short moral-ity." If Williams accepts the usual definition of a morality as a psychomachia in which Vice and Virtue battle for man's soul, that soul belongs to Dr. Cukrowicz. The name, he tells us, means sugar, and he is described as glacial and icy, superficial attributes of sugar. Through the saints' martyrdom, Dr. Cukrowicz may be redeemed; sugar and ice perhaps dissolve in faith, as the doctor announces a kind of belief in Catherine's story. Implicitly rejecting Violet Venable's vice—cruelty through bribery—he can save Catherine, thus rewarding her inability to hate or to lie. Since the play ends on this hint of possible reward for virtue, the final shock is diluted by the sudden suggestion that God means love, truth, justice.

God has been the most anomalous image in *Suddenly Last Summer*. Sebastian and Dr. Cukrowicz both seek God—Sebastian in cruelty and the doctor in surgical cures. Mrs. Venable, refusing to fly to her husband's deathbed, begins her cable: "For God's sake." She protects Sebastian from his God, who seems thirsty for his millions. Hunting Catherine down, Mrs. Venable forces her into a Catholic (or Episcopalian?) nursing home, but that does not seem to shake Catherine's belief in her own story.

St. Catherine was beheaded, and Williams' Catherine is threatened with lobotomy, but both remain true to their faith. Saint Sebastian was beaten to death after recovering from his arrow-wounds. Williams' Sebastian is battered to death near a beach named for the saint. Even before his death, Sebastian Venable saw himself as a martyr to a cruel God, and Catherine's repetitions of "Suddenly Last summer" gives his death incantatory importance. The final blazing whiteness of the scene evokes the transcendence associated with saints.[13] However Williams defines morality play, he invests his garrulous grotesques with religious aura in a drama where the threat of martyrdom (Catherine's) is heard through a report of martyrdom (Sebastian's).

GOD'S NATURE REMAINS IN THE BACKGROUND OF *Suddenly Last Summer*, but God is the most surprising of the several additions by which Williams expands his 1948 short story, "The Night of the Iguana," into a three-act play in 1961. The short story focuses on the iguana and three humans. At the beginning of World War II, the only guests at the Costa Verde hotel in Mexico are two writers and a Mississippi spinster painter (age thirty), Miss Edith Jelkes, who undergoes an experience in compassion when the elder writer attacks her sexually. The elder writer (age thirty) of the story becomes the play's thirty-five year old T. Lawrence Shannon, formerly an Episcopal minister, but prey to the desires of the flesh. Locked out of his church for calling God "a senile delinquent," Shannon conducts "tours of God's world." During the play, he swears by God about a dozen times; he sees God in cruelty and storms. By the end of the play, after a brief spiritual communion with Miss Jelkes (rechristened Hannah and aged to forty), Shannon seems to find peace, while she asks God for peace.

Like the story, the play focuses on the loneliness of God's creatures. But dramatic expansion dilutes that loneliness. The hotel Patrona of the short story becomes an American widow, Maxine Faulk. Hannah Jelkes, still a painter and spinster, now travels with her ninety-seven year *young* grandfather (named Nonno for nonage) who is a minor poet. The cast is swelled, too, by Mexican lovers of Maxine, a Rubenesque Nazi family, and two members of an off-stage busload of Texas Baptist females— all of whom function largely as comic relief, with minimal relevance to plot or theme.

Comic Texan drawls, comic German accents, and local Mexican are background for two contrasting rhythms—clipped colloquialisms and leisurely flow. Williams' main characters are typically garrulous, each in his own idiom, and neither of them strains after images. Shannon and Maxine speak with pointed brevity. Shannon swears by great Ceasar's ghost and often exclaims: "Fantastic!" Flowing phrases belong to Hannah Jelkes. In the play's central conflict between the realistic and the fantastic, the rhythms help highlight the opposition and similarity of Shannon and Hannah. Their names are homonymic; they both need sedatives; they are both haunted—the one by a spook and the other by a blue devil. Most telling are their respective responses to life:

SHANNON: Yeah, well, you know we—live on two levels, Miss Jelkes, the realistic level and the fantastic level, and which is the real one, really. . . .
HANNAH: I still say that I'm not a bird, Mr. Shannon, I'm a human being and when a member of that fantastic species builds a nest

in the heart of another, the question of permanence isn't the
first or even the last thing that's considered . . . necessarily?
. . . always?

These contrasting rhythms sustain the first two acts of the
play, but they are interrupted by three monologues in the third
act: Hannah describes the House for the Dying in Shanghai,
Shannon describes coprophagists in a nameless tropical country, and Nonno recites his last poem—in which the persona
wishes for the courage of an orange branch. Mood pieces, these
three monologues depict human endurance, but that subject is
tangential to the central loneliness. The monologues overbur-
den the final act, which is already strained by Hannah's two-
stage confession.

In Williams' short story, the compassion of Miss Jelkes is
awakened first by the captive iguana and then by the abortive
sexual assault of the writer who is equated with the iguana. In
the play, Hannah arrives with compassion full-grown. It has
evidently been born at some time between her two "love experiences." As an adolescent, she was accosted by a man in a movie
theater, and she screamed, though she subsequently refused to
press charges. Much more recently, two years ago on a sampan
ride, she acceded to a request for her undergarment by a traveling salesman fetichist. To both incidents, Shannon comments:
"Fantastic!" They inspire him with a desire to share his life with
Hannah.

She realizes that this is not realistic, and she urges him instead
to free the iguana, whose symbolism Shannon enunciates: "See?
The iguana? At the end of its rope? Trying to go on past the end
of its goddam rope? Like *you!* Like *me!* Like Grampa with his last
poem!" After he frees the iguana, Shannon thrice calls it God's
creature. As Hannah has found faith in "one night . . . communication" between strangers, Shannon now sees God's hand in all
His creatures. At the personal level, each of them pronounces
the play's too evident moral.

HANNAH: Accept whatever situation you cannot improve.
SHANNON: When it's inevitable, lean back and enjoy it.

By the end of the play, Shannon, having freed the iguana, will remain with Maxine while Hannah will travel on without her grandfather, who dies. Each will accept the inevitability of his situation—the more readily perhaps for their brief night of spiritual communion.

THOUGH WILLIAMS IS OFTEN CALLED A POETIC PLAYwright, all the plays examined (and most of those not examined) accept the realist convention of psychologically and sociologically coherent characters, grotesque though they may be. These grotesque characters are exceptionally verbal, given to a degree of imagery that is unusual in American realistic drama. In a few of his plays, Williams combines verbal with theatrical imagery to insist upon a symbolic resonance beyond the realistic surface —*Glass Menagerie, Streetcar Named Desire, The Rose Tattoo, The Night of the Iguana.* There is also a more candidly symbolic strain in his playwriting, bordering on allegory. His first excursion into this domain was the short *Ten Blocks on the Camino Real,* revised and expanded in 1953. With modification, Williams continued the non-realistic form in *The Milktrain Doesn't Stop Here Any More* and his two "Slapstick Tragedies." In contrast to their experimental, often expressionistic form, these plays use crisp, colloquial dialogue.

Though five years separate *Ten Blocks on the Camino Real* from the first Broadway production of *Camino Real,* no substantive change occurs. The earlier play is subtitled "A fantasy," and the fantastic elements are increased in the full-length play. The hero in each play is Kilroy, whose name derives from the ubiquitous American soldier of World War II; in Williams' plays, however, he is not a soldier, but an ex-Golden Gloves winner. He speaks in American slang of the 1940's, which contrasts with the more literary locutions of such characters as Marguerite Gautier, Jacques Casanova, Baron de Charlus, a gypsy daughter Esmeralda, Don Quixote, and a sinister Mr. Gutman. In the shorter play, Kilroy appears on seven of the ten blocks; in the longer one, he is present on eleven of the sixteen blocks, his importance steadily increasing as the play progresses. Moreover, a prologue suggests that the entire play is a dream of Don Quixote, and Williams' Expressionistic technique is thus indebted to Strindberg's *Dream Play*, often considered the first Expressionist drama.

A quest play like *The Dream Play*, *Camino Real* mirrors Kilroy's quest by the separate quests of Jacques Casanova, Proust's Baron de Charlus, Lord Byron, and the arch-dreamer Don Quixote. Trapped in sixteen blocks of no man's land, all these dreamers are rejected from the Royal Way, so that they are compelled to stray on the Real Road—as Williams puns on the Spanish and English meanings of "real." There are three possible exits from this country of fantasy: escape in an airplane appropriately named Fugitivo; bold egress into the desert of the Terra Incognita; death and degradation at the hands of the sinister Streetcleaners who deliver corpses to a medical laboratory. In the diffusion of scenes, action centers on the Camino *Re*al; none of the major characters reaches the Fugitivo, Lord Byron sets out for Terra Incognita, Baron de Charlus falls to the Streetcleaners, and, in his fidelity to Marguerite Gautier, Jacques Casanova will spend eternity shuttling back and forth from Royal Way to Real Road. But Kilroy, ex-champ and ex-Patsy, pure-hearted lover of an ever-renewed Virgin, becomes garbage for the Streetcleaners, guinea pig for the medical students, to be resurrected as the companion to Don Quixote in his venture into Terra Incognita.

Williams summarized the play's theme: *"Camino Real* doesn't say anything that hasn't been said before, but is merely a picture of the state of the romantic non-conformist in modern society. It stresses honor and man's sense of inner dignity which the Bohemian must re-achieve after each period of degradation he is bound to run into. The romantic should have the spirit of anarchy and not let the world drag him down to its level."[14] In the play itself, Esmeralda, the gypsy's daughter, who is a prostitute and always a virgin, utters much the same sentiment in more determinedly colorful idiom: "God bless all con men and hustlers and pitch-men who hawk their hearts on the street, all two-time losers who're likely to lose once more, the courtesan who made the mistake of love, the greatest of lovers crowned with the longest horns, the poet who wandered far from his heart's green country and possibly will and possibly won't be able to find his way back, look down with a smile tonight on the last cavaliers, the ones with the rusty armor and soiled white plumes, and visit with understanding and something that's almost tender those fading legends that come and go in this plaza like songs not clearly remembered, oh, sometime and somewhere, let there be something to mean the word *honor* again!" Not only does the prayer embrace the literary characters of the play, but it uses the clichés of romantic literature—heart, love, green country, armor, plumes, legends, songs, honor. Camille accuses Casanova: "Your vocabulary is almost as out-of-date as your cape and your cane." And the charge can be made against much of Williams' dialogue.

What distinguishes Kilroy, however, is his colloquial innocence in this literary company. Announced as "the Eternal Punchinella," Kilroy arrives with his concrete idiom: "I just got off a boat. Lousiest frigging tub I ever shipped on, one continual hell it was, all the way up from Rio. And me sick, too. I picked up one of those tropical fevers. No sick-bay on that tub, no doctor, no medicine or nothing, not even one quinine pill, and I was burning up with Christ knows how much fever. I couldn't make them understand I was sick. I got a bad heart, too. I had to retire from the prize ring because of my heart. I was the light heavy-weight champion of the West Coast, won these gloves!— before my ticker went bad." More than two decades after the original version of the play, when its staging no longer seems inventive, the play's spine lies in Kilroy's idiom. His slang has dated with his legend, so that Williams' wandering American is a pathetic anachronism, who talks too much, but who endears himself to us because all that talk is a whistling in the dark at the human condition.

Other than Kilroy, only the Gypsy speaks vigorously in the cynical language of commercial enterprise, which has dated less than Kilroy's slang. Before the farcical scene in which the Chosen Hero Kilroy courts the Prostitute Virgin Esmeralda, the Gypsy summarizes the action: "There's nobody left to uphold the old traditions! You raise a girl. She watches television. Plays be-bop. Reads *Screen Secrets*. Comes the Big Fiesta. The moonrise makes her a virgin—which is the neatest trick of the week! And what does she do? Chooses a Fugitive Patsy for the Chosen Hero! Well, show him in! Admit the joker and get the virgin ready!"

As the concreteness of Stanley overwhelms Blanche's esthetic abstractions and clichés, the commercial vigor of the Gypsy and the visual menace of the Streetcleaners overwhelm the ethical abstractions and clichés of the literary characters on Camino Real. But with determined optimism, Williams gives the final inspiring words to Don Quixote, in whose shadow walks Kilroy. Earlier, on Block X, faithful Jacques Casanova had attempted to convince faithless Marguerite Gautier: "The violets in the mountains can break the rocks if you believe in them and allow them to grow!" Though there is no evidence of belief on Marguerite's part, we last see her rising from the bed of her young lover to invite Jacques from Skid Row to her sumptuous hotel. As they embrace, Don Quixote raises his lance to proclaim: *"The violets in the mountains have broken the rocks!"* The old idealist *"goes through the arch with Kilroy."* Clearly, Williams intends triumph for the grotesque Bohemians, in spite of stale slang and stale literary phrases.

As in his more realistic dramas, Williams plays upon a theatrical symbol—the heart. Kilroy's heart is as large as a baby's head, and Kilroy himself calls it a "ticker" in this land where time is running out. Lord Byron describes how Trelawney "snatched the heart of Shelley out of the blistering corpse!" Byron disapproves of Trelawney's action, asking: "What can one man do with another man's heart?" Jacques Casanova responds with passion; speaking for himself and all lovers, he takes a loaf of bread and accompanies his words with actions—twisting, tearing, crushing, and kicking the heart-loaf. By Block XV, Esmeralda has done all this to Kilroy's heart, and he lies dead on a dissecting table. When his heart is removed, it is seen to be the size of a baby's head, and it is made of solid gold. Kilroy rises from the operating table, grabs his heart, and escapes from the laboratory to the loan shark, where he pawns his heart for gifts for Esmeralda—romantic to the last. When she rejects him and the gypsy ejects him, Kilroy joins Don Quixote on Skid Row, with words that summarize the action more truly than the violets in the mountains: "Had for a button! Stewed, screwed and

tattooed on the Camino Real! Baptized, finally, with the contents of a slop-jar!—Did anybody say the deal was rugged?!"

COMPARABLE COLLOQUIALISM IS RARE IN WILLIAMS'
more realistic plays, but in his most recent work—a combination of realism and fantasy—he has sought a popular idiom, with
a minimum of the pretentious images that spring so readily to
the lips of his garrulous grotesques. *The Milktrain Doesn't Stop
Here Any More* (1963) is based on Williams' short story with a
pidgin English Title, "Man Bring This Up Road." Though
much of the dialogue (as well as the name Sissy Goforth) is
transferred intact from story to play, Williams invents tough
talk for Sissy, the ex-stripper, even while he underlines the
symbolic meaning of the whole. Williams' foreword declares
that the play has been "rightly described as an allegory and as
a 'sophisticated fairy tale.'" One may quibble at the word "sophisticated," but the allegorical quality is instantly conveyed in
the names of the two main characters. The seventy-two year old
millionairess, Sissy Goforth, is a sissy about going forth from
this world, and she herself dwells on the pun of her name: "Sissy
Goforth's not ready to go forth yet and won't go forth till she's
ready. . . ."

The erstwhile poet, present maker of mobiles, is named Chris
Flanders (as opposed to Jimmy Dobyne of the short story). Flanders Field is an obvious association with death in battle, and
Chris suggests both Christ and St. Christopher, the patron saint
of travelers. Influenced perhaps by the Angel of Death in Albee's *Sandbox*, Williams calls Chris the Angel of Death because
he is present at the death of rich dowagers. In spite of these same
central characters, however, the play changes the focus of the
story. In the latter, Sissy drives the poet out to the oubliette
while she plans a big party; in the later work, Chris becomes a
kind of ministering angel at the death of Sissy Goforth.

Much more than in the story, the two opposing characters are
distinguished by their dialogue; the rebellious cynicism of Sissy
is opposed to the calm formality of Chris. Blackie, Sissy's secretary not present in the story, calls Mrs. Goforth a "dying monster," but for all her egotism, Sissy is the most attractive

character in the play, because of her determined spit and fire: "Hell, I was born between a swamp and the wrong side of the tracks in One Street, Georgia, but not even that could stop me in my tracks, wrong side or right side, or no side."

Though Chris claims that Sissy and he have reached "the point of no more pretenses," his rhetoric is still pretentious as he affirms that he has ceased to believe in reality, and only human communication can restore that belief. Sissy, on the other hand, does not pretend, admitting candidly that she wants a last love; impecunious though he is, Chris is too proud to perform this office: "I wouldn't have come here unless I thought I was able to serve some purpose or other, in return for a temporary refuge, a place to rest and work in, where I could get back that sense of reality I've been losing lately." A few minutes later, however, Chris admits that he came because, as Sissy phrases it: "You've been tipped off that old Flora Goforth is about to go forth this summer." In a passionate monologue, Sissy denies that she is dying, but she clings to Chris as she dies. Chris assures Sissy's secretary that the end was peaceful.

Between story and play, Williams has shifted sympathy from the young man to the dying dowager. Avoiding the pathetic helplessness of such earlier characters as Laura, Blanche, or even Kilroy, Williams summons our admiring pity for a tough spirit. An older version of Maggie the Cat, and in more desperate straits, Sissy Goforth is imbued with "fierce life." But her life—with the many repetitions of her reluctance to "go forth" —cannot carry the play, whose conflict is diluted by a movie gangster, stage Italian servants, and Kabuki stagehands, none of them bearing any relation to the basic form. In his realistic plays, moreover, Williams' imagery was unusual and sometimes arresting; in such a determinedly experimental play, however, Sissy's tough talk is overwhelmed by Chris' airy platitudes and the visual business on stage. In spite of a striking scene or two —Sissy greeting the Capri Witch, Sissy on the point of death— the various gothic elements are never integrated into a whole.

IN HIS PREFACE TO *Slapstick Tragedy*, WILLIAMS associates *Glass Menagerie*, *Camino Real*, and these short plays of

1965 as "diversions" which share "experimentation in content and in style, particularly in style." *Glass Menagerie* uses narrator and flashback; *Camino Real* is a fantasy of legendary characters; *Slapstick Tragedy* is composed of two separate short plays, a miracle and a saint's legend. The kind of experimentation changes with the years.

The Mutilated, a miracle play, contains a feud between Celeste Delacroix Griffin, shoplifter and prostitute (that her name belies), and Trinket Dugan, whose breast was amputated. Comic dialogue is heavily based on their need for alcohol, love, and friendship on Christmas Eve. Like the verbal thrusts of the Capri Witch and Sissy Goforth in *The Milktrain*, these two denizens of tawdry Hotel Wonder fling insults at each other. Given Trinket's mutilation, breasts echo through their dialogue. Celeste, proud of her firm symmetry, picks up a scornful metaphor of Sissy Goforth, proud of her own firm symmetry:

SISSY: Some women my age, or younger, 've got breasts that look like a couple of mules hangin' their heads over the top rail of a fence.

CELESTE: . . . many women past forty or even thirty have boobs like a couple of mules hanging their heads over the top rail of a fence.

By Christmas Day, Trinket Dugan, having felt a lump and pain in her single breast, emerges from being "dug in," and offers hospitality to a destitute Celeste. As the two women, differently mutilated, drink cheap wine, they feel the presence of the Virgin. Suddenly, Trinket loses lump and ache, and the two women kneel in praise, sharing the ecstasy over the miracle, as Christmas Carolers enter singing. From Rotrou to Claudel, playwrights have found that miracles are untractable on stage. In this faithless age, it is hard to share the ecstasy of Williams' mutilated women.

Gnädiges Fräulein is German for the Blessed Virgin, but in Williams' second slapstick tragedy, the name belongs to a grotesque creature who, to gain the attention of a seal-trainer, caught in her mouth fish intended for a trained seal. Gradually, Gnädiges Fräulein has had to catch her fish (traditional symbol for Christ) before less and less distinguished audiences, until she performs on the Southernmost Florida Key, in rivalry with the dangerous cocalooney birds. For a change in Williams' work, the play's grotesque protagonist is almost speechless, and we learn about the Gnädiges Fräulein from Molly, the boarding-house keeper, and Polly, a society page columnist. While coca-looney birds and a blonde "erotic dream" of an Indian strut picturesquely on the stage, the two old crones rock out their spiteful gibes. As in *Milktrain*, the religious symbolism is im-posed upon a vigorous idiom, but the dialogue lacks develop-ment and tension. Like Sissy Goforth, Molly recalls a Dixie Doxie, and like Chris Flanders, the Gnädiges Fräulein loses her sense of reality. This time, however, death does not arrive to restore reality. In the final scene, Molly and Polly have stolen the fish from the blinded Fräulein, and Indian Joe has deserted her to share the fish with the old crones. As the three sinners partake of the fish, the indomitable Fräulein hears the whistle of the fishing-boat, and she *"starts a wild, blind dash for the fish docks."*

Hardly the "wildly idiomatic sort of tragedy" that Williams claims it is, the play does abound in malicious colloquial comedy against which we see the pathos of his most grotesque character, the Gnädiges Fräulein. More than *The Mutilated*, this play uses the slapstick of farce. But the word "tragedy" is wrong for these slight pieces in which grace is granted.

In spite of his prolific output, Tennessee Wil-liams is narrow in range. Most of his plays are set in Southern United States, which he contrives to give an exotic hue. Most of his plays focus on protagonist-victims who manage to combine humor with deformity. Unlike the monosyllabic characters of many American realistic plays, Williams' grotesques are luxuri-ously loquacious—with incantatory repetitions and self-con-scious images. Williams uses set, music, light, rhythm, image to impose symbolic meaning upon his realistic surfaces; the more blatant the symbolism, the more frail the play. Like Tom in *Glass Menagerie*, Williams has "a poet's weakness for symbols." The emphasis should be placed on the word "weakness." Insistence on symbols weakens the dramatic drive of several Williams' plays—*Summer and Smoke, The Rose Tattoo, Suddenly Last Summer, Cat on a Hot Tin Roof, Night of the Iguana, The Milktrain Doesn't Stop Here Any More, Slapstick Tragedy,* and *Kingdom of Earth.* Williams' symbolic imagery is most effective when its weakness is built into the fabric of the drama—the stale nostalgia of Amanda in *Glass Menagerie,* the cultural yearning of Blanche in *Streetcar,* the dated slang of Kilroy in *Camino Real.* In these plays, the inadequacies of Williams' lyricism function thematically and theatrically, to evoke our sympathy for his garrulous grotesques.

As Miller moves a limited step beyond O'Neill in his use of colloquial rhythms and idiom, Williams reacts against O'Neill in his profuse images and relatively complicated syntax. Pithy or lyrical as suits the character, Williams' dialogue endowed the American stage with a new vocabulary and rhythm. Though his lines lack the taut coherence of Southern poets like Ransom or Tate, and though his plots lack the human complexity of Southern novelists like Faulkner, Welty, or O'Connor, Williams gave Southern grotesques dignity on the Broadway stage. Even the farcical *Rose Tattoo* is peopled with giants by comparison with *Tobacco Road.* Though shocking sexuality rather than human warmth may account for his Broadway success, Williams has managed to combine shocking sexuality with human warmth, sometimes in the same play. His major instrument in this combination is distinctive dialogue that embraces nostalgia, frustration, sadness, gaiety, cruelty, and compassion. Like O'Neill and Miller, Williams wrote few organically flawless dramas. He does not often hammer like O'Neill, he does not often preach like Miller, but he too often indulges in gratuitous violence and irrelevant symbol. At his best, however—*Menagerie, Streetcar,* first version of *Cat, Iguana* and even *Camino Real*—Williams expands American stage dialogue in vocabulary, image, rhythm, and range.

5 / The Verbal Murders of

EDWARD ALBEE

Collectively, O'Neill with his realistic idiom, Miller with his varied inflections, and Williams with his functional imagery brought American dialogue to a maturity that was Edward Albee's birthright. Albee-playwright was born at the age of thirty, with perfect command of contemporary colloquial stylized dialogue.

Albee's intensely American yet original idiom is striking if we compare a passage from Albee's first play, *The Zoo Story* (1959), with the competent translation into German, the language of its first production.

But good old Mom and good old Pop are dead . . . you know? . . .[1] I'm broken up about it, too . . . I mean really. BUT. That particular vaudeville act is playing the cloud circuit now, so I don't see how I can look at them, all neat and framed. Besides, or, rather, to be pointed about it, good old Mom walked out on good old Pop when I was ten and a half years old; she embarked on an adulterous turn of our southern states . . . a journey of a year's duration . . . and her most constant companion . . . among others, among many others . . . was a Mr. Barleycorn.

Ja—oh, weh und ach—, Mammi und Pappi sind tot, und ich weiss nicht, ob ich es ertragen könnte, sie dauernd vor mir zu sehen, fein säuberlich eingerahmt. Nebenbei bemerkt, oder vielmehr gar nicht nebenbei: Mammi ist Pappi weggelaufen, als ich zehneinhalb Jahre alt war. Sie hatte sich auf eine ehebrecherische Fahrt durch unsere Südstaaten begeben. Der Ausflug dauerte ein ganzes Jahr. Der be-

ständigste unter ihren Reisegefährten war, wie sich später heraus-
stellte, ein Mister Barleycorn.

The cloud circuit vaudeville act is absent from the German, as
are the ironic rhythmic resonances of the repeated "good old."
And it is not even clear that the only fidelity of Jerry's mother
is to whiskey.

Albee combines this vividly colloquial diction with a seemingly leisurely indirection. In the work of the other three
dramatists, dialogue was examined in Aristotelian terms: how
did it further the plot? How did it reveal character? How did it
delineate thought (usually interpreted as theme)? These questions are still useful for Albee's plays, and yet the dialogue of *The
Zoo Story* sounds absurdly disjunctive. But under Albee's dis-
junction lie an eventful plot, coherent characters, and thematic
consistency.

The main theme of *The Zoo Story* is communication. A "per-
manent transient" tries to communicate with a proper publisher, whom he meets one Sunday on a Central Park bench.
One human being tries to communicate with another. Being a
highly unorthodox individual, Jerry uses highly unorthodox
means of communication—entirely verbal at first. Early in *The
Zoo Story*, Jerry informs Peter: "I took the subway down to the
Village so I could walk all the way up Fifth Avenue to the zoo.
It's one of those things a person has to do: *sometimes a person has
to go a very long distance out of his way to come back a short distance
correctly.* " (my italics) Jerry's long walk enables him to describe
his methodology. Jerry could have gone to New York City's
Central Park Zoo by the cross-town bus, but, deliberately in-
direct, he chose a circuitous route, "a very long distance out of
his way to come back a short distance correctly." As Hamlet is
"but mad north-north west," Jerry walks "northerly," seeking
by indirection to find direction out, seeking by indirection to
communicate with Peter. At the verbal climax of the play, Jerry's dog story, he uses the same pointedly clumsy phrase to
describe his indirection: "THE STORY OF JERRY AND THE DOG!
. . . What I am going to tell you has something to do with how
sometimes it's necessary to go a long distance out of the way in
order to come back a short distance correctly." When we hear

131

DIALOGUE IN AMERICAN DRAMA

the dog story, we are already familiar with Jerry's "out of the way" dialogue and its two main rhetorical patterns, pointed thrusts and digressive monologues.

The dog story is an analogue for the titular and thematic zoo story, which Jerry does not narrate, though he predicts that it will be in the newspapers and on television. Jerry's dog story is a parable, as Albee's *Zoo Story* is a parable. In the latter, vagrant confronts conformist on a park bench; in the former, man confronts animal in a dark hallway. Jerry is vagrant and man; conformist Peter replaces the animal as Jerry's friend-enemy. Jerry views Peter as he does the dog—with sadness and suspicion; Jerry tickles Peter as he tempts the dog—into self-revelation; Jerry forces Peter to defend his premises as the dog defends *his* premises; Jerry hopes for understanding from the dog ("I hoped that the dog would . . . understand") and from Peter ("I don't know what I was thinking about; of course you don't understand.") As the dog bit Jerry, Peter stabs Jerry.

However, the dog's hostility to Jerry begins the dog story whereas Peter's hostility to Jerry is only gradually aroused in *The Zoo Story*. The dog's hostility is at the surface of his animality, but Peter's hostility is calculatedly manipulated by Jerry, whose physical assault on Peter is comprised of five actions—tickling, shoving, punching, slapping, and immolating himself on the knife. But the physical assault has been prepared by Jerry's skillful verbal assault: "I have learned that neither kindness or cruelty by themselves, independent of each other, creates any effect beyond themselves; and I have learned that the two combined, together, at the same time, are the teaching emotion." Jerry combines the two in his education of Peter, with cruelty more immediately evident than kindness.

After Jerry's verbal attack, a terrified Peter screams when Jerry opens his knife: "YOU'RE GOING TO KILL ME!" But Jerry's intention is more subtle. *"Jerry tosses the knife at Peter's feet"* and urges him to pick it up. Once the knife is in Peter's hands, Jerry taunts him into using it. He slaps Peter each time he repeats the word "fight." Since Peter is a defensive animal (when pressed) and not an attacker, Jerry *"impales himself on the knife."* Though Jerry, wounded, screams like a "fatally wounded animal," he dies like a man—talking. In dying, Jerry comes to partial self-

132

recognition through his stream of associations: "Could I have planned all this? No . . . no, I couldn't have. But I think I did." His final broken phrases reflect the disjunctive quality of his behavior.

Jerry's fragmented life and speech contrast with Peter's coherence and order. Peter's effort to light his pipe triggers Jerry's first taunt: "Well, boy; *you're* not going to get lung cancer, are you?" With this thrust, Jerry exposes Peter's caution. At the same time, he introduces death, one of the play's themes, into the dialogue; he will harp on that theme in his account of his parents and aunt, in the dog story, and, finally, in his own death. Only in dying does Jerry shift from cruel to kind words, reassuring Peter that he is "an animal, too." The "too" is significant; Peter and Jerry are both animals, as are the seals, birds, and lions at the zoo; as are the parakeets who make Peter's dinner and the cats who set his table. In his dog story, Jerry says he put *rat* poison into the hamburger bought for a pussy-*cat*, so as to kill the landlady's *dog*. We see no animals on stage, but they recur thematically in the dialogue. Thus, animals become interchangeable. Albee's *Zoo Story*, the story that is not told, generalizes that men are animals; beneath an illusion of civilization, they live in rooms that resemble zoo-cages. They may use words and knives instead of fangs and claws, but they still can kill.

As Gilbert Debusscher has shown, this aspect of *The Zoo Story* is reminiscent of Tennessee Williams' *Suddenly Last Summer*. In both plays, too, "the cleverly interrupted monologue moves forward first by jerky and monosyllabic staccatos, then through the largo of long confessional passages, toward an unbearable tension which is resolved in a violent and sensational climax."[2] In both plays, that climax is a kind of mystical ecstasy—erotic, religious, but above all thematic.

By his climactic death, Jerry finally communicates with Peter, teaching him that men are brothers in their animality. However, Jerry does more than reveal Peter's animality to him. Like the Old Testament Jeremiah, whose cruel prophesies were a warning kindness to his people, Albee's Jerry may have educated Peter in his relation to God. Jerry occasionally introduces biblical notes: "So be it." "And it came to pass that . . ." "Amen." Before the dog story, Jerry exclaims: "For God's sake." After

133

DIALOGUE IN AMERICAN DRAMA

poisoning the dog, Jerry promises its owner that he will pray, though he does "not understand how to pray." At the end of the dog story, Jerry recites a list of those with whom he has tried to communicate—a list that begins with animals and ends with God, anagram of dog. In his cruel-kind deviling of Peter, Jerry calls on Jesus, and Peter replies with a "God damn" and a "Great God" almost in the same breath.[3]

This undercurrent of religious suggestion is climaxed by the final words of the play. Toward the beginning, Peter reacted to Jerry's unconventional life story with "Oh, my; oh, my." And Jerry sneered: "Oh, your what?" Only after the impalement is Jerry's question answered—by Peter's whispered repetitions: "Oh my God, oh my God, oh my God."—the only words Peter speaks while Jerry dies, thanking Peter in biblical phrases: "I came unto you and you have comforted me." After Jerry's revelation of Peter's animal nature, and Peter's subsequent departure according to Jerry's instructions, we hear "OH MY GOD!" as an off-stage howl—the final proof of Peter's animality, but also of his humanity, since he howls to his God. Jerry, who tells an animal story, closes the play by echoing Peter's "Oh my God" in the difficult combination demanded by the stage direction: "*scornful mimicry and supplication.*" That tonal combination is Jerry's last lesson in the pedagogy of cruel kindness. Much of his scornful wit has been mimetic, and yet the wit itself is an inverted plea for love and understanding; the very word "understand" resounds through the play.

Because life is lonely and death inevitable, Jerry seeks communication in a single deed of ambiguous suicide-murder. He stages his own death, and by that staging, he explodes Peter's illusion of civilization, converting him into an apostle who will carry the message of man's caged animality—the zoo story. Jerry's death brings us to a dramatic definition of humanity—born with animal drives but reaching toward the divine. Though this definition is at least as old as Pascal, Albee invests it with contemporary relevance through his highly contemporary idiom.

With gesture and language, Jerry teaches Peter. The relationship of the two men is not simply non-conformist versus conformist, but teacher and student, realist and illusionist, man and

fellow-man. Shifting from intimate questions to intimate revelations, Jerry opens a new world to Peter. Even in his dying
speech, Jerry does not sentimentalize, and he remains partially
mocking as he narrows down to the final spaced syllables: "Oh
. . . my . . . God." Homosexual interpretations of *The Zoo Story*
miss its wide resonance, but there *is* love in Jerry's pedagogy—
a love rooted in animality and straining toward the divine.

IN *The Death of Bessie Smith* (1959), ALBEE CHANGES
both structure and texture, but his dialogue continues to combine associational monologues with lethal thrusts. Based on a
newspaper story of the death of the Negro Blues singer, *The
Death of Bessie Smith* is documentary in origin—a unique phenomenon in Albee's work. But his Bessie Smith is a presence
and not a character in his play, whose most sustained character
is a voluble young Nurse. Lacking Jerry's pedagogic kindness,
the Nurse's dialogue is vitriolic, and yet she is not responsible
for the death of Bessie Smith.

In the eight scenes of the play, Albee attempts to counterpoint
two story-threads—the trip North of blues-singer Bessie Smith,
and the Nurse's sadistic control of a Southern hospital. The
Nurse story overshadows that of Bessie Smith, who is known
only through the dialogue of her chauffeur-companion, Jack.
Albee gives names to the sympathetic Negroes—Jack, Bernie,
Bessie Smith—whereas he type-casts the white world—Nurse,
Father, Intern, light-skinned Orderly, Second Nurse. Named
and unnamed characters are alike in their loquacious inaction.
As Paul Witherington has noted, they talk about doing things
which they do not do.[4]

The Nurse is the only coherent character in *The Death of Bessie
Smith,* and she coheres through her scornful verbalizations. To
her father, she sneers: "I'll tell you what I'll do: now that we
have His Honor, the mayor, as a patient . . . when I get down
to the hospital . . . If I ever get there on that damn bus . . . I'll
pay him a call, and I'll just *ask* him about your 'friendship' with
him." The Nurse goads her mulatto orderly: "Tell me, boy
. . . is it true, young man, that you are now an inhabitant of
no-man's-land, on the one side shunned and disowned by your

brothers, and on the other an object of contempt and derision to your betters?"

About half way through the play, Jack's car, with Bessie Smith as passenger, crashes off stage. On stage the Nurse carries on a bored telephone conversation with a second Nurse at another hospital. It is this second Nurse who is indirectly responsible for the death of Bessie Smith, but we do not learn this till the end of the play.

In the two longest of the eight scenes (sixth and last) the cynical but conformist Nurse engages in a thrust-and-parry dialogue with the liberal Intern. At his rare dialectical best, the Intern is as cruel as the Nurse. Though ideologically opposed to her, he desires her—a desire inflamed by her taunts. When his sneer about her chastity evokes her threat to "fix" him, he combines admiration with vengefulness: "I just had a lovely thought . . . that maybe sometime when you are sitting there at your desk opening mail with that stiletto you use for a letter opener, you might slip and tear open your arm . . . then you could come running into the emergency . . . and I could be there when you came running in, blood coming out of you like water out of a faucet . . . and I could take ahold of your arm . . . and just hold it . . . and watch it flow . . . just hold on to you and watch your blood flow . . ." The carefully cadenced pauses augment the cruelty of the words.

The death of Bessie Smith occurs off stage, between the last two scenes of the play. In the brief seventh scene, the Second Nurse refuses hospital admission to Bessie Smith, injured in an automobile accident: "I DON'T CARE WHO YOU GOT OUT THERE, NIGGER. YOU COOL YOUR HEELS!" Similarly, when Jack brings Bessie Smith to the central hospital in the last scene, the Nurse refuses admission to the singer. As the Intern and Orderly rush out to Bessie in the car, Jack tells the Nurse about the accident, and she recalls the Intern's wish that he might watch while her blood came out "like water from a faucet." But it is Jack who has watched the ebb of the life-blood of Bessie Smith. When the Intern and Orderly re-enter, *their uniforms are bloodied,* and Bessie Smith is dead.

In *The Death of Bessie Smith* nurses do not tend the sick; they converse at hospital admissions desks, refusing care to the injured. "Mercy" is merely an expletive without meaning. The Nurse says that she is sick of things; the word "sick" is on everyone's tongue. But it is Bessie Smith who dies of the sickness in the South. The Nurse speaks of her letter opener in the Intern's ribs, of a noose around his neck, but it is Bessie Smith who dies violently. The Nurse likes Negro blues, but she will not lift a finger to save a Negro blues-singer; rather, she mocks dead Bessie Smith, singing until the Intern slaps her. Albee's play indicts the whole sick South for the murder of Bessie Smith; his setting is a Southern hospital in which no one is well, but only Bessie Smith dies. Nevertheless, the singer's story is fragmentary, and we are left with a more vivid impression of the verbal duelling of Nurse and Intern; this is often gratuitous skirmishing in a loosely constructed, morally earnest drama.

By contrast, satiric caricature is Albee's main technique in *The Sandbox* (1959) and *The American Dream* (1960). Both monologues and thrust-and-parry exchanges contain the clichés of middle-class America. The implication is that such clichés lead to the death of Grandma, who represents the vigorous old frontier spirit. In her independence, Grandma resembles Jerry or the Intern, but age has made her crafty, and she has learned to roll with the punches. In both *The Sandbox* and *The American Dream*, Mommy delivers these punches verbally, and yet she does not literally kill Grandma.

Of the relationship between the two plays, Albee has written: "For *The Sandbox*, I extracted several of the characters from *The American Dream* and placed them in a situation different than, but related to, their predicament in the longer play."[5] *The Sandbox* is named for the grave of Grandma, the first-generation American, and *The American Dream* is named for the third-generation American, a grave in himself; in both plays, murderous intention is lodged in the middle generation, especially Mommy. In *The Sandbox*, Mommy and Daddy deposit Grandma in a child's sandbox, as Hamm deposited his legless parents in ashbins in Beckett's *Endgame*. Half-buried, Grandma finds that she can no longer move, and she accepts her summons by the handsome Young Man, an Angel of Death.

137

In *The American Dream*, Ionesco is a strong influence on Albee. Like *The Bald Soprano*, *The American Dream* thrives on social inanities. Like Ionesco, Albee reduces events to arrivals and departures. As in *The Bald Soprano*, a mock-recognition scene is based on circumstantial evidence—husband and wife in the Ionesco play, and in the Albee play, Mrs. Barker and the American family for whom she barks. Albee also uses such Ionesco techniques as proliferation of objects (Grandma's boxes), pointless anecdotes (mainly Mommy's), meaningless nuances (beige, wheat, and cream), cliché refrains (I don't mind if I do; how fascinating, enthralling, spellbinding, gripping, or engrossing.).

Within this stuffy apartment of Ionesco motifs, Albee places a family in the American grain, with its areas for senior citizens and its focus on money. When Mommy was eight years old, she told Grandma that she was "going to mahwy a wich old man." Sterile, Mommy and Daddy have purchased a baby from the Bye-Bye Adoption Service, that puns on Buy-Buy. Mommy spends much of her life shopping (when she isn't nagging Daddy or Grandma). In *The Sandbox*, Mommy and Daddy carry Grandma to *death*, but in *The American Dream*, Mommy nags at Grandma's *life*. She informs a feebly protesting Daddy that he wants to put Grandma in a nursing home, and she threatens Grandma with a man in a van who will cart her away. Mommy treats Grandma like a naughty child; she discusses Grandma's toilet habits, warns her that she will take away her TV, worries about her vocabulary: "I don't know where she gets the words; on the television, maybe."

And Grandma, who is treated like a child, repeats the phrases we learn as American children: "Shut up! None of your damn business." Grandma tells the story of the family child to Mrs. Barker. Since "the bumble of joy" had eyes only for Daddy, Mommy gouged his eyes out; since he called Mommy a dirty name, they cut his tongue out. And because "it began to develop an interest in its you-know-what," they castrated him and cut his hands off at the wrists. Our acquaintance with Mommy has prepared us for Grandma's account of Bringing up Bumble. But more painful than the mutilations are the ailments it subsequently develops, because we can hear in them Mommy's cruel

American platitudes: "it didn't have a head on its shoulders, it had no guts, it was spineless, its feet were made of clay." This is Mommy's more insidious castration, nagging the child into a diminutive Daddy, who is "all ears," but who has no guts since he "has tubes now, where he used to have tracts." Daddy's organs are related to housing, on the one hand, and television, on the other—both mass produced in modern America, and both part of the modern American dream life. In *The American Dream*, like father, like son. Daddy "just want[s] to get everything over with," and his bumble-son does get everything over with, by dying before Mommy can complete her murder of him.

In *The American Dream*, it is an off-stage bumble that predicts Grandma's death, as an off-stage rumble announces Grandma's death in *The Sandbox*. Like the bumble, Grandma escapes Mommy's murderous malice by a kind of suicide. As Jerry turns Peter's reluctant threat into the reality of his death, Grandma turns Mommy's repeated threats into the reality of her disappearance from the family. Mommy is even more conformist than Peter, so that she cannot perform deeds of violence herself. Daddy has been devitalized on an operating table, so that Grandma has to be threatened by a proxy murderer—the man in the van.

When a handsome Young Man arrives, Grandma is alone on stage, and she instantly recognizes the American Dream shaped by Mommy. He shares only appearance and initials with the Angel of Death in *The Sandbox*, but he has the same meaning. The American Dream is an Angel of Death who is linked to both the mutilated bumble and to Grandma. In a confessional monologue, the Young Man tells Grandma of a twin "torn apart" from him, so that it seemed his heart was "wrenched from his body," draining him of feeling. As his twin brother was mutilated physically, the American Dream is mutilated emotionally.

When Mrs. Barker intrudes upon this confrontation of the numb young modern man with the vigorous old frontier spirit, Grandma introduces him as the man in the van, Mommy's bogey-man. Asking him to carry her boxes, Grandma follows the Young Man out. Boxes and sandbox are coffin and grave; the

139

American Dream leads but to the grave, and Grandma, accepting her fate, goes out in style—escorted by a handsome swain whose gallantry replaces feeling.

Though minatory Mommy later admits that "There is no van man. We ... we made him up," she readily accepts the American Dream as a replacement for Grandma. Thus, the "comedy" ends happily, though Grandma is dead to Mommy: "Five glasses? Why five? There are only four of us." In spite of Mommy's malice—expressed in the clichés of contemporary America—Grandma and bumble manage to die their own deaths.

In the conversation between a sympathetic Grandma and an ambiguous American Dream, Albee dilutes his satire. In spite of Grandma's pithy frontier comments and her asides on "old people," Grandma does not openly oppose Mommy. Since the Young Man is first caricatured, then sentimentalized, his long speeches sag. He will "do almost anything for money," and he tries to sell us the sad story of his life. Apparently ignorant of the mutilations to his twin brother, he describes his parallel loss of sensation that has resulted in his inability to love. In spite of Albee's rhythmic skill, this abstract statement of losses is duller than Grandma's pungent summary of the mutilation of his twin, and this dulls the edge of Albee's satire. In spite of the Young Man's warning that his tale "may not be true," the mutual sympathy of Grandma and the American Dream is incongruously maudlin. Albee makes an effort to restore the comic tone by bringing back Mommy and Daddy with their mindless clichés, and the play ends with Grandma's sardonic aside: "everybody's got what he wants ... or everybody's got what he thinks he wants." The word "satisfaction" has threaded through the play, and the American family finally snuggles into its illusion of satisfaction.

IN *Who's Afraid of Virginia Woolf?* (1963) SUCH ILLUsion is less satisfactory, and it is expressed in a more varied and vitriolic idiom. As in Albee's earlier and shorter plays, however, murderous dialogue leads obliquely to murder. As the shadow of death lay over the sunny afternoon of *The Zoo Story*, death lies like a sediment in Martha's gin, Nick's bourbon, Honey's brandy, and mainly George's bergin. George claims that "the favorite sport is musical beds" in New Carthage, but the sport that commands our attention is elaborate word play in a diapason whose dominant note is that of death. And yet this death-dipped gamesmanship—the word "game" is repeated over thirty times—exposes an anatomy of love. Despite the presence of four characters, the play's three acts focus on the relationship of George and Martha, who express their love in a lyricism of witty malice.

Games do not formally begin in Act I, in spite of its title, "Fun and Games." However, the "fun" of stylized questions, exclamations, repetitions, and repartee involves us immediately in the verbal play of George and Martha. During the first few minutes of the drama, Martha calls George cluck, dumbbell, simp, pig, blank, cipher, and zero. George addresses Martha as "dear" and "love," but his offhand accusations relate her to animals—braying, chewing ice cubes like a cocker spaniel, and yowling like a sub-human monster. Through the swift first act, the dialogue rises toward a dissonant duet: Martha chants about George's failures while he tries to drown her voice in the party refrain, "Who's afraid of Virginia Woolf?" Toward the end of Act III, "Exorcism," George and Martha reach "a hint of communion." Despite their exchange of insults, George and Martha are *together* at the end of Acts I and III—the first mercilessly comic and the last mysteriously serious. During the three acts, neither of them can bear the extended absence of the other; each of them praises the other to Nick. Separated between Acts II and III, both George and Martha, independently, think of *A Streetcar Named Desire*. (Martha refers to *The Poker Night*, the original title of Williams' play, and George quotes the Spanish refrain of the Mexican flower-vendor.) However aggressive they sound—both utter the word "No" like a staccato tom-tom—George and Martha are attuned to one another, and they need one another.

George and Martha have cemented their marriage with the fiction of their son. Except for their inventive dialogue, they are outwardly conformist; privately, however, they nourish their love upon this lie. George's playlong preoccupation with death hints that such lies must be killed before they kill.

The distinctive love duet of George and Martha contains Albee's theme of death. Early in Act I, George tells Martha *"murderously"* how much he is looking forward to their guests. Once Nick and Honey are on scene, George shoots Martha with a toy gun, and then remarks that he might really kill her some day. In Act II, Nick and George exchange unprovoked confessions: Nick reveals intimacies about his wife and her father, but George's anecdotes center on death. He tells of a fifteen-year old boy who had accidentally shot his mother; when the boy was learning to drive, with his father as teacher, he swerved to avoid a porcupine, and he crashed into a tree, killing his father. Later in Act II, Martha summarizes George's novel about a boy who accidentally killed both his parents. Martha's father had forbidden George to publish the novel, and George had protested: "No, Sir, this isn't a novel at all . . . this is the truth . . . this really happened . . . TO ME!" George reacts to Martha's mimicry with a threat to kill her, and he grabs her by the throat. Athletic Nick, who resembles the American Dream both in physique and lack of feeling, tears George from Martha, and she accuses her husband softly: "Murderer. Mur . . . der . . . er." But George's stage murder will be performed verbally rather than physically.

While Nick and Martha disappear upstairs, drunk Honey voices her fear of having children, and George needles her: "How you do it? [sic] Hunh? How do you make your secret little murders stud-boy doesn't know about, hunh?" And George proceeds to plan the "secret little murder" of his child of fantasy. In Act III George and Martha declare "total war" on one another, and Martha vows "to play this one to the death." The death happens to a fantasy son, who, by George's account, swerved his car to avoid a porcupine, and crashed into a tree. George's imaginary child and his perhaps imaginary father died in precisely the same way.

Though George fires a toy gun at Martha, then tries to throttle her; though she leaps at him when he kills their child; though Honey shouts: "Violence. Violence." four times, the only stage murder is verbal. Such murder is oblique, and George leads up to it obliquely, with his "flagellation." The idiom that has nurtured their love will serve also to kill the illusion at its heart.

Martha may have downed George with boxing-gloves, but he outpoints her with words. He corrects her misuse of "abstruse" for "abstract," "something" for "somebody," "it" for "him." George insists upon "got" as a correct past participle. He builds balanced periodic sentences, for example his use of triplets in his description of Martha's drinking habits. Martha mocks him as Dylan Thomas, but the very name suggests an appreciation of George's language. Twice, Martha summarizes: "George and Martha: sad, sad, sad." but George and Martha speak the wittiest lines of American drama—economical, euphonic, and perfectly timed for our gaiety rather than sadness.

The sado-masochistic marriage of George and Martha is sustained through their verbal dexterity and their imaginary child, which save them from conventional academic mediocrity. Far from a *deus ex machina*, the child is mentioned before the arrival of Nick and Honey, when George warns Martha not to "start in on the bit about the kid." By that time, they have been sparring in their recurrent pattern, Martha cutting George with his lack of success and George striking at Martha's age, drinking, and promiscuity.

Guests heighten the pitch of the George-Martha exchange, as they move frankly into games. Though George has twice cautioned Martha not to mention their child, he himself is tantalizingly evasive when Nick asks whether they have children. While Martha is upstairs changing, she evidently tells Honey about their son, and that is the change that sets this evening off from similar evenings in the life of George and Martha. Once revealed, their son must die.

But George perceives this only at the end of Act II, and Martha struggles against it. Through two full acts, the couple spars verbally, with Nick as goad. Martha uses the child in Strindbergian fashion, suggesting that George might not be the father of the child. Unlike Strindberg's Captain, however, George is not vulnerable to this blow about their "bean-bag," but he is extremely vulnerable to Martha's taunts about his lack of success. As Martha mouths the phrase: "A great . . . big . . . fat . . . FLOP!" George breaks a bottle and clutches its splintered neck—a gesture that he may have learned from Blanche Dubois in *A Streetcar Named Desire*. But the jagged glass does not prevent Stanley's attack on Blanche, nor does it prevent Martha's attack on George.

143

Act II introduces some variations in the verbal fencing: George and Nick toward the beginning, Martha and Nick in the middle, and George and Honey at the end. But the bedrock remains George versus Martha. They have a momentary fling in French; they speak of their child in sexually insulting terms. George invents taunts: "Book dropper! Child mentioner!" These taunts summarize the two lies of George's own life—the murder of his father, which is the expression of the end of childhood, and the murder of his son, which may be the expression of the end of marriage. Martha's accusation against George —"Murderer. Mur . . . der . . . er." points both forward and backward in the play.

George charges Martha with "slashing away at everything in sight, scarring up half the world," and she claims that that is the reason he married her. Each insists that the other is sick—a leitmotif of this play as of *The Death of Bessie Smith*. In the prelude to their declaration of "total war," each marriage partner assaults the other's dominant fantasy:

MARTHA: . . . before I'm through with you you'll wish you'd died in that automobile, you bastard.

GEORGE: *(Emphasizing with his forefinger)* And you'll wish you'd never mentioned our son!

Each predicts the other's wish to renounce lies, implying an embrace of truth, but predictions are only obliquely fulfilled in *Who's Afraid of Virginia Woolf?!*

SNAP—sound, word, and gesture—becomes a stage metaphor in the destruction of lies, which may lead to truth. Martha snaps her fingers and informs George: "It's snapped, finally. Not me . . . it. The whole arrangement." She rhymes "snap" with "crap," and uses the word insistently, repetitively, to announce the beginning of their "total war." But George plays more intricate variations on the theme of snapping. His Act III entrance is delayed and mysterious— *"a hand thrusts into the opening a great bunch of snapdragons."* *"In a hideously cracked falsetto"* he chants: "Flores; flores para los muertos. Flores." In Williams' *Streetcar*, the Spanish words denote the end of the relationship of Blanche and Mitch. Comparably, George seems to announce the end of their relationship, as built upon an illusory son. After Martha lies that Nick is not a houseboy, George *"flourishes the flowers,"* shouting "SNAP WENT THE DRAGONS!!!" Then George throws the snapdragons—his flowers for the dead—at Martha, one at a time, stem-first, spear-like, as he echoes her "snaps" at him. St. George slew the dragon; Albee's George slays with hothouse snapdragons and the word "snap."

Before throwing the snapdragons, however, George starts a story about an eccentric moon on a Mediterranean trip, which he claims was a graduation present from his parents. "Was this after you killed them?" asks Nick. *"George and Martha swing around and look at him."* Then George replies ambiguously: "Truth or illusion. Who knows the difference, eh, toots?" Martha charges: "You were never in the Mediterranean . . . truth or illusion . . . either way." Only after Martha tells George that he cannot distinguish between truth and illusion, does he pelt her with the snapdragons. Martha repeats the dichotomy: "Truth or illusion, George. Doesn't it matter to you . . . at all?" This time George doesn't throw anything as he answers her: "SNAP!" And with relish, he sets the scene for snapping their common illusion, in preparation for the possibility of truth.

In his triumphant enactment of the murder, George snaps his fingers for Nick to join the final game, Bringing Up Baby; the ambiguous gerund embraces introduction, education, and vomiting. George himself claims that they have been playing Snap the Dragon, before beginning Peel the Label. Thus, Snap the Dragon becomes Bringing up Baby becomes Peel the Label, as George snaps his fingers for Honey to support his outrageous boast that he ate the death telegram. Death rites are accompanied by snaps, involving all four characters.

The death scene and its aftermath contain the most perfectly cadenced dialogue of a remarkably rhythmed drama. Rhythm abets meaning in George's attack on Martha's illusion. So zealous is he in punishing Martha that it is difficult to believe in the purity of his corrective purpose. George and Martha fire a salvo of mutual sexual accusation. Before breaking the news of the son's death, George joins Martha in a discordant duet, as at the end of Act I. Martha begins a sentimentalized account of the life of their son, while George begins to recite the Requiem Mass. Then Martha shifts to innuendoes against George, and George uses their son as a weapon against her. In harmonious discord, Martha invokes the purity of their son in "the sewer" of their marriage, while George chants the Mass in Latin. As George lingers over his announcement of their son's death, Martha at first reacts with fury but soon wilts like the scattered snapdragons. Suddenly, Nick reveals his illumination about their child, asking: "You couldn't have . . . any?" And George replies: "*We* couldn't."—a sentence that Martha echoes with Albee's scenic direction: "*A hint of communion in this.*" It is the broadest hint we have. At the departure of Nick and Honey, the dialogue narrows down to monosyllables; the playlong repetitions of "No" dissolve into a series of affirmatives (with two exceptions, in which George denies the rebirth of illusion). When George hums the title refrain, Martha admits that *she* is afraid of Virginia Woolf—a woman afflicted with a madness that drove her to suicide.[6]

Martha's fear is understandable. Whatever will George and Martha do now that their bean-bag is dead, their illusion exorcized? Since Albee once planned to give the Act III title, "The Exorcism," to the entire play, we know that he attaches importance to it. To exorcise is to drive out evil spirits, and in New Carthage the evil spirits are the illusion of progeny—Honey's imaginary pregnancy and Martha's imaginary son, which terminate in a "Pouf." These imaginary children live against a background of repetitions of the word "baby" in reference to adults.

The illusions of Martha and Honey are both child-connected, but they differ in cause and effect. Honey seems to have forced Nick into a marriage which "cured" her of a psychosomatic pregnancy. During marriage, her "delicacy" is the apparent reason they have no children. Without truth or illusion, they live in a vacuum of surface amenities. But when Martha indulges in an idealized biography of her son (before George kills him), Honey announces abruptly: "I want a child." She repeats this wish just before Martha shifts from the son as ideal biography to the son as weapon against George. Though Honey's conversion is sudden (and scarcely credible), it seems to be sustained.

For George and Martha, the exorcism is less certain, less complete, and far more involving. The marriage of Nick and

Honey kills their illusion, but the illusion of George and Martha is born in wedlock, perhaps because they could have no real children and Martha "had wanted a child." Martha's recitation indicates that the conception of the child—intellectual and not biological—may have originated as a game, but the lying game expressed their truest need. The imagery associates their son with classical and Christian divinity—golden fleece and a lamb —but such imagery also links the fathers of the two women, who emerge as calculatingly diabolic. An ambiguous creation through most of the play, son Sunny-Jim is killed on the eve of his maturity—an inverse Oedipal act by which George hopes to rid his domain of sickness.

Uninteresting in themselves, Nick and Honey function as foils and parallels of George and Martha: the syllabic similarity of the names, the parallel fantasies of the women, the similar yet opposing professions of the men, and the cross-couples advancing the plot. Without Nick, Martha's adultery would not have driven George to murder their son; without Honey, George could not have accomplished the murder. Albee's repetitions of "True or False" and "Truth versus Illusion" emphasize truth, but it is problematical whether truth can be sustained in the world of the play, and Albee leaves it problematical, refusing Martha the easy conversion of Honey. Unless the Act III title, "The Exorcism" is ironic, however, George and Martha construct a new relationship on the base of Truth—"Just . . . us?" —though their gifts seem more destructive than constructive. Dawn breaks on Martha's fear, and our lasting impression of the play is not of exorcism but of the exercise of cruel wit.

In *Who's Afraid of Virginia Woolf?* Albee exhibits rare mastery of American colloquial idiom. Since colloquialism is usually associated with realism, the play has been viewed as realistic psychology. But credible motivation drives psychological dramas, and Albee's motivation is flimsy: Why does George stay up to entertain Martha's guests? Why, for that matter, does she invite them? Why do Honey and Nick submit to being "gotten?" Why do Nick and George exchange confessions? Drinking is only a surface alibi, but the play coheres magnetically only if we accept the *Walpurgisnacht* as a *donnée*. These four people are brought together to dramatize more than themselves.

Of his novel, George says: "Well, it's an allegory, really—probably—but it can be read as straight, cozy prose . . ." No one has called Albee's prose "cozy," but it too has been viewed as "straight" realism, sometimes of "crooked" sexuality.[7] Like George's novel, however, Albee's drama is "an allegory, really —probably." In an interview, Albee himself affirmed: "You must expect the audience's minds to work on both levels, symbolically and realistically."[8]

Albee sets *Who's Afraid of Virginia Woolf?* in a realistic living-room in a symbolic New Carthage. Carthage (meaning "New City") was founded in the ninth century B. C. by a semi-legendary, deceitful Dido, and it was razed to the ground in 146 A. D. By the fifth century, it had again become a power which St. Augustine called "a cauldron of unholy loves."[9] Albee uses the historical conjunction of sex and power as spice for the American stew he simmers in his cauldron. He himself suggested: "George and Martha may represent the Washingtons and the play may be all about the decline of the West."[10] Nick was named for Nikita Kruschev. In spite of a tongue-in-cheek tone, Albee's hints are borne out by the play.

Albee's unholy lovers are George and Martha, whose names evoke America's first and childless White House couple. As the legendary George Washington could not tell a lie, Albee's George murders in the name of Truth. George describes his fictional son as "Our own little all-American something-or-other." Albee thus suggests that illusion is an American weakness. American drama has been much concerned with illusion, but Albee's America is representative of contemporary Western civilization. George *"With a handsweep take[s] in not only the room, the house, but the whole countryside."* He speaks French, Spanish, and Latin in the play, and he echoes President Kennedy's "I will not give up Berlin." George characterizes the region as "Illyria . . . Penguin Island . . . Gomorrah . . ." Realm of fantasy, realm of social satire, realm of sin—George's condemnatory geography shows an academic foursome in the decline of a romantic mythology, love in the Western World.[11] A humanistic George opposes a mechanized Nick. George can see the handwriting on the wall, and it is the penmanship of Oswald Spengler, whose book George flings at the chimes that become a death knell. On one broad level, then, *Who's Afraid of Virginia Woolf?* is in the American tradition of dramatized illusion: O'Neill's *Iceman Cometh*, Williams' *Streetcar Named Desire*, and Miller's *Death of a Salesman*.

Albee also reaches out beyond America into an examination of the nature of love, which may be his metaphor for Western civilization. The games of the play—Humiliate the Host, Get the Guests, Hump the Hostess, and Bringing up Baby—suggest a miniature society, and though George mocks his own Napoleonic stance, he *is* preoccupied with history. But his anemic humanist yearnings tend to be submerged in his playlong vitriolic idiom.[12] His views of history are simplistic—the construct-a-civilization speech; his views of science are simpleminded—the mechanical Nick-maker. George wants to defend Western civilization against its sex-oriented, success-oriented assailants—"I will not give up Berlin."—but his defense of life and love is centered in his invective rather than his scrotum. An attacker rather than defender, George is more effective *against* illusory dragons than *for* bastions of civilization. And George's limitations limit the resonance of Albee's play. Despite his keen ear for American idiom, Albee can scarcely bring new social standards to the White House. Martha is finally reduced to her fear, and George to his post-murder "It will be better. . . . It will be . . . maybe." But when has "betterness" emerged from murder, even if the victim is imaginary?

ALBEE CLAIMED THAT *Tiny Alice* (1965) IS A MYStery play in two senses of the word: "That is, it's both a metaphysical mystery and, at the same time, a conventional 'Dial M for Murder'-type mystery."[13] But the play's one murder—the Lawyer's shooting of Julian—takes place before our eyes, without detective story mystery. Instead, the mystery of what is happening on stage dissolves into the larger mystery of what happens in the realm of ultimate reality. Governing both is a conception of mystery as that which is forever hidden from human understanding.

Albee's protagonist is Brother Julian, who claims to be "dedicated to the reality of things, rather than the appearance," but

149

who has to be violently shocked—shot to death—before he recognizes reality, and even then he tries to convert it into familiar appearance. Using the disjunctive technique of Absurdism and the terminology of Christianity, Albee drapes a veil of unknowing over his mystery. Thus, the play is nowhere in place and time, though the flavor is American and contemporary. The three stage settings are fantastic, and Miss Alice's millions are counted in no currency. Time moves with the fluidity of a dream, and yet it is, as the Lawyer claims: "The great revealer." Except for pointed references to Julian's "six blank years," Albee obscures the *passing* of time; the Lawyer says that Miss Alice's grant is a hundred million a year for twenty years, and after Julian is shot, the Lawyer offers the Cardinal "two billion, kid, twenty years of grace for no work at all." The play may thus last twenty years between the twelve "tick"s in the Lawyer's opening gibberish and Julian's dying question: "IS IT NIGHT . . . OR DAY? Or does it matter?"

Of the five characters, two have names, two are named by their function, and one—Butler—bears the name of his function.[14] Albee has denied that the name Alice stand for Truth and Julian for Apostasy, but he cannot expunge such associations for us. Named or unnamed, however, all characters are locked into a function: Brother Julian into service to his God, the Cardinal into service to his Church, and the castle trio into service to their deity, knowable only as the mouse in the model. Servants of Tiny Alice, they appear to master the rest of the world. Their dialogue suggests that, like the trio in Sartre's *No Exit*, they are bound in an eternal love-hate triangle. Their mission is to deliver victims to Tiny Alice, at once a reduced truth and a small obscene aperture into an aspect of being.[15]

Their victim is Julian, a lay brother, who is a kind of Everyman. As in a medieval Morality, we are involved in the conflict within Everyman's soul, but we are aware too of our world in which that conflict resonates. Rather than Virtue versus Vice, Albee's Julian becomes a battlefield for Truth versus Illusion.

Though Julian is at the center of the play, Albee delays introducing him. Instead, the drama begins with personifications of power à la Jean Genet: Cardinal and Lawyer, sacred and profane, church and state, buddies and enemies, with a long past behind them. We first see Julian at the castle, in conversation with the Butler, whose symbolic function is a stewardship based on his serving of wine, Christian metaphor for blood. Butler also offers Julian water, tea, coffee, before port and champagne— sweet and effervescent forms of wine—and, appropriately, Butler tries to sweeten the ineluctable claims of Tiny Alice upon Julian. Butler guides Julian through the wine-cellar of the castle, and he pours champagne at Julian's wedding, which is his last supper.

As in earlier plays, Albee builds his dialogue with thrust-and-parry exchanges and monologues, but he uses them somewhat differently; the verbal skirmishing often ends in a draw, and the monologues sound explicit but are buried in the central mystery, which is unknowable. As in earlier plays, Albee's thrust-and-parry dialogue leads obliquely to murder. The master verbal fencer of *Tiny Alice*, the Lawyer, shoots Julian, but Miss Alice is the principal agent of his undoing, and she, as the Lawyer remarks, was "never one with words." Rather, she acts through surprises: the old hag turns into a lovely woman; un-prompted, she confesses to Julian her carnal relations with the Butler and the Lawyer; abruptly, she inquires into Julian's sex life; before marrying and abandoning Julian, she alternates a mysterious prayer with an address to "someone in the model." She cradles the wounded Julian, making *"something of a Pietà."* At the end she is cruel and kind; her last words are "Oh, my poor Julian"; yet she leaves him to die alone.

Miss Alice's seduction of Julian is accomplished through deeds rather than words, but Julian himself translates the erotic into a highly verbal mysticism. He defends his loquacity to Miss Alice: "Articulate men often carry set paragraphs." In each of the play's three acts, Julian indulges in a rhapsodic monologue that does not sound like a set paragraph, since its rhythms are jagged. Like the disjunctive monologues of *The Zoo Story*, the cumulative effect is apocalyptic, but Julian's apocalypse is sexu-ally rooted, *lay* brother that he is (Albee's pun). In Act I, Julian describes a perhaps hallucinatory sexual experience with a woman who occasionally hallucinated as the Blessed Virgin. Not only does Julian speak *of* ejaculation; he speaks *in* ejacula-tions. Julian's mistress with an illusory pregnancy recalls the illusion-ridden women of *Virginia Woolf;* as the imaginary child of that play is an evil spirit to be exorcized, the imaginary pregnancy of the hallucinating woman of *Tiny Alice* proves to be a fatal cancer. And even as Julian confesses to Miss Alice what he believes to be his struggle for the real, she tempts him with her own desirability—very beautiful and very rich.

In Julian's Act II monologue about martyrdom, he shifts his identity—a child, both lion and gladiator, then saint and the hallucinating self of the Act I monologue—all couched in imagery that is sexually suggestive. While Julian describes his eroto-mystical, multi-personal martyrdom, Miss Alice shifts her attitude, first urging Julian to marry her, then spurring him to sacrifice himself to Alice, whom she invokes in the third person.

In Act III, Julian, who left the asylum because he was persuaded that hallucination was inevitable and even desirable, embarks on his final hallucination, which ends in his real death. Abandoned and dying, Julian recollects (or imagines) a wound of his childhood, as Miss Alice in her prayer recollected (or imagined) being hurt in *her* childhood. Alternately a child and the hallucinating woman who called for help, Julian is forced to face himself in death—the prototypical existential confrontation. With phrases of the Thirteenth Psalm, Julian very slowly and desperately dissolves Miss Alice into Tiny Alice into the Christian God. Unable to accept the words of the lucid Lawyer: "There is Alice, Julian. That can be understood. Only the mouse in the model. Just that."—Julian recoils from the hermetic, dust-free vacuum of Tiny Alice, from the unblinking eyes of the phrenological head: "Ah God! Is that the humor? THE ABSTRACT? . . . REAL? THE REST? . . . FALSE." Unable to laugh at such absurd humor, Julian reverts to Christian illusion, to traditional images that protect him from the reality of abstraction, which is death.

Julian calls on deity in the words of Christ on the cross: "ALICE? MY GOD, WHY HAST THOU FORSAKEN ME?" As a "great presence" engulfs him, Julian takes the crucifixion position, injecting his God into Alice: "God, Alice . . . I accept thy will." Albee's play opens on Genet's satiric Balcony, but it closes on the Blackness of Ionesco's dying king; both Julian and Bérenger go down fighting against predatory death, but they both go down. On a throne, or crucified, or whimpering in bed, Every-man is food for Tiny Alice who devours in mystery.

Julian's three experiences pivot on his confusion between illusion and reality: the sexual experience may have been a hal-lucination; the experience of martyrdom has haunted Julian's imagination, and he dies in an evocation of Christ, the martyr, which may be his last illusion. Rhythms of ecstatic agony and the image of blood link the three experiences, or the three de-scriptions of experience, which perhaps become experience *through* description.

Between his three monologues as within them, Julian's speech is fragmentary, interrogative, and recapitulatory. In contrast to the sinewy syntax of the Lawyer, Julian's sentence fragments are heavy with gerunds, adjectives, efforts at definition through synonyms. As Jerry's indirection mirrored the theme of *The Zoo Story*, Julian's phrasal fragmentation mirrors the theme of *Tiny Alice*, and that fragmentation functions partly as synecdoche.

"In my Father's house are many mansions," said Christ (*John* XIV, 2) and in the mansion of Tiny Alice are many rooms. True to his heredity and calling, Brother Julian praises library, chapel, and wine-cellar—all with religious associations. Alone in the library after his wedding, he recalls the childhood loneli-ness of an attic closet. But all rooms belong to Tiny Alice, and space does not contain them. When the fire in the model an-nounces a fire in the chapel, Julian asks Miss Alice: "Why, why did it happen that way—in both dimensions?" After his wed-ding, Julian likens the disappearance of people to "an hour elaps[ing], or a . . . dimension." And shortly after shooting Julian, the Lawyer remarks to his old buddy-enemy, the Cardi-nal: "We have come quite a . . . dimension, have we not?" In *Tiny Alice* dimensions are diffused and confused; one does not move, as in the Great Chain of Being, from an animal dimen-sion, to human, to angelic, to divine. Rather, all dimensions are interactive, and point to the whole metaphysical mystery in its more private parts.

Those parts are sexual, but Albee also suggests them through verbal insistence on birds and children—vulnerable both. Bird imagery embraces everyone: the play opens with a nonsense address to birds; the Cardinal has cardinals in his stone-and-iron garden; the Butler speaks of swallows "screeping"; the Lawyer's poem is said to have the grace of a walking crow; Miss Alice is first visible in a *wing* chair, and she later envelops Julian in the "great wings" of her robe; Julian is variously a "bird of pray," a "drab fledgling," and a "little bird pecking away in the library," summarizing his piety, innocence, and sexual vulnerability. At times, too, the characters act like children, or they summon recollections of childhood. Julian is often and explicitly called "little," and in his dying soliloquy, he becomes a little boy calling for his cookie. All these lines suggest the helplessness of birds and children in the world of Tiny Alice, who is at once mouselike, monstrous, and feline.

Like imagery and fragmentation, the tone of Albee's dialogue is complex. Familiar is the stinging salaciousness of the opening scene between the Cardinal and the Lawyer. This functions symbolically, since the Cardinal-Church is the son of a whore, and the Lawyer-State eats offal and carrion. The titillation of these disclosures is counterpointed against the formality of the syntax—first-person plurals, avoidance of contractions, emphasis on prepositional nuance, and self-conscious word-play (the eye of an odor). Only rarely does the Lawyer slip into a vigorous Americanism that underlines his malice: "Oh, come on, your Eminence." "You'll grovel, Buddy. As automatically and naturally as people slobber on that ring of yours." "Everyone diddled everyone else." "We picked up our skirts and lunged for it! iiiiii! Me! Me! Gimme!"

The Lawyer, who evokes Satan for the Cardinal, is the chief instrument of Albee's mutilating dialogue. Not only does he thrust at the Cardinal; he sneers endearments to the Butler, and he woos Miss Alice as "clinically" as he fondles her. At his first meeting with Julian, he belittles the Cardinal and humiliates Julian. After shooting Julian, the Lawyer directs the death-scene, without pity for the dying martyr. The Butler accuses the Lawyer: "You're a cruel person, straight through; it's not cover; you're hard and cold, saved by dedication; just that." And yet, both the Cardinal and the Butler speak of the Lawyer as "good," for he *is* good in his dedication to Tiny Alice.

The cross-relationships of the five characters of *Tiny Alice* are more complicated than in *Virginia Woolf:* the Cardinal and the

Lawyer loathe each other, Miss Alice detests the Lawyer, and the Lawyer has never liked the Butler. The Cardinal may have had carnal relations with the Lawyer and with Julian; Miss Alice has had the Butler and the Lawyer as lovers; in Julian's presence, the Butler and the Lawyer address each other with words of endearment; the Lawyer and the Butler play at being the Cardinal and the Lawyer, the Butler plays at being Julian the victim, Miss Alice takes the very name of Tiny Alice. Julian is, successively, the Cardinal's secretary, the Butler's protegé, Miss Alice's husband, the Lawyer's victim. And Julian alone seems to be mortal.

As in Albee's earlier plays, violent death leads to a revelation of a deeper layer of reality. Miss Alice tells Julian pointedly: "Accept what's real. I am the illusion." Finally, Miss Alice will be Alice *missing*, as want [desire] of emphasis becomes a lack of emphasis. And yet, the Butler who makes this semantic point, has mocked Julian: "Six years in the loony bin for semantics?" The Lawyer and Butler debate Julian's fate almost as a semantic exercise: Will he be pushed "back to the asylums. Or over . . . to the Truth," which is Tiny Alice.

Julian's wedding day becomes his death day. Earlier, Julian used pious clichés for a business deal: "That God has seen fit to let me be His instrument in this undertaking." Dying, Julian flings the same word at the Lawyer, as an insult: "Instrument." The play reveals the Lawyer as the instrument of absurd reality, which is Tiny Alice. Julian, on the other hand, is first and last the instrument of his own imagination. He is both Everyman and the victim of the "awful humor" of Tiny Alice, precisely because he claims to reject illusion for reality. *That* is his illusion, with which he commits himself to an asylum. And rather than accept the reality of Tiny Alice, he is ready to commit himself again, but is prevented by the Lawyer's fatal shot. The cynical lucid Lawyer has already foretold the pattern of Julian's final behavior, mixing the formal and the colloquial in the same speech: "face the inevitable and call it what you have always wanted. How to come out on top, going under."

Because he bends his imagination to embrace the inevitable, Julian achieves the difficult martyrdom he seeks. On stage, the long dying scene borders on the ridiculous, as Julian's initial resistance to the inevitable *is* ridiculous. But, "going under," he summons the heroic illusion of his culture; not a "Gingerbread God with the raisin eyes," but a human god crucified for man. Julian dies in imitation of Christ, deaf to Tiny monstrous Alice who comes thumping and panting to devour him. The play ends on Alice, truth, reality, after Julian has been crucified in his illusion, but our lasting impression is that of a hero—vulnerable, loquacious, even ridiculous, but nevertheless heroic in the intensity of his imagination.

EVEN PUZZLED AUDIENCES HAVE BEEN INVOLVED IN Julian's plight, which the Butler describes: "Is walking on the edge of an abyss, but is balancing." Albee's next play, *A Delicate Balance* (1966) is named for that perilous equilibrium. Like *Virginia Woolf*, the play presents a realistic surface; as in *Virginia Woolf*, a love relationship in one couple is explored through the impact of another couple. There is enough talking and drinking to convey the impression of a muted, diluted *Virginia Woolf*. Both plays end at dawn, but the earlier play contains "Exorcism." The later play dramatizes what Albee has called "arthritis of the mind."[16]

Each of the six characters of *A Delicate Balance* "is walking on the edge of an abyss, but is balancing"; a middle-aged marriage is balancing, too, until a makeshift home in a "well-appointed suburban house" is threatened by both family and friends. In Friday night Act I, terror-driven friends seek refuge in the family home; in Saturday night Act II, the master of the house, Tobias, assures his friends of their welcome, but his daughter Julia reacts hysterically to their presence. In Sunday morning Act III, the friends know that they are not welcome, know that they would not have welcomed, and they leave. The delicate balance of the home is preserved by an "arthritis of the mind."

The play begins and ends, however, on a different delicate balance—that of the mind of Agnes, mistress of the household, wife of Tobias, mother of Julia, sister of Claire. In convoluted Jamesian sentences, she opens and closes the play with doubts about her sanity; at the beginning, she also extends these doubts to an indefinite *you*—"that each of you wonders if each of *you* might not . . ." And as we meet the other members of the family, we can understand the wonder: Claire the chronic drunk, Julia the chronic divorcée, and Tobias who heads the house. Though Agnes starts and finishes the play on her doubts about sanity, each of the acts dramatizes the precarious stability of the other members of the family: first Claire, then Julia, and finally Tobias. In each case, the balance is preserved, a little more delicate for being threatened.

However perilously, the family is bound together by love. In Claire's words to Tobias: "You love Agnes and Agnes loves Julia and Julia loves me and I love you . . . Yes, to the depths of our self-pity and our greed. What else but love?" Agnes, who blames the others for their faults, describes such blame as the "souring side of love" in this drama about the limits of love.

Agnes early characterizes the family to Tobias: "your steady wife, your alcoholic sister-in-law and occasional visits . . . from our melancholy Julia." But her description is only a first approximation: her own steadiness is severely strained, Claire insists that she is not "a alcoholic," and Julia is more hysterical than melancholy. By Act III a harassed Tobias, having suffered his passion, offers a contrasting description of the same family: "And you'll all sit down and watch me carefully; smoke your pipes and stir the cauldron; watch." He thus groups wife, daughter, sister-in-law as three witches, or the three fates "who make all the decisions, really rule the game . . ." And who preside over the term of life until death cuts it short.

As in other Albee plays, death lurks in the dialogue of *A Delicate Balance*, but death is not actualized in this play. Violence is confined to a single slap, a glass of orange juice poured on the rug, and an ineffectual threat with a gun. In words, however, Claire urges Tobias to shoot them all, first Agnes, then Julia, and herself last. Agnes suggests that Claire kill herself, and Claire in turn asks Agnes: "Why don't you die?" It is this sisterly exchange between Claire and Agnes that inspires Tobias to his digressive monologue, his cat story. Because his cat inexplicably stopped liking him, Tobias first slapped her and then had her killed. Out of the depths of his greed and self-pity, he had her killed.

Like Jerry's dog story, Tobias' cat story is an analogue for the play of which it is part. As Tobias kills the cat, he will effectively kill his friends, Harry and Edna, when he denies them a home. As Claire and Agnes approve his conduct toward the cat, Claire and Julia will approve his conduct toward Harry and Edna. The death of the cat maintains Tobias' delicate emotional balance in spite of his bad conscience, and the departure of Harry and Edna will maintain Tobias' delicate family balance in spite of his bad conscience.

The threat of death is almost personified by Harry and Edna. Julia tries to aim her father's gun at the visitors, and Agnes calls their terror a disease and a plague. In demanding that Tobias make a decision with respect to Harry and Edna, Agnes reminds him of the intimate details of their sexual life after the death of their son, Teddy. She addresses Tobias as "Sir," with a servant's deference to a master. But this master gives no orders, and it is Harry and Edna, conscious of their own mortality, who decide to leave, taking their plague with them.

A Delicate Balance is itself in most delicate balance between the cruel-kindness of its surface and the mysterious depths below, between a dead child and a new dawn, between ways of loving and ways of living. Albee has posed his equilibrium discreetly, without the symbolic histrionics of *Tiny Alice*, without the corruscating dialogue of *Virginia Woolf*. At the most general level, the arrival of Harry and Edna raises the question of the limits of love; Tobias says to Harry: "I find my liking you has limits . . . BUT THOSE ARE MY LIMITS! NOT YOURS!" Harry and Edna push each family member to his limits. Before their arrival, Agnes thanks Tobias for a life without mountains or chasms, "a rolling, pleasant land." But the plague can attack rolling, pleasant lands, and it is carried by one's best friends.

In Harry and Edna, Albee creates Janus-symbols, for they are at once Tobias and Agnes, and their friend-enemies. Described in the Players' List as *"very much like Agnes and Tobias,"* Edna and Harry live in the same suburb and belong to the same club. They are godparents to Julia, as Tobias and Agnes are her parents. When Harry serves drinks, Agnes remarks that he is "being Tobias." When Edna scolds Julia, Albee's scenic direction indicates that she *"becomes Agnes."* Just before leaving, Edna speaks in the convoluted formal sentences of Agnes.

Otherwise, however, Harry and Edna do not sound like Tobias and Agnes, and they did not look like them in the original production supervised by Albee. Edna weeps whereas Agnes rarely cries; Edna shows desire whereas Agnes conceals it. As clear-sighted Claire (Albee's pun) points out to Tobias, all he shares with Harry is the memory of a summer infidelity with the same girl. Tobias denies being frightened, while fright ambushes Harry and Edna. Harry admits honestly what Tobias conceals clumsily: "I wouldn't take them in." When Harry and Edna finally depart, Agnes lapses into a rare cliché: "Don't be strangers." to which Edna replies: "Oh, good Lord, how could we be? Our lives are . . . the same." Rather than being *like* Tobias and Agnes, Harry and Edna are the *same* as Tobias and Agnes —minus a family.

Terror drives Harry and Edna from their house because a couple is inadequate bulwark against emptiness; they are free of the blood-ties which protect us from the loneliness of self and the encroachment of living death. Harry and Edna arrive after a family conversation about the bonds of love; their terror has no cause: "WE WERE FRIGHTENED . . . AND THERE WAS NOTHING." They were frightened *because* there was nothing.

In *Who's Afraid of Virginia Woolf?* George and Martha conceived an imaginary child to sustain their love; in the autumn of their lives Harry and Edna find themselves engulfed by nothing. As Tobias and Agnes would be, were the void not filled with the *repetitive* failings in the family: Agnes and Claire both call Tobias' anisette "sticky"; Agnes says of both Claire and Julia, separately, that either she will come down from her room, or not; Claire and Julia both contrive to apologize accusatively. The game of musical recriminations is what keeps the family love alive, and this is what Harry and Edna need—what they *want*, in the most insistent pun of the play.

In dramatizing the failure of love, which is death, Albee is ascetically sparing of vivid imagery and dazzling dialogue. Though he does not quite indulge in the fallacy of imitative form, he seems to imply that a drama with emptiness at its center, must echo in hollowness. Each time two characters start to thrust and parry verbally, the spark is damped. Each of the characters apologizes at least once, snuffing out verbal fire-

159

works. Damped, too, are the few threads of imagery—the household, childhood, helping, and sinking. So fragile is the sensuous quality of the imagery, that it seems mere verbal repetition. All the characters refer to the house as they all recall a childhood before "Time happen[ed]." Help is usually mentioned in connection with invisible servants, though Agnes says tentatively to Harry and Edna: "If we were any help at all, we . . ."

Rhythm and rhyme emphasize the feelings of fragmentation and displacement. Claire's comic anecdote about the topless bathing-suit is emblematic of her fragmented life. Agnes comments obliquely on the thin surface of all their lives: "It's one of those days when everything's underneath." Claire claims that they all submerge their truths, then turns to Edna: "Do *you* think we can walk on water, Edna? Or do you think we sink?" Edna is *"dry"* as she replies: "We sink." All the drinking in all three acts reveals their ineffectual efforts to develop gills.

Sparing his imagery, Albee plays upon the verb *want* to sustain the delicate balance. Its double meaning, wish and lack, were already suggested in *Tiny Alice*, and Albee exploits this ambiguity more fully in *A Delicate Balance*. Claire wishes Agnes to die but doesn't know whether she wants it. Hysterical, Julia shifts from "they [Harry and Edna] want" to "I WANT . . . WHAT IS MINE!" Agnes asks Harry and Edna pointedly: "What do you *really* . . . *want*?" And some minutes later, Edna replies, playing on the same verb: "if all at once we . . . NEED . . . we come where we are wanted, where we know we are expected, not only where we want." Harry insistently questions Tobias: "Do you *want* us here?" And in Tobias' final aria, he shifts from: "I WANT YOU HERE!" to "I DON'T WANT YOU HERE! I DON'T LOVE YOU! BUT BY GOD . . . YOU STAY!"

Love is lack and love is wish in *A Delicate Balance*, and Albee suggests that the human condition is to be bounded by want—lack and wish. *"The living-room of a large and well-appointed suburban house. Now."* is where we live in contemporary middle-class America. Not a social America, however, but a metaphysical Kafkaesque America, the leading nation in the decline of the West. The play's American resonances are muted: Republicans and Reno are brief guideposts; Alcoholics Anonymous and tax deductions are possible markers. American slang and imagery are used apologetically:

CLAIRE: . . . the shirt off your back, as they say.
JULIA: As they say, I haven't the faintest.
AGNES: . . . the fatal mushroom . . . as those dirty boys put it.
TOBIAS: You're copping out . . . as they say.

The "regulated great gray life" is greater, grayer, and more regulated in America, but it reaches out tentacularly over the whole world.

Each of the sisters uses her own distinctive rhythm to state the play's theme.

AGNES: There *is* a balance to be maintained, after all, though the rest of you teeter, unconcerned, or uncaring, *assuming* you're on level ground . . . by divine right, I gather, though that is hardly so.
CLAIRE: We can't have changes—throws the balance off.

The death of their son, Teddy, has thrown off the balance in the home of Tobias and Agnes, who teetered in a household that gradually took on the balance of a home again. Rather than upset the balance, Claire and Harry both lie to Agnes about the infidelity of Tobias. Rather than upset the balance, the family members play out their identity patterns, with only momentary shifts: Agnes poses as Julia's father, Tobias imitates Julia's hysteria, Claire plays a Tobias who explains to a judge the murder of his family, Julia spouts the opinions of her most recent husband, and Claire may be the nameless upended girl whom Tobias and Harry seduced one "dry and oh, so wet July." Identity itself is in delicate balance in this "regulated great gray life." Edna speaks of and for them all when she summarizes her recognition of the delicacy of all balance, which is life: "It's sad to come to the end of it, isn't it, nearly the end; so much more of it gone by . . . than left, and still not know . . . still not have learned . . . the boundaries, what we may not do . . . not ask, for fear of looking in a mirror."

In generalizing the predicament of his characters into the human condition, Albee relies on biblical associations of "house," as on associations of the names of the two couples, and of the three days between Good Friday and Easter Sunday, when Christ suffered his passion. Harry means torment, and clear-sighted Claire calls him "old Harry," which is a nickname for the devil; in contrast, Agnes is the lamb of God. The two couples, who are the same, range from angelic expressions of love to diabolic noncommitment. The other two names, Tobias and Edna, figure in the Book of Tobit; by angelic intervention Tobias was able to marry Sara, though her first seven bride-grooms died before possessing her; the mother of Sara was Edna. Albee's parallels with the Book of Tobit are obscure; neverthe-less, the Book of Tobit is concerned, like *A Delicate Balance*, with ties of blood and with the burial of the dead. Albee's Tobias is occasionally called Toby or Tobe, and like his biblical eponym, he is faced with the problem of Being.

A number of biblical references to "house" illuminate this family in the "well-appointed suburban house:"

For I know that thou wilt bring me to death, and to the house appointed for all living. (*Job* XXX, 23)

Thus saith the Lord, Set thine house in order; for thou shalt die and not live. (*Kings* XX, 1; *Isaiah* XXXVIII, 1)

If a house be divided against itself, that house cannot stand. (*Mark* III, 25)

But biblical prophets and patriarchs were men of great faith whereas Albee's Tobias wants that firm ground, and he quivers in the delicate balance of which his wife is fulcrum. For that is the house he has moulded, under the illusion that it has moulded him.

Like *Virginia Woolf*, *A Delicate Balance* ends at dawn, and dawn's meaning is again problematical. In spite of exorcism, Martha continues to fear Virginia Woolf; in spite of the ful-crum, the delicate balance might not last through a morning that Tobias implies is "very late at night." On the stage of *A Delicate Balance*, moreover, the pale language serves to pale dawn's light. Though Agnes apologizes for being articulate, she and Tobias tend to talk around subjects. Though Claire mocks Tobias: "Snappy phrases every time." she utters the play's few snappy phrases. Written in a minor key, *A Delicate Balance* lacks the lethal dialogue that has become Albee's trademark, but death nevertheless hangs heavy in the atmosphere.

IN ADAPTING GILES COOPER's *Everything in the Garden*, Albee tries a combination of the injurious repartee of *Virginia Woolf* and the stilted phrases of *A Delicate Balance*. Though Albee had earlier adapted two novels—Carson MacCullars' *Ballad of the Sad Cafe* (1963) and James Purdy's *Malcolm* (1965)—*Everything in the Garden* (1967) in his first adaptation of a play, and his dialogue changes are instructive. Most obvious is the transfer from English to American suburbia, with its corresponding idiom. The Madame's name is changed from Mrs. Pimosz—"like primrose, but have no *r's*"—to Mrs. Toothe, whose bite pierces to blood. Jack, the victim who is buried in the garden, is changed to a witty narrator who addresses the audience directly, before and after his death. Both plays—Cooper's and Albee's—too easily indict a comfort literally built on corpses—the "everything" that is buried in the garden, but the dialogue of Albee's indictment shows his habitual rhythms. The wife's reaction to the Madame's offer uses his characteristic pauses:

Cooper: You must see I can't take money from you like this.
Albee: Look, you . . . you can't just . . . *give* me money like this. I can't just . . . take money from you.

Or the husband's curtain line, when he learns the source of his wife's wealth:

Cooper: Farrow and Leeming! Acton here. I want a case of champagne and two bottles of brandy. Can you deliver them this afternoon?
Albee: . . . and . . . and . . . so, so, so, scotch, and . . . bourbon, and . . . *(Full crying now)* . . . and gin, and . . . gin, and . . . gin, and . . . *(the word* gin *takes a long time now, a long, broken word with gasps for breath and the attempt to control the tears)* . . . g-i-i-i-n, and . . . *(Final word, very long broken, a long howl)* G——i——i——i——i——n——n——n——n. *(Curtain falls slowly as the word continues.)*

Though adaptations permit Albee to exercise his muscular dialogue, their thematic facility is unworthy of him. Like his sketch, *Fam and Yam*, they are evidence of self-indulgence.

In "two inter-related plays," *Box* and *Quotations from Chairman Mao Tse-Tung*, Albee engages in quite different verbal exercises —different from anything he or any other playwright has attempted. For the first time, Albee's murderous thrust-and-parry dialogue vanishes completely, as each of his characters retreats into a solipsistic monologue.[17] Nothing happens on stage; or rather, only the dialogue happens, but the threat of death is implicit in that dialogue.

Box presents us with the titular box that takes up *"almost all of a small stage opening."* While we look at the box, in a constant bright light, we hear the disembodied voice of a woman, which *"should seem to be coming from nearby the spectator."* In the second of the two inter-related plays, *Quotations from Chairman Mao Tse-Tung* (about eight times the length of *Box*), an ocean liner appears within the outline of the box; aboard are four characters —Mao, who addresses us from the ship's railing, a stationary Old Woman who also addresses us directly, a Long-Winded Lady in a deck chair who addresses herself to a silent clergyman in his deck chair. The articulate trio is soon joined by brief phrases from the disembodied voice of *Box*. In the final *Reprise* we see the silhouettes of the four figures of *Mao*—now silent— as we hear a selection of about half the original *Box* monologue.

In *Virginia Woolf*, Albee counterpoints the Requiem Mass against a drunken conversation; in *Tiny Alice*, he integrates the Thirteenth Psalm into Julian's dying monologue. But in *Quotations from Chairman Mao Tse-Tung*, Albee makes unparalleled use of quotation—not only selections from Mao's Red Book, but over twenty stanzas of Will Carleton's "Over the Hill to the Poor-House." And since we have already heard the phrases of *Box*, three of the four voices recite familiar material, all of which functions as background for the only personal story of the play, associationally narrated by the Long-Winded Lady.

Though the voice of *Box* does not emanate from the box, it uses the cube as its point of departure, and since all we see is a box, verbal associations spring readily for this word—prison, coffin. Albee has already used boxes in *The Sandbox* and *The American Dream*, where they are associated with Grandma, the dying frontier spirit. There is a faint echo of this in *Box*, where a woman's voice reaches us from outside the box, close to us. We are not yet boxed in, but the threat is visually before us throughout the woman's monologue.

The voice belongs to no empiricist, for it moves almost immediately beyond what our senses perceive, to the *possibility* of a rocking chair in the box, to generalizations about crafts, and on to art. Through a lyric threnody of loss, the voice suggests that art is powerless to prevent catastrophe—"seven hundred million babies dead"—and that the very practice of art is a kind of corruption in a time of disaster. And yet, art gives us "the memory of what we have not known," introduces us to experience we cannot otherwise know, as sea sounds can frighten the land-locked. In a world where "nothing belongs," art strives for order.

Mao opens the second play with a fable from Chapter XXI of the Red Book, which glorifies the Chinese masses. Mao then moves on to Communist theory and tactics, growing more and more aggressive in vocabulary, though *"his tone is always reasonable"* and his purpose always pedagogic. Many of the quotations are drawn from Chapter VI of the Red Book, "Imperialism and All Reactionaries are Paper Tigers." In that chapter and in Albee's quotations, the arch-imperialist is the U. S., so that Mao's final words damn America: "People of the world, unite and defeat the U. S. aggressors and all their running dogs." Mao's patiently positive attitude culminates in an injunction to widespread murder.

The Old Woman, who *"might nod in agreement with Mao now and again,"* is not so repetitive in her chant, and Albee stipulates that *"she is reciting a poem,"* even though its subject matter is very close to her. In other words, her poverty is evident in her shabby clothes and the simple food she eats in our presence, but she is not necessarily identical with the persona of Will Carleton's poem. That persona uses limping, heavily accented, rhymed hexameters to complain about the events that sent her "over the hill to the poor-house." Widowed, she loses five of her six children as, one by one, they go out to live their own lives. After the sixth child marries, she is successively rejected from the homes of each of her children, and finally she is sent to the poor-house, inspiring her final maudlin prayer: "And God'll judge between us; but I will al'ays pray/That you shall never suffer the half I do today."

Mao has given us a formulaic system, the Old Woman a formulaic lament, but the Long-Winded Lady is entirely original and personal. She starts with an incomprehensible splash, imagining the reaction of "theoretical . . . onwatchers." Associationally, she has a childhood memory of breaking her thumb, then a more recent recollection of a taxi going wild. As she entered with a plate of crullers on the bloody scene (recalling Marie Antoinette and her *brioches* in the face of famine), the Long-Winded Lady comments on the utter inadequacy of any response to disaster. More and more, the theme of death links her disparate associations; uncle, sister, and husband speak of death, and her husband was aware of the perpetual process of dying before he was attacked by the agonizing cancer that killed him. Though his dying is now over, "his *death* stays." And it is with that death that the Long-Winded Lady lives, having no communion with her daughter, and no relationship with anyone else. Finally, toward the end of the play, the Long-Winded Lady describes the opening splash in detail. It is *her* splash, but she describes it without a single "I." She fell off an ocean liner (like the one on which we see her) *splash* into the ocean. Ironically and improbably, however, she did not sink but was rescued. After congratulations came questions: Could anyone have pushed her? Did she throw herself off? Try to kill herself? The Long-Winded Lady closes her monologue and the *Mao* part of Albee's play with a half-laughing denial: "Good heavens, no; *I* have nothing to die for." It is a brilliant twist of the cliché: "I have nothing to live for." We live—most of us—by natural momentum, but voluntary death demands a dedication beyond the power of the Long-Winded Lady—or most of us.

As the disembodied woman's voice opens the "inter-related plays," so it closes them in a "reprise." But between *Box* and *Reprise*, Albee expunges catastrophe from the Voice's monologue, having suggested disaster in each of the three separate monologues of *Mao*. *Reprise* retains the *Box* images of music, birds, order, and an art that hurts. Though the Voice is matter-of-fact, even *"schoolmarmish,"* it is lyrical in the hint that emotion alone invests events with meaning, and yet the emotion of art is unable to act meaningfully upon any event. Pain can merely be contained by order—"Box."

From Chekhov on, we have been familiar with characters who talk past each other rather than engaging one another in dialogue. But in *Mao* each of the characters is completely unaffected by the other's speech, gives no evidence of hearing the others. And there is no plot connection between the speeches, as there is in Beckett's *Play*. But theme, tone, and contiguity give rise to associations of meaning for us, as the characters speak singly.

Death is the theme that unites the three visible and audible characters—the holy crusade of Mao, the old widow, and the very personal description of dying in the monologue of the long-winded widow. But though death sounds in these monologues, the notes are subtle and discontinuous. Thus, the Old Woman is absent from the following threnodic strain:

MAO: A revolution is an insurrection, an act of violence by which one class overthrows another.

VOICE, FROM BOX: When art begins to hurt, it's time to look around. Yes it is.

LONG-WINDED LADY: And *I*, he said, *I*—thumping his chest with the flat of his hand, slow, four, five times—*I* . . . am *dying*.

Each of the four voices is distinctive and unique, and yet they may be paired by tone or style. Mao and the Old Woman recite ready-made phrases; the Long-Winded Lady and the Voice speak searchingly, punctuating their discourse with pauses and images. Yet, the Voice is schoolmarmish as Mao is pedagogical; each of them comments on the nature of reality, but their realities are different. By contrast, the persona of the Old Woman and the Long-Winded Lady gradually reveal life stories; both are widows, and both are touched by death. In addition to these pairs, the three women's voices may be grouped by pathos; they sing in a minor key. Masculine Mao, on the other hand, is positive and optimistic, and the masculine clergyman is silent.

Thematically, death binds these four voices, and stylistically repetition is their common technique. Mao emphasizes single words or ideas by reiteration; the Old Woman does not recite Carleton's poem straight through, but chooses certain lines or stanzas to linger over and dwell upon; occasional phrases of the Long-Winded Lady recur—above all "dying"; after the initial performance of *Box*, all the words of the disembodied voice are repetitions, and the final *Reprise* means repetition. The *Reprise* joins end to beginning in a kind of musical parallel for a box, but since music moves in time, repetition itself becomes thematic through strains of dialogue.

Because the Long-Winded Lady alone has a personal, a *dramatic* monologue, she is at the center of the play. Seeking the counsel of a silent clergyman, she is threatened by the two other figures on this ship of fools—the ruthless system of Mao and the maudlin poverty of the Old Woman. Long-winded, unrooted, she is a middle-aged, middle-class Miss America, that last corrupt and dying outpost of Western civilization. Unlike George and Julian, who also represent the Western tradition in Albee's plays, the Long-Winded Lady utters no words of optimism or heroism. She can merely offer the stuff of her life to a silent and therefore ineffectual representative of God. Like Joyce's distant artist paring his fingernails, a disembodied voice embraces all experience in the order of art. But the question nags as to whether Albee's particular art is drama.

EDWARD ALBEE IS THE MOST SKILLFUL COMPOSER OF dialogue that America has produced. His very first play showed thorough mastery of colloquial idiom—syntax, vocabulary, and above all rhythm. With adroit combinations of monologue and witty repartee, Albee dramatizes human situations. He never permits his characters to lapse into discussion, and he rarely inflates them with abstraction. Almost always, he mirrors the meaning of events in the rhythm of his dialogue: Jerry's indirection, George's surgery, Julian's fragmentation, the Long-Winded Lady's long wind. Difficult as marriage is *within* his plays, they contain unusually harmonious marriages of sound to sense.

But suspicion is born of Albee's very brilliance. His plays are too well crafted, his characters too modishly ambiguous, his dialogue too carefully cadenced. This is not to say that he writes perfect plays—whatever that may be—but his surface polish seems to deny subsurface search, much less risk. Again and again, O'Neill stumbled and fell in the darkness of his dramas; even the final achievements lack grace, but their solidity endures. Miller has probed into his own limited experience and into his own limited view of the experience of his time, but his plays sometimes give evidence of reaching to his limits. Williams expresses his guiltiest urges, and though the very naiveté of his guilt restricts the resonance of his plays, he does agonize toward religious resolution. Albee's plays are not devoid of suffering, and in any case one cannot measure the quality of a play by some putative pain of the playwright. Nevertheless, Albee's craftsmanship recalls the meditation of the disembodied voice of *Box:* "arts which have gone down to craft." And it is particularly ungrateful to turn his own finely modulated words against Albee. But just because his verbal craft *is* so fine, one longs for the clumsy upward groping toward art.

6 / Less Than Novel

In ANALYZING PLAYS OF AMERICA'S BEST KNOWN PLAYWRIGHTS, I was able to focus on the dialogue because the dramas themselves are so familiar. In turning to the plays of America's novelists and poets, I will have to provide introductions to largely unfamiliar material, and I therefore begin with an apology for tedious but necessary plot summary. Necessary because it is only against the background of America's most skilled writers that we can evaluate the achievement of the dramatists.

Drama, an ancient art in Western tradition, and fiction, a relative newcomer, both move through time. But fiction, like its ancestors the epic and romance, has considerably more temporal freedom. It may allot less than a hundred pages to a century, as in Virginia Woolf's *Orlando;* or a single day may need seven hundred sixty-eight pages, as in James Joyce's *Ulysses.* Drama, in contrast, has to be played in counterpoint with real theater time; though different periods may elapse *between* scenes, movement *within* the dramatic scene usually imitates the flow of clock time. I suspect that a difference in temporal sensibility may help explain the fact that novelists rarely write dramatic dramas. Not that they haven't tried.

During the nineteenth century, before the development of mass media, American novelists might look to the stage for added income, but they committed their serious concerns to novels. Fiction-writers Bret Harte, Henry James, William Dean Howells, Mark Twain turned to drama for profit; occasionally, they tried to convert their novels into plays. Though twentieth century novelists also had affairs with the theater, these were less purely commercial, since the big money had shifted to the mass media. Novelists were rarely involved in screen-plays of their novels, but they were often involved in their dramatization. Thus, Zona Gale recast *Miss Lulu Bett* in dialogue form; Sinclair Lewis called on George Kaufman to help him perform a similar operation on *It Can't Happen Here*, and he collaborated with Lloyd Lewis on an original play, *The Jayhawker*. Sentimentalizing his stories, Ring Lardner worked on musicals: *Elmer the Great* with George M. Cohan and *June Moon* with George Kaufman. Langston Hughes collaborated with David Martin to adapt his *Simple Takes a Wife* into *Simply Heavenly*. When Sherwood Anderson's fictional powers were waning in the 1930's, he tried to straitjacket his earlier works into dramatic form—*Winesburg, Ohio* and *The Triumph of the Egg*. Conrad Aiken adapted his *Mr. Arcularis* for the stage. Richard Wright enlisted the aid of Paul Green in dramatizing *Native Son*. Norman Mailer singlehandedly tried to cramp *The Deer Park* into a review for the stage. William Faulkner wrote *Requiem for a Nun* largely in dialogue form, without intending it for the stage, but Albert Camus staged it in French. William Saroyan began his playwriting career by expanding and dramatizing a short story, "The Man with the Heart in the Highlands," followed in quick succession by five other plays about beautiful people who live quixotically on love. Edward Albee has dabbled in missionary work, converting from novels to plays James Purdy's *Malcolm* and Carson McCullars' *Ballad of the Sad Cafe*, the latter as sentimental as McCullars' dramatization of her own *Member of the Wedding*. John Steinbeck has produced what he called "play-novelettes:" *Of Mice and Men, The Moon Is Down*, and *Burning Bright*. Although he made large claims for this form, it is indistinguishable from fiction. None of these hybrids contributes anything new to the dialogue of drama, and the plays are diminished versions of the fiction.

Over and above such Procrustean plays, however, several significant novelists have made sporadic efforts at direct dramatic impact, and in the 1960's the Ford Foundation encouraged such efforts, so as to improve the quality of American drama. With the single exception of Thornton Wilder—if we can consider him a novelist—no twentieth century American novelist has sustained an allegiance to drama, and few novelists have produced plays of dramatic interest. Even inept, however, these plays instruct us in the craft demands of the theater. In spite of its long acquiescence to commercialism, the American theater does demand skill—a skill that the novelist cannot master with his left hand.[1]

THEODORE DREISER

As might be expected, Dreiser's interest in drama was not primarily commercial. With earnest industry, Dreiser produced plays as he did poems, short stories, articles, autobiography, along with the novels for which he is remembered. He wrote his plays during that intense creative period between 1911 and 1916, during which he published little, but conceived most of his major works. And yet, his plays are poor stuff. Beginning with short plays at about the same time that O'Neill was writing his first short plays, Dreiser tended toward dreariness or fantasy. He went on to write only one full-length—very full-length—drama, *The Hand of the Potter*, which H. L. Mencken compared to a jelly-fish, for lack of structure.

Structure is not evident in Dreiser's 1916 volume of ten short *Plays—Natural and Supernatural*, and yet a jelly-fish is scarcely the metaphor that springs to mind for the work of this consistently tough reporter. Somewhat surprisingly for a writer usually pigeon-holed as a naturalist, the Supernatural plays dominate the Natural by a ratio of seven to three. However, all ten plays reflect Dreiser's somewhat simplistic view of the chaos of nature and the relativity of morals. The individual plays scarcely merit summary or commentary, but the subject-matter is bold for its time. In the three Natural plays, for example, the titular *Girl in the Coffin* has died of an abortion, *The Light in the Window* illuminates greed and divorce among the rich, *Old Ragpicker* is a case history of a deranged derelict. Little more than vignettes, these plays are untheatrical and undramatic dialogues that make extravagant demands on scene designer and audience. Dreiser's language thuds through the short pieces that do not accumulate the clumsy power of the novels. Flat statement, repetition without climax, authorial intrusion dull the focus. For example, Dreiser's scenic direction calls for the father of the dead girl in the coffin to *"break out fiercely,"* and he explodes at some length: "Damn it, there's some rotten coward, some beast, some low-down scoundrel has ruined my girl. I don't know who he is. But I want to know! I want to find out! I want to find him! I want to kill him! It's the only thing I do want. Until I've done that, this strike can go to hell. You can go to hell. They all can go to hell." In spite of "damn," "hell," and a strike background, the dialogue gathers no force from the monosyllabic repetitions, which are deployed toward no climax.

And yet, the Natural plays are phonographically honest, even to dialect and swearing. But the Supernatural plays, in which Dreiser waxes poetic, are embarrassing. In *Laughing Gas* a doctor under the effects of an anesthetic declaims: "A thing of the spirit, this, plainly. I suppose I am a test, but how futile so to be. Round and round and round, an endless, pointless existence. Yet I cannot help myself. I must live. I must try. I do not want to die. *(He makes a great effort, concentrating his strength on the thought of life.)* Oh, how ruthless and indifferent it all is! Think of our being mere machines to be used by others!" Loaded with abstractions, burdened with Victorian inversions or expletives, the dialogue buries the occasionally interesting idea.

Examples of such poetastership proliferate through the Supernatural plays. In *The Spring Recital,* an Organist declares: "This passage always makes me think of moonlight on open fields and the spicy damp breath of dark, dewy wood, and of lilacs blowing over a wall, too. So suitable, but I would rather live than play." In *Phantasmagoria,* the Lord of the Universe commands: "Oh, ho, ho, ho! Oh, ho, ho, ho! Death! Death! Death! Thou dearest death! Bring thou me heaps of dead— the endless slain! Breed winged and forked things, horrors all! Bring thou me shames, despairs, disasters, with which to torture and slay! Go forth! Go forth! Sweep thou with Hate, with Rage, with Despair, with Fear! Breed me vast powers of evil, and still vaster! Rank thou me them rank on rank—file by file! *(He thinks on tortured forms.)* Make me armies of horrors,

173

of woes, of immedicable griefs!" One longs for a red pencil.

Apprentice-works of the kind that O'Neill had the wisdom to destroy, Dreiser's short plays show no evidence of theatrical intention. But Dreiser wrote his four-act *Hand of the Potter* (in 1916) to challenge the American theater of puritanical melodrama or flimsy farce, as his *Sister Carrie, Jennie Gerhardt,* and *The Genius* had challenged American publishing. The American theater was even more irrelevant than publishing to the realities of the young twentieth century. Though several Ibsen plays were produced in New York in the turn-of-the-century years, his dramas were seldom revived in the second decade of the twentieth century, and even the anodynous realism of a James A. Herne died with him in 1901.

Dreiser's title, *The Hand of the Potter,* is taken from that non-realistic poem, which was also a favorite of Eugene O'Neill— *The Rubayiat:* "What! did the Hand then of the Potter shake?" Dreiser implies an affirmative answer as he paints a Jewish immigrant family whose misery and misfortunes recall those of the Selicke family at the dawn of realistic drama in Germany. The Potter's shaking hand created Isadore Berchansky, who has molested one little girl before the play opens, and who closes Act I with the (off-stage) rape and murder of a twelve-year old child, after he leers lustfully at his sister and niece. When one recalls the shock effect of the rape scene in *Streetcar Named Desire* as late as 1947, it is hardly surprising that Dreiser could find no producer for his *Hand* until the intrepid Provincetown Players undertook it in 1921. By then, Dreiser had published the play (in 1918).

Though Mencken's metaphor of the play as a jelly-fish is incongruous for this view of tenement life in New York City, form *is* conspicuous by its absence. As in his novels, Dreiser attempts to bulldoze us into a consciousness of natural chaos and moral relativity. The rapist-murderer, one of ten children (of whom six are alive), is a loving son who informs us of his misfortunes in improbable soliloquies, which attempt to be phonographically faithful to uneducated urban speech: "I ain't no good, much. I don't amount to nothin'. Here I am of a Saturday afternoon when everybody else is off sportin' around, an' I ain't got no place to go, an' no work, an' no money. . . . I know I'll

do sompin wrong pretty soon. I feel it. I can't help it. I ought
to kill myself, but I ain't got the nerve, that's what's the matter!"
Isadore has been beaten in an insane asylum, mistreated in
prison; he cannot find work, and he cannot control his overpow-
ering lust. Hunted by the police, urged by his family to commit
suicide, he performs a last courageous deed; he urges his land-
lord's daughter to flee from him: "Get out, kid! Quick! Quick!
Get out, I tell you, before I do sompin! Get out! You don't know
me! Can't you see? Quick! Quick! Hurry!" Then, locking himself into his room, he turns on the gas before he can harm
anyone else. The last we hear him say is: "I ain't all bad, an' I
don't wanta die, but—oh—"

Painstaking (and painful in the clumsy, inaccurate use of Jewish dialect), Dreiser records with an unselective ear. Dull as the
Berchansky family would be on stage, they acquire credibility
in the reading—powerless parents, unselfish lame sister,
selfishly sensual sister (who judges her brother in nineteenth
century rhetoric: "I knew him of old."), and above all deranged
Isadore, who "wanted to live just like other people an' be
happy." Though the Act III trial scene is theatrically tedious,
there is again a fictional honesty in the refusal of each member
of the Berchansky family to testify against Isadore. But Dreiser
is not content with journalistic observation, and, paradoxically,
it is an Irish journalist who speaks Dreiser's own philosophy, in
verbose and inept brogue: "Aal men are naht balanced or normal be their own free-will an' say-so, any more than they're free
an' equal in life, an' that's naht at aal. They're naht aal endowed
with the power or the will to do an' select, aal the rules ave the
copybooks to the contrary nahtwithstandin'. Some are so con-
stituted mentally an' physically that they can't do otherwise
than as they do, an' that's what ye never can get through the
average felly's brain, nor through the average newspaper's,
ayther. Most people have a few rules, a pattern, an' everybody's
supposed to be like that. Well, they're naht. An' naathin' will
ever make 'em exactly alike, ayther—ayther aal good or aal bad,
or a little ave waan or the other, accordin' to anybody's theory.
Nature don't work that way. An' nature makes people, me
young friend, me an' you *(he taps him on the chest)* an' every waan
else, an' she don't aalways make us right ayther, by a damned

sight." Dreiser's moral bludgeoning is so thorough that we can scarcely revive for father Berchansky's moving final line: "Vy pull at de walls of my house? Dey are already down." Moving in spite of inconsistency of *v* for *w*, of the correct use of the difficult English preposition "at," of the English position of the adverb "already." Finally, *The Hand of the Potter* accumulates fictional veracity, but the dialogue is unspeakable, rendering the play unplayable.

Thomas Wolfe

Dreiser made no other forays into drama, but his theatrical venture was not an isolated phenomenon for fiction writers. Of the novelists who gained attention during the 1920's, only Thomas Wolfe trained himself as a playwright. He devoted eight years (1918–1926) very largely to the genre that he subsequently abandoned. While a student at the University of North Carolina, Wolfe studied playwriting with Professor Frederick Koch, then spent three years at Professor George Baker's famous 47 Workshop at Harvard. Though he evidently left some three thousand pages of manuscript in dramatic form, he completed only two full-length plays, *Mannerhouse* and *Welcome to Our City*.[2] He began *Mannerhouse* in 1920 and *Welcome to Our City* in 1922, revising constantly while submitting the plays to the Theatre Guild, the Provincetown Playhouse, and the Neighborhood Playhouse. Though the plays were favorably regarded, they were not produced.

Mannerhouse traces an old Southern mansion through a prologue and two acts, covering a century in time, during which language does not change. In the Prologue, Mr. Ramsay founds his house upon the subjugation of Negroes and the prayers of a local minister. In the following two acts, the house—both literal and dynastic—falls victim to the Civil War and its aftermath.

The play's protagonist, Eugene Ramsay, is patterned on Hamlet. Son of General Ramsay—to the manor and the manner born—he comments cynically upon the romantic fervor of the Southern heritage: "To be quite frank, Mother, I have a sort of proprietary interest in my own hide which you so generously are offering up to the careful inspection of an enemy who will not hesitate to shoot it full of holes."

General Ramsay has two sons—the opposing brothers of Romantic literature; one marches gladly off to war, whereas Eugene goes reluctantly. Father and reluctant son express their conflict in iambic meter and pseudo-Elizabethan language. But poor whites and Negro slaves speak Southern dialect. While aristocratic Southerners arm to repel the Northern invasion, poor white Mr. Porter rejects participation: "Hit ain't my war . . . I don't fight for yore niggers, Mr. Ramsay."

Eugene Ramsay is in love with a Major's daughter, Margaret, but his Hamlet stance leads him to ironic bawdiness: "Why, this is a good season for fruit. Are your melons ripe, lady?" He soon shifts to passionate declarations, as self-indulgently rich as the descriptions in Wolfe's later fiction. After he returns from the war, Eugene intensifies his Hamletic spleen, telling the Major: "You must not reveal this to anyone, but I have found out what men do to one another when they go to war. *Earnestly.* Major, you may believe it if you like, but they shoot one another." To the Major's daughter, Margaret, Eugene declares that he is dead and can feel nothing for her. In echoes of *Hamlet*—"You loved me once."—the lovers part, and Eugene prepares himself for the end of Mannerhouse. The dying General, knowing that the energetic, commercial-minded Mr. Porter can save his estate, wills the house to him, and gives himself a last rhetorical command: "The truce is ended! Go where they call you, Pilgrim, on the road."

The final scene occurs several years later. Porter gives orders for Mannerhouse to be demolished by two carpenters who joke like the gravediggers in *Hamlet*. A mad Eugene participates in the destruction, rejecting Margaret's tearful plea. Pulling down one of the Mannerhouse's main columns, Eugene buries himself, as he shouts for Tod, his father's ex-slave and the descendant of kings: "Here was a house. It was by you begun; by you it must be ended." Mr. Porter stabs Tod, who manages to *"break [Porter] in his mighty grip."* as he falls. Mannerhouse buries three men—the mad prince of the house, his poor white heir, and the black kingslave. The least credible aspect of this Jacobean tragedy on Southern soil is that the Theatre Guild was seriously considering production.

Welcome to Our City is similarly violent, in Expressionist style. The ten scenes are set in the modern South. Old Southern aristocrats and nouveau riche whites are firmly united to deprive the Negro of any rights, and the particular right they are after is Negro land, which they wish to exploit. Their greed is directed especially toward the old Rutledge mansion, owned by mulatto Dr. Johnson, who stubbornly refuses to sell at any price. Wolfe's plot becomes confused as the scion of the Rutledges, another cynical Hamlet, rapes Johnson's daughter; a tubercular writer comments on the action and runs off to Paris before racial conflict erupts; a governor is elected on the platform of God and good weather; a Northern Negro spurs the Southern Negroes to rally round Dr. Johnson. Rather than give up the Rutledge manor, Dr. Johnson burns it down. He is shot, and Rutledge watches him die.

Threading through the diffuse play is the question that was posed by much Expressionist drama: What is a man? But posed in the American South, the question probes to the Negro condition. Early in the play, a coarse white real estate agent declaims: "You know I've always said the Nigger is the original missing link. He's like a monkey in many respects. He apes all the tricks of the white man." The writer expounds in Shakespearian vein: "What a piece of work is a god! How valiant in despair! How mighty in defeat! In all his pained and thwarted beauty, how like a man. The ruin of the sun, the broken shard of overthrown light, on tiger feet he carries his fierce flame through the victorious dark!" The imagery suggests the Negro's African heritage, but nothing else in the play supports this passage. Rutledge's final words over the corpse of Dr. Johnson, the Negro who resisted him, link up to the early speech of the real estate man: "Poor fool! So still! So still! Why did you choose to become a man?" In spite of its sympathetic portrait of oppressed Negroes, *Welcome to Our City* (originally called *Niggertown*) is an inept play in its lack of focus and its unskilled medley of idioms.

Like Dreiser in the Supernatural plays, Wolfe tried to poeticize his dialogue, as opposed to the realistic surface that dominated theater speech by the 1920's. His vocabulary is more varied than that of Dreiser, and his model—the Elizabethans—far richer than that of Dreiser—the Victorians—but he produced unplayable hybrids, a graft of Hamlet on the history or problem play.

JOHN DOS PASSOS

WHEN WOLFE TURNED FROM DRAMA TO FICTION, HE VIRTUALLY turned from social commitment. Dos Passos, on the other hand, is a tireless social commentator, whatever the genre. The introduction to his collected plays is a diatribe against the commercial theater, which is disparagingly compared to a socially meaningful theater: "A really national or municipal theatre will be a social service, not a business. Such a theatre can play an important part in creating the new myth that has got to replace the imperialist prosperity myth if the machinery of American life is ever to be gotten under social control. If the theatre doesn't become a transformer for the deep high tension currents of history, it's deader than cockfighting. To such a theatre, that certainly does not exist now, and that perhaps will never exist, I respectfully dedicate these plays."

His first play, *The Garbage Man*, was written in 1923, before Dos Passos had found his fictional voice. Like O'Neill, Wolfe, and Elmer Rice, Dos Passos at this period saw Expressionism as a more viable form than Realism in which to register social protest. German Expressionist plays tend to be stridently social (e.g. Toller) or, stemming more directly from Strindberg, to focus on the poetic quest of the protagonist (e.g. Kaiser's *From Morn to Midnight*). Dos Passos mixes the two streams, and writes a confusing play.

Tom and Jane, childhood sweethearts, rebel against their middleclass environment, but it is never clear why they find it inadequate. The death of Jane's mother—Death appears as the Family Practitioner—frees her to go off with Tom, but when an accident stops their train—Death now appears as a Man in Black Overalls—Jane leaves Tom pretentiously: "Love is like filling your hands with water at a spring when you're thirsty. . . . You put your lips down to drink and it's gone. You can't pack it away

179

in mothballs like a dress suit to wear on great occasions." They live their separate lives for a while, Jane becoming a Broadway star, and Tom a tramp. The Death character appears to Tom as A Man in the Stovepipe Hat who inveigles him to take part in a holdup. Fleeing from the police, Tom seeks shelter near Jane's house at the very moment that she faces the Death-figure, now disguised as the titular Garbage Man: "The dump's full of the likes of ye, pretty things that git thrown out, bits o' colored papers that flutter and rustle in the cart. The city'd be cluttered and stinkin' if I didn't do my job." Tom rescues Jane from the Garbage Man, and they go off to some indeterminate region. The play ends:

> TOM: Where are we going?
> JANE: Somewhere very high. Where the wind is sheer whiteness.
> TOM: With nothing but the whirl of space in our faces.

It is not even clear whether they are alive or dead, wandering in these uplifting images that suggest nothing concrete. Dos Passos' Production Note indicates that he feels the play rests upon popular forms such as musical comedy, but, far from popular, the dialogue of the protagonists is painfully literary. A poetic quest play demands a poet—Brecht's *Baal*, Strindberg's *Road to Damascus*, even Williams' *Camino Real*—but Dos Passos is a journalist. What we best remember in Dos Passos' novels are the journalistic inserts that build a society—the Camera Eye, headlines, biographies. But the maudlin love story of *The Garbage Man* barely reflects the society in the background, while the dialogue is inflated by pseudo-poetry and Expressionist sighs.

Dos Passos clings to realism in his next two plays, the one focused on a family and the other on a place. *Airways, Inc.* (1928), as its title suggests, deals with a big business corporation, but it deals even more with the disintegration of a family under capitalism. When the play opens, the mother is dead, and the father is a has-been; Martha keeps the home for him and her three brothers—Claude a conservative clerk, Elmer an airplane pilot and mechanic, and Eddy a factory-worker. Martha is in love with and loved by Walter Goldberg, a union organizer, but they do not marry because of difference of religion and duty to her family. During the course of the play, the father commits suicide, Elmer has a serious accident, Walter is executed on a false murder charge, and Claude prospers in Airways, Inc.

The play is agit-prop melodrama: capitalist sympathizers are stupid and vicious, whereas the few radicals are humane and selfless. Unlike old-fashioned theatrical melodrama, however, violence is banished off stage, while the dialogue rambles on stage. Walter Goldberg tries to enlist our sympathy for the downtrodden: "You'd have to be a jew like me to understand. You've heard of the Pale. Every one of us has something fenced up way down in us. We've been in prison for two thousand years. I have the mind of a jailbird, that's why a prison can't hurt me. That's why we throw ourselves into every movement of freedom. That's why I feel the slavery of the workers, I feel it as a worker and I feel it as a jew. Oh, you can't imagine the overheated stuffiness of life at home on the East Side when I was a kid. We were all jailed in poverty and Judaism and in old customs and hatreds and wornout laws." Dos Passos' juxtaposition of Judaism and the Pale is unintentionally comic, but Walter's preaching is dull. Neither image nor rhythm is distinctive in this reasoned "that's why."

Though Dos Passos avoids direct didacticism in his Depression play, *Fortune Heights* (1933), the diction is again dull, because Dos Passos has no ability to make us care about his characters. Or perhaps we find their diction dull because we do not care about his characters. There is, of course, no more facile criticism than to say that a play has or has not convincing or credible characters. And yet, this is a particular problem of realistic drama with a social orientation, if it is not to be a tract in dialogue form. We may debate about whether or not *Death of a Salesman* is a tragedy, but we do so only because we care about Willy. We may or may not respond to a play with Aristotelian pity and terror, but if we do not respond with *any* emotion, mere dialogue cannot create a drama.

In *Fortune Heights*, Owen Hunter owns a filling station on a national highway, but the property is heavily mortgaged; nevertheless, he feels enough self-confidence in ownership to plead that his estranged wife Florence return to him. With alacrity, hard times turns various characters into holdup men, and by the end of the play Owen and Florence, with a baby, are expelled from their home. Owen intones the moral: "All we want to do's to dope out some way to live decent, live, you and me and the kid. Gettin' rich is a hophead's dream. Live, that's what's up to us . . . a man's that easy to kill. . . . We'll walk along the road, we'll think of somethin'. We'll make somethin' turn up. We'll meet others on the road in the same fix. We got to find the United States." This hesitant speech of Dos Passos' mid-westerners recalls that of O'Neill's New Englanders, but Dos Passos is never able to focus on the large, dramatic character; his eyes are busily darting all over the worn canvas. In the silent final scene of the play, Owen and Florence join an enormous crowd *"on the march after a job, after a home, after a new order."* But the play ends as a Real Estate agent shows "their" filling-station to a couple just like them: "One man's misfortune is the next man's opportunity. You may be the man success has marked to win." We are left, finally, with these cynical words undermining our view of the marching crowd. But neither words nor march evolves dramatically from the play's action.

At about the time he wrote *Fortune Heights,* Dos Passos was working on *USA,* where he found the journalistic voice for which he is celebrated; he conveys a cross section of a big city in the grip of depression, through Camera Eye, Newsreel, biographies, legends, headlines. And he had the wisdom not to attempt drama again.

F. Scott Fitzgerald

Unlike Dreiser, Wolfe, and Dos Passos, Fitzgerald turned to theater for the very money whose lavish spending distinguishes his novels. But money is absent from his single play, a comedy. *The Vegetable or from President to Postman* (1923) builds three laborious acts upon an anecdotal situation. Act I establishes Jerry Frost as a hen-pecked Vegetable, whose ambitions are to be president, to marry, and to be a postman in that order. Having attained the second goal, he drinks the brew of his bootlegger and has a fantasy that he is president; he behaves with farcical ineptitude that occasions his impeachment. Only in Act III does it become evident that Jerry's presidency was a drunken dream.

After frightening his wife by leaving home, Jerry returns as a postman—all ambition spent because realized.

Though the play is tedious, Fitzgerald does sustain an easy conversational idiom, but in this comedy the scenic directions are funnier than the dialogue: *"That couch would be dangerous to sit upon without a map showing the location of all craters, hillocks, and thistle-patches."* Jerry's wife, Charlotte, *"has begun this row as a sort of vaudeville to assuage her nightly boredom."* But her husband-baiting scarcely assuages *our* boredom. The other characters are too monochromous to evoke more than an initial smile; Jerry's doddering, bible-quoting father; Charlotte's romantic sister; her fiancé from Idaho, and the Conman-bootlegger, Mr. Snooks. The potpourri has occasional moments of charm, but Fitzgerald did not take his comedy seriously enough to sustain the fun. One has only to compare his Washington scene in Act II with Kaufman's libretto for *Of Thee I Sing* or Kanin's *Born Yesterday*— neither one a comic masterpiece—to see Fitzgerald's heavy hand on detail. Relying on stock types as he never does in his fiction, Fitzgerald fails to give the comic dialogue a biting edge.

L a n g s t o n   H u g h e s

LANGSTON HUGHES IS USUALLY CALLED A POET, BUT HE TRIED TO father all genres of American Negro literature. Actively engaged in theater, he wrote and collaborated in at least twenty plays over a period of forty years—more concerned about production than publication. Only recently, five of his plays have been made available by Indiana University Press; two of these are musicals and fall outside the purview of drama. But *Mulatto* (1931) and *Little Ham* (1935) show some of Hughes' fictional gifts.

In her study, *Negro Playwrights in the American Theatre 1925–1959*, Doris Abramson finds that Negro playwrights tended to use established rather than experimental dramatic forms, and she singles out Langston Hughes in this respect: "Langston Hughes's *Mulatto* (1935) [production date], surely the best play written to that date by a Negro, reads more like a nineteenth- than a twentieth-century work."[3] Though it may read that way, however, it does not sound that way. One has only to compare the dialogue of a nineteenth-century character, Aiken's Uncle Tom, with that of Hughes' Negro characters to hear a new fluidity and independence. Aiken's Tom speaks in biblical rhythms: "Mas'r, if you was sick, or in trouble, or dying, and I could save you, I'd *give* you my heart's blood; and, if taking every drop of blood in this poor old body would save your precious soul, I'd give 'em freely. Do the worst you can, my troubles will be over soon; but if you don't repent, yours won't never end." Hughes' Cora, another service Negro, uses more distinctive dialect, rhythm, and imagery: "Oh, Lawd, have mercy! *(Beginning to cry)* I don't know what to do. De way he's acting up can't go on. Way he's acting to de Colonel can't last. Somethin's gonna happen to ma chile. I had a bad dream last night, too, and I looked out and seed de moon all red with blood. I seed a path o' living blood across the house, I tell you, in my sleep. Oh, Lawd, have mercy!"

Mulatto, as the title indicates, is a melodrama about miscegenation. The plot focuses on the mulatto son of a Southern Colonel and his Negro housekeeper-mistress. Though they have been cohabiting for some thirty years and have several other children, their youngest son Robert is the first to reject his demeaning position. Act I traces Robert's fight for dignity and the Colonel's rage at his insubordination. At the end of the first act, Robert leaves the Colonel's mansion by the forbidden front door, and the Colonel starts after him with a loaded pistol. His mistress, Cora, falls on her knees and pleads: "He's our son, Tom. Remember, he's our son." And the curtain falls with perfect melodramatic timing.

But Hughes' second act rejects suspense and thrills. In the first scene, father and son are literally at each other's throats, so that mulatto Robert chokes his white father. Neither cringing with fear nor weeping with remorse, Robert takes his father's gun and walks proudly out of the house. But the inevitable lynching posse gathers, and Robert's doom is a foregone conclusion. Alone with the corpse of the man she has served for thirty years, Cora delivers a long accusation of him and the white "master race." No longer servile, she concludes: "Damn you Thomas Norwood! God damn you!" In the lucidity of her sorrow, she is no longer praying for mercy.

In the final scene, the hunted Robert comes back home to die. After another violent accusation against the dead Colonel, Cora (deranged with grief) parts from her son.

CORA: I was waiting for you, honey. Yo' hiding place is all ready, upstairs, under ma bed, under de floor. I sawed a place there fo' you. They can't find you there. Hurry—before yo' father comes.

ROBERT: *(Panting)* No time to hide, ma. They're at the door now. They'll be coming up the back way, too. *(Sounds of knocking and the breaking of glass)* They'll be coming in the windows. They'll be coming in everywhere. And only one bullet left, ma. It's for me.

CORA: Yes, it's fo' you, child. Save it. Go upstairs in mama's room. Lay on ma bed and rest.

ROBERT: *(Going slowly toward the stairs with the pistol in his hand)* Goodnight, ma. I'm awful tired of running, ma. They been chasing me for hours.

CORA: Goodnight, son.

The muted courage of the end contrasts with the overcharged dialogue—white and black—of the rest of the play. A more sensational version of *Mulatto* was the only Broadway success by a Negro playwright during the first half of the twentieth century.

Of the other two plays in the Indiana University Press edition of Hughes, *Soul Gone Home* is merely an expanded anecdote, and *Little Ham* an amusing comedy. Little Ham is a Harlem Don Juan, long on sweet talk though he is small in stature. Living by his wits, on the fringe of the law, he never loses poise or aplomb. Ham's wit energizes the play, and Hughes is not above typical Broadway humor of the 1930's. Thus, Ham describes someone as "married—but she's broad-minded." A white detective, having just arrested a Negro, declines Ham's offer of a shine: "We got one, that's enough." Written by a white playwright, *Little Ham* would be stale and insulting—with its comic love story of a little man and a huge woman (named, inevitably, Tiny), with its picture of gay and irresponsible Negroes. But no white playwright could have given us insights into a Negro beauty parlor, the Savoy Ballroom, the numbers racket, and the closed society of Harlem sports. Certainly Hughes will be remembered for his poems rather than for his fiction or plays. Nevertheless, his skill in dialogue, his dramatic range even without depth, and his sustained interest in a Negro theater have born fruit in the 1960's.

ERNEST HEMINGWAY

ACTION-PACKED THOUGH HIS FICTION IS, HEMINGWAY WROTE ONLY one drama, *The Fifth Column*, while in besieged Madrid in 1937. Produced by the Theatre Guild in 1940, it is closely tied to its setting and has been virtually (and understandably) ignored by admirers of the writer. Its dialogue resembles that of *Farewell to Arms*—clipped, brittle, and occasionally brutal; its protagonist is a rough sketch for Robert Jordan, sacrificing himself for ideals he believes mainly through his gut. Philip Rawlings, the play's protagonist, is one of the first versions of a stock type of the mass media, from Humphrey Bogart through Marlon Brando, Jimmy Dean, and Bob Dylan—a tender tough guy who is irresistibly attractive and morally admirable—by the standards of the surrounding context. He expresses himself with colloquial economy.

The combination of physical violence and sexual daring, conveyed through simple declarative sentences, bears the unmistakable Hemingway signature. Swift pacing is achieved by dividing each of the three acts into at least three scenes, but this division sacrifices intensity. A "lost generation" feeling of futility is achieved by circularity of effect; in the play's second scene, when the plot begins, we learn that Philip is with a Moorish prostitute; as the play ends, Philip calls for the Moorish prostitute to join him after her bath. In the play's long body, however, Philip falls in love with luscious blonde American Dorothy Bridges, who tempts but does not swerve him from dedication to the Loyalist cause in the Spanish Civil War. Bourgeois Dorothy is the fleshpot that Philip renounces to pursue counter-espionage against the Fascist Fifth Column, which is destroying Madrid from within the city.

Philip Rawlings poses as a drunken playboy while he carries

on his deadly work, and Dorothy is half dumb blonde and half wholesome American home girl. Alone under the bombardment, the couple converses in clipped phrases:

DOROTHY: I feel safe with you.
PHILIP: Try to check that. That's a terrible phase.
DOROTHY: But I can't help it.
PHILIP: Try very hard. That's a good girl.

At night with Dorothy, especially in bed, Philip talks of the "horrors" and of marriage. With his colleagues, however, Colonel Antonio and fellow-spy Max, Philip speaks like a tough soldier. Of German Max, he says: "A comrade with his teeth gone in front? With sort of black gums where they burn them with a red-hot iron? And with a scar here?" The two idioms, tough and tender, would seem to be mutually exclusive, but Philip occasionally manages to combine them: "I'd like to marry her because she's got the longest, smoothest, straightest legs in the world, and I don't have to listen to her when she talks if it doesn't make too good sense. But I'd like to see what the kids would look like." Hemingway's heroes are more impressive when silent and active, since their phrases can be flabby as their muscles never are.

Determined to break with Dorothy, Philip calls her a commodity, then kisses her good-bye. Dorothy asks: "You—you—you don't want the commodity?" And he replies: "I can't afford it." The cut is clean. When Philip turns to the Moorish prostitute in his room, Max leaves because he cannot stand cruelty. It is unclear whether Max is reacting against Philip's completed cruelty to Dorothy, or his future cruelty to Anita. What *is* clear is that Philip is too well known as a counter-espionage agent, and therefore is doomed.

In spite of occasional incisive lines and swift repartee, *The Fifth Column* is a simplistic melodrama. The world is divided not into good Loyalists and evil Fascists, but into good tough men who die with style and bad soft men who whimper and cower. And both kinds are vulnerable to tall blondes whose name, as Hemingway admits in his introduction to the play, "might also have been Nostalgia." Hemingway adds: "But if being written under fire makes for defects, it may also give a certain vitality."

187

Unfortunately, theatrical vitality cannot be guaranteed through even the highest moral price—the courage to create under fire.

JAMES BALDWIN

THOUGH BALDWIN TOOK PART IN NO WARS, HE DISPLAYED COMPARA-ble courage in his two plays. Escaping from his native Harlem to Paris, Baldwin escaped from escape in his first novel *Go Tell It on the Mountain*, after which he returned to America. Then, as he records in the published version of his first play, *The Amen Corner* (1955): "But when I came back to sell my first novel, I realized that I was being corraled into another trap; now I was a writer, a *Negro* writer, and I was expected to write diminishing versions of *Go Tell It on the Mountain* forever." He hoped to avoid that trap by turning to dramatic form. Ironically, however, *The Amen Corner* emerges as a "diminishing version" of *Go Tell It on the Mountain*.

One of the sub-plots of *Go Tell* becomes the main plot of *The Amen Corner*: the novel's Florence rejects Frank because of his joyous impracticality, and the play's Margaret rejects Luke because of his joyous irreligion. Florence loses Frank to another woman who informs her of his death in war, and she returns to the Church during the single day's action of *Go Tell*. But though she returns, she does not take her loss gracefully, and she is not redeemed by her preacher-brother. Her last words in the book are a threat to her brother: "When I go, brother, you better tremble, 'cause I ain't going to go in silence." In contrast to this credible bitterness, Margaret of the play comes to understand that love is more important than righteousness: "It's a awful thing to think about, the way love never dies!" Baldwin has pointed out that this was the first line of the play to be written, and he seems to have fallen prey to its facility.

Instead of the complexity and compassion of the novel, Baldwin writes a thin play. Father and son are aligned against preacher Margaret, who is supported by a sister functioning much like a confidante of French tragedy. The minor characters are cardboard comics who speak piously and act selfishly. Not only do the play's characters lack density, but their dialogue lacks the condensed richness of the speech of Baldwin's first novel. Margaret's dry sermons hardly bear comparison with the fire-and-brimstone experiences of Gabriel or John in *Go Tell* (which bear comparison with the sermon in Joyce's *Portrait of the Artist*). The sulky monosyllables of the play's adolescent David lacks the brilliance of Roy, John, or Elish—three distinctly individual boys of the novel. Luke, Margaret's jazz musician husband, comes closest to uttering Baldwin's message of love in the play: "Everytime you see a man, you think you got to go digging for some pork chops." or "You know, the music don't come out of the air, baby. It comes out of the man who's blowing it." But Luke's dying words are maudlin: "When your arms was around me I was always safe and happy." How much truer are the words that form Florence's last memory of Frank in the novel: "You just kindly turn out that light and I'll make you to know that black's a mighty pretty color."

"Amen," as Margaret explains in the play, "means Thy will be done. Amen means So be it." And the play's Amen Corner proves to be a vicious corner, where love is subordinated to an orthodoxy. The metaphor may also be turned against Baldwin in his first play, where rich rhetoric is subordinated to the orthodoxy of the commercial theater—three acts with proper climax, virtue (in the guise of love) triumphant.

Baldwin not only returned to writing fiction, but he also wrote moral and moving essays. Though the more militant Blacks have been hard on him, Baldwin forced his generation— black but especially white—to face the question of what it is to be a man, and of what we have a right to demand of other men. In his justly celebrated essay, "Everybody's Protest Novel," (1949) he pointed out that Richard Wright's Bigger Thomas (of *Native Son*) and Uncle Tom of the famous Cabin were opposite sides of the same cold coin, reducing man's warm complexity to a current Cause.

By 1964, when Baldwin wrote *Blues for Mr. Charlie* in response to Elia Kazan's suggestion that he work in the theater, a younger generation had taken up the black cause. White and black youths of all faiths and none "freedom rode" in the South. The assassination of Emmett Till (which was the kernel of Baldwin's play) was followed by that of Medgar Evers, then of three Northern-

189

ers. In the midst of such carnage, Baldwin produced his play, brooding over whether he would be able "to draw a valid portrait of the murderer."

But such portraits are better committed to a more documentary form of drama, such as Duberman's *In White America* or Weiss' *Song of the Lusitanian Bogey.* Younger black playwrights, in contrast, are writing "plays of black consciousness set in the context of black theatres that operate within black communities."[4] In offering *Blues for Mr. Charlie* to New York's Actor's Studio, Baldwin in effect accepted their naturalistic staging, psychological violence, and middle-class professionalism. In that context, his play of our uncivil war is inadequate.

It is inadequate, however, not in black-versus-white terms but in the flatness of *all* characters, black and white, who fall too easily into the rhetoric expected of them. Lyle Britten, the murderer, is the character that troubled Baldwin most; as a result, we come to understand him too rationally—the likable man's man with his manly language and yearning for sons; the heritage of economic frustration and the present dependence on Negro trade; the vague fidelity to the dead code of Southern chivalry, which forces him to shoot two Negros, with seeming reluctance. It is all too neatly explained, allowing no room for the monstrous sadism with which such murders have actually been perpetrated. "I had to kill him," Lyle Britten pleads. "I'm a white man! Can't nobody talk that way to *me!*" Are we to assume that there would have been no murder if Richard had addressed Britten subserviently?

Only slightly less credible is Baldwin's white liberal, Parnell James. He is the inevitable Southern aristocrat, who talks reform of race relations, but finally supports the white Southern code. Because Parnell will not contradict a lady—Lyle Britten's wife—the murderer is furnished with the stock alibi, attempted rape. But then Parnell's liberalism might be expected to be only skin-deep, since its entire basis seems to be a youthful infatuation with a teen-age black beauty: "I got sick wanting to take her in my arms and love her and protect her from all those other people who wanted to destroy her." Hardly the spirit of social protest.

And yet, Baldwin must have been thinking of rebellion when

he chose the name Parnell as opposed to his friend Britten. Or is it merely that a woman is the undoing of both Parnells, the Southern liberal and the Irish Nationalist? After the witness-stand lie of Baldwin's Parnell, he obtains Britten's private confession of the murder and then asks to join the Negro march of protest against the court verdict of *innocent:* "Can I join you on the march, Juanita? Can I walk with you?" Like a schoolboy offering to carry his girl's books, in nineteenth century American fiction. And as in nineteenth century fiction, Juanita replies: "Well, we can walk in the same direction, Parnell. Come don't look like that. Let's go on." Is she leading him back into liberalism? Forward into rebellion? Or where?

If the white portraits are incredible, the black portraits are insulting. Most of them speak (and presumably think) of little but sex or love, often confused. Richard Henry, the victim, is the most confused and confusing of all the characters. Is he the smart-assed ex-Southerner, whose murder is nevertheless a crime? Is he the courageous new Black who stands for the coming revolution? Understandably hating whites, he brags to his black friends about his white women. Eldridge Cleaver has made us understand rape as a weapon, but Baldwin has written five essays to show that the monomania of Bigger Thomas makes poor fiction. Yet Baldwin's Richard Henry is an avatar of Bigger.

Richard's white-women and gun-toting boasts are ambiguous but believable; what is sentimentally unbelievable is Juanita's pure love: "You said you were lonely. And I'm lonely too." After his murder, she explains: "[Richard] needed me and he made a difference for me in this terrible world—do you see what I mean?" It is too easy to be *told* what she means, but nothing in the play *dramatizes* Richard's attraction for women, or his totality as a man. This could be turned to dramatic point, were Baldwin to emphasize that Richard's death is as monstrous as if he *had* been a significant rebel. The problem is that Baldwin himself isn't sure. Richard Henry doesn't have the physique of the legendary John Henry, but he claims the sexual prowess of myth, while languishing in a sentimental pure love. Like some of today's rebellious Blacks, Richard sasses the white community in their own uninventive sexual terms. And he goes to his death rather than change his tune. Is this a moral and courageous triumph? The words that trigger Britten's shot are: "And *I* know your women, don't you think I don't—better than you!" Feeding the portrait of a cliché Negro, which Baldwin himself has decried, Richard Henry dies. Richard's final taunt punctuates Baldwin's own confusion about his protagonist: "Okay. Okay. Okay. Keep your old lady home, you hear? Don't let her near no nigger. She might get to like it. You might get to like it, too. Wow!" Not only does this implicitly deny the truth we know—that Richard has never approached Britten's wife—but why might Britten like "it?"

The play contains other Negro stereotypes—the benevolent Granny, the pious preacher, and love-inspiring Juanita, all of whom tell lies on the witness-stand. Only the Uncle Tom character tells the accusing truth: "He killed him. I know it, just like I know I'm sitting in this chair. Just like he shot Old Bill and wasn't nothing, never, never, never done about it!" The repetitions have the ring of conviction. But what do they mean in the context of the play? That even an Uncle Tom, or especially an Uncle Tom, is more trustworthy than a white liberal on the witness-stand?

Baldwin has described *Blues for Mr. Charlie* (which may be paraphrased as "dirge for the white man") as "one man's attempt to bear witness to the reality and the power of the light." But light never shines through stereotyped roles and hackneyed rhetoric. Baldwin's witness is too important to trickle into such clichés. His novels capture what he claims he tried to put into the play—"something ironic and violent and perpetually understated in Negro speech." But the dialogue of his plays too often sinks to the merely saccharine, the temper tantrum, and the overstated in both Negro and white speech.

SAUL BELLOW

ON THE SURFACE, SAUL BELLOW OFFERS A COMPLETE CONTRAST TO James Baldwin—the comic vision as opposed to the tragic, Jewish idiom as opposed to Negro—but they both reflect the urban melting-pot of modern America, where melting is being obstructed by stubborn precipitates. And they took similar paths to drama. Each began by publishing a relatively simple play related to the fiction, and each produced a more complicated work at the suggestion of a theater professional.

More modest than *The Amen Corner*, Saul Bellow's *Wrecker* (1954) is an anecdote expanded to one-act play. A railroad flat on the East Side of New York City—"the woman's temple, the man's asylum"—has been condemned to destruction, and a husband ebulliently proceeds to wreck his home. When the play opens, however, the wrecking activity is merely a series of off-stage crashes; on stage the man's wife and mother discuss his neurosis, wife more sympathetic than mother, who nags like the stereotypical Jewish mother: "I see he's passing up an opportunity to make your life easier because he wants to play like a boy. Treasures! People ought to be forced to be their age. What if he put on a sailor suit and told you he was going to sail his little boat in Central Park pond? What a sex the males are!"

A City Employee enters the apartment and reacts indignantly to the freelance wrecking: "Lady, for one thing wrecking is a licensed occupation. You can't just go wreck. You have to know how." He leaves in anger, convinced of the husband's madness, and the mother follows him to try to pacify authority. Alone, husband and wife disagree about the necessity to wreck their home, for the wife recalls their past with nostalgia, the husband with scorn. He insists that wrecking is heroic activity: "Does it say anywhere that Achilles ever built anything? Or Ulysses? They tore down Troy and killed everyone in it. Who were the heroes of the war? The fellows who dropped bombs on cities. A hero destroys the links with the past when they bother him. He frees himself from what other men have done before him." In his enthusiasm, the husband smites the ceiling, and the chandelier drops on his head. Out of her concern for the stunned husband, the wife takes up the wrecking mission, but the blow has made the husband cautious. Attacking the bedroom, the wife declares exultantly that "maybe the best way to preserve the marriage is to destroy the home." And the husband answers mildly: "It may well be."

Constricted within a realistic framework, *The Wrecker* lacks the farcical savagery of a play like Ionesco's *New Tenant*, and even in its brevity it lacks focus, since there is no dramatic reason for the presence of the husband's mother or the City Employee. Nor is there sufficient exploration of the relationship to the past that necessitates the wrecking. Though the husband-and-wife switch of attitudes is farcically funny, it lacks meaning. Nevertheless, the very theme of research into the past, rendered with a Jewish intonation, will form the basis for Bellow's full-length play, written between 1959 and 1964, at the suggestion of playwright Lillian Hellman.[5]

In a note to the published version of *The Last Analysis* (1965), Bellow explains that the play is "not simply a spoof of Freudian psychology" but "the mind's comical struggle for survival in an environment of Ideas." The specific stage mind belongs to Philip Bummidge né Bomovitch and called Bummy, who is a successful comedian turned "*Existenz*-Action-Self-analyst." The titular last analysis is to be performed on himself by himself, before a closed-circuit television audience, in the hope of converting people to his theories through their laughter at his analysis. More than personal survival is at stake, since Bummy is a missionary at heart: "I want to persuade them, move them, stun them . . ."

Act I consists of preparations for the broadcast, and Act II contains the broadcast and aftermath. Though Bummy has been conducting an unproustian *Recherche du temps perdu*, he is more hospitable to earlier avatars of him*self* than to *other* people of his past—wife, son, sister, mistress, cousin, and midwife. Vultures all, they contrast with his present associates who believe in him —Imogen the ex-Playboy bunny and Bertram an ex-rat exterminator. As in Bellow's novels, all the play's characters are horrendously verbal, and, as in the novels, the protagonist is instantly identified by a sensitivity of soul expressed in rich idiom.

Bummy, who plays Lazarus and Christ among his many roles, progresses from death to birth during the course of the play. When we first see him, he is draped in a sheet which may be a winding-sheet, like that of Beckett's Hamm in *Endgame*. In spite of obstacles, the television broadcast proceeds on schedule. As the broadcast ends, Bummy is reborn to the accompaniment of Handel's "Hallelujah Chorus," which modulates into "America the Beautiful," for Bummy's rebirth is symbolic of a new

194

humanity and a new America. The trauma of rebirth silences him; after the vigorous dialogue of the earlier scenes, that silence underlines the climax.

An auto-didact, Bummy builds his idiom on fragments of Western culture—Freud, Jung, Aristotle, Greek and biblical myth, biology and psychology. His cousin Winkleman complains: "The suckers had their mouths open for yucks—he fed them Aristotle, Kierkegaard, Freud." And Bummy tells his son how his clowning led him to *Angst:* "Have you ever watched audiences laughing? You should see how monstrous it looks; you should listen from my side of the footlights. Oh, the despair, my son! The stale hearts! The snarling and gasping! . . . My work? It's being stolen from me. . . . Destruction appears like horse-play. Chaos is turned into farce, because evil is clever. It knows you can get away with murder if you laugh." By the end of Act I, our laughter is climaxed by Bummy's crucifixion; stapled to the wall as Christ, Bummy undercuts the famous last prayer, intoning: "Forgive them, Father, for, for . . . What comes next?"

In his television broadcast, Bummy casts family and "friends" in their murderous comic roles—a hoodlum partner, a flapper sister who doubles as Bummy's mother, an Oedipal son who functions as his father, a balls-busting wife, a faithless mistress dressed as a chorus girl, a cousin as little Lord Fauntleroy, the rat-catcher who is a generalized mother figure, and a comically sadistic midwife in a wheelchair. The roles are related to the reality of Bummy's past. Bummy analyzes his own illness: "The Pagliacci gangrene! Caused as all gangrene is by a failure of circulation. Cut off by self-pity." Unlike Bellow's Herzog, who also wallows in self-pity, and who channels his tears into letters to the great individuals of our culture, Bummy broadcasts his psychic biography and achieves a catharsis out of which a new man is born—comically, on the stage, against the tragic background of history.[6]

As Bummy directs and acts in his "scientific" program, the assembled actors criticize the performance (à la Pirandello), but Bummy's retainers praise him.

GALLUPPO: You think you sell this? I'd walk out. Worst show I ever saw.

MAX: It's like a lecture at the New School, but crazier.
IMOGEN: Every word of it is clear to me.
BERTRAM: Plain as day.
WINKLEMAN: Take it from me, the industry is hard up for novelty.
  There is something here for the great public.

Cousin-lawyer-crook-Lord Fauntleroy-Winkleman is right. After the show, the successful producer Fiddleman arrives with checks and contracts. But Bummy remains pure as a newborn babe. Dictating new and profound notes to Imogen, he scarcely recognizes the clamoring voices out of his past. When he does, he catches these human rodents in a giant net and whisks them off stage. With his faithful Imogen and Bertram of Shakespearean resonance (the one reborn and the other accepting his reborn wife), Bummy will found the Bummidge Institute of Nonsense, where the Kalbfuss Palace of Meats stands. Death will always be converted to a symbolic birth.

T. S. Eliot wrote of Henry James that his mind was so fine, no idea could violate it. Bummy's mind, in contrast, is so coarse that it laps up every attractive or humane idea. And it does so with a voluble eloquence that is rare on the American stage. There are notes of Bert Lahr, Zero Mostel, Theodore Reik, and Rollo May in Bummy, and yet he is very much his own man. All Bellow's protagonists have a family resemblance, but there are no identical twins in the family.

For all Bummy's panache, however, the optimistic end lacks conviction. Bummy is not at his best on closed-circuit television, and we tend to agree with the vulturous detractors rather than with the invisible audience who have been moved as by Billy Graham. Bummy's wife Bella explains: "How could we doubt him? But it's like being in the orchestra. You play oompa-oompa-oompa, but out front it's Beethoven." We, however, remain in the orchestra, and we hear no Beethoven. We laugh at the zany happy ending of farce, but we balk at farce with an abrupt redemptive message. The protagonists of Bellow's novels—Augie March, Henderson, Herzog, Sammler—learn how to blend their memories and malaise into the possibility of a new human and humane momentum. Though they find the grace to go on, they do so without Bummy's explicit panacea. They end as

Bummy began—with the affliction of Humanitas, and no Pollyanna's nurse them for our health. In Bummy, Bellow creates a big man for the American stage, but he is still a pygmy compared to the heroes of the novels, who tower through depth.

MARK HARRIS

UNLIKE SAUL BELLOW, WHO TRIED AN APPRENTICE HAND AT A PLAY even before being officially encouraged, Mark Harris and John Hawkes became playwrights through a Ford Foundation grant, enabling each of them to work with the Actor's Workshop of San Francisco. Harris, like Bellow, comes from an urban Jewish background, and his one play, like Bellow's *Last Analysis*, reflects this. Like Bellow, too, Harris writes in a comic vein; even the title confirms this: *"Friedman & Son* [1962], a political topical patriotical musical historical comedy in three acts, adapted by Mark Harris from the private papers of his late lamented father, and commemorating the election of Vice-President Lyndon B. Johnson, with an extended author's preface describing autobiographical revelations."

Like Harris himself (as he tells us in the "extended author's preface"), the play's protagonist is a happily married writer who has become a stranger to his father. The preface also suggests that Harris' play is half apology for his estrangement from his now dead father and half wish-fulfillment for the reunion they never had. That reunion is engineered, in the play, by an unscrupulous finagler, Schimmel, whose profession is organizing testimonial dinners. Fantasy scenes of these dinners provide a variant upon the play's realistic surface. Schimmel, by far the most colorful character of the play, is not even mentioned in the extended preface.

Act I contains Schimmel's efforts to persuade the writer-protagonist to finance a testimonial dinner for the father he has not seen in five years. Act II contains Schimmel's efforts to persuade the father to finance a testimonial dinner for his famous son, a writer. Act III contains the confrontation of father and son, the exposure of Schimmel's shameless lies, and the emergence of the truth of Schimmel's lies, a father-son esteem.

But father and son are more vivid in Harris' preface than on stage. Like Gregory Solomon in Miller's *Price*, Schimmel attracts through wisdom disguised as comedy.

Conjuring up elaborate testimonial dinners, Schimmel is fertile in invention, repeating like incantations: "Imagine, if you will . . ." and "Devise in your mind . . ." When the prospective client demurs, Schimmel urges: "In Russian—you speak no Russian—in Russian is an old expression . . ."—which he follows by an American platitude. Occasionally his wisdom is explicit: "Never mind *of course*. Don't tell me *of course*. In the house of the son of an immigrant, such as your father, such as me, English is by no means spoken *of course*. Words are hard come by. In the house of the son of an immigrant the dictionary is the whole connection to life."

Like Miller's Solomon in a play focused on a family, Schimmel usurps the stage in a play focused on a father-son relationship. Too articulate and spirited for his dramatic importance, he grows tedious when we are presented with the literal scenes of his fantasy. Schimmel's gift is verbal, not visual. His eloquence drowns out both father and son, each of whom appears in two acts whereas Schimmel dominates all three. And three acts are many for colorful idiom only sporadically linked to plot and theme. Especially when plot and theme are probed more deeply in preface than in play, however comic.

JOHN HAWKES

LIKE HARRIS, JOHN HAWKES TURNED TO DRAMA AS A RESULT OF A Ford Foundation grant for work with a resident theater; he wrote *The Innocent Party* and *The Wax Museum* during 1964–1965, while in residence with the Actor's Workshop, and the other two plays were completed in 1965. All four plays stress Hawkes' obsessive theme—the decline of white Protestant America—a decline riddled with lust and violence. One play, *The Wax Museum*, is set in Canada, and the other three in Southern United States, the decay of whose culture has pervaded twentieth century American fiction. The four short dramas are similarly constructed: a shocking confrontation mounts in intensity to an ambiguous finale. Except for *The Innocent Party*, the confrontation is limited to two characters, but at least one of these two plays several roles, for the plays, like Hawkes' fiction, imply that reality consists of improvised motives accumulating into a role.

The Innocent Party is a punning title; literally, it refers to a tequila party given by Phoebe for her brother, his wife, and their daughter, when she visits them after seven years. Metaphorically and ironically, the title designates the daughter Jane, who is described in the List of Characters as "part tomboy and part Aphrodite-as-young-girl, and as such approaches a mythic force." Coveted by the masculine millionairess aunt, surrendered by her selfish impoverished parents, Jane seems to be the innocent victim of both, until she establishes her cold control of all relationships. The predatory aunt bows to the predatory niece.

The play's dialogue—lyrical but taut—reveals the failure of the three adults and of the fantasy-life of the adolescent, in a derelict motel with a dry swimming-pool. The dialogue of Jane's parents exposes their emotional bankruptcy; Edward keeps reassuring his wife that she is a lovely woman of whom he is proud, but she wavers between complaint, arrogance, and confession of "the barren condition of my body." Millionairess Phoebe's abandon is heard in easy slang; she addresses everyone as "baby," and she undertakes Jane's initiation, first by contrasting the motel's dry pool with her marble swimming-pool in which handsome young men play water polo, and finally by forcing Jane to dance—"Baby, you know the score. So let's get down to business." After condemning the "pee-pot morality" of Jane's parents, Phoebe falls unconscious. Alone on stage, Jane dances beautifully, and we hear the sounds of water in the swimming-pool. When dawn's light breaks, Jane repeats a long lyric monologue that she has spoken early in the play—imagining water in the swimming pool. But whereas the climax of the first recitation was the reflection of her own face in the fantasy water, Jane terminates the second recitation and the play as she smiles directly to the audience: "I look into the swimming pool and try to see our faces in the water." The play has dramatized a *rite de passage* from solitude to togetherness, though it is left ambiguous as to *who* is together in an adult world where there are no innocent parties. But Jane has also progressed from the innocence of pure experience to the reflection that is art.

The Wax Museum is more pointedly erotic, but it too dramatizes a development from solitude to togetherness. In a wax museum Bingo, a young attendant, fondles George, a wax figure of a Royal Canadian Mountie. Sally Ann, a virgin, interrupts them while her fiancé Frank visits the Chamber of Horrors in another room. The entire play consists of the erotic education of Sally Ann by Bingo, using the wax figures as props: "Blood and ecstasy, that's the ticket." Bingo keeps comparing and contrasting the wax George with the absent but living Frank, and by the end of the play, the two young women change clothes (both revealing red brassieres). It is Bingo who answers Frank's off-stage call, while Sally Ann begins to fondle the wax George, repeating the very terms of endearment with which Bingo opened the play. An expanded anecdote, *The Wax Museum* uses insidiously grotesque idiom to show how close we are to the wax dummies we create.

The Undertaker and *The Questions* were written in that order, and the one is a preparation for the other. The first, according to Hawkes, is a "farcical melodrama" based on the father's suicide in his novel, *Second Skin*. In spite of the provocative (and debatable) genre designation, the play does not modify the meaning of the novel's suicide scene; insistence upon farcical effects of dialogue robs the death of its fictional intensity and mystery.

The Questions, on the other hand, achieves intensity because death remains mystery. Again there is a dialogue between two people. Man and Girl reconstruct a family—a Southern couple and their adolescent daughter, involved with an Englishman who may have been the mother's lover. On stage, the one who is questioned is clearly the daughter, and the questioner is ambiguously the father. The fate of the mother and her (possible) lover is left in doubt, and yet death is the innuendo behind the probing questions. Death is also an ostensible subject, as both Man and Girl talk about "the kill," which is the end of a foxhunt. Though questioner and questioned give different descriptions of that hunt, they seem to agree on the kill, as the Girl asks the Man: "Listen—my story was just as good as yours. I mean, they were the same, weren't they?" As in Hawkes' novels, one has the feeling that the truth of fiction emerges through desperate lies.

During the course of the two versions of the story, the fox is compared to the Englishman who, in turn, is compared to an iron Negro figure before the mansion. Through the questions, we witness the breakdown of the father's Puritan, humanitarian traditions before the triple threat of the foreign, the native foreign, and the animal. Both the sensual Mother and the worldly wise daughter—"The last mockery of an ingenue"—are compared to nuns, and the Girl's final words are: "But listen—according to Papa the silly virgins always beat the moral barbarians at their own game, so I guess we won . . ." "We" has emerged as the scheming, seeming flower of Southern womanhood, but the identity of the moral barbarians is obscure. The playlong anguish of the questioning Man suggests him as the loser, and he is possibly a moral barbarian, since his fantasies contain animality and morality. However, the theatrical urgency of Hawkes' play rests upon the relentless crescendo of suggestive questions, which builds the fatal foursome for us, even though we do not know their fate or their final significance. Dialogue alone dramatizes emotion; in the repeated phrase of the Man: "death, grief, anguish, a life of emotional oblivion."

GERTRUDE STEIN

UP TO THIS POINT IN THE CHAPTER, NOVELIST-PLAYWRIGHTS HAVE been examined chronologically. In conclusion, however, chronology will be violated in order to contrast three writers born in the nineteenth century. Though all three wrote novels, they were less committed to fiction than most of the writers considered in this rubric. Gertrude Stein's idiosyncratic plays are only now beginning to find an audience; Djuna Barnes wrote brief melodramas early in her career and a verse tragedy some four decades later; Thornton Wilder has attained popular success as novelist and playwright.

Of all the playwrights in this book, Gertrude Stein is most

mysterious to me. Her plays have received no attention from drama critics and small attention from Stein critics, but she herself was conscious of writing a radically original kind of drama. One of her *Lectures in America* is entitled "Plays," by which she meant mainly *her* plays. In that lecture she criticizes traditional theater (which she visited often as a child but rarely as an adult); its great fault, she felt, is a delay between the emotions presented on stage and the emotions aroused in the audience: "Your sensation as one in the audience in relation to the play played before your sensation I say your emotion concerning that play is always either behind or ahead of the play at which you are looking and to which you are listening."[7] Stein wrote that one experienced *completion* in exciting scenes of real life; in the theater, on the other hand, the experience was that of *relief.* I do not fully understand what she meant by these two words, but, having read her plays (and seen one), I would guess that the artificial manipulation of dramaturgy produces relief at the play's resolution and conclusion, whereas absorption in life's unpredictable immediacy effects a feeling of completion. In her own plays, Stein sought to evoke the feeling of completion by robbing the reader-spectator of his preconceptions of dramatic form.

Before Stein turned to plays, however, she had achieved in fiction the "prolonged present" of *Three Lives* and the "continuous present" of *The Making of Americans.* Her earliest plays seem to be a development of her prose portraits, which set forth a person in his essential presentness. She wrote in her lecture on plays: "In my portraits I had tried to tell what each one is without telling stories and now in my early plays I tried to tell what happened without telling stories so that the essence of what happened would be like the essence of the portraits, what made what happened what it was."[8]

In Stein's first play, *What Happened* (1913), *nothing* happens; there is no story, and there are no individual characters to whom anything could happen. Parodically, *What Happened* is divided into the five acts of classical drama, but each act consists of discreet sentences or series of phrases. Numbers in parentheses seem related to the number of sentences to be spoken and may also indicate the number of speakers for each group of sentences.

Usually, a rhythmic change accompanies the announcement of
the number. Often nonsensical, always disjunctive, the sentences contain sound play and repetition. Though the sentences
are not always complete, an overall rhythm emerges from simple declaration—subject-predicate, subject-predicate, with *is*
often repeated.

What Happened is the first of seventeen plays contained in the
volume *Geography and Plays* (1922). Twelve plays are specifically
designated as plays; in addition, we find a dialogue, a monologue, two curtainraisers, and a frolicsome playlet subtitled a
tragedy. In length, the plays vary from the one-page *Curtain-
Raiser* to the twenty-seven page *Mexico*. Donald Sutherland,
Stein's most illuminating critic, claims that this first group of
plays is "based largely on Spanish movement, which is very
intense, inclined to the vertical and a very narrow field. It is
essentially vibration and a constant reversion to the beginning,
it has very little development or wandering or discursiveness."[9]
The plays seem to me to wander, since they have no center, but
if narrowness is vertical and Spanish, one may classify the plays
as Spanish, especially since the dialogue makes occasional references to Spain—paticularly Mallorca. Purist admirers like Sutherland would undoubtedly frown at imposing interpretation on
the deliberate non-sense of the dialogue, but I nevertheless find
social satire in such plays as *Do Let Us Go Away, For the Country
Entirely*, and *Please Do Not Suffer*. In *Mexico*, the frivolous small
talk culminates in the reduction to small talk of the experience
of a bombardment:

William King. Are you pleased with everything.
Certainly I am the news is good.
Marcelle Helen. How do you do I have been in a bombardment.
So you have.
And were you evacuated.
We did not leave our village.
We asked the consul to tell us what he thought.
He said that there was nothing to fear.
Nothing at all.
So he said.
Very well today.
Oh yes the wind.

Usually, however, there is no climax but a flat present time throughout the play. Combined with Stein's emphasis on present time is her concern with relationships in space—perhaps inspired by her affinity for the painting of Cezanne and Picasso. The very title *Geography and Plays* suggests that geography and theater are linked through spatiality. Like geography, like landscape, Stein's plays are compositions in space and for space.

In her lecture on plays, Stein states that her second group of plays, published in *Operas and Plays* (1932), was evoked by the landscapes of the French countryside at Bilignin: "I felt that if a play was exactly like a landscape then there would be no difficulty about the emotion of the person looking on at the play being behind or ahead of the play because the landscape does not have to make acquaintance."[10] As a landscape relies on the relation between things in nature, her plays should contain similar relations. Donald Sutherland finds that these French-inspired plays are "concerned with a more complex, discursive, wandering, conversational movement."[11] The plays of *Operas and Plays* tend to be longer than those of the first volume, and that alone makes for a more discursive, wandering movement, and for complication if not necessarily complexity.

As a group, the second volume contains more variety. Four operas and two movies are clearly labelled as such, but the remaining sixteen pieces are not all designated as plays, and *Old and Old* does not seem to me to be one. *Objects Lie on a Table* (1922) resembles a still life more than a landscape, and *The Five Georges* (1931) is closest to normal dramatic dialogue because of its witty repartee. Even the title *They Must. Be Wedded. To Their Wife.* (1931) shows Stein's desire to fragment sentences, which characterizes the dialogue of that play and parts of others. *Say It With Flowers* (1931) incorporates phrases, long sentences, and scenic directions into the dialogue, combining them with familiar sound play and repetition.

Most of Gertrude Stein's remaining plays are found in the posthumously published *Last Operas and Plays*.[12] The operas of this volume are better known than the sixteen plays, but since the former were intended as librettos, to be sung to music, they do not fall into the purview of drama. The plays themselves span nearly three decades, from the 1917 *Exercise in Analysis* to the 1945

Yes Is for a Very Young Man; several of them would provide full evenings in the theater.

The early plays in this volume are relatively short and devoid of individual characters; the dialogue consists of short sentences of social chitchat. *A Circular Play* (1920), as Lawrence Kornfeld's 1967 production proved, is a felicitous whimsy based on sound association and incremental repetition. *Paisieu* (1928), a longer play, is subtitled "A Work of Pure Imagination in which No Reminiscences Intrude." Since reminiscences rarely intrude in Stein's drama, this is a facetious title for cheerful playing with the name Geronimo. In the many short scenes, there is no designation of who speaks the lines, and the lines themselves seem to be more determinedly devoid of meaning than in the earlier plays. Syntactically, the sentences are fragmented or problematical, such as: "Does which and dulled made which she knows that is is the same and she was that which was a pleasure." Short sentence-paragraphs suggest a rather rapid rhythm of give-and-take for most of the play's dialogue, but the finale is a long paragraph which demands to be spoken in a rush that robs the words of denotative sense.

Three so-called Historic Dramas, written in 1930, designate individual characters, and that may be the root of the historicity. In these plays the more conversational mode returns, with hints of social satire in the disconnectedness of the trivia.

The plays of 1932 contain short phrases or sentences, as confirmed by one of the titles, *Short Sentences*. *A Play of Pounds*, whose title seems unrelated to its contents, is particularly abstract, containing no characters, no proper names, few objects, and few refrains. In *A Manoir* phrasal repetition is parallelled by repetition of act-numbers or scene-numbers, but the scenes themselves are not repeated.

Like *Paisieu*, *Byron a Play* (1933) is a long play on a name. It is at the same time, as Carl Van Vechten points out in his introduction, "more of a discussion of playwriting rather than an actual play."[13] But Stein's plays permit no clear boundary between the two, and the play offers such Steinian dramatic criticism as "a theater is a place," "This which I think is a play is a play," "I feel I know now what a play is there are many kinds of them." The name-play in *Byron* seems to me both lighter and more extended than in *Paisieu*. Stein exploits sound play on the name, Byron.

The two plays of 1936, *Listen To Me* and *A Play Called Not and Now*, are focused thematically by more than a name; central to the former is counting and to the latter a party. Both plays incorporate description and narration into the dialogue, and *A Play Called Not and Now* introduces direct dialogue with he said's and she said's. *Listen To Me* combines description and dialogue in an almost Pirandellian play about the play. Sweet William and his genius and his Lillian are at once characters and subjects of the play. Words are both entities and numbers of syllables. Nameless characters comment on themselves:

The second character. There is a second character.
The third character. There is a third character.
The fourth character. There is a fourth character.
The fifth character. There is no fifth character.

Counting syllables and characters is a recurrent motif in this witty play that embraces numbers, words, and people—a universe.

In sharp contrast to these striking plays of 1936, Stein's last play is almost conventional. The original title, *In Savoy*, is less arresting than the subsequent *Yes Is for a Very Young Man* (1945), subtitled "A Play of the Resistance in France." Alice B. Toklas affirms that Stein "considered it a play like any other—except perhaps for its quality—and that the characters were portraits and of ordinary people."[14] And that is perhaps what is wrong with it. The people are too ordinary, and the plot, if not quite "like any other," loses particularity in its concern for authenticity.

In this play of the French Resistance, husband and wife are divided in their reactions to the German occupation; American lady helps the Resistance, but husband's young brother is too young to understand, and at first he says Yes to the German occupation of France. By the end of the play, he is no longer a very young man, and he has learned to say No, leaving for Germany to organize the resistance of prisoners. The play's narrative line is thin, the characters are barely sketched, and the dialogue echoes ordinary speech. Sprinkled through the play, however, are lines of pure Stein: "Yes, yes is for a very young man and you Ferdinand, you are a very young boy, yes you are, yes is for a very young one, a very young man, but I am not so young, no I am not, so I say no. I always say no. You know, Ferdinand, yes you know that I always say no." Within the realistic mode, it is difficult to imagine a tone for such characteristic Steinian repetition, contradiction, and sound play.

Gertrude Stein's drama is a reaction against the whole dramatic tradition. In order to plunge the reader-spectator into the immediate *thereness* of her continuous present, Stein stripped her plays of plot, character, event, theme, subject, and meaningful dialogue. Instead, she gives us disjunctive and rhythmic dialogue, often spoken by undesignated voices. Disoriented, we must respond to the words' immediacy. Sometimes the linguistic exploration in the dialogue takes a spatial pattern on the page and suggests a different spatial form in the theater. Though Stein was probably not familiar with the work of Appia, Artaud, Craig, or Meyerhold, she too was engaged in spatializing the theater. But her space was filled with words, estranged from their denotative meaning.

Djuna Barnes

With the exception of Gertrude Stein's last play, her considerable dramatic output is governed by her view of drama as immediacy of experience, and she expressed that view over a period of three decades. In contrast, Djuna Barnes, who belonged to what Gertrude Stein called "the lost generation," wrote very different plays at the beginning and end of her writing career. An art student who moved toward poetry, fiction, and drama during World War I, she worked with the Provincetown players and published three one-act plays in *A Book* (1923). As melodramatic as O'Neill's early shockers for the same acting group, Barnes' plays did not eventually lead her toward her own experience, as did those of O'Neill.

Two of the three plays use that stock character of late nineteenth-century melodrama, A Woman with a Past. In *Three from the Earth* (1919) such a woman is confronted by three brothers

207

who ask for the return of their father's letters to her; after some stilted cross talk (replete with "Hush!" "Ah ha!"), she gives the letters to the youngest brother. The curtain falls on the shocking revelation that he is her son.

In *To the Dogs*, Gheid Storm vaults through Helena Hucksteppe's window, pleading for her love. But she responds with such discouragement as "Must I, who have spent my whole life in being myself, go out of my way to change some look in you?" Cowed, the misnamed Storm retreats and leaves the house; it is not clear which of the two is going "to the dogs."

The Dove turns shock into anecdote. The play is named for a delicate young girl living with two old maid sisters who collect knives, guns, and romantic fantasies. The Dove is the obverse of her name, since she desires not peace but murder. After taunting each of the sisters in turn, she alone uses a gun—to shoot at a painting of prostitutes.

It is impossible to consider these plays seriously, in their modish poses and pseudo-poetic dialogue. The sure touch of Barnes' novels seems to come from some other mind. But nearly four decades after these dubious plays, Djuna Barnes again turned to drama. Still melodrama in that the emotion seems to exceed the vehicle, the dialogue of that vehicle is distinctive— different from anything else written by Djuna Barnes, and different fron any other play of the twentieth century.

The title *Antiphon* (1958) suggests an archaic and static form, for an antiphon is a verse reply, as in an antiphonic hymn. Elizabethan in phrasing, the drama is antiphonal in several scenes; that is to say, a verse speech calls forth its immediate reply, rather than fitting into an overall action. Though the verse of *The Antiphon* is archaic, setting and plot are relatively modern—the one recalling Eliot and the other Yeats. Like Eliot's *Family Reunion*, *The Antiphon* is set in an English country house; curiously, the date of production of *Family Reunion* is the date within *The Antiphon*—1939, the beginning of World War II. The war is the play's present, but the characters are mired in the past, as in Yeats' *Purgatory*. In both plays, a woman has betrayed her aristocratic heritage by lust for a commoner.

In three acts, *The Antiphon* reveals sexual sin and a hint of expiation. To seventeenth-century Burley Hall, a visible ruin on stage, come Miranda and her coachman-companion from Paris; Augusta and her two sons have been summoned from America by a third son, Jeremy. Augusta is the Burley who has been disloyal to her lineage, marrying an improbable American Mormon, Titus Higby Hobbs of Salem. (The name is resonant of usurpation, materialism, witchcraft, etc.) Seductive and sadistic, Titus has tortured his wife, brutalized his three sons, offered his daughter for rape by a middle-aged Cockney. Dead now, his memory is stronger in Burley Hall than that of the nobles who inhabited it.

His memory and his heritage. Even before we see Augusta at the beginning of Act II, we learn that her two merchant sons, Dudley and Elisha, plan to murder her. Jack Blow, the mysterious coachman, may be having an affair with Miranda, who has a checkered past as actress, writer, and woman of the world. Only Augusta's brother Jonathan, who never left Burley Hall, is free of rancor and suspicion. Jeremy, the third son, is nowhere to be seen.

The heavily imaged verse embraces all three acts of the drama, but the theatrical mood of each act is different. Act I is Jack Blow's exposition through hint and metaphor. Act II contains accusations and occasional defense; towards the end, the stage acquires the visual interest of a masque; by lamplight, Dudley and Elisha don pig's and ass's masks in order to taunt Augusta and Miranda, mother and sister, in a grotesque dance. Pitying both mother and sons, Miranda interposes herself between Augusta and Dudley, but they are interrupted by the entrance of Jack Blow with a doll's house, a miniature of Hobbs' Ark, the family home in America. Unlike the miniature castle of Albee's *Tiny Alice*, which reflects the mysterious present, Hobbs' Ark reveals a palpable past—Titus and his seven mistresses, seventeen-year old Miranda's rape arranged by her father. Voyeurs at this latter crime, Dudley and Elisha apparently renounce their murderous intention. Jack Blow and Jonathan wait in the wings while the Act III antiphon concentrates on a daughter and a mother who has been charged: "You made yourself a *madam* by submission."

Accusing self and the other, both women recognize self in the other as they slowly mount the wide staircase. At the top,

Augusta realizes that her sons have abandoned her in Burley Hall, but she refuses to accept the limits of her daughter and home. Rapidly descending the stairs, Augusta accuses Miranda of a plot and rings a giant curfew bell down upon them both. Her brother Jonathan and the erstwhile coachman, actually her son Jeremy, enter to view the catastrophe. Jeremy muses: "But could I know/ Which would be brought to child-bed of the other?" Together, mother and daughter have been born into death. In Jeremy's words, "This is the hour of the uncreate."

But matter extracted from manner betrays *The Antiphon* more than most plays. The seventeenth-century speech reflects the theme, carrying conviction of the Burley past. Djuna Barnes' lines tease with echoes of Webster and Tourneur, and yet the idiom is original. In Yeats' *Purgatory* we have the Old Man's word that "Great people lived and died in this house." But in Barnes' *Antiphon* the language imposes those people upon us.

As in her novel *Nightwood*, Djuna Barnes makes some effort to differentiate the speech of the several characters: Jonathan is brief or descriptive; Jeremy-Jack Blow is racy and witty; Dudley and Elisha are American, practical, obscene; suitably, Augusta and Miranda are similarly sensitive. In spite of differences, all six characters utter free pentameters, freer images, and the two women use a syntax that is perhaps too convoluted to be understood in the theater.

Unlike T. S. Eliot, who forced his verse into the mold of modern conversational prose, Djuna Barnes resolutely resurrects techniques of Elizabethan drama—soliloquy, aside, catalogue, pun, and above all metaphor. At its worst, the imagery swallows denotative sense: "It's true the webbed commune/ Trawls up a wrack one term was absolute." More often, though, the imagery concentrates paragraphs of dialogue: "The world is cracked—but in the breach/ My fathers mew."

There are few sustained threads of imagery, but these few are significant. Miranda is often a voyager or traveler; Augusta is both hunted and hunter. The word "rate" is frequently used by and of the mercantile brothers, and the mocking word "free" damns the dead father, Titus. Several times, Jeremy-Jack Blow breaks into a refrain: "Hey, then who/ Passes by this road so late." For it is late in the day of these children in their fifties, late in the day of the ancient Burley family, and of European civilization at the beginning of World War II. There is no hint of rainbow at the end of this holocaust, for Hobbs' Ark has been built by a monster, and monstrous crimes have been enacted in it. The Latter Day Saint was a devil, infecting his nobly born wife and genetically affecting his children. And yet this modern Noah, whose progeny people the earth, *has* built an ark. It is only after his death that his children strip him naked, but he has already cursed them with the consciousness of sin. Miranda the admirable dies in that consciousness, but Dudley and Elisha thrive on it, and Jeremy, unlike the passionate prophet Jeremiah, *"with what appears to be indifference leaves the stage."*

The dialogue of *The Antiphon* is astonishing. As drama, *The Antiphon* has many flaws: Jack Blow's opening exposition is obscure; descriptions are gratuitous of Augusta's sister Elvira and of Titus' mother Victoria. Even the coupling of Miranda's ruin with a Paris ruined by war is skillful in its horror rather than organic in its link. Too often, connotations muffle denotations; sound buries sense. In spite of these serious faults, however, *The Antiphon* contains extraordinarily rich diction and varied rhythms. For literary accomplishment, the play begs comparison with Eliot or Yeats. But unlike their plays, *The Antiphon* has not yet—1970—tempted theatermen. Which implies its own critique of the play, or of the theater.

Thornton Wilder

Djuna Barnes has yet to find a theater audience. Gertrude Stein is only now being acclaimed by devotees of Happenings. Thornton Wilder knew success in his own time. Like Stein and Barnes, Wilder worked in both narrative and dramatic form. But unlike their drama, that of Wilder shows the novelist's hand. Often described as an experimental playwright, Wilder has written lucidly about the novelty of his own drama: "The theatre has lagged behind the other arts in finding the 'new ways' to express how men and women think and feel in our time. I am not one of the new dramatists we are looking for."[15] On the contrary. Under a surface of "new ways"—partly borrowed from fiction—Wilder has smoothed over "how men and women think and feel in our time."

In contrast to his novels, which adventure into other times and places, Wilder sets his major plays in America. His earliest plays, however, published in 1928, the year after he won a Pulitzer Prize for *The Bridge of San Luis Rey,* ranged over various literary landscapes. Inspired by Dreiser's *Plays of the Natural and the Supernatural,* Wilder's *Angel That Troubled the Waters* consists of sixteen three-minute plays for three actors. The plays draw upon history, legend, and invention; the staging directions are elaborate, the dialogue pretentious, and the plays are interesting only as evidence of Wilder's early disinclination for the dominant realist mode, which prefigures his lifelong rebellion against the box-set. A quotation from the title play illustrates the mixture of fin-de-siècle atmosphere with didacticism:

> THE ANGEL: I must make haste. Already the sky is afire with the gathering host, for it is the hour of the new song among us. The earth itself feels the preparation in the skies and attempts its hymn. Children born in this hour spend all their lives in a sharper longing for the perfection that awaits them.
>
> THE NEWCOMER: Oh, in such an hour was I born, and doubly fearful to me is the flaw in my heart.

More mannered than the dialogue of Dreiser's "supernatural plays," that of Wilder also drowns its substance.

Having traveled to study non-realistic staging in France and Germany, Wilder showed considerably more dramatic skill in his second volume of plays, *The Long Christmas Dinner and Other Plays* (1931). The three least interesting plays are Pirandellian in their treatment of the fictional process and its problematic relation to life. The three other plays experiment with stage space and time.

The titular *Long Christmas Dinner* is ninety years long; between 1840 and 1930, we are introduced to four generations of the Bayard family in a Midwestern town. Influenced perhaps by the Heaven and Hell of medieval drama, Wilder places a Birth Portal and a Death Portal at stage left and right. On stage the characters age before our eyes, and then move toward death. Individuals are expendable, but the long Christmas dinner continues, with its conversation about the meal, the weather, the sermon, and the passing of time. Three generations of Bayard men ask whether diners prefer white or dark meat; three generations of Bayard women remark that every twig is encircled with ice.

Against this repetitive dialogue, Wilder counterpoints change within individual lives, as well as change from generation to generation. Thus the first Mother Bayard, who can still remember the Indians, dwells in the past, whereas the last Mother Bayard, who moves East to her children, thinks of their future. As the years pass, Roderick Bayard speaks with increasing formality. Charles Bayard, head of the firm after Roderick's death, echoes his father's phrases even to wanting his son in the family firm. But he is more successful and more ruthless than his father, as revealed in this passage: "Perhaps an occasional war isn't so bad after all. It clears up a lot of poisons that collect in nations. It's like a boil." Charles' two sons break the family pattern, since one is killed in World War I and the other runs away from "the first family of this city." Two lonely old women share a penultimate Christmas dinner—widow and spinster. At the last dinner, the spinster reads a letter from the widow visiting in the East, where a new family is beginning.

As *The Long Christmas Dinner* condenses time, *Pullman Car Hiawatha* condenses the cosmos into a train trip from New York to Chicago. The play's title suggests a combination of aboriginal America and mechanized speed; among the characters are humans, towns, planets, and hours who are philosophers and archangels. A Stage Manager governs this motley mixture, and that Stage Manager is, as Wilder was later to describe the Stage Manager of *Our Town*, "a hang-over from a novelist technique." Omniscient, he sets the scene, plays minor parts, introduces non-realistic and even non-human characters, and regulates the exchange of dialogue. Except for the slight Negro dialect of the Pullman porter and the quotations from philosophers and poets, the characters speak in deliberately undistinguished American phrases. Fields and towns (such as Grover's Corners, Ohio), living, dead, and imaginary figures declaim briefly. Oblivious to them, the Pullman passengers brood about their separate cares —health, love, business, insanity, and death. A woman passenger is eased into death by the archangels Michael and Gabriel, whose words are inaudible to us. The night hours quote briefly from Plato, Epictetus, and St. Augustine. Just before the train reaches Chicago, the Stage Manager orchestrates an incomprehensible chorus: "*The human beings murmur their thoughts; the hours discourse; the planets chant or hum.*" Though the play returns to human America at the end, this chorus foreshadows Wilder's more sustained juxtapositions of the trivial and the universal, expressed in comprehensible words.

A slight play (though Wilder's own favorite), *The Happy Journey to Trenton and Camden* departs from verisimilitude in its use of a nearly bare stage and a Stage Manager. Thus, an automobile consists of four chairs, as the Kirby family travels seventy miles in twenty minutes of playing time. The Kirby's are mildly ungrammatical in speech, as is the Stage Manager in his several small roles; they use folksy colloquialisms such as "I declare," "go along now," and "rest easy." This homespun quality contrasts with the energetic slickness of the advertisements that they read aloud from billboards along their route. Less ambitious than *The Long Christmas Dinner* or *Pullman Car Hiawatha*, *The Happy Journey* also reaches for a larger meaning through the married daughter's close brush with death, and the evocation of Washington as the family passes through Trenton.

In *Our Town*, COMPLETED SEVEN YEARS LATER IN 1938, there is no comparable historic reference, but references to death punctuate the three acts of the play. And the point of these references is to evoke an appreciation of life. Wilder has commented on his most popular play: "[*Our Town*] is an attempt to find a value above all price for the smallest events of our daily life."[16] Rather than small events, however, Wilder gives us small people, and it is mainly the omniscient, omnipresent Stage Manager—that "hang-over from a novelist technique"—who seeks to impress us with the value of "our daily life." Throughout the play, his dialogue swings in pendulum-fashion from the play's specifics to cosmic significance.

"Our" town is Grover's Corners, New Hampshire, transplanted from Ohio in *Pullman Car Hiawatha* to New England, which is richer in early American tradition. Three decades after Wilder wrote the play, Grover's Corners is one of the best-known towns in American literature. *Our Town* has been widely translated and anthologized; it is a favorite in high school and community theaters. Discovering that life imitates art, *Life* magazine ferreted out such a town in South Dakota in 1962. But *Life's* seal of approval merely emphasizes Wilder's pernicious portrait of turn-of-the-century America.

Pernicious because it invites self-congratulation. *Our Town* focuses on two middle-class WASP families, entirely and smugly self-sufficient as families and inhabitants of Grover's Corners. And the play at large barely hints at the suffocating limits of their world. The greeting card parents and celluloid adolescents are ignorant, innocent, and without individuality. Even the family names—Webb and Gibbs—differ only by a consonant or two. Doctor Gibbs and Editor Webb are virtually interchangeable, even to their hobbies in history. Plump mother and thin mother *are* interchangeable, stringing imaginary beans. Though each family has a boy and a girl, "same ages," their sex fizzes into strawberry ice cream sodas in Grover's Corners. Economic competition and outright theft are unknown. Though Editor Webb claims that "they spend most of their time talking about who's rich and who's poor," we are idyllically spared such talk. A doctor's son thus becomes a farmer without a murmur of objection from his family. At seventeen, a boy breaks into tears of remorse because he didn't help his mother chop wood. At sixteen, a girl thinks her father and all men are perfect. Though the Gibbs family complains of the difficulties of the father-son and mother-daughter relationships, we see no such difficulties in *Our Town*. A church organist drinks to drown his troubles, but we never learn the nature of those troubles, even though they drive him to suicide. (There is a vague hint that the "troubles" may be musical genius.) The town has a jail, but the policeman is everybody's friend. The "plants" in the audience who ask about social injustice, culture, or beauty in Grover's Corners are put in their place by Mr. Webb's tolerant good humor, so that "our town" emerges as wiser and better than any place we know, and yet Wilder contrives to give us the impression that this bovine existence *is* what we know, and that its value is "above all price."

Crucial to this idealized portrait is the self-consciously simple staging. Originally played with conventional sets, *Our Town* was poorly received in the very New England of its setting—the citified town of Boston. Wilder then leaned upon his experiments in one-act plays and suggested the innovation of an almost bare stage to emphasize the deliberate placeless generalization of the play. As Wilder was later to write: "The box set stifles the life in drama,"[17] and "the bareness of the stage releases the events from the particular."[18] In its new undress, *Our Town* appealed to critics surfeited with the details of realistic sets, and *Our Town's* suggestion of cosmic profundity appealed to critics surfeited with the problem plays of the depression. *Our Town* won the Pulitzer Prize and, subsequently, the heart of a country seeking an imaginary innocence.

Like Dylan Thomas in *Under Milk Wood*, Wilder attempts to link the town-protagonist with large cosmic forces. But the poet Thomas presents a mystical vision through his metaphysical imagery, Welsh rhythms, and cyclical structure. Wilder's language is as bare as his stage. Thomas drew upon the lyric fertility of his poems, but Wilder consciously tailored his material to the group mind of the great number who attend the theater. Universal experiences are suggested by the titles of the acts: I Daily Life, II Love and Marriage, III Death. But all three experiences (with marriage inevitably linked to love) are so universalized that they lose specific meaning.

Francis Fergusson has accurately summarized the inadequacies of *Our Town*: "The characters . . . are clichés of smalltown life rather than individuals; the language they speak . . . is distressingly close to that of plays written for high schools and Sunday schools, or to the soap operas of radio. . . . [Wilder] hardly imagines them as people, he rather invites the audience to accept them by plainly labeling them as sentimental stereotypes of village folksiness. . . . The distance between the life onstage, which the audience accepts because it is so familiar in this sense, and the idea which the author has in mind is too great. The 'greater number' blubbers at the platitudes of character and situation, while the author, manipulating his effects with kindly care, enjoys the improbable detachment of the Mind of God."[19]

"The Mind of God" is Wilder's addition to the cosmic address which he borrows from Joyce's *Portrait of the Artist as a Young Man;* Stephen Dedalus wrote: "Stephen Dedalus, Class of Elements, Clongowes Wood College, Sallins, County Kildare, Ireland, Europe, The World, The Universe." Rebecca Webb tells her brother about a letter her friend received from a minister; it was addressed: "Jane Crofut; The Crofut Farm; Grover's Corners; Sutton County; New Hampshire; United States of America; Western Hemisphere; the Earth; the Solar System; the Universe; the Mind of God." This address concludes Act I; though the act contains Daily Life, it reaches finally toward the Mind of God.

Joyce's artist, paring his fingernails, views his creation from a divine distance, whereas Wilder deliberately immerses us in pathos, even while he seeks to generalize its meaning. Thus, the first description of our town ends at the cemetery. Even before we hear them speak, we learn that Dr. and Mrs. Gibbs are now dead. No sooner do we see Joe Crowell delivering papers on stage than we learn that he died back in World War I. Because of this shared omniscience, the Stage Manager causes us to share his sense of recollection of this idyllic town—"You all remember what it's like."—and the old-fashioned, unadorned diction reënforces this sense.

Except for Professor Willard's brief pedantic remarks, all the characters use a modified New England dialect. The omniscient descriptions of the Stage Manager are punctuated with "there"'s, "that"'s, "there comes," and "thank you."'s Everyone indulges in such reassuring colloquialisms as "I declare," "look sharp," "I reckon," "what do you know," "go along with you," "Oh, hush-up-with-you," and "that's a fact." We hear such well-worn sentences as "The important thing is to be happy." "There's a lot of common sense in some superstitions." "I'd rather have my children healthy than bright." "People are meant to go through life two by two." "You don't want to be the first to fly in the face of custom." Even the dead speak in clichés: "That ain't no way to behave!" "They don't understand."

Imagery is rare in our town, but tends to be drawn from animals. Rebecca Gibbs compares herself to a sick turkey, Dr. Gibbs says his wife has the voice of an old crow, Mrs. Webb scolds her children for "gobbling like wolves," and she recalls that she went into marriage "blind as a bat." Only the Stage Manager attempts a mildly original image toward the end of Act I: "The day's running down like a tired clock." One repetition almost becomes an image by meaningful position; in Act I Mr. Webb asks Emily: "Haven't any troubles on your mind, have you, Emily?" And she replies: *"Troubles,* Papa? *No."* Just after her death in Act III, Emily exclaims: "I never realized before how troubled and how . . . how in the dark live persons are." But the effect is diluted by Emily's previous remark, which praises a Ford that "never gives any trouble."

Deliberately prosaic, Wilder's language occasionally achieves hypnotic quality through Steinian repetition. Wilder himself has called attention to the recurrence of large numbers in the dialogue—hundreds, thousands, millions. The Stage Manager says in Act I: "There's some scenery for those who think they have to have scenery." And: "You can go and smoke now, those that smoke." Though the courtship of George and Emily is maudlin, it is almost credible when couched in Steinian repetition: "All the girls say so. They may not say so to your face, but that's what they say behind your back." Gertrude Stein used her repetitions to imitate the texture of experience; she relies on specific verbs or nouns, as in the famous "rose is a rose is a rose." Wilder skirts emptiness when he applies the repetitions to abstraction, as in the sermon of the Stage Manager (as minister) in the Act II wedding, and in the omniscient introduction to the Act III funeral. The former begins: "There are a lot of things to be said about a wedding; there are a lot of thoughts that go on during a wedding." And ends: "And don't forget all the other witnesses at this wedding—the ancestors. Millions of them. Most of them set out to live two-by-two also. Millions of them." It is a sobering thought only for those unaccustomed to thinking. The funeral remarks give non-thinkers a comfortable feeling of having thought along with great minds: "Now there are some things we all know, but we don't take'm out and look at'm very often. We all know that something is eternal. And it ain't houses and it ain't names, and it ain't earth, and it ain't even the stars . . . everybody knows in their bones that *something* is eternal, and that something has to do with human beings. All the

greatest people ever lived have been telling us that for five thousand years and yet you'd be surprised how people are always
losir.g hold of it. There's something way down deep that's eternal about every human being." "Something" is hardly a mile-
stone for depth.

Dante in the *Purgatory* (to which Wilder acknowledges a debt)
conveys eternity through the presence of his recollecting spirits,
but Wilder's spirits are almost disembodied. Detached from and
superior to the living, they mitigate the effects of death. As the
Act II wedding had a hint of sadness, the Act III funeral has a
tinge of happiness. Emily's recognition is juvenile: "Oh, earth,
you're too wonderful for anybody to realize you." In *Our Town*,
emotions are not mixed so much as flattened, under the tender
omniscience of the Stage Manager.

Wilder's deliberate exploitation and repetition of cliché has
been ascribed to the influence of his friend Gertrude Stein, and
yet the language of *Our Town* is similar to that of *The Happy
Journey to Trenton and Camden*. The probability is that Stein
confirmed his own rejection of the strained poeticism of his
earlier plays, but he was guided by her to convey the significance of the apparently insignificant. This risks the imitative
fallacy, since Wilder uses undistinguished language to sing the
glories of the undistinguished. The play's international success
suggests that insignificance is ubiquitous, particularly when it
masquerades as significance. The homely American diction appeals particularly to contemporary Americans who wish to believe in their own wholesome roots.

As *Our Town* REFLECTS WILDER'S ADMIRATION FOR
Gertrude Stein, *The Skin of Our Teeth* reflects his admiration for
James Joyce. Between these plays influenced by two experimen-
talists, Wilder wrote *The Merchant of Yonkers*, adapted from a
farce by Johann Nestroy, which in turn was adapted from an
earlier farce by John Oxenford, and which incorporates some
dialogue from Molière's *Miser*. But Wilder wears his learning
lightly, and *The Merchant of Yonkers* is his least pretentious play,
thriving on joyous adventure (especially in the revised version,
The Matchmaker).

It has been claimed that Wilder's emphasis shifts, between *The Merchant of Yonkers* (1938) and *The Matchmaker* (1954), from a male to a female protagonist who was not present in his main source, Nestroy's *Einen Jux will er sich Machen*. Actually, however, the dialogue is more evenly distributed among all the characters in the revised version, aphorisms are sharpened, repartee is exchanged more swiftly, and mockery of the box-set is increased. Thus, the scenic directions are more detailed for the four different sets—one for each act of the farce. In both versions of the play, each act contains a long soliloquy of direct address to the audience: Act I—Vandergelder, Act II—Cornelius, Act III—Malachi (Melchoir in the first version), and Act IV—Dolly. Other than the rearrangement of a few phrases in Vandergelder's speech, the first three soliloquies are virtually the same in the two versions, but the difference in Dolly's speech is instructive. In both versions, she addresses her dead husband to announce her coming marriage to Vandergelder. In *The Merchant of Yonkers*, Dolly is didactic, but in *The Matchmaker* she has learned through suffering. Thus Wilder omits from the revised script: "Inside of all of us nice people are the seeds of quarrels, lawsuits, and wars, too. It's nice people, also, who tear their fellow men to pieces." A few moments later, the Dolly of *The Merchant of Yonkers* re-joins the human race, with Steinian repetition of Wilderian abstraction: "As for me, I've decided to live among them. It was a perfect marriage that taught me to accept the human race. . . . If you accept human beings and are willing to live among them, you acknowledge that every man has a right to his own mistake." In *The Matchmaker*, however, Dolly expatiates upon *her* mistake, and what she learned from it: "I wasn't always so. After my husband's death, I retired into myself. . . . And one night, after two years of this, an oak leaf fell out of my Bible. I had placed it there on the day my husband asked me to marry him; a perfectly good oak leaf—but without color and without life. And suddenly I realized that for a long time I had not shed one tear; nor had I been filled with the wonderful hope that something or other would turn out well. I saw that I was like that oak leaf, and on that night I decided to rejoin the human race."

Since *The Matchmaker* is a farce, Wilder wisely limits his solilo-

quies; farce demands physicality—ridiculous clothes and posi-
tions, concealment and chases, disguises and mistaken identity
—and this he supplies. Though the ubiquitous bed of French
farce is absent from *The Matchmaker*, Wilder makes fun of an
American Puritan heritage—money-making and propriety.
Vandergelder is Dutch thrift; Dolly Gallagher Levi is a descendant of Abie's Irish Rose; Irish Irene Molloy couples with Dutch
Cornelius Hackl, as the fair young ingenue keeps complaining
that she doesn't want all these romantic adventures. The rollicking has been helped by music in *Hello Dolly*.

For centuries, plagiarism has been the life-blood
of the theater, and one can only complain when the theater is
anemic. Plautus, Molière, Oxenham, and Nestroy may lie behind the frothy surface of *The Matchmaker*, but the froth justifies
the theft. The encyclopedic erudition of James Joyce may lie
behind *The Skin of Our Teeth*, but does it *nourish* Wilder's play,
as the *Hellzapoppin* techniques certainly energize it?

Campbell and Robinson tabulate the debts of *The Skin of Our
Teeth* to *Finnegans Wake*:[20] among them are the circular structure
of the whole, the basic family unit, the recurrence of periodic
catastrophes, the opposition of wife-mother to maid-temptress,
and the incorporation of a mythic heritage into the daily life of
the present. Under a self-imposed "necessity of treating
material understandable by the larger number,"[21] Wilder simplifies Joyce. And onto the mythic structure he grafts a burlesque of the conventions of the box set, so that visual high-jinks
supplement the conceptual pyrotechnics of Joyce.

Joyce himself relies on Vico for his four stages in the cycle of
history, but Wilder's three acts present three catastrophes—
glacier, flood, and war—from which the human race (Greek
anthropos) escapes by the skin of its teeth. Though the pattern is
repetitious, Wilder implies development as well. In its Act I
infancy, humanity is threatened by a purely external disaster
(though Henry-Cain has killed his brother), and it survives
through a combination of courage and practicality. In Act II the
implication is that the storm arrives—as in biblical times—to
punish man for his sins; the third black disc goes up as Antrobus

and Sabina-Fairweather retire into her cabana. Mankind is saved through grace rather than works, for the refuge-ship is waiting off the pier. Act III opens on the armistice after an unnamed war, which is obliquely linked to Henry's aggressiveness—"Henry *is* the enemy. Everybody knows that." Written during World War II, *The Skin of Our Teeth* ends on a determinedly optimistic note, as Mr. Antrobus intones: "Maggie, you and I will remember in peacetime all the resolves that were so clear to us in the days of war. We've come a long ways. We've learned. We're learning." And at the very last, Sabina repeats her opening lines, then turns to the audience: "This is where you came in. We have to go on for ages and ages yet. You go home. The end of the play isn't written yet." We might be in Genet's dizzying *Balcony* up to this point, but the final uplift is pure Wilder: "Mr. and Mrs. Antrobus! Their heads are full of plans and they're as confident as the first day they began,—and they told me to tell you: good night."

Though Wilder exhibits some linguistic versatility in this play, the ground rock of the dialogue remains folksy Americanisms, as in *Our Town*. Mrs. Antrobus never deviates from its plain simplicity; Mr. Antrobus and Sabina return to it after their occasional excursions into other idioms—swearing drunkard and Kiwani-type politician in the one case, maid of melodrama and false soubrette in the other. Early in the play the human plight is made immediate through American slang— "knock on wood," "catch as catch can," "skin of our teeth," "tight squeeze."

In its peril, Wilder's symbolic family is meant to represent the human race throughout Western civilization, but the sustained joke of the play is that this modern American family keeps referring to its prehistoric past in the present tense. Thus, we have the comic incongruity of a modern news release to announce the ice age; the political convention, whose watchword is "Enjoy yourself," precedes the flood; a radio address parodying the Gettysburg Address precedes the Fortune Teller's warning that the Antrobus family should seek shelter in the ark. Only in Act III does the comic element flag, and simplistic didacticism follows the war.

Though Wilder has acknowledged his debt to Joyce, he has

said nothing of a debt to Pirandello, and yet *The Skin of Our Teeth*, like Pirandello's Theater Trilogy, suggests that the flux of reality will always intrude into the conventions of theater. Wilder's "group mind" Pirandello matches his "group mind" Joyce; rather than the complexities of the tension between roles and reality, Wilder reduces his breaking of theatrical illusion to the several censorious interruptions of Sabina-Miss Somerset. Comic in Acts I and II, her interruptiveness becomes the Act III climax. We are asked to believe that a seasoned (if foolish) actress stops the father-son struggle on stage because she fears an actual murder: "Last night you almost strangled him. You became a regular savage. Stop it!" Method actors, Antrobus and Henry recite their biographies to explain their stage violence. And Sabina, who in Act III moralizes as piously as Mrs. Antrobus, flays us all: "We're all just as wicked as we can be, and that's the God's truth." After that little excursion to the pulpit, Wilder returns us to the onward-and-upward path; after all, the Antrobus family lives in Excelsior.

Wilder also leans on Pirandello to enunciate the wisdom of the ages. When seven actors (seven!) take sick, they are replaced by four theater employees, to act as philosopher-hours. Wilder explains the fantasy that he borrows from his *Pullman Car Hiawatha*: "just like the hours and stars go by over our heads at night, in the same way the ideas and thoughts of the great men are in the air around us all the time." In addition, Wilder suggests that Time, Philosophy, and Human Courage are relevant not only to actors on stage, but to all of us who work in and out of the theater.

Wilder does not trust our response to his carefully chosen quotations from Spinoza, Plato, Aristotle, and Genesis to prove that we all exist in the Mind of God and that suffering ennobles us. Therefore, Mrs. Antrobus underlines the moral in two separate speeches: "Too many people have suffered and died for my children for us to start reneging now." And: "The only thought we clung to was that you were going to bring something good out of this suffering." As in Act I, it is she who gives her husband the strength to preach on his own: "All I ask is the chance to build new worlds and God has always give us that. And has given us voices to guide us; and the memory of our mistakes to warn us." After the inventive staging, the occasionally parodic dialogue, and the genial comedy of prehistory in modern suburbia, Wilder closes the play in Sunday School.

IN SUBSEQUENT PLAYS, WILDER TRANSPOSES CLASSICAL myth and biblical legend into homey Americanisms. He himself has decided against publishing his *Life in the Sun* (1955), a version of the Alcestis myth, and excerpts in print confirm the wisdom of his decision.[22] He has also embarked upon two different cycles of one-act plays, of which several have been produced. Judging from productions, one must again congratulate him for modesty and tact; critical comment is therefore unwarranted. Though Wilder's box office success is not surprising, serious critical attention is—Bogard, Corrigan, Gassner, Goldstein, Hewitt.[23] One of the best read playwrights, Wilder reduces the questions of the past and the experiments of the present to wholesome lessons. His rebellion against the box set has toppled no orthodoxy. At his best when he capers freely around the stage—*The Matchmaker*—he has a dangerous soporific effect in *Our Town* and *The Skin of Our Teeth*, because their facile comfort masquerades as cosmic significance. After his major plays were written, Wilder published an article entitled "Toward an American Language," in which the following sentence is found: "The United States is a middle class nation and has widened and broadened and deepened the concepts of the wide and the broad and the deep without diminishing the concept of the high."[24] Neither wide, nor broad, nor deep, and above all not high, Wilder's plays are smugly self-congratulatory of a country that O'Neill called "the greatest failure."[25] Out of that failure (and his own) O'Neill wrenched his masterpieces; on a middle class nation, Wilder bases his homilies.

IN HIS 1957 INTRODUCTION TO AN EDITION OF HIS THREE major plays, Wilder declared: "The novel is pre-eminently the vehicle of the unique occasion, the theatre of the generalized one."[26] Though Wilder has tried to make this statement true, significant modern novelists have used the unique occasion as a pebble in a pond, and ripples spread wide over the pond when the pebble is thrown by Proust, Joyce, Kafka, Faulkner, Beckett —to choose very different novelists. The major American dramatists have also sought a general meaning through particular occasions. Neither O'Neill, Miller, Williams, nor Albee has been content with the unique occasion; in their best plays, generalizations rest upon specific, if not unique occasions—the more specific, the more general—paradoxical though that sounds.

The plays of twentieth century American novelists *have* tended to be vehicles of the unique occasion—from Dreiser's embryonic American tragedy, *The Hand of the Potter*, to Hawkes' fictional reënactment of tragedy, *The Questions*. There is no point to enumerating the plays of this chapter—without exception inferior to the fiction. Though the reasons for this vary with the novelist, one may hazard the generalization that the dramatic dialogue of the novelists was inadequate to construct the specificity of the stage occasion. Flat, pretentious, or digressive, the phrases often seem to be depersonalized. On stage appears the anomaly of words rambling around a unique occasion, without *people* functioning in time to build the occasion by means of the words. Since Wilder concentrates determinedly (in *Our Town* and *The Skin of Our Teeth*) on the generalized occasion, he makes small claim to unique plot or character. In addition to generalizing all occasions—birth, marriage, catastrophe, and death—he has tried to generalize his cast of characters too; the wholesome American family is at the center of his plays, secure and optimistic in the face of small and large events, which the family members are scarcely able to distinguish. Neither in his facile universals nor in the factitious uniqueness of these part-time playwrights has there been deep penetration into "how men and women think and feel in our time"—for the illumination of those men and women who *do* think and feel.

7 / Poets at Play

THOUGH PROSE HAS DOMINATED English LANGUAGE DRAMA OF THE last two centuries, poets have sporadically tried to reclaim terrain. Yeats and Eliot, two of the most accomplished poets to write in English in the twentieth century, committed much of their creative energy to drama, but no comparable American poet showed such dedication.[1] At intervals through the twentieth century, however, differently gifted American poets turned to plays. These efforts are too numerous and often too slight to merit detailed examination, but some attention should be paid to the plays of poets who have produced some quantity of verse of quality.[2] Since poets are virtuosos of language, we might expect their dramatic dialogue to derive the advantage of their talent. As in the case of novelists, however, poets seem to write plays with their left hand. But more poets than novelists have attempted plays; hence a long and choppy chapter.

Of American poets born before the turn of the twentieth century, Wallace Stevens ventured briefly into drama at the beginning of his long career, and Robert Frost at the end of his. Ezra Pound "arrang[ed] beauty into the words" of Ernest Fenollosa's translations of Japanese Noh plays and produced his own translation of Euripides' *Women of Trachis*. William Carlos Williams and E. E. Cummings flirted with the dramatic form, whereas Robinson Jeffers and Archibald MacLeish sustained a certain devotion to it. Yet none of these poets created a single play of the quality of their best lyrics.

WALLACE STEVENS

THREE PLAYS OF STEVENS WERE PRODUCED, AND TWO OF THESE HAVE
been published—*Three Travelers Watch a Sunrise* (1916) and *Carlos
among the Candles* (1917). The very titles designate static situations, and the brief plays are more literary than theatrical. Even
as literature, their subject is abstract—the relation of imagination to reality. Thus, the two plays predict Stevens' major
theme, and they also predict his distinctive idiom—concise
metaphor in *Three Travelers* and meditative exoticism in *Carlos*.

The Three Travelers who watch a sunrise are parable Chinese traveling through a wooded hill in Eastern Pennsylvania.
Served by two Negro Property Men, they don, respectively, red,
blue, and green silk robes, while discussing philosophic attitudes toward reality. Though they speak similarly and formally,
the three Chinese think differently: the first Chinese tends to see
truth as objective, the Third Chinese as subjective, and the Second believes that there is a necessary interpenetration of the two
ways of viewing reality: "But when the sun shines on the earth,/
In reality/ It does not shine on a thing that remains/ What it
was yesterday./ The sun rises/ On whatever the earth happens
to be."

What "the earth happens to be" when the stage sun rises is the
last resting place for a young man who has hanged himself
during the night. That same night, the First Chinese sang a
ballad of a young lady and her maid, who dream of a young
gentleman far away. Even as the Chinese analyze the ballad—
"But it is a way with ballads/ That the more pleasing they are/
The worse end they come to."—they remark that a young Italian has disappeared with his neighbor's daughter. When the
First (objective) Chinese discovers the body of the hanged man,
he recognizes an avatar of the young gentleman of the ballad.
The Third (subjective) Chinese orders the stage bushes to be
taken away, and behind them is found the grief-stricken girl of
the ballad—become real for the Chinese. Alone on stage, the
Third (subjective) Chinese reiterates, in the metaphoric language that characterizes Stevens, the necessity of interaction
between reality and imagination. Music, color, and the incanta-

tory quality of the lines—all these try to theatricalize the tantalizing evanescence of reality in a fragile play, famous in its time for winning a contest for poetic plays sponsored by *Poetry* magazine.

As in *Three Travelers Watch a Sunrise*, illumination is at once literal and metaphoric in *Carlos among the Candles*; the imagination illuminates reality. Thus, candles, lanterns, and sunrise serve illumination in *Three Travelers*; in *Carlos among the Candles* the entire action consists of the lighting and extinguishing of candles, and the entire dialogue consists of Carlos' reactions to the different effects of light. As the three Chinese perceive different aspects of reality, so during Carlos' playlong monologue he perceives different aspects of reality through the changing light of the candles. And as an external reality intrudes upon the travelers' sunrise, so external reality intrudes upon Carlos' contemplation; a gust of wind extinguishes several candles, and Carlos acquiesces to the reality of darkness: "Oh, ho! Here is matter beyond invention."

The body of the play, and all its dialogue, traces the invention of Carlos, couched in the idiom of an esthete, where only the syntax is simple in the rhythmically varied prose: "I was always affected by the grand style. . . . It is in the afternoon and in the evening . . . in effects, so drifting, that I know myself to be incalculable, since the causes of what I am are incalculable. . . . Here there will be silks and fans . . . the movement of arms . . . rumors of Renoir . . . coiffures . . . hands . . . scorn of Debussy . . . communications of body to body. . . . Imagination wills the five purple palmations of cinquefoil. . . . The extinguishing of light is like that of old Hesper, clapped upon by clouds." The arch qualities of Carlos' verbal invention undercut his final submission to uninvented reality—"matter beyond invention."

In a letter to Harriet Monroe, editor of *Poetry*, Stevens commented on his theatrical intention: "A theatre without action or characters ought to be within the range of human interests. Not as a new thing—a source of new sensations, purposely, only; but naturally, normally, why not?"[3] Why not? Because Stevens was unable to make his plays natural and normal; instead, they are arch and *recherché*, without the redeeming discoveries of his poems.

ROBERT FROST

ROBERT FROST WAS FOND OF TELLING AN ANECDOTE ABOUT STEVENS and himself which embraces even their slight plays. Traveling together, the two poets were ill at ease in one another's company, and Stevens charged Frost with writing poetry that fastened on to subjects. In fact, Stevens' subjects disappear into metaphor, whereas those of Frost are firmly on the surface of his works.

The subjects are announced in the very titles of Frost's plays, *A Masque of Reason* (1945) and *A Masque of Mercy* (1947). The word "masque" implies the plays' lack of drama, but it conceals their excessive talkiness. To adumbrate his subject matter, Frost draws upon the Bible—the Job story for the first masque and the Jonah story for the second.

A Masque of Reason is a triangular discussion between Job, his wife, and God. The Devil appears only as a sapphire wasp, and he is almost mute. Husband and wife recognize God because He looks like Blake's picture of Him, and we recognize Job as Job by the early references to his trials. In the modern manner with myth, Job is our contemporary because he speaks our American idiom, and yet that idiom—as in Frost's poetry—is as formal as it is simple, correct in its New England terseness. God Himself comments on His language: "I should have spoken sooner had I found/ The word I wanted. You would have supposed/ One who in the beginning *was* the Word/ Would be in a position to command it./ I have to wait for words like anyone."

In this discursive masque, the discussion centers on Job's unremitting search for reason behind God's actions. Job's wife, in contrast, wants to know the reason for all actions, and she charges God: "All You can seem to do is lose Your temper/ When reason-hungry mortals ask for reasons." In Frost's play, however, God's temper is under better control than that of the humans, and indeed the characters are remarkable for their old-fashioned courtesy toward one another, considering what is at stake. Job compliments God on being human, and Job's wife cheerfully helps Satan. It is she who insists upon the traditional final tableau—Job front and center between God and the Devil. As in the Bible, Frost's Job is given no reason for human misery,

229

so that the play might more properly be called *A Masque of non-Reason.*

A Masque of Mercy, in contrast, yields positive intimations of mercy, but they are only capriciously present. And the moral is not as neat as in *A Masque of Reason.* There are again four characters, but this time the dialogue is more evenly distributed among them—Jonah, Paul, a bookstore owner named My Brother's Keeper, and his wife Jesse Bel. The drama begins when Jonah intrudes upon the threesome of old acquaintances. Frost's Jonah is trying to escape his career of prophecy because God never carries out his threats of delivering justice. During the course of the play, however, Jonah comes to appreciate mercy above justice. At the last, he is carried to the foot of the cross by Paul and Keeper, and he acknowledges: "Nothing can make injustice just but mercy."

Though the final substitution of New Testament mercy for Old Testament justice is clear enough, the verbal progress is devious through the several allegorical oppositions. Nearly twice as long as *A Masque of Reason,* the Mercy Masque is sometimes redundant or digressive. Trivial subjects such as urban living, didactic preaching, crass commercialism, interpretation of dreams enter fleetingly; anachronistic remarks have a contemporary cuteness; the husband-wife bickering of Keeper and Jesse Bel supply conventional comedy. Abstractions punctuate the theological dispute—not only justice and mercy, but fear, courage, sacrifice, evil. And yet concreteness is achieved through the specifics of the New York bookstore scene and the adroitness of the strict iambic pentameter.

In his introduction to the *Collected Poems,* Frost claims that there are only two meters in the English language—"strict iambic and loose iambic." He is one of the few strict iambicists of the twentieth century, and his combination of simple diction with strict meter endows these discursive dialogues with a certain tension. (Even the scenic directions scan perfectly: *"The door here opens darkly of itself."*) It is obvious, however, that the brief plays are of interest only because they were written by a considerable poet in another genre.

230

ROBINSON JEFFERS

A CONTEMPORARY OF STEVENS AND FROST, JEFFERS DIFFERS FROM them in his long free lines and his unrelieved solemnity. Though he turned to dialogue more often than they did, it was originally with no thought of theatrical performance. Only his *Medea* (1946) was specifically intended for the stage—an adaptation of Euripides at the request of actress Judith Anderson, who had already played in Jeffers' first dramatic poem, *The Tower Beyond Tragedy* (1925). Besides *Medea*, Jeffers wrote five poems in dialogue form, all of them subsequently performed.

The Tower Beyond Tragedy is Jeffers' version of the *Oresteia*. Divided into three parts, the dramatic poem is faithful only to the surface events of Aeschylus. Jeffers' Agamemnon is swiftly slain off-stage; when his followers attempt vengeance, Clytemnestra offers her body to them, turning their murderous drive to lust: "I have not my sister's,/ Troy's flame's beauty, but I have something./ This arm, round, firm, skin without hair, polished like marble; the supple-jointed shoulders:/ Men have praised the smooth neck, too,/ The strong clear throat over the deepwide breasts . . ." While Clytemnestra, slowly stripping, offers herself to the soldiers, dead Agamemnon's voice is heard in the throat of Cassandra. Then, like the cowboy of Western films, Aegisthus appears in the nick of time to rescue Clytemnestra; the two lovers subdue the city, decreeing death for Orestes and Electra, who flee. In Part II, eight years later, brother and sister return. After Orestes kills Aegisthus and Clytemnestra, Cassandra (who is still alive) prophesies: "I have seen on what stage/ You sing the little tragedy; the column of the ice that was before on one side flanks it,/ The column of the ice to come closes it up on the other: audience nor author/ I have never seen yet: I have heard the silence: it is I Cassandra." Whereupon Orestes murders her too.

In Part III, Electra offers herself to Orestes, tempting him to rule Argos with her. But he passes beyond his tragedy and all tragedy, evidently attaining a kind of transcendence through his rejection of passion. A narrative voice closes the published poem: "To [Orestes] who had climbed the tower beyond time, consciously, and cast humanity, entered the earlier fountain."

In this conclusion, images are confusing, but Jeffers' approbation for Orestes is unmistakable. Jeffers himself explained his intention: "Orestes, in the poem, identifies himself with the whole divine nature of things; earth, man, and stars, the mountain forest and the running streams; they are all one existence, one organism. He perceives this, and that himself is included in it, identical with it. This perception is his tower beyond the reach of tragedy; because, whatever may happen, the great organism will remain forever immortal and immortally beautiful. Orestes has 'fallen in love outward,' not with a human creature, nor a limited cause, but with the universal God."[4]

Though Jeffers was to write more speakable dialogue, he was not to modify the long, image-strewn lines, spoken by towering characters. Even with Judith Anderson in the role of Clytemnestra, it is difficult to take the strip-tease seriously; Cassandra's prophecies are tedious in their generalizations of doom (and were cut in the Broadway production); Electra and Orestes regurgitate Freud. The determined loftiness of *The Tower Beyond Tragedy* robs its dialogue of humanity, but then Inhumanism came to be Jeffers' creed.

Nevertheless, Jeffers' next dramatic poem, *Dear Judas* (1929), exhibits his most sustained concern for mere human beings, even though Jesus, Mary, and Judas are hardly typical human beings. Jeffers himself thought that his play imitated the Japanese Noh form, in which ghosts at a haunted place re-enact their lives and deaths. However, Jeffers' re-enactment is heavily verbal, lacking the grace of the Noh's culminating dance.

Jeffers explained that in the title, *Dear Judas:* "The emphasis should be on the word 'dear'—'dear' Judas—the man was dear to Judas even while he was being betrayed by him."[5] In turn, Judas held the human race so dear that he betrayed Jesus rather than watch Him destroy that race.

Since Jesus uses many biblical phrases, and Mary sounds like an unusually self-effacing Jewish mother, Judas carries the burden of Jeffers' rhetoric and imagery, in his usual long uneven lines: "My soul is dark with images, and all are dreadful,/ Sword, scourge and javelin, and the Roman gibbet,/ Women dying horribly in hopeless birth-pangs, men dying of thirst and hunger, the miners dying in the mines/ Under the stinking torches, in summer by the Red Sea, consumed with labor in the metal darkness;/ And the angles eaten with rust, and the blood-striped backs, of the oars in a thousand galleys: it would be salvation/ To think that I could willingly bear the suffering— if it were possible—for all that lives, I alone:/ I dare not think so." For all the generalized and impersonal description of the suffering, it is unusual for a Jeffers character to express any pity at all.

Jesus, in contrast, does not express pity, but he leads the mob to rebel against the indignities of their condition, and Judas turns against him when Jesus' charity gives way to indignation, his self-doubt to certainty of his divine mission. Turning from the warnings of Mary, Jesus declares his destiny: "I have seen the angels of God." In a long monologue, he forgives Judas for the coming betrayal, and he enunciates his faith: "Dear Judas, it is God drives us./ It is not shameful to be duped by God. I have known his glory in my lifetime, I have *been* his glory, I know/ Beyond illusion the enormous beauty of the torch in which our agonies and all are particles of fire."

For about three-fourths of the play, Jeffers depicts an intense relationship between his three ghosts, but once Jesus is cru-cified, Lazarus delivers Jeffers' own message of the final immer-sion of the merely human in the large inhuman universal: "Let him [Judas] and the other [Jesus],/ Their pain drawn up to burning points and cut off, praise God after the monstrous manner of mankind./ While the white moon glides from this garden; the glory of darkness returns a moment, on the cliffs of dawn."

Neither quite Christian in theme nor quite Noh in form, *Dear Judas* is exceptional in Jeffers' canon because of the sympathy for small human emotions—particularly those of Judas and Mary. In spite of Jeffers' rhetorical monologues, gratuitous images, and final didacticism, individual moments achieve a dramatic inter-play which reappears nowhere in Jeffers' work.

The very titles *At the Fall of an Age* (1931) and *At the Birth of an Age* (1935) indicate the complementary nature of Jeffers' next two dramatic poems. Both are drawn from relatively obscure leg-ends, and the legends spring from different traditions—the one Greek and the other Germanic. In the earlier play, the age which falls is that of Helen and Mycenean Greece, to be replaced by Athenian rationalism. In the latter play, a new age takes as its symbol the Hanged God of Norse mythology, which exalts suffering above the endless series of betrayals and counter-betrayals in the previous age. Both poems are steps along Jeffers' Inhumanist way—a kind of latter-day Stoicism in which man redeems himself by objectifying his experience and viewing it in the light of inhuman durability.

In *At the Fall of an Age*, this Inhumanist view is espoused by the dead Achilles and his Myrmidons. Basing his plot on Pausanius' description of Helen's death at the hands of Queen Polyxo, whose husband was killed at Troy, Jeffers is able to indulge freely in his elemental characters, since there is no extant tragedy containing them. Thus, Helen is the obvious symbol of beauty, and no one knows it better than she. Her desire to live is praiseworthy, since she is seeking the permanence of beauty. When she is hanged, however, beauty does not die, since the townspeople worship the tree of her undoing, and they avenge her death, killing Polyxo. Into this agon of Helen versus Polyxo, Jeffers introduces a dead Achilles who, like Orestes in *The Tower Beyond Tragedy*, achieves transcendence through his acceptance of death and his denial of lust.

In *At the Birth of an Age*, it is Gudrun who achieves this kind of transcendence. Since her brothers killed her husband Sigurd, Gudrun betrays her brothers to her new husband, Attila the Hun. After they are slain, she takes her own life, and once dead, she becomes prophetic. Hearing the apocalyptic message of the Hanged God, she accepts his Inhumanism: "Without the pain, no knowledge of peace, nothing. Without the peace,/ No value in the pain." What is not clear is how the play's action leads to her concluding lines: "I will enter the cloud of stars,/ I will eat the whole serpent again."

Jeffers proceeded to express the oppressive symbolism of rocks, sun, stars, and wild animals in non-dramatic poems which can accommodate them better, and he did not again turn to drama until Judith Anderson successfully played Clytemnestra in 1941 in his *Tower Beyond Tragedy* (written in 1925). When a New York producer wished to star her as Medea, Jeffers agreed to adapt Euripides' tragedy. Predictably, Jeffers viewed the Greek tragic heroine as a woman of elemental passions whose violence should teach us to rise above mere human emotion.

Since Euripides' Medea is already a creature of large passions, Jeffers emphasizes this through imagery which derives from fire, water, minerals, and above all animals. Medea uses a dog image both for Creon and Jason: "You saw me low on my knees before the great dog of Corinth; humble, holding my heart in my hands/ For a dog to bite—break this dog's teeth!" And "Or if I could fire the room they sleep in, and hear them/ Wake in the white of the fire, and cry to each other, and howl like dogs."

More than the Medea of Euripides, that of Jeffers savors her revenge. In Euripides, Medea's specific plan is formulated and revealed right after the scene with Aegeus, which convinces her of men's love of their children. In Jeffers we do not know the details until after the event, but they are suggested by such obvious symbols as a mare who tears a stallion apart with her teeth and Medea's description of the golden robe: "That robe of bright-flowering gold, that bride-veil, that fish-net/ To catch a young slender salmon—not mute, she'll sing: her delicate body writhes in the meshes,/ The golden wreath binds her bright head with light: she'll dance, she'll sing loudly;/ Would I were there to hear it, that proud one howling." Rhyme and repeated vowels emphasize the savagery of Medea's desires.

The first messenger from the palace reports the joyous acceptance of Medea's gift, building suspense till Medea sends her old Nurse for the sadistic description of the deaths of Creusa and Creon. Unlike Euripides' Medea, that of Jeffers barely hesitates before killing her children. After the deed, Medea taunts Jason, showing him her blood-stained hand: "The wine I was pouring for you spilled on my hand—/ Dear were the little grapes that were crushed to make it; dear were the vineyards." Not coolly inhuman, Medea delights in the details of her horrible vengeance.

For a woman of such sadistic pleasure, her proud and moral conclusion seems incongruous. Medea declares that Jason would betray his sons' bodies for silver, punctuating the play's view of Jason as a calculating seeker of power. Medea, in contrast, has been true to her passions, and strong in her truth. Instead of her final appearance as a kind of goddess *ex machina*, as in Euripides,

Jeffers' Medea stands up tall to collect the bodies of her sons, intoning the final lines of the play: "Now I go forth/ Under the cold eyes of heaven—those weakness-despising stars:—not me they scorn." Clumsy as the compound adjective is, the words confirm her strength. In the context of Jeffers' work, we suspect that he admires his psychopathic heroine, who knows none of the womanly weakness of the Euripidean character. And yet the lush lines root her strength in the psychopathology of sadism. Hell hath no fury like a woman scorned, and Jeffers savors that fury, rewarding her finally with stars that do not scorn her.

A woman scorned is also the subject of Jeffers' last dramatic poem, *The Cretan Woman* (1954). The Cretan woman is, of course, Phaedra. Like Racine, Jeffers focuses on her, rather than on the pure and cold Hippolytus. And yet Jeffers borrows a Chorus from Euripides and retains the goddess Aphrodite, who announces: "We Gods and goddesses/ Must not be very scrupulous; we are forces of nature, vast and inflexible, and neither mercy/ Nor fear can move us. Men and women are the pawns we play with; we work our games out on a wide chess board,/ The great brown-and-green earth."

Aphrodite sets the plot moving. Phaedra declares her love to Hippolytus, who rejects her. Phaedra tells Theseus that Hippolytus has raped her, and in anger he stabs his son, whose dying words to Phaedra are: "I despise you." To Theseus: "My poor father." Off stage, Phaedra hangs herself, and Theseus prays to Poseidon to resurrect his son. But the dead do not live again, and Aphrodite smilingly delivers the final Inhumanist message to us: "In future days men will become so powerful/ That they seem to control the heavens and the earth,/ They seem to understand the stars and all science—/ Let them beware. Something is lurking hidden./ There is always a knife in the flowers. There is always a lion just beyond the firelight." But the warning is an addendum; it does not grow out of the action.

Jeffers uses myth to illustrate his Inhumanism—his view that man's grandeur lies in his stubborn and Stoic resistance to the petty ills and delights that flesh is heir to. Man achieves greatness only if he can view himself in the light of the inhuman—mountains and oceans, redwoods and boulders, hawks and lions. Though this rather puerile philosophy furnishes Jeffers with his rhythms and images, it is not only antipathetic to the modern temperament which tends to focus on the human, but it is antipathetic to dramatic form, whose imagery must be integrated into theater, whose rhythm must be spoken by actors. A nostalgia for poetic drama and thirst for operatic acting may explain the awe that greeted production of *Medea*, but today Jeffers' dramatic and undramatic poetry is most instructive as negative example, despite occasional regional revivals in California.

E. E. Cummings

The antithesis of Jeffers in theme and style, E. E. Cummings also reacted against modern American materialism. But rather than seek refuge in Inhumanism, Cummings exploited human and popular forms in his two excursions into drama. After writing poems, reviews, and a novel, Cummings turned to drama, publishing *him* in 1927. It was produced at the Provincetown Playhouse in 1928, but the group that launched O'Neill virtually sank Cummings as playwright. Variously interpreted as a burlesque show or a comedy about a man who married a dumb wife, *him* has been accumulating readers rather than audiences through the years, although it draws upon performance forms such as circus, vaudeville, jazz, and barker-salesman.

Him, the protagonist of Cummings' play, is at once a sensitive artist and a modern wise guy, attempting to discover his basic identity and his role in life. His wife-mistress, Me, is both help and hindrance in that quest. Cummings immerses the quest in such profuse verbal variety that the plot is often hard to follow. Eric Bentley's interpretation of the play is inspired by the painted backdrop, in which a Doctor is anesthetizing a woman.[6] Thus, the basic situation of the play may be Me's anesthetic-induced fantasies while she is giving birth to Him's child. Though this interpretation is possible, it reduces the play to a rational, realistic structure; moreover, Me does not seem capable of the imaginative flights of Acts II and III of Cummings' play.

Basically, Cummings' scenes are suggestive rather than explicit: beginning and end of the play explore the Him-Me relationship, whereas the bulky middle satirizes contemporary American civilization, largely by means of dialogue. Cummings' play overflows Me's literal consciousness, but birth images thread through the various idioms of the play, emphasizing the thematic importance of origins. As one of the Weird Sisters says: "Life is a matter of being born." And being born—literally and symbolically—is the matter of Cummings' play.

There are three levels of dialogue in *him*, and all three are comically oriented, with an underlying serious intention: 1) the probing conversations between Him and Me, 2) the near non-sense of the three Weird Sisters, and 3) a variety of dialects and idioms that mock modern America. All three levels are heard in the three acts of the play, but verbal diversity energizes the middle act—a play within the play, ostensibly written by Him, who is a poet-playwright.

Acts I and III of *him* are constructed with a certain symmetry. The five scenes of Act I alternate in pendulum fashion between the disjunctive pronouncements of the Weird Sisters and the general problems of the Him-Me couple; scenes i, iii, and v belong to the Weirds, scenes ii and iv to the couple. Though Act III is not quite so neat in the deployment of its seven scenes, there is comparable alternation; the Weird Sisters dominate scenes ii and iv; the problems of Him and Me are central to scenes i, v, and vii; scene iii is a *Walpurgisnacht* at Les Halles in Paris, and scene vi is a Vanity Fair in an American circus—both scenes sustaining the caricature America that is presented in Act II. Thus, scenes iii and vi of Act III depict the mindless world of Act II, whereas the rest of Act III depicts the mental world of Act I.

Act I opens and closes on the trivial non sequiturs of the Weird Sisters, describing a circle from the hippopotamus in scene i to the hippocampus in scene v. Not only zoology but history, geography, cuisine, figure in their small talk. In scene iii the three Weirds read Him's palm, telling his fortune in cryptic terms but cliché phrases. Logical nonsense, their gnomic syntagmae suggest that today's three Fates can merely utter disconnected slogans, whose ultimate import is weird. The first names of the Weird Sisters are Stop, Look, and Listen, and these injunctions recur throughout the play in which no one stops, looks searchingly, or listens attentively—except Him and Me. As the ancient Fates spun man's life from birth to death, Cummings' Weirds rock and knit, but they no longer control man's life. When Me is discovered with her newborn baby, the Weirds protest in unison: "It's all done with mirrors!" Though they do not realize it, this line—their last in the play—links them to Him's description of the hero of *his* play, "Mr. O. Him, the Man in the Mirror."

Mirror and window are fixed in adjoining walls of the stage room, symbolizing interior and exterior, microcosm and macrocosm. As the room rotates through the course of Cummings' play, we see mirror and window in different perspectives, but they remain in fixed relationship to one another. Speaking into the mirror, Him and Me express their relationship, while the window becomes our ear upon the many voices in American society. Me is window-oriented and Him mirror-oriented, but neither is allegorically fixed to window or mirror, and their respective speeches delineate a whole character. Me is direct, puzzled, intuitive. Him, always self-conscious, is a ham-actor and a poet-poseur. The first person and third person pronoun-names seem ironic, since Me does not focus upon herself, and Him does. Him awes and irritates Me by drawing upon the vocabulary and rhythms of advertising, genetics, soap opera, automobile mechanics, murder mysteries, metaphysics, geometry, and especially the circus. The rapid succession of references is a preview of his Act II play within the play, where a different idiom will pervade each scene.

In Act II, Him and Me become voices in the dark; they are the only voices in scene i, and they punctuate every other scene but the last one. In these scenes, presumably written by Him, the Doctor plays a major role, and he changes verbal style with his changes of role.

Each of Him's eight scenes parodies a different kind of popular entertainment, and Cummings' play thrives on this burlesque of theatrical rather than literary forms. Though Him's Act I references to theater are Aristotelian—"pity and terror incorporated," "I've got the machine who's got the god?"—his Act II play is composed of vaudeville skits. Him presents his play to Me as a rollicking farce, "How Dyuh Get that Way?"

Though his comments to Me introduce each new scene, there is no apparent order to the sequence. Scene ii presents stage drunks, followed by a caricature virgin reciting a testimonial for a laxative. Scene iii is a virtual monologue of a patent medicine salesman, appropriately declaimed by the Doctor. Scene iv is a parody of O'Neill's *Great God Brown* (produced in 1926, the year before *him* was published) as murder mystery. In scene v, the dramatization of the Frankie-and-Johnny blues song is punctuated by a self-appointed censor who inveighs against obscenity in a 320-word sentence of self-righteous cant. Scene vi presents us with an Englishman carrying his Unconscious in a trunk on his back; like the Medusa-head, the mere sight of it kills, so that we see the successive deaths of a detective speaking stage New Yorkese and a policeman speaking the same dialect. In scene vii two cigar-smoking, balloon-carrying tycoons carry on monosyllabic conversations aboard an ocean liner. Scene viii lavishly presents sycophantic homosexuals fawning on Mussolini in a Rome designed after Boston's Old Howard Burlesque House. In the final scene of Act II, an Interlocutor (played by Him) attempts to convince a Gentleman (played by the Doctor) of the misery of the masses, but only direct confrontation with hunger awakens the Gentleman to its reality. Once aware of people's plight, the Gentleman removes his clothes and declares that he has just been born. Lacking the caricature quality of the other scenes, this serious interlude is incongruous and unconvincing. But the final incident reflects mockingly on the main action of Cummings' play. Instead of the Doctor attending the birth of Him's baby, the Doctor *is* the newborn baby in Him's play.

Though Act III brings us back to the frame play, several Act II characters enter scene iii as tourists, and all the Act II characters reappear in Act III, scene vi—but not until Him and Me have taken up the burden of their personal relationship. When Him leaves Me, the disjunctive dialogue of the Weird Sisters seems especially suitable for the situation of the protagonists. In this final act, there is no realistic basis for the *Walpurgisnacht* scene Au Père Tranquille in Les Halles of Paris. In keeping with the name of the establishment, everyone is asleep until the bell wakens them to action. After some tedious conversation, meant to reveal the vapidity of the American bourgeois tourist (including the Gentleman of Act II, scene ix, Will and Bill of Act II, scene iv), Him enters with the cabbage from which he claims recent entry into the world—another variant upon the birth theme.

Him, back from Paris, meets Me by accident, but he seeks to invest that accident with meaning. Through dream and memory, he arrives at a hesitant understanding of their relationship. No longer indulging in verbal display, Him couches his new understanding in abstractions: "I cannot feel that everything has been a mistake—that I have inhabited an illusion with you merely to escape from reality and the knowledge of ourselves." His soul-searching is interrupted by the vulgar voice of a Circus Barker, full of concrete images: "Ladies un gentlmun right dis way step dis way evrybudy tuh duh Princess Anankay tuh duh Tatooed Man tuh duh Huemun Needle tuh duh Missin Link tuh duh Queen uv Soipunts tuh duh Nine Foot Giun tuh duh Eighteen Inch Lady tuh duh Six Hunduh Pouns uv Passionut Pullcrytood tuh duh Kink uv Borneo dut eats ee-lectrick light bulbs!" Played by the Doctor, this hunch-backed Circus Barker spews a long sales pitch at the characters of Act II. Him's Act II play is replaced by these Circus freaks, who provoke brief conformist comments from the spectators. Then the Barker announces the final freak, "the Huemun Form Divine," and it proves to be Me with a newborn baby. The dreamlike associations of an anesthetized woman of the backdrop and the zigzag path of Him's stage pilgrimage result dramatically in this baby, which inspires a fond look from Me, a cry of horror from Him, and which crystallizes Me's intuitive acceptance as opposed to Him's obsessive intellection.

In the final scene of Cummings' play, back in the room with window and mirror (imaginary as at the beginning), neither Him nor Me refers to the events of the play we have seen. Instead, Me indicates to Him that the imaginary fourth wall of the room is in fact the real theater audience. She summarizes and undermines illusionistic theater: "They're pretending that this room and you and I are real." The final lines of the play attempt to reconcile the dichotomy between window and mirror by embracing all the occupants of the theater.

241

HIM: I wish I could believe this.
ME: You can't.
HIM: Why?
ME: Because this is true.

But like the real theater audience, who pretend the actors are real characters, reality must accommodate the mirror of poetic truth. As Him has come to value Me's intuition above knowledge, Me seems to embrace Him's need of more than literal truth. Through the series of disjunctive scenes, Cummings' *him* makes a simple point—that a child is born of creativity, which is in turn a compound of truth and love. The loquacious bulk of the play, however, dwells on the uncreative, untruthful, unloving aspects of American life. Avant garde for its time, *him* today appears self-indulgent in its verbal flow. As Denis Donoghue wrote of Cummings: "He seems to write in the hope that what he hates will be obliterated by the sheer profusion of his words."[7]

Less profuse, Cummings' five-scene *Santa Claus* (1941) also ends in victory for feeling and creativity. Lacking *him*'s fantasy and satire, *Santa Claus* is a rather childish allegory subtitled "A Morality." In medieval morality plays, Vice and Virtue struggle for the soul of Everyman, and Cummings bases his modern Morality on a comparable psychomachia. The Vice figure is Death, and the Virtue figure is Santa Claus, but we do not know this until the end of the play. Instead of an Everyman figure, Death and Santa Claus are each in search of salvation. Exchanging masks, each ventures out in the guise of the other. Since the morality play is built on their basic opposition, though, each retains his own viewpoint. The sentimentalities of Santa Claus are challenged by the snappy slang of Death, but virtue triumphs. Death is lynched by a mob whose existence he denied, and Santa Claus is reunited with the Woman who is Love. This finale has been contrived by their child, who penetrates all disguises.

Santa Claus is a pretty fairy tale for the very young. Denis Donoghue pointed out (in admiration): "Most of the thought of the play is in the slogans and the ideas which are invoked, in all reverence, to destroy the slogans."[8] But the references are ready-made. For a grownup audience, Understanding has to *earn* its triumph over Knowledge, and Love over ubiquitous Death. A Morality is no longer an adult genre.

WILLIAM CARLOS WILLIAMS

LIKE CUMMINGS, WILLIAMS WAS FITFULLY INTERESTED IN THEATER; he took part in many plays during the course of his active life, but he has published only four dramas, written between 1940 and 1960. The best known of these is *Many Loves* (1942), which ran for over a year (1959–1960) in the repertory of the Living Theatre at a time when they were committed to verse drama.

Williams himself has summarized the structure of *Many Loves:* "[*Many Loves*] is made up of three completely unrelated sequences, written in prose—one forming the substance of each act—and a counter-plot, in modern verse, which binds them together. The theme of each 'playlet,' and of the counterplay, is love—of a sort.

In the first sequence, a young man loves an older, married woman. In the second, a young man and young woman of high school age—comparable to the lovers of Romance—are assailed by the girl's father. [The girl seeks solace in the arms of a Lesbian.] In the third of these prose playlets, an older man and a younger woman engage in a mild intrigue.

In the counter-play, the love is between two men, an elder and another, younger one. Here the dramatic action hinges on the necessity for the younger, who is the author of the three short pieces, to get the older man, his presumptive backer, to finance the production of his play—but without concessions. For the poet-playwright is in love with and about to marry his leading lady, a fact which he tries to keep secret from his enamored backer. The discovery of this love by the backer supplies the climax and catastrophe of the play."

In today's theater we no longer consider that plays on the same theme are "completely unrelated." Williams achieves independent actions in the three playlets within the larger play, and he creates a distinctive idiom for each playlet—colloquial urban speech in the first, colloquial farm dialect in the second, and colloquial suburban conversation in the third. Williams uses his distinctive short free line for the verse that links the three plays. Williams' well-known dictum from *Patterson*—"No ideas but in things."—proves to be viable for the stage. In the frame play of *Many Loves*, playwright Hubert and angel Peter voice several ideas about drama, but the ideas arise from the "things" that we see—the three short plays within the frame, in each of which love fails.

In the first play, a married woman has had an affair with a boy about to be drafted. He leaves her with the phrase: "So long. I'll send you a post card." Another boy of draft age declares his love for her, and the married Serafina replies: "You've got a crust." Her final words to him are: "Good-bye, sucker!" The flat language submerges sentimentality, but the very spareness submerges resonance as well. Only a rabbit, which has been killed for Serafina's pregnancy test, looms symbolically in this city warren.

The second playlet is more ambitious, since Williams sketches three generations of the disappearing farm life of New Jersey. The action moves from the worn-out farm family—"You're like to do him an injury, Pete, shoving a man of his age around thata way."—to teen-agers who seek escape from their farm heritage —"You bring his little girl home at five in the morning—with the reputation you got. And you want him to meet you with a brass band, I suppose, and a bunch of flowers." As in his poems, Williams finds an image for this moribund farm life—the farm itself, which will be transformed by the new owner, a successful New York City businesswoman, a Lesbian. As the city Lesbian announces that she will buy the farm, the old owner dies in his sleep. The Lesbian takes his teen-age grandchild in her arms: "It's all right, darling. I'll take care of you." The cliché phrases contrast with the unusual visual image (for 1942)—the embryonic Lesbian love, the dead man who has loved his farm, and the middle-aged couple who have betrayed both generations.

The third playlet offers a comparably telling contrast; as the suburban housewife tries to seduce her pediatrician, the woman's child interrupts them with the single word: "Daddy." During the course of the talky playlet, however, the pediatrician functions like a psychiatrist while Clara, the married woman, rambles associationally through her life. She in turn serves to stir the doctor's memories; and both sets of memories are ignorant of the meaning of love. The woman is resentful that a child has resulted from her own effort to find love: "This isn't a hundred and fifty years ago. These are modern times—people don't have babies like that any more. Isn't that what causes war, too many babies?"

The woman finds talk restful, but the doctor finds it an evasion: "And pretty soon we'll all be dead forever and never have opened our eyes wide once—wide, that is, to see what actually . . . starved as we live, because we never, never, never, never took a chance among the five or six thousands or million people of our small personal world to know them actually and individually . . . what actually the creature in the next bin is doing or feeling." As in Williams' poetry, the flat language sings through careful deployment of sound—the variety of vowels and consonants, contrasting with repetitions—actually, ever, never. The image of the bin links the last play to the warren image of the first; the child who interrupts the erotic scene is carrying a toy rabbit *"almost as big as herself."* We are all rabbits, implies Williams, except for our rare moments of love.

The three playlets dissolve into a fourth, the counter-play that involves the characters of the frame play. The elegant verse of the frame contrasts with the hesitant prose of the playlets. After a scene in which the actress Alise threatens to shoot the homosexual Peter, who is jealous of her, Peter assents to a heterosexual wedding between playwright and actress, and he sends for a minister and champagne. When Alise announces that she is going to have a baby, the Minister responds: "Yes, yes,/ of course, my dear, what else is marriage for?" Not only are the many loves linked thematically, but Alise's announcement of pregnancy links the frame play to the pregnancy motif in each of the playlets—the rabbit test of Serafina, the fear of teen-age Ann, Clara's dislike of children. The minister's reply is all-inclusive; Nature's purpose is the propagation of the race, and to this the "many loves" must be accommodated: "What else is marriage for?" The unhappy loves of the playlets converge to be reversed in the climactic marriage of the frame.

Williams' next play, *A Dream of Love* (1948), is a more problematical examination of marriage. Intended for Broadway, the
play treats that stock subject, a lovers' triangle. Williams pref-
aces his play with a quotation from Symonds' translation of
Agamemnon; Menelaus, abandoned by Helen, dreams of her love.
But Williams' play does not quite parallel this classical lovers'
triangle. The Menelaus-character is a Doctor's wife, and Helen
is a middle-aged doctor who loves his wife. Paris becomes a
young married woman whom the Doctor takes to a hotel room,
and the Doctor dies during their adulterous interlude, undertaken to renew his relationship with his wife. The grief-stricken
wife is confronted by her rival, and she reacts hysterically. Neither eating nor resting in the week since the Doctor's death, the
wife falls into an exhausted sleep and dreams of the Doctor, who
recounts the details of his love affair in the hotel room. He
speaks of poetry before making love, and this suddenly erupts
into the Civil War on stage. When the wife awakens to answer
the telephone, she says firmly: "The doctor isn't here. No!"
With these words, the wife resumes her own life, minus a
"dream of love."

Like Williams himself, the play's protagonist is a doctor-poet.
In the early days of his marriage, the protagonist had written a
Williams-like poem about a dream of love:

>   —a dream
>   we dreamed
>   each
>   separately
>   we two
>   of love
>   and of
>   desire—
>
>   that fused
>   in the night—
>
>   A dream
>   a little false
>   toward which

now
  we stand
    and stare
transfixed—

All at once
    in the east
rising!
    All white!

a locust cluster
a shad bush
    blossoming

And so
  we live
  looking—

a dream
    toward which
we love—
at night
    more
than a little
    false—

We have bred
we have dug
we have figured up
our costs
we have bought
an old rug—

We batter at our
unsatisfactory
    brilliance—

There is no end
    to desire—

Only in her dream does the doctor's wife come to understand that there is indeed "no end/ to desire." Nowhere does the play's dialogue match the poem's lyricism, as the reality of love nowhere matches its dream. The long drawn out explication of the poem adds no drama to the play. Husband and wife, mistress and lover, and above all wife and mistress speak in the banal idiom of Broadway and Hollywood triangles, which betrays instead of illustrating the poem at the heart of the play. Moreover, the intensity of the triangular situation is diffused by too much dialogue assigned to minor characters—a Negro maid, a Milkman, the husband of the mistress of the Doctor. One need only contrast Williams' triangle with that of Beckett in *Play*, to see the achievement of a dramatic poet in this stale domain.

Williams engaged in only that one flirtation with Broadway, but the political climate of the Joe McCarthy era inspired him to return to the device of the play within the play. *Tituba's Children* (1950) deals with the same subject as Arthur Miller's *Crucible*, which followed it by three years. Like the well-known Miller play, the drama is melodrama—all the good guys are against the witch-hunt. Although Williams and Miller both focus on a single protagonist-victim, Williams' play leaves an effect of confusion.

In each of Williams' two acts, a scene in 1692 is followed by a scene in 1950, and yet the earlier scenes do not quite fit within the frame of the modern ones. In Scene 2, set in a night-club in modern Washington, a Hallowe'en entertainment deals, improbably, with the Salem trials. The witch-hunt is parallelled by the twentieth-century persecution of Mac McDee, a young State Department liberal. In the seventeenth-century scene, the Negro servant Tituba is frightened into testifying that the children were bewitched, and her testimony helps condemn the early liberals. In the twentieth-century scene, a good-natured night-club entertainer comforts McDee while his wife is bearing twins in a hospital. Though she says nothing to damage him, caricature reactionary senators use her to soil the reputation of the young liberal. Finally, twentieth-century McDee is arrested, and seventeenth-century Giles Cory is condemned.

Like Miller after him, Williams researched his material. In spite of the title, however, the Salem part of Williams' play does not focus on Tituba, and it is difficult to recognize the modern senators as her children. The atmosphere of hysteria is synthetic rather than tense. Williams makes almost no concession to seventeenth-century English, and his direct quotation from contemporary testimony is not integrated into the language of his play, as the seventeenth-century trial is not integrated into the modern framework. The innocent McDee, the good-hearted Stella, and the night-club entertainer Tony occasionally speak in verse lines, but the rhythms are too subtle to be heard on stage.

Reading the testimony of those years, one often has the feeling of witnessing a bad melodrama written in stale language, but this places even greater responsibility upon the playwright—that his language be sufficiently memorable to expose the cruel clichés for what they are. The final flat lines of Williams' chorus fail by their didacticism:

> It is useless. You cannot divert
> the doom which the blood of brother
> and brother has brought upon us.
> Some day we shall be wiser.

If the Salem scenes were meant to dramatize "the blood of brother/ and brother," they are too diffuse to carry conviction. And there is nothing in the play to justify the (ironically?) optimistic conclusion. In contrast, the old ballad of Giles Cory rings out more meaningfully than Williams' dialogue, which is an unfused medley of direct documentary quotation, worn political cliché, abrupt lyric flight, and heavy night-club humor. More than in his other two plays, Williams' effort at wide idiomatic inclusion results in confusion. The dialogue jangles when he tries to imitate *Patterson's* richness.

In 1952, after suffering his first paralyzing stroke, Williams began his last play, *The Cure*. Increasingly debilitated, he nevertheless completed it in 1960. A triumph of will-power, it should be viewed only as such.

249

DIALOGUE IN AMERICAN DRAMA

Archibald MacLeish

MacLeish is easily the most successful poet turned playwright of the generation born in the last years of the nineteenth century—largely because of a single play, *JB*. But MacLeish's devotion to the theater has lasted through four decades, since he published *Nobodaddy* in 1926 and *Herakles* in 1967, with six plays (or dramatic poems) falling between those years.⁹ Two of his plays are based on classical myth, two on the Bible, and the other four are frankly contemporary. Changing rhythm and idiom for the different plays, MacLeish might appear to be gifted with what T. S. Eliot called "the third voice of poetry—when [the poet] attempts to create a dramatic character speaking in verse."¹⁰ In most of his plays, however, MacLeish's characters tend to speak a similar verse, which sometimes resembles MacLeish's own lyric voice.

Nobodaddy is omitted from the list of plays on the flyleaf of the recently published *Herakles*, so that discussion is inappropriate when the author evidently does not wish to claim the play. But passing mention may be made of aspects that prefigure *JB*, also a biblical play. The title, *Nobodaddy*, derives from Blake, who gave this name to those who pay lip service to God, but who are really of the devil's party. In MacLeish's play, the designation is ambiguous, but it seems to point to the absent God. The first two acts recount the Fall of Adam, as we listen to him listening to the temptations of the invisible devil; in the third act, Cain, provoked by Abel's unquestioning orthodoxy, slays his brother. Eve endures through the whole play, offering her love first to Adam and then to Cain, both of whom wish to be as gods.

In his Foreword to *Nobodaddy*, MacLeish calls it a "poem," and all three acts of the poem contain static discussions before momentous deeds—Adam's eating the apple and Cain's murdering Abel. Early in *Nobodaddy*, Adam declares: "I am a god. I say I am a god." By the end of the poem, Cain, having killed his brother, defies God and even implies his non-existence: "Where are you, god? Where are you, god? Speak to me—" But God does not speak. As the poet says in his Foreword, MacLeish is dealing with "the condition of self-consciousness in an indifferent universe." And the indifferent universe has no voice.

In the socially conscious 1930's, MacLeish shifted his dramatic concern from self-consciousness to social consciousness, writing *Panic* (1935), *The Fall of the City* (1937), and *Air-Raid* (1939). The titles summarize the subjects. The particular panic is the reaction to the bank failures of 1933. Financier McGafferty first refuses to panic in a time of crisis and finally shoots himself rather than face the accusations of the mass of poor people. The play is influenced by Expressionist counterpoint between a mechanical, monstrous protagonist and the mass of men he wrongs. MacLeish's preface is influenced, on the other hand, by T. S. Eliot's essay on the nature of dramatic poetry. MacLeish rejects blank verse, substituting trochaic lines with five accents and any number of unaccented syllables. In his preface, he theorizes; "The rhythms of contemporary American speech . . . are nervous, not muscular; excited, not deliberate; vivid, not proud. . . . The voices of men talking intently to each other in the offices or the mills or on the streets of this country *descend from* stressed syllables; they do not rise *toward stressed* syllables as do the voices of men speaking in Shakespeare's plays." Hence iambs give way to trochees and dactyls in *Panic*.

Rarely has a practising poet been deafer to spoken rhythms. Not only does MacLeish analyze rhythms out of context of meaning, but his arbitrary disposition of accents creates the staccato telegraphese of Expressionism; the hiccuping rhythm serves the tickertapes of *Panic*, but it fragments stage speech, as in the following example of McGafferty's address to fellow financiers: "Yes and twenty more. And why? What's done it?/ Who's behind it? That's the question gentlemen." At other times, an incongruous blank verse rhythm peeps through the falling lines, as when McGafferty's mistress speaks of love: "Have we not given love and taken it?/ What *did* we give and take then? What's the thing/ Given and taken in a bed at night but/ Love? What other have you ever wanted?" Since MacLeish himself did not reuse this rhythm for subsequent plays, no more need be said of its thudding monotony.

In *Panic*, idiom matches rhythm, for McGafferty piles up nouns as though to replace the fortune he has lost. Cleanth Brooks has compared McGafferty to a driver whose automobile has stopped, but, who, knowing nothing about mechanics, orates about the engine. [11] McGafferty also cuddles loquaciously in the back seat, and his suicide resembles a flat tire.

Both *Fall of the City* and *Air Raid* are radio plays with a collective protagonist. In the former, a city does not defend itself against its enemy; in the latter, village women do not take shelter from an enemy air raid. Since both plays are indefinite in locale, the first was hailed as prophetic of the Austrian *anschluss*, and the second was related to the disaster at Guernica. Rather than conveying the concreteness of history, however, both plays contain a people's disbelief in the war that destroys them; ironically, the disbelief carries more conviction than the destruction, grown familiar as our daily food in our own era.

In the two years that separate these two plays, MacLeish's hopes for radio drama rose and fell. Though these plays have been produced on stage, they are self-indulgent in elocutionary effects that ring hollow in the theater. [12] The Announcer, for example, is superfluous where we can see what he describes, and the Chorus is heavy in its pontifical stance. Though the plays treat social violence, they are dramatically static, lingering too determinedly on sound play, facile generalization, hammered repetition, and pastoral description.

After more than a decade of public service, MacLeish turned again to dramatic form in the 1950's, and his first two efforts are, like the radio plays, almost bare of visual appeal. Like the radio plays, too, they are determinedly poetic in their idiom. And like the radio plays, *The Trojan Horse* (1952, subtitled a poem rather than play) is socially oriented. As in *Fall of the City* and *Air Raid*, the collective protagonist, Troy, brings about its own destruction. Against the advice of Laocoon, and misinterpreting the advice of Helen, the Trojans admit the treacherous horse, and the play closes on Cassandra's predictions of doom. Formal and rhetorical, MacLeish's verse ranges through loose trimeters, tetrameters, and pentameters; there is too much rhythmic variation for the slight play, and there is no apparent reason for the variety. Often skillful in itself, the verse does not respond to the drama of events, and the entire dialogue seems to reach us across a great distance.

MacLeish followed *The Trojan Horse* with a different kind of verse play, *This Music Crept By Me Upon the Waters* (1953), taking its title from Shakespeare's *Tempest*. Denis Donoghue has summed up the fusion (and occasional confusion) of theme and atmosphere: "The pervading mood of the play arises from those circumstances in which a person of utmost sensitivity feels the impact of elemental forms."[13] In *This Music*, the elemental forms are a full moon upon the Caribbean, and the pervading mood is one of awe. In a cast of ten, nine characters are sensitive to the extraordinary quality of this particular moonrise; we actually hear the reactions of four characters, and we hear about the other six.

So moved are two of the characters, Elizabeth and Peter, that they decide to build a life upon their common (but not shared) response to the moon. Though they are willing to leave their respective spouses, they do not wish to injure them, and Peter returns from the inspirational to the quotidian when his wife is suddenly missing. Not in peril, she has been cooking potatoes in the kitchen, but the possibility of her loss dissipates Peter's exultation, and Elizabeth closes the play: "Yes,/ And Ann's potatoes. Are you coming, Peter?" The Shakespearean title thuds down to earthy potatoes.

As Donoghue points out, this kind of mood play derives from Maeterlinck, and Elizabeth quite appropriately quotes from Apollinaire. But Maeterlinck and Apollinaire sustain their moods through metaphors that harmonize with their total decorum. MacLeish, on the other hand, makes impossible demands upon his propped or lighted moon, and his characters react with what Donoghue aptly calls "strained metaphors."[14]

> ELIZABETH: [The moon] burns like silence in a mirror.
> ALICE: Between the slidings of the sea a syllable.

These are typical post-Symbolist images, but they are incongruous on the tongues of these jet-setters *(avant la lettre)*. Instead, MacLeish can sometimes capture the brittle quality of conversation:

> OLIVER: God, will they never come? I'm starving.
> It must be going on for nine.
> CHUCK: It's eight.
> OLIVER: Not by the belt I buckle.

Though MacLeish does not supply a spectrum of styles for the ten characters of this brief play, he does distinguish between the least sensitive, Harry Keogh, and the most sensitive, Elizabeth.

KEOGH: Keeps his cocktails in his car,
    The thoughtful bastard.
ELIZABETH: Each minute like the last that will be:
    Each like the first that ever was.

It is in the broad middle eight characters that MacLeish makes errors in diction, and there is too much broad middle against which to highlight the poetic sensitivity of Elizabeth. Nevertheless, the mood play taught MacLeish to use words to build a specific mood, curbing his tendency toward prolixity.

This lesson stood him in best stead for his most successful play, *JB* (1958), his humanistic version of the biblical Job story. As in *Nobodaddy*, written thirty years earlier, MacLeish is concerned with "the condition of self-consciousness in an indifferent universe." In the interval, MacLeish learned to personify the indifference of the universe as divinity, and he has distributed the self-consciousness between several characters, though the central awareness is that of JB, the modern Job.

Structurally, MacLeish modifies the biblical story by the addition of a frame play involving two actors, Zuss and Nickles, who are obscurely driven to stage the drama of Job. By means of the frame, MacLeish seeks to emphasize both the timeliness and the timelessness of the biblical theme; Zuss puns on Zeus with its resonances of classical divinity, and the name of the Satan figure, Nickles, at once suggests the colloquial Old Nick and the modern world of nickels and dollars.

In the original published version, *JB* is divided into a Prologue and eleven scenes; for the New York production, the play was shortened to two acts. At the suggestion of New York director Elia Kazan, conflicts were sharpened, speeches tightened, events speeded, and the conclusion was more sharply focused on JB.[15] As in the case of Tennessee Williams' *Glass Menagerie*, it is unfortunate that the acting version of *JB*—the playwright's final revision—is less widely circulated than the reading version.

Our first impression is that of the world as circus. *"The raking of the rings and the hang of the canvas give a sense that the audience too is inside the huge, battered, ancient* [circus] *tent."* In the acting version, the opening lines—broken and hesitant tetrameters—belong to two Roustabouts who set the tent up for this night's show. When Zuss and Nickles enter, with their balloons and popcorn, we see them as part of the modern circus, but they lose no time in announcing the old Job story: "Here's where Job sits —at the table."

The two Roustabouts are indistinguishable in their first brief tent-raising appearance, but they are consistently differentiated in their subsequent roles. As soldiers who announce the first catastrophe to Job and Sarah—the death of their son, David— they speak crudely, except for a lyric touch by the Second: "How, by night, by chance, darkling .../ By the dark of chance . . ." As reporters who announce to Job and Sarah the automobile accident in which two of their children die, the Roustabouts add cruelty to their crudeness, and the Second Reporter waxes poetic: "There's always someone has to—someone/ Chosen by the chance of seeing,/ By the accident of sight—/ Having witnessed, having seen . . ." As Policemen who announce to Job and Sarah the rape and murder of their youngest daughter, they understate the news, and again it is the Second Policeman who expresses himself in imagery: "Out in the desert in the tombs/ Are potter's figures; two of warriors, / Two of worthies, two of monsters./ Ask them why. They will not answer you . . ./ Can the tooth among the stones make answer? . . ./ Can the seven bones reply? . . ./ Death is a bone that stammers . . . a tooth/ Among the flints that has forgotten." In the last appearance of the Roustabouts, as Civil Defense Officers, the Second actor lapses into metaphor: "Two words. I don't know what they mean./ I have brought them to you like a pair of pebbles/ Picked up in a path or a pair of/ Beads that might belong to somebody." And it is he who sounds the biblical: "I ONLY AM ESCAPED ALONE TO TELL THEE."

Though these poetic touches are unsubtle, they do dovetail with the colloquial dialogue of the First Roustabout to obtain the timely and timeless effect that MacLeish clearly seeks. Moreover, the Second Roustabout's repetition of the biblical line

255

prepares for the Act II displacement of the two messengers of disaster by the biblical Comforters. Not only do events conspire cumulatively against JB, but people too; for all their crudeness, the two Roustabouts are less cruel than the three complacent Comforters.

In their first appearance, the Comforters squat close to Job as "in the Blake etching," and MacLeish caricatures them verbally as Blake does, graphically, but MacLeish draws his caricatures in a contemporary context—psychiatrist, labor leader, and collarless cleric. Each of the three Comforters uses professional jargon—"Guilt is a/ Psychophenomenal situation," "*History* is justice," "Happy the man whom God correcteth!" Each of the three Comforters states his inflexible position with verbose rhetoric, so that it is not always clear what that position is, but its inflexibility is always clear. Man cannot know guilt because his actions are determined—whether by Freud, Marx, or God. These comfortless Comforters speak in dimeter rhymes, chanting without thought, reducing the magnificence of creation to a repulsive image: "We watch the stars/ That creep and crawl/ Like dying flies/ Across the wall/ of night! . . . And shriek! . . ./ and that is all." Only after they leave does JB make his most impassioned plea to God, to be answered by the biblical Voice out of the Whirlwind, whose words MacLeish selects, aligning them in rough tetrameters.

The biblical Comforters depart before we hear the Voice, which is only vaguely sensed by the Chorus of Women that MacLeish invents. That Chorus enters late in Act I—victims of a bombardment, like JB and Sarah. Unlike the Messengers, the Chorus offers human warmth to JB; unlike the Comforters, the Chorus makes no judgments; unlike JB, the Chorus asks no questions of God. Appropriately, they speak unrhetorically—complaining, curious, and compassionate. They simply endure, and they help us understand JB's final acceptance of his own suffering.

The different idioms of Chorus, Comforters, and Messengers insist upon the modernity of the Job story, but MacLeish's main bid for contemporary relevance lies in the playlong exchange between Zuss and Nickles. Ostensibly actors in the biblical drama, they paradoxically become more involved in the story as their roles diminish to those of spectators. Though the speech of Zuss is always dignified, that of Nickles can snap into slang (rejuvenated as he is between the reading and acting versions of the play).

The two actor-vendors feel compelled to stage the Job story, but their roles have evidently not been assigned. Zuss plays God "naturally," but Nickles first assumes that he will be Job. Embarrassed, Zuss informs him that "there's always/ Someone playing Job," and that Nickles is to be Zuss' opposite. Like Goethe's Mephistopheles, Nickles is the spirit who always denies, and much of the play's energy derives from his sardonically negative comments upon JB's righteousness. And yet, his philosophic nursery rhyme, twice repeated, is not negative, and it describes the conduct of *JB* rather than that of Satan, upon whom Nickles is modelled: "If God is God He is not good,/ If God is good He is not God;/ Take the even, take the odd,/ I would not sleep here if I could/ Except for the little green leaves in the wood/ And the wind on the water." Reductive as the lines are, they do pose the problem of evil, and they do suggest a pastoral, almost pantheistic acceptance of good *and* evil. Rhythmically and dramatically, the jingle contrasts sharply with the Distant Voice, which is heard shortly afterwards: "WHENCE COMEST THOU?" The Voice awes both actors into a realization that they are playing something larger than their roles, and it evokes their attitudes that will be consistent through the rest of the play —Zuss cleaves to the Book, but Nickles rebels against the script. Near the end as near the beginning, Nickles undercuts Zuss' eloquent panegyrics to God.

ZUSS: Infinite mind in midge of matter!
NICKLES: Infinite mush!

ZUSS: searchless power
    Burning upon the hearth of stars—
NICKLES: Where did I put that *popcorn* . . .

During the course of the action of the play within the play, Nickles' idiom varies from the succinct contemporary "That's our pigeon." to the factual presentation of disasters—"a daughter raped and murdered by an idiot!"—to his final Satanic wishful thinking, "Job will fling it in God's face/ With half his guts to make it spatter!/ He'd rather suffocate in dung,/ Drown in ordure—"

But of course neither Job nor JB suffocates in dung, drowns in ordure. The biblical Job puts Satan behind him; MacLeish's JB says neither "Yes in ignorance" nor "No in spite." Though Nickles recited a rhyme about "little green leaves in the wood," his negative spirit prevents him from recognizing the green leaves on Sarah's branch, which will confirm JB's positive acceptance of life and love, in spite of loss. The play within the play, the dramatization of the Job story, ends in triumph—for JB, Job, and, by implication, the human race.

Traditionally, a play within the play creates distance toward the inner play, and MacLeish manipulates such distance with skill. We first hear the voice of JB after listening to the imposing words of biblical Job and Satan. Suitably, JB establishes his Job-connection through delivering the Lord's Prayer at a Thanksgiving feast. Immediately, however, the dialogue plummets to trivia; this is no Keatsian feast of St. Agnes, but home-grown American food described in homey Americanisms, liberal with imprecise adjectives. JB's wife Sarah calls him Job, but he speaks like a caricature American business executive; his energy is subsumed by initials—J.B. In the "lucky story," a family legend, Job is "J.B." to the envious Patrick Sullivan.

The story itself—an old one—is told theatrically, and it harmonizes thematically with the play's presentation of a humanist Job. JB's family likes the story as evidence of JB's faith in God's power; Sullivan, resenting God's world, has to call upon God to forbid that world. This is literally taking the name of the Lord in vain. And it prefigures JB's final action by negative contrast. When JB comes to resent God's world, he forgives God and ignores Him, accepting a new life in human terms. As various hostile theologians have pointed out, MacLeish recasts biblical Job in the mould of a humanist hero.[16] But MacLeish's JB grows to heroism.

In the opening Thanksgiving scene, JB speaks like a fatuous American tycoon. Without the pretentiousness of McGafferty of *Panic*, he is nevertheless smug in his very simplicity, his taste running to lucky stories and family rhymes. When JB lingers in the dining-room, his lapse into metaphysics is incongruous: "Caught as we are in Heaven's quandary/ Is it we or they are gone/ Under the grass tree,/ Under the green tree." But "green" picks up the theme of Nickles' rhyme and predicts the pantheist end.

Before the end, JB is assaulted with the series of disasters, to which he reacts with clichés: "It isn't true. . . . It . . . happened . . ." and "God, let me die. God, let me die." But JB doesn't die, and he subsides into acceptance, reciting the biblical words. The most moving passage in the play calls on Shakespeare as well as the Bible, when Sarah abandons JB.

JB: THE LORD GIVETH . . . Say it!
SARAH: THE LORD GIVETH
JB: THE LORD TAKETH AWAY . . .
SARAH: Takes!
        Kills! Kills! Kills! Kills!

Afterward, Sarah elaborates too loquaciously on the point she has already made with Lear's passion. And afterward, neither she nor JB relax their high rhetorical stance.

At the suggestion of Elia Kazan, director of the Broadway Production, Sarah's role was reduced in the final scene, but her role is still important. It is she who, earlier, has picked up Nickles' mocking sound play on "God" and "good," and it is she who finally arrives with "the small green branch" that fulfills the green hints of Nickles and the family rhyme. In the heroic humanism of the finale, MacLeish forces his imagery, as in Sarah's account of her rejction of suicide: "I thought there was a way away/ Out of the world. Out of the world./ Water under bridges opens out of the world. Out of the world./ Closing and the companion stars/ Still float there afterwards. I thought the door/ Opened into closing water." The lines convey neither the feeling nor the meaning of despair, but the repetitive *statement* of a desire to be "out of the world."

Kazan insisted that the play's climax should come through JB rather than Sarah, and MacLeish attempted to provide that climax in the acting version, partly through imagery: "Blow on the coal of the heart, poor Sarah." This is a blurred echo of Yeats' great lines: "Whatever flames upon the night/ Man's own resinous heart has fed." Nevertheless, it *is* an image and not an abstraction. The final lines of JB, however, which are the final lines of the play, are inflated with abstraction: "We *are* and that is all our answer./ We are and what we are can suffer./ But . . . what suffers loves. And love/ Will live its suffering again,/ Risk its own defeat again,/ Endure the loss of everything again/ And yet again and yet again/ In doubt, in dread, in ignorance, unanswered,/ Over and over, with the dark before,/ The dark behind it . . . and still love . . . still love." The single image of "dark" is inadequate to anchor these abstractions that sound, not like poetry, but like a sermon.

It might be argued that the humanistic choice of MacLeish's JB justifies a human language that *should* sound inadequate by contrast to the biblical words of a theistic Job, but this is the wrong kind of inadequacy. A humanistic JB needs concrete human imagery, rather than abstraction. During the heroic growth of MacLeish's JB, he graduates from homely smug cliché to rhetorical abstraction, without ever enunciating the specifics of his suffering. For all the subtle touches in the outer frame, MacLeish's drama fails by the inadequacy of his JB— not inarticulacy but inadequacy. Like Willy Loman and Blanche Dubois, JB claims too much for himself through his language. But whereas the linguistic poverty of Willy and Blanche enriches the total meaning of their plays, that of JB impoverishes his play. The Bible restores wealth and family to Job, and MacLeish follows the Bible in that respect. But he robs his JB of a "pure and naked . . . affirmation of the fundamental human thing" precisely because affirmation is draped in strained abstraction.[17]

MacLeish's verse play based on a humanized Bible was followed by *Herakles* (1967), based on a humanized Greek tragedy. An author's note informs us that MacLeish leans on Euripides: "As the generation of Euripides knew the myth, it was after the Labors had been accomplished and the dog dragged from the gate of death that Herakles, unknowing, killed his sons." Much more pointedly than in his *Trojan Horse*, MacLeish insists upon the relevance of Greek myth to us, and he returns to rhetorical dialogue to do so.

The tragedy by Euripides splits sharply in two: in the first half, we have the triumphant return of the hero in time to rescue wife and sons from their enemy; in the second half, the hero, mad, slays wife and sons. MacLeish uses a similar structure: in the first half of his play, an American scientist, fresh from Nobel Prize, comes to Athens; the city causes him to think about the heroism of Herakles, and in the second half of the play, the scientist's wife and daughter visit the Delphic Oracle, where they witness the drama of Herakles and Megara. Like Euripides, MacLeish juxtaposes triumph and madness, godlike exploits and domestic failure. As MacLeish's JB becomes Job, his Professor Hoadley becomes Herakles, but the identity is less clear.

Language and women link the two halves of MacLeish's play; Mrs. Hoadley, her small daughter, and the daughter's governess appear in both acts. In both acts, all characters speak formal modern English, rhythmed in loose tetrameters. We find in both parts the pastoral imagery that characterizes MacLeish's non-dramatic work. Sea and sun, stones and vegetation punctuate the dialogue of the main characters. As usual in MacLeish, such imagery alternates with abstraction that states his meaning rather than dramatizing it. Thus, Hoadley's impassioned portrait of Herakles is intended also to represent the modern scientist, and it is bare of imagery: "Herakles who won't put up with it,/ won't give in to it, won't despair,/ or hope or trust or anything—who struggles—/ dares to struggle—dares to overcome—/" Mrs. Hoadley's response prefigures that of Megara in Act II, both bare of imagery: "To want the world without the suffering is madness!/ What would we be or know or bear/ or love without the suffering to love for?" Similarly, in Act II, Megara's metaphysics is so abstract that it sounds like parody: "If truth were only true because it/ happened to have happened what would/ truth be? Anything can happen."

In the hubris of Hoadley and Herakles, MacLeish returns to one of the earliest themes of his drama—the desire of Adam and Cain of *Nobodaddy* to be like gods. During the forty years that separate the two plays, MacLeish learned to characterize more concretely, to focus his still verbose dialogue on stage action, and to pare his lines to comprehensibility in the theater. But *Herakles* lacks the attractive colloquialisms of the Roustabouts, Chorus, and Nickles of *JB*.

261

As in *JB*, MacLeish tries to theatricalize through a play within the play; the three modern females and their Greek guide are an audience to MacLeish's version of the second part of Euripides' tragedy. But the moderns are not integrated into the myth, and the myth itself seems flaccid by inevitable comparison with the rendering of Euripides. Compare, for example, the expression of this point in the action:

HERAKLES: The man who cannot bear up under fate
                could never face the weapons of a man.
                I shall prevail against death. I shall go
                to your city. I accept your countless gifts.
                For countless were the labors I endured,
                never yet have I refused, never yet
                have I wept, and never did I think
                that I should come to this: tears in my eyes.
                But now, I see, I must serve necessity.
                                  (Arrowsmith translation)

                Roll up pity for myself like dogs in carrion!
                  A man is made for anger isn't he?—
                to stand up, strike back,
                fight in the snow—fall in the tricks of light
                in the wild air—ills encountered
                everywhere that ills befall,
                fear befalls . . .

Euripides builds up slowly to the tears that accompany a father's long lament in the lines that follow the quoted passage. But despite questions, exclamations, and interruptions, MacLeish's character seems incapable of grief, which is reserved for Megara (who is not killed with her sons). Like Sarah in *JB*, Megara pleads for human love—"Only human/ hands can bury what we have to bury." But Herakles is not JB; he spurns Megara in order to vie hubristically with the Oracle.

Both his unregenerate hubris and Megara's humility are phrased in MacLeish's characteristic combination of strained metaphor and simple abstraction. In spite of an incantatory effect through repetition, the play's finale is abstract. Mrs. Hoadley pleads (apparently to the Oracle): "Let me go back to my life wherever my/ life was or is or will be waiting/ wandering up and down from the one/ morning to the other morning,/ from the one despair to the next, from the hope in/ this day to the hope in that one . . ./ Oh, release me from this mortal story!" Though the pun on "mortal" is meaningful—human and deadly —the picture of daily life is generalized into meaninglessness. Similarly, JB's choice of human endurance lacks specific detail. In both plays, MacLeish imposes humanism upon his characters, beyond the concrete grasp of his characters. Their generalized rhetoric is not grounded in concrete dirt.

Perhaps MacLeish has been so successful in the theater because he is a simple rather than subtle poet. In spite of a recent tendency to simplify human experience into the immediately "relevant," the great verbal artists have always given us new insights into the *complexity* of experience. All of us have gone on living in spite of evil, in spite of loss, but the great artist leaves us a little richer in spite of evil, in spite of loss. MacLeish resembles Wilder in the determination of his simplistic optimism, optimism that is often associated with the American temperament, but that is undermined by America's greatest artists.

KENNETH REXROTH

A DECADE OR SO YOUNGER THAN MACLEISH, TWO OTHER POETS turned to myth to dramatize a somewhat vaguer humanism— Kenneth Rexroth and Paul Goodman—and both poets were produced by the Living Theater. In 1951, Rexroth published four verse plays in a single volume, *Beyond the Mountains*. All four plays are based on extant Greek tragedies, but in form they are modeled on Japanese Noh plays. Like Noh plays, they contain few characters in rich costumes, as well as Chorus and Musicians, and each drama is climaxed by a dance. As in Noh plays, too, Rexroth's stage is almost bare, but his language is more profuse in imagery. Rather than the duologues of Noh, Rexroth uses the three speaking parts of Classical drama.

The first of Rexroth's plays is called *Phaedra*, and it presents the basic story of Euripides' *Hippolytus*. After Phaedra's dance, Hippolytus responds voluptuously to her love, which then erupts into a *pas de deux*. Theseus accepts the situation with equanimity: "What are you talking about? You mean/ You gave her comfort in my absence?/ Look, my boy, I am a man of the world./ What do you think I thought would happen?" But Phaedra and Hippolytus are less accepting, and each commits suicide, to the petulant distress of Theseus: "why should things like this/ Have to happen to me all the time?"

In an Author's Note, Rexroth explains that "Phaedra and Hippolytus achieve transcendence but are destroyed by impurity of intention." Rexroth is probably drawing on the Zen teachings behind Noh, in which the dance leads to *yugen*, a kind of transcendence. In the American play, however, the deaths of the lovers seem dictated by Greek myth rather than a search for transcendence; Phaedra impales herself upon a sword, and Hippolytus is trampled to death by a bull. The final words of the Chorus are full of gnomic morality that the drama has not theatricalized: "Impure intention is damned/ By the act it embodies./ Each sinned with the other's virtue./ They go out of the darkness,/ Onto a road of darkness./ The wind turns to the north, and/ The leaves rattle. An unknown/ Bird cries out. And the insects/ Of a day die in the starlight." The wisdom is sententious and the images facile; they have not been earned in action.

Iphigenia at Aulis again follows the story of Euripidean tragedy, with different nuances. Rexroth's Iphigenia, who has been her father's mistress, and who kindles the desire of an innocent Achilles, has a vocation for transcendence. Therefore it is she who sends her lover off to Troy, and she who forces her father to sacrifice her. Though we scarcely need Rexroth's note that "Iphigenia marches straight to transcendence," the note implies that this is a noble fate, whereas the play gives us a distastefully manipulative woman. To her father, she says: "We live here tonight with my head/ In your lap, my hands in your beard;/ We are the oldest kind of lovers." And to Achilles: "Dear, I am only a young girl./ Now I am clothed in your heart. You/ Are clothed in mine. We cannot part." Iphigenia leads them each in a dance, so that it becomes difficult to believe the admiring words of the Chorus: "Heaven has taken her. She/ Has gone into the bright world." The closing words of the Chorus contrast the fate of Iphigenia with that of Helen: "Aeneas and

Odysseus/ Wander, lost in a new world./ Helen dies in a brothel." But the contrast is more vivid than the play, in which events are stated without dramatic development.

The titular *Beyond the Mountains* is composed of two plays, *Hermaios* and *Berenike*. Despite the exotic Hellenism of the names, however, the plot is that of the *Oresteia*. Hermaios is an Agamemnon who is killed (along with his Cassandra) by his wife-sister and her lover, his and her brother. Berenike is an avenging Electra who seduces and kills the Aegisthus-figure; the Orestes-figure is reluctant to murder his mother, who therefore impales herself on his sword. But the special poignancy of what Rexroth calls "the same root types, the same dramatic figures" is that they are the last Greeks, since they are conquered by the Huns, who finally dominate the stage in a *"wild, acrobatic military dance."* Orestes and Electra (who go by the names of Menander and Berenike) change places, respectively, with the beggar and the prostitute who form the first Chorus in all the plays.

These root types are reminiscent of Yeats, who ended his last play, *The Death of Cuchulain*, with what "the harlot sang to the beggar-man." To this day, Yeats' dance plays—that modified form of Noh—tax actor and audience beyond most capabilities. And even though Greek myth is more familiar than Celtic myth, Rexroth lacks the atmospheric tension evoked by Yeats' dialogue. It would be otiose to compare Rexroth with the greatest English-language lyric poet of the twentieth century, but the American's determination to load his lines with passionate images undercuts the static intensity of the Noh-form he has chosen. The short lines carry too heavy a load of images to drive the drama. As dialogue poems, however, they present piquant variations on Greek tragedy.

Paul Goodman

In contrast to Rexroth, a poet who gave vent to dramatic utterance in only one slim volume of brief plays, Paul Goodman is a man of many professions and books, who declared: "If I had my choice I would write mainly for the theatre." He claims that he has not in fact written *mainly* for the theater because the theater has been unreceptive to his plays, spread over two decades, during which he has also written novels, criticism, poems, and essays. In 1941 he published his first volume of plays, *Stop-Light*. The five plays are patterned on the Noh: a traveler comes to a particular place, meets a spirit connected with the place, who dances; the dance evokes a new perception in the traveler. A chorus comments on the event. In all five plays, Goodman uses blank verse for most of the dialogue, though there are occasional shorter lines and some prose.

In the first two plays, the Traveler bears the name of the author, Paul, and the next three feature Poet, Cyclist, and Driver. The Traveler is thus an Everyman, who takes part in an event expressed through the dance of a ghostly character. In *Dusk*, a woman, Esther, expresses her undying love for a dead lover, and the Traveler comes to the realization that such perfect images of love fade at dawn. In *The Birthday*, the Birthday itself dances, teaching Paul the meaning of mortality. In *The Three Disciplines*, a Demon of Boundaries dances separate dances for chess, music, and algebra; but the Poet-Traveler is unable to write, for he has learned nothing about life. In *The Cyclist*, a Poem dances to alleviate the Cyclist's fear of a storm, and in *Stop-Light*, a Road Spirit dances an automobile accident, causing the Driver-Traveler to meditate on the preciousness of life.

Goodman's introduction to the volume begins: "Perhaps the deepest distinction between the noh-play and our western drama is that the former imitates a State, of the soul or of nature, and the latter an Action." All Western imitators of Eastern static drama have had to depend heavily upon dance or music, and only Yeats was able to compose poetry that was itself so gestural and musical that his own question is evoked: "How shall we know the dancer from the dance?"

It is difficult to imagine Western performance of the Noh-plays of lesser poets than Yeats, and this is particularly difficult in the case of Goodman, who writes unformal contemporary idiom in loose pentameters. The effect is incongruous, of conversation in a strict form, as in Paul's exclamation: "Poor cousin! used to be my mother's sister's daughter,/ now hardly a human-being, compelled this way and that."

Goodman himself must have realized that Western audiences would not readily accept his version of the Eastern form; in the same year that he published the five dance poems—1941—he wrote a more conventional drama of action, *Jonah*. A five-act play based on the Old Testament, *Jonah* translates Scripture into comedy, mainly through the range of Jonah's dialogue, which, as Goodman notes, runs "from marriage-broker jokes to meditations on first theology." The prophet replies to the Angel's summons: "I'm always awaking when there is a loose connection between the body and the soul. No wonder I have a short temper. . . . It should happen to a dog to be a prophet of the Lord of Hosts." Jonah complains to the Angel with clichés of bitter Jewish humor: "The matter he's asking what's! I'm sixty-five years old and my only well-wisher is the undertaker. What's the matter! I walk in the street and B. says to A., 'You think you got *tsures?* Wait! Here comes Jonah.' I show up at a wedding and the bride has a miscarriage. What's the matter."

Like Frost's Jonah, that of Goodman is discontented with his prophetic role. Trying to deceive the Lord by going to Tarshish instead of Nineveh, Jonah is thrown overboard in a storm and is swallowed by the whale. In the stomach of the whale, the Angel visits Jonah, who is dressed as a tailor, and they enact the old Jewish joke that Beckett was to use as Nagg's story in *Endgame*. The Angel orders a pair of trousers from Jonah and then complains: "But for God's sake, Tailor! such a long time! In six days the Lord God made the whole world, and you take two weeks for a pair of pants!" To which Jonah replies: "My good fellow—so you'll *look* at the world, and you'll look at this pair of pants."

Somehow the Angel guides a ragged Jonah into Nineveh, a city like New York, which lionizes the prophet and registers various degrees of skepticism about his warnings of doom. God spares the city, and Jonah's pride is wounded. But the Angel mollifies him with Jonah's favorite Yiddish word, *nebich*: "Should not I spare Nineveh that great city, wherein are eight million persons who, if I may say so, cannot discern between their right hand and their left, and also much cattle? *Nebich?*" Which Jonah has previously defined as "It means—it means that this big deal that you have is as *nothing* compared with a little

267

secret that *I* know; so really there is no need for me to feel the
burning resentment that I do feel; and anyway, I have my own
ideas about the value of that little secret such as it is. *Nebich!*"
A fiddler of the Lord who never quite climbs as high as the roof,
Jonah carries Goodman's comic intent, though the play has
longueurs. We watch Jonah learning humility, and Goodman has
claimed in his preface that "teaching and learning are im-
mensely worth watching, and more important than what is
taught or learnt."

In *Faustina* (1948) the learning-teaching process is more arduous, without comic relief. Faustina, wife of Emperor Marcus
Aurelius, lusts so strongly for the Gladiator, Galba, that sexual
intercourse after each day's combat does not slake her appetite.
For all his determined Stoicism, Marcus Aurelius experiences
sexual jealousy. Faustina inveigles the Emperor to have the
gladiator killed, but he proceeds to do it in his own way, by
trying to convince Galba of the worthlessness of life so that he
will desire his own death. When slow-witted Galba realizes that
he is condemned, he screams for help, and yet he comes to
understand the Emperor (and to echo his speech pattern) before
he is killed. The Emperor's teacher then kills himself in horror,
and the Emperor himself finally calls for help.

Faustina's passion is expressed in free blank verse into which
rhythm she forces all who address her. Marcus Aurelius, on the
other hand, usually speaks a syntactically simple prose, with
occasional quotations from *The Golden Book.* In the scene where
the Emperor tries to convince the gladiator of the benefits of
death, Goodman writes that the playwright's problem is "the
desperate search for the right use of speech altogether. The
problem poses itself as follows: Why should a protagonist in
tragic extremity waste his time and breath in talking, just because this is a theatrical convention? . . . Both the gladiator and
myself come to a thought that allows us to speak again: namely,
that under certain circumstances it is *pleasant* to use words and
feel the flow of reasons." But this is equivocation, depending
upon the definitions of "certain circumstances" and of "pleasant."

It is not the circumstances that fail to justify Goodman's use
of language, but his language that fails to convince us of dra-

matic circumstance. Many of Goodman's essays focus on people as much as ideas; paradoxically, the plays focus on ideas rather than people or events. Jonah, a worldly wise New York Jew, is perhaps his most credible character, but even he lives and quips in shadowy circumstances. The exoticism of Faustina and the rationalism of Marcus Aurelius seem only peripherally related to the events of their play. However the learning and teaching process may interest Goodman, he has burdened his dialogue with too much discussion.

Turning back to the Bible in 1955, Goodman wrote *The Young Disciple*, which he claims to be inspired by his "psychological analysis of the Gospel of Mark." The play also resembles Yeats' *Resurrection*, in which a rational reaction to Christ is opposed to an irrational. Goodman's titular Young Disciple is the most determined of rationalists, loving the enigmatically designated Our Master for his humanity. The Young Disciple explains his attitude: "I cannot exist in the extraordinary; I cannot live in extreme situations. I have to live on from hour to hour and from day to day. As usual. As usual. I cannot rely on the extraordinary." Suitably suspicious of metaphor, the Young Disciple scorns miracles and their seduction of the mob. After the crowd stone Our Master to death, the Young Disciple cries out: "You have killed a saint!" Now that He is dead, the crowd acquiesces to its guilt. The Young Disciple then feels himself becoming part of the very crowd he despises: "I am aware how I denied him. I have been astonished *not* out of my wits. I am almost at home here with these superstitious people. I do not love them, but that will come in time. And found our church."

In a note to the play, Goodman writes that he tried to emphasize "the pre-verbal elements of theatre: outcries and gasping, bawling and giggling, trembling, breathing hard, throwing tantrums and throwing punches." This is the language of his crowd. In reading, one cannot judge the effectiveness of such "pre-verbal" speech, but the verbal dialogue is heavy with rationalization and abstraction, often in syntactically awkward prose. The three Wise Ones (including a woman) and the Young Disciple speak in simple sober sentences for the most part, but Our Master tries to energize the word. In one of his first lines, he says: "It is true, I feel powerless here. I doubt that I am powerless, but that is neither here nor there. How would I know until I come to act? I feel like the adolescent who comes to his first fuck and can't get a hard-on." Before his death, Our Master offers a joyful wooing song to the world; both he and the Young Disciple express their love for the world as "fucking." The last we see of Our Master is his "Dance of Awareness of Himself and the Compresence of the Others"—a search for the *Yugen* of Noh, though the play is structured in the three acts of Western dramatic form.

In the preface to his collected plays, Goodman acknowledges: "Almost always I say it pretty literally as I mean it." The various dramas that Goodman mentions as influences upon him—Racine, Irish vaudeville, Moralities, Noh—do not say things "literally:" Racine, thin in imagery, is strict in rhyme and rhythm; Irish vaudeville joins gesture to joke; Moralities are strict in their allegory, expressed in metrical lines; Noh plays depend on music, dance, and often mask. Goodman's dramatic dialogue is usually philosophical, punctuated by slang or verse. He neither ennobles nor patronizes his characters, who tend to be reasonable, intelligent men—like himself. The cumulative effect of his essays—however one may disagree about details—presents a man committed to human community. But this is a difficult man to theatricalize, no matter how one tries to imbue the verb with the atmosphere of stylized Oriental tradition. Western theater is traditionally more active, and American drama has been active to the point of violence. It lends itself clumsily to reasonable and intelligent speech.

RICHARD EBERHART

FAR LESS CATHOLIC IN HIS TASTE THAN GOODMAN, RICHARD EBERhart wrote six verse plays about the problem of writing plays. Of his first play, *Triptych*, which dates from the mid-1930's, Eberhart said that it was "little but fantastic talk." The triptych are three people, with three different attitudes towards esthetics, particularly the esthetic problem of writing a play. One man espouses airy imagination, another concrete common sense, and the woman is impatient with art. After the woman leaves them, the men conclude: "We have come to no conclusion./ Conclusion is too inclusive./ To(o) crude warfare my food is air." The word play—to, too—is indicative of the literary quality of the dialogue, which leads to no action.

Even when Eberhart adds action, this literary quality pervades his other plays, written during the 1950's. *The Apparition* (1951) submerges the action in a frame play in which three couples discuss the possibility of creating a dramatic action. The author-actor, named Robin Everyman, wishes to incarnate Everyman, who, in twentieth-century America, has to be called John. To John of the inner play, far away from home in a hotel room, appears a young woman. John thinks of seducing her; she thinks of retiring to a nunnery. But the action ends with neither seduction nor decision; was she appearance or apparition? The on-stage audience complains that this is very thin theater, and yet it moves them to become a chorus, engaging in a "unifying, unified ritual." Robin Everyman closes the play with a promise of more to come: "Since we feel tragical, we'll try another comedy."

Slight as *The Apparition* is, Eberhart worked at the verse dialogue. The critical couples of the frame play speak in loose tetrameters, but John and the girl of the inner play speak in contemporary conversational blank verse. Rhythms and idioms of outer and inner play are contrasted. Thus, Eberhart manipulates his characters through the intellectual discussions in a way that is at variance with his credo of spontaneous poetic inspiration. Unlike Pirandello, the master of theater about theater, Eberhart does not weave the esthetic dialogue into the dramatic fabric. There is so little action in the inner action, and so much discussion of that little, that this piece too is "little but fantastic talk."

In the preface to his collected plays, Eberhart writes of his two *Preambles* (1954): "I conceived these two pieces as somewhat Shavian prologues or preambles to a full action to come." In each play, two men discuss a play-to-be—Poet and Author in the first Preamble, Author and Consulting Author in the second. In each Preamble, one of the men wishes to write large, in terms of the great works of the past, whereas the other tries to give practical advice in terms of contemporary taste. In the first play, there is a burlesque of the *Faust* motif: "Take this penknife and slit your wrist./ Here is an eye-dropper. Take out some blood/ And I will put it in this Parker 51." In both plays, the moderate men comment ironically upon the lavish aspirations of the would-be poets—which are those of Eberhart's own poetry. Both poets speak in capital letters about Love and Death—two of Eberhart's main poetic themes, as indeed of many poets.

As in the frame play of *The Apparition*, the discussions are learned and occasionally witty, referring to Job, Oedipus, Aristotle, and sometimes parodying well-known lines, as for example: "A noble thing in prison it is to suffer/ The wings and sparrows of outrageous torsion." Though the duologues of both Preambles probably reflect Eberhart's own preoccupations when he turned to drama, the erudite urbanity undercuts any feeling of concern with the problem of how a modern poet approaches the theater.

In the preface to his collected plays, Eberhart implies that the Preambles were followed by "the full action" of *Visionary Farms* (1955). A play within the play, *Visionary Farms* uses the three discussing couples of the frame of *The Apparition*. Of the fifteen scenes of *Visionary Farms*, two—first and fourteenth—are given to the esthetic commentary of the frame characters, but the bulk of the action involves the characters of the inner play. The totality has the effect of a blend of low-keyed Pirandello and Toller.

The inner play's Visionary Farms are born of the dishonesty of Hurricane Ransome. Hired as a clerk in the Parker Company, he secretly borrowed five dollars from the company funds. Unable to explain this sum on the books, Ransome began to juggle accounts until the company grew rich. However, we learn this expositorily only after half the play is over; Scene VI closes on Ransome's long confession, which ends: "My wife, my child, Mr. Parker, Adam Fahnstock,/ How could I do it? How could I betray you?/ It is the evil getting me from the inside./ The slightest, innocent-seeming insinuation/ When it all began, back in 1914,/ Has grown in my hand to my most monstrous sin./ I am bound upon a wheel of fire./ There is no end to the agony I am in."

But precisely because he *states* it, Hurricane Ransome does not dramatize his agony. Earlier, Eberhart has portrayed Ransome as a dynamo of energy. In Scene II, he amazed a Sunday School class by dipping a silver dollar into hydrochloric acid, so as to show the children the literal blackness of money. Though Ransome is not present in Scene III, Parker and Fahnstock praise his practical ingenuity that has enriched the company. In Scene IV, we watch that practical ingenuity in action, as Ransome instructs a veterinarian to disguise a rooster as a champion-bird: "Success is a trick." But when Ransome's tricks are discovered in Scene X, he is sent to prison. Parker, panicking at the loss of reputation, forces Fahnstock into bankruptcy although he knows that the latter's wife is dying of cancer.

Up to this point of the inner play, it is reminiscent of anti-capitalist Expressionist plays. The three business partners are type-characters defined by their commitment to their business; they have some slight individuality—Ransome's enterprise, Fahnstock's family feeling, Parker's business paternalism—but they are all cogs in the system, which Eberhart satirizes faintly. His theme grows fuzzy when a scene is wasted on Ted Parker's love of fast cars, and another scene on a Jewish furniture merchant instructing his daughter in tolerance. At the end of Scene XII, two of the frame spectators comment on the inner play: "What actually happens is strange and evocative,/ A long complexity, edging toward a sort of order." But neither "complexity" nor "order" characterizes the simplistic play we have been watching.

Scene XV opens with the abrupt entrance of an Author named Richard Eberhart, who confesses: "My execution never mated my deep passions/ and so I leave you with a semi-illusion,/ A hint of greatness in a waste of folly." The mention of "a hint of greatness" is more disarming than the hint itself, and Eberhart's subsequent commentary is more acute than the meditations of his spectator-characters: "But the whole piece, while it is an effort toward true tragedy, seems to me to be more nearly a tragi-comedy." Tragi-comedy has many definitions, but Eberhart's comedy is largely and heavy-handedly satiric. Unfortunately, the tragic intention often emerges as comic—Ransome's soliloquy, Parker's ruthlessness, Fahnstock's familial

273

sentiments, and the Latinate generalizations of the on-stage spectators.

The final scene—Ransome in jail—was added at the request of actors in a Seattle production of the play. Such spontaneous composition is in accord with Eberhart's theory of poetic creation, but his scene undercuts the meaning of his play. Energetic and unrepentant, Ransome organizes the prison to make profit; he rejects both his parole and the position of Warden. Finally, the on-stage audience define him: "He seems to have become a myth of the society/ That forged him real and brassy as itself." In this final scene, Ransome does ring out real, brassy, and attractive. The implication is that he represents a similarly attractive and energetic culture; profit and progress thus become desirable goals, but this patently contradicts the bulk of the play, not to mention Eberhart's stated intention of "true tragedy."

The play's confusion is mirrored in the dialogue: the moral Ransome of Scene II sounds like a caricature preacher: "If you do good you will be a shining brightness." Fahnstock and Parker sound like Sunday supplements;

FAHNSTOCK: Just think, I started from the bottom, on nothing.
Now twenty years later, due to industry
And hard work, I own thirty-five per cent of the stock.

PARKER: We partake of the greatness of America
And nothing can stop us.

Fahnstock's family feeling comes straight from soap opera: "We have had a wonderful and loyal family." Ransome at work utters American business clichés: "The only way to make money is to spend money." "I'll bet I'll win that bet." "We want the land carpeted with chickens." "Speech, nothing. I am a man of action." But the edge of this satire grows dull because there is too much of it. After such satire, it is impossible to take Ransome's soul search seriously: "Sometimes I have to think out loud/ To keep from sort of getting the creeps." Although Ransome's prison vigor is appealingly concrete, it cannot be harmonized with a tragic intention.

The three couples of the frame play attempt to focus our

reactions, but they introduce another idiom—that of erudite criticism—which further blurs the play's focus. Eberhart claims in his preface that this chorus "was conceived as a sophisticated surround and atmosphere to the inner action, which is complete in itself." Too complete in satire, incomplete in consistency, the play's dramatic development is not illuminated by Eberhart's comment.

In his next play, *The Mad Musician,* Eberhart blends the same choral characters with poetic passages written earlier; these were "yoked together during the mid-fifties." In contrast to the learned language in tetrameters of the frame of *Visionary Farms,* Eberhart simplifies diction and rhythms to those of modern suburbia. The inner play, on the other hand, is complicated; in seven scenes, it is the biography of a boy who becomes the titular mad musician. Curbed and spurned by father and mother, he is discouraged by his teacher, pronounced mad by the College Psychiatrist, and analyzed by a Professional Psychiatrist. In free rhymes, another Chorus comments on the wide meaning of the action, while the frame Chorus comments on the action. Robin Everyman, again the author, is accused of basing his biographical portrait too closely upon the life of Pendleton, an actual composer. Still another chorus—two college students —comment on what might have happened. Finally, the mad musician, having married far from home, becomes a Vedantist and is jailed for being a conscientious objector. As the frame chorus comments upon this unexpected turn of events, the composer Pendleton enters with policemen, to arrest Robin for libelous use of his life. And so the play ends with this old Pirandellian twist on the reality of fiction.

A slighter work than *Visionary Farms, The Mad Musician* is too frail to support the twists of plot, the variety of rhythms and vocabulary, and the juxtapositions of realities and illusions. The Hamletian soliloquies of the mad musician, which probably date from the 1930's, are particularly pretentious in context, and the suburban conversation of the outermost frame trivializes all the action. Eberhart himself admitted that the play's parts were "yoked together," but they were not unified.

Devils and Angels (1962), an even slighter play, is Eberhart's comedy to offset the effort at tragedy, *Visionary Farms.* An author, seeking the happy marriage of Robin and Beryl Everyman, decides to write a play about lovers. Before he can begin, however, the Devil enters to wrestle with him and convince him of the power of intellect. After the Devil conquers the Author, an Angel enters to convince him of the power of Intuition. The Author's wife interrupts both confrontations with bulletins about their sick child. Two swift staccato scenes—one between professors and the other between national figures—illustrate the temptations of power. As the Author defends Free Will, a Consulting Author argues for Determinism—in wordy terms. At the end, Devil and Angel hover protectively over a two-year-old baby who wails "Waldo, Waldo—" for the Emersonian Oversoul. The play-to-be is still to be, as Intellectual Devil and Intuitional Angel always divide humanity.

In Eberhart's last play, his tetrameters are very free, and they are free also of the erudite humor of the earlier plays. Frankly allegorical, the last verse play is Eberhart's most integrated effort at colloquial dialogue, straining neither for metaphor nor abstraction. But the new suppleness of his stage verse did not inspire Eberhart to continue in the dramatic genre.

JAMES SCHEVILL

FOR THE NEXT GENERATION OF AMERICAN POETS—THOSE BORN BEtween World War I and the 1929 crash—drama continued to be an avocation. Occasionally, as in the cases of James Schevill and Robert Lowell, translation brought the poets to drama. After rendering Corneille's *Cid* in English rhyming couplets, Scheville turned to history for his own first play, *The Bloody Tenet* (1958).

In spite of its documentary basis, however, *The Bloody Tenet* resembles Eberhart's plays in incorporating a play within the play. The frame play presents a confrontation between a middle-aged Journalist and a voluptuous Evangelist who preaches in a Temple of Radiant Redemption. The Journalist accuses her of setting up separatist churches that weaken Christianity: "Isn't there a risk of turning religion into Public Relations/ With your March for Christ and your follow-up systems?" Ecstatically, the

Evangelist invokes Roger Williams, "the founder of religious freedom," but the Journalist accuses her of bending the real Williams to her own designs. This contemporary debate about Williams dissolves into a 1635 setting.

In the inner play, we hear the seventeenth century charges against Williams, who defends himself in the titular "Bloody Tenet." We see Williams with his wife; we witness his two dreams, about an Indian Chief and about an English Lord; we hear some of his trial as it was set down in the record; and finally, we find Williams facing the Journalist and the Evangelist of the frame play. Even while his seventeenth century sentence to exile is pronounced, Williams refuses to choose between the Evangelist's praise of him and the Journalist's criticism. While a background choir sings the hymn, "Wondrous Love," Williams, speaking in imaged verse, reaffirms his faith in individual paths to God.

Schevill's first play does not blend the disparate dialogues— the earnest Journalist, the satirized Evangelists, the dry ideology of Williams' contemporary opponents, Williams' imaged speech alternating with abstractions. Both frame and interior plays are written in loose blank verse, with little difference between seventeenth and twentieth century characters. Though his seventeenth century opponents accuse Williams of ornate speech, the images are drawn mainly from nature and the Bible and do not lend themselves to theatricalization. Nor, though Williams is called a dreamer, does Schevill theatricalize his dreams, which consist entirely of words—his self-defense to the Indian chief, Canonicus, and his self-defense against the accusations of his one-time patron, Sir Edward Coke. In his trial, Williams is charged with "tak[ing] the Bible as mere figures!" when he compares the world to a wilderness in which the gentle and innocent are victimized. But for most of the trial, as for most of the play, ideological issues are discussed and debated in abstract terms. The rare imagery does not focus a drama which deals with issues of only tangential contemporary relevance.

The frame play nevertheless provided Schevill with a model for the theatrical confrontation which was to serve him more effectively in his next two plays, paired as *American Power* (1964). In both *The Space Fan* and *The Master*, a man faces a woman, each an Expressionist type-character. Schevill subtitles *The Space Fan* a play of escape, and *The Master* a play of commitment, but the subtitles are ironic; the protagonist of the first play is a sympathetic escapist from American power; the protagonist of the second play is unsympathetically committed to American power. The combined moral would seem to be that escape is healthier than commitment for America, but the plays are not moralistic and can be enjoyed theatrically.

Because Melinda Davis is an amateur Space Fan who receives and transmits messages from and to outer space, the government has sent an investigator to ascertain her intentions. Melinda describes her space as "A new language of sounds and music." But she and the Investigator engage in an exchange of more familiar language, drawn mainly from science fiction (although the moon landings have made these terms less fictional). Through her determined eccentricity, Melinda converts the Investigator to her carefree, enjoyable hobby; she and the Investigator laugh happily as they incinerate the conformist literature of contemporary America—"Bank stubs . . . savings book . . . Identification card with finger prints and photo!" At the last, to electronic music, they join in a formal dance. The Investigator realizes the importance of his calling: "For the first time in my life, I feel that I've become a real investigator." They speak a few banal words of love as they dance, and a woman's voice sings offstage: "The shapes our searching arms/ make in the empty air/ are women's bodies/ that when the wind and rain/ possess our sight/ we have that grace to touch,/ those white shapes to know,/ and keep a sanity/ for love." Both the rhythms and images are reminiscent of the lyrics in Yeats' Plays for Dancers, but the lines relate only tangentially to the contemporary, conversational idiom of the play itself.

The same lyric opens *The Master*, to which it seems not at all related. In this play, an attractive young woman, the Candidate, comes to an imposing man, the Master, to study for a degree of General Mastery. The Master proceeds to put the Candidate through her paces, with rapid physical movement accompanying the dialogue. During the course of the examination, the Candidate becomes army officer, Indian squaw, Minute Man, Southern rebel, corpse. After this swift series of words and movements, the Master indulges in a long autobiographical monologue, and the Candidate responds with a matching conformist autobiography of the "ideal average woman." To jazz rhythms, the dialogue resumes its quick repartee as the Master questions the Candidate, sometimes in nonsense-riddles. Through a mimed baseball game, the Master leads the Candidate to an appreciation of American power. Then, enacting an old couple, they display the emptiness of their consumed consumer lives—dead long before their actual deaths: "At the Senior Citizens' Center, they have square dancing. It's a leisure world. Old age should be a long vacation." In the final Eagle sequence, they dance sensuously to their joint vision of American power, making a mockery of the love lyric with which the play began. In spite of the disjunctive scenes, the play is coherent in its satiric theatricalization.

Schevill's published volume of plays is named after the last one to be written, *The Black President* (1965). Called a "song-Scenario," containing sixteen songs, it is nevertheless a drama whose main meaning is carried by dialogue. The plot centers on Moses Jackburn, an American black who is captain of a facsimile slave-ship manned by blacks of many countries: "We sail in the slow, black ship of slavery to show you that the past must not be forgotten, that the future must be different if man is to survive." A flashback scene shows Jackburn's family in the South. A return to the present gives him a love scene with a Spanish girl, Carla.

When Jackburn anchors his ship in the Thames and demands to see the Prime Minister, he is met with pious platitudes and firm refusals. Instead, an English lord threatens him with hypocritical courtesy; the ship can leave peacefully or be forced out to be sunk in international waters. Instead, a millionaire offers to buy the ship and put it in a museum; the ship that symbolizes suffering is viewed as a commodity. Jackburn appears to yield, but after insulting the millionaire, he dresses formally to surrender his ship. However, he orders the ship blown up rather than surrender it.

While waiting to be extradited to America, Jackburn is visited by Carla, and they have a fantasy of their life together; she helps him campaign for the presidency—the first black president of the United States. When Carla leaves him, Jackburn returns to reality: "God damn the campaign! You hear me? It's all a pile of shit! You can't laugh off a black skin. You can't laugh the world into peace. They'll train you, they'll beat you, buy you into order. When I get back to New York, I'm going off and hide in the loneliest, black room in the city. I'm going to be the original invisible man! All of you bastards who are trying to fix up the world can go stuff yourselves! You hear me?" But these bitter words are diluted by a final song, ending optimistically: "Maybe somewhere there's a little light."

The earnest purpose of *The Black President* is less theatrical than the whimsy of *The Space Fan* or the gestural repartee of *The Master*. In *The Black President*, blacks and whites, Africans and Europeans and Americans, all speak in the same educated idiom. Nowhere do we find the rage of LeRoi Jones, the humor of Ed Bullins or Langston Hughes. This is not to legislate that a white dramatist cannot write about blacks, but it is to suggest that these blacks are not distinguishable from whites. And if that is a point of the play, then more should have been made of the point. Though Schevill has unusual visual and musical imagination for a poet, his most potent dramatic tone remains satire.

ROBERT LOWELL

LOWELL IS THE MOST GIFTED POET OF HIS GENERATION TO TURN TO the stage. Like Schevill, he came to drama through translation, but the way was prepared by the dramatic turn of his lyrics after 1957, with their loosened rhythms and simplified syntax. By the time Eric Bentley commissioned him to translate Racine's *Phèdre* (1961), he had already been thinking about speakable verse. His comment on his translation illuminates his own verse plays: "[Racine's] poetry is great because of the justness of its rhythm and logic, and the glory of its hard, electric rage. I have translated as a poet, and tried to give my lines a certain dignity, speed, and flare."[18]

In 1967, working from a prose rendering of *Prometheus Unbound*, Lowell completed an "imitation" in highly lyric prose—

syntactically varied, inventive in sound play, and lush in imagery. As Lowell's Phaedra was rendered through Freud, his Prometheus has a contemporary existential consciousness. His language has invigorated two classical tragedies for speakers of English, but his most significant dramatic achievement is the three plays grouped as *The Old Glory*.

New England, the birthplace of the poet, is also the birthplace of the phrase "Old Glory" as a synonym for the United States flag. A Captain William Driver apparently applied the term to his ship's standard when he sailed from Salem, Massachusetts, in 1831. The three plays of *The Old Glory* are rooted in New England, with the first two actually set there. Ostensibly dealing with early American history, Lowell's three plays examine that history through the fiction of Hawthorne and Melville, and he focuses on the image of a flag. Lowell has dramatized stories whose cumulative significance equates Old Glory with its rhyme-word "gory."

Two of Lowell's three plays—those based on Hawthorne's stories—take place in colonial times, but Lowell sees the United States already present in seventeenth-century Puritan Massachusetts, as in eighteenth-century Revolutionary Boston. Lowell's third play, based on Melville's novella *Benito Cereno*, foreshadows the Civil War and our contemporary racial strife. Conceived as a whole, the three plays of *The Old Glory* comment on contemporary America in contemporary language. All three dramas contain a single act of mounting tension. All three dramas close on violence whose reverberations still ring loudly in our ears. Far from a patriotic celebration, these three plays accommodate the ambiguities of revolutionary action, and they do so in the most controlled verse of American drama.

Endecott and the Red Cross, the first play of the trilogy, takes its title from a Hawthorne short story, but Lowell's drama also draws upon another Hawthorne story about Endecott, "The Maypole of Merry Mount," as well as upon Thomas Morton's *New English Canaan*. Lowell places the two Hawthorne stories in sequence, using Morton's account as background for both. Moreover, since first publication in 1965, Lowell has expanded the play to "give supporting force to *Benito Cereno*."[19] The Africans of the latter play are parallelled by the Indians of the former; the Puritans are dedicated to their destruction, whereas Morton tries to befriend them. This Indian subplot blurs the central conflict of Endecott versus Morton, and it slows the play's dramatic drive. The most discursive play of the trilogy, *Endecott and the Red Cross* is even talkier in the revised version. Thus the thematic balance of *Endecott* against *Benito Cereno* is achieved at the cost of the former's dramatic focus.

By combining the two Hawthorne stories in sequence (in both versions of the play), Lowell follows Endecott's display of momentary softness with his lasting hardness. Unlike Hawthorne, Lowell provides his protagonist Endecott with an antagonist Morton—an opposition derived from Morton's historical denigration of Endecott as "Captain Littleworth." Like Hawthorne and Morton, Lowell shows us the carefree sensuous life at Merrymount, and again like Hawthorne and Morton, he shows us the Manichean Puritan doctrine in action, contrasting the two cultures. Morton himself described Puritan arrogance and cupidity: "They [the Puritans] differ from us something in the creede too, for if they get the goods of one, that is without, into their hands, hee shall be kept without remedy for any satisfaction: and they beleeve that this is not cosenage. And lastly they differ from us in the manner of praying: for they winke when they pray, because they thinke themselves so perfect in the highe way to heaven that they can find it blindfold: so doe not I." (Book III, Chapter XXVII). And so does not Robert Lowell.

Leaning on Morton's account, Lowell suggests that Anglicans and Puritans shared an allegiance to commerce; mercantile words therefore punctuate the ethical conflict of the drama— money, pay, cash, trade, profit. Above the commercial undercurrent, however, principle shines in Lowell's play; patriotism is never a simple matter of pounds and pence, as in Brecht's plays. Not money but a flag is the most insistent image of Lowell's three plays, and the flag is first mentioned in conjunction with Endecott. When the Anglican minister, Mr. Blackstone, asks about Endecott's loyalty to the Crown, Thomas Morton replies:

> I don't know. He might give you a kick in the ribs.
> I know this, though: Endecott is an Englishman,

> he carried our flag, the Red Cross of England,
>   against the Spaniard.
> He'll never defy England. He's as loyal there as I am.

Lowell's free verse emphasizes the importance of the play's first coupling of Endecott and the Red Cross, through the internal rhymes—know, know though; the syllabic similarity of "Endecott" and "Englishman"; the insistence on "Englishman" and "England."

When Endecott first comes on stage—about one-third of the way through the play—he is followed by a soldier bearing the English flag. Glancing at the banner of Merrymount, Endecott observes: "There are flags and flags./ This one at Merry Mount sags pretty badly,/ it bulges in the belly." Rhyme, assonance, alliteration, and repetition build to the "bulging belly" image, which implicitly condemns the sensuous life of Merrymount.

The word "flag" recurs about a dozen times in the dialogue, with increasing frequency toward the end of the play. But just before ordering his soldier to tear down the British flag fastened to the Maypole, Endecott calls the flag a standard: "Bring me our standard,/ the Red Cross of England!" Since it is "our"s, the soldier fears to tear the flag from the staff, and Endecott, with a laconic "It's nothing," *"cuts the Red Cross from its staff."* Hawthorne's story ends at this climactic point: "And forever honored be the name of Endicott! We look back through the mist of ages, and recognize in the rending of the Red Cross from New England's banner the first omen of that deliverance which our fathers consummated after the bones of the stern Puritan had lain more than a century in the dust."

Lowell, too, recognizes in Endecott's act "the first omen of that deliverance," the American Revolution, but act and actor are more equivocally portrayed. Alone on stage at the last, Lowell's Endecott *"lifts the fallen Red Cross of England with his foot,"* admitting: "It's strange I was in such an unmanly terror about a flag. . . . It's a childish thing."

Lowell's Endecott can remember his days at court in London. He remembers his beautiful wife who died young, and whose death turned him into a man of action. Needing doctrine for his acts, he chose the sternest faith to sustain him as a soldier.

Highly self-conscious, Lowell's Endecott recognizes the reasons for his faith, but he cannot prevent his nostalgic memories. Therefore, he consistently undercuts the cruel punishments pronounced by the rigid Elder Palfrey (whose fanaticism is more comprehensible in the revised version). Differing, Endecott and Morton are both reasonable men, less intransigent than those representatives of polar ideologies, Elder Palfrey and Mr. Blackstone. To Endecott's "Flags of a hundred colors,/ they're all made of cloth." Elder Palfrey counters: "There's one faith and one flag."

This is the signal for Endecott to tell Elder Palfrey his dream, in which Endecott is Elder Palfrey, preacher and executioner. The dream—invented by Lowell—is relevant to the twentieth as to the seventeenth century, for it is a dream of men who commit cruel deeds in the name of stern religions; it is a dream of countering cruelty with cruelty. As Elder Palfrey in his dream, Endecott executes every man in sight, but two men spring up for each one felled, and the flag waves over the carnage: "Green grass, blue sky; and in all that vacancy,/ our flag, the Red Cross, was knocking and hacking in the wind." As so often in drama, Endecott sees clearly through the dream's symbolism, and he prophesies that the king will act so as to cause him to harangue his soldiers and incite them to rebellion. Thus, he begins to confirm instead of undercutting Palfrey's punishments. Though he is angered by Morton, he decides on open rebellion only after he hears Mr. Blackstone's "authoritative and logical words."

Endecott's own words, except for the dream description, have been so sober and soldierly that his "hollow, dishonest harangue" rings out in colorful contrast. Hawthorne's Endecott inveighed: "But what think ye now? This son of a Scotch tyrant —this grandson of a Papistical and adulterous Scotch woman, whose death proved that a golden crown doth not always save an annointed head from the block." Lowell builds climactically upon this substance:

Will Charles Stuart stop us? That savage,
that Scotchman, that peacock who spends more money
on clothes than any woman in the Kingdom?

Yet Charles had excellent forebears:
King James, who slobbered, his life the life of a bitch,
one uninterrupted heat for the glittering boys?
Or Queen Mary? She did what James dreamed of,
a world whore, a French agent, a common murderess,
who blew her husband up with powder.
Her death at the block shows us perhaps how treacherously
the Divine Will overshadows her grandson's crown.

Assonance, alliteration, and irony serve the rebellious dema-
gogue. His picture of men in power casts a shadow upon his
own power, and predicts the violence and corruption of power
throughout Lowell's trilogy. Understandingly as Lowell por-
trays Endecott, he is not quite as ready as Hawthorne to honor
that name forever.

Hawthorne himself takes a more ambiguous attitude toward
the protagonist of his haunting story, "My Kinsman, Major
Molineux." Hawthorne's very first paragraph summarizes the
violence that greeted British deputies in Massachusetts during
the fifty years before the American Revolution, and the whole
story implies mob violence or lynch law behind any revolution.
The protagonist, eighteen-year old Robin, has come to the city
to seek his fortune through the support of his kinsman, Major
Molineux, British governor of the colony. Within the few hours
that Robin spends in the city streets, his country innocence
dissolves into complicity in the killing of his kinsman.

So, too, in Lowell's play, *My Kinsman, Major Molineux.* In
Endecott and the Red Cross, Lowell conflated three sources to pose
a dramatic conflict—flexible Morton versus inflexible Endecott.
In this second play of the trilogy, Lowell hews close to a single
source, Hawthorne's story; theatrically, this takes the form of an
Expressionist quest play, with Robin a kind of American Everyman. In Hawthorne's story, each of Robin's adventures is a
discreet event; after Robin sees his kinsman, however, "in tar-
and-feathery dignity," the people he has met become "fiends
that throng in mockery around some dead potentate." And he
joins that fiendish mockery. In Lowell's drama, Robin's quest
seems less concrete and more symbolic. The setting is at once
more particular—Boston on the eve of Revolution—and more

general—Hell. To bind the disjunctive short scenes, Lowell abandons the free verse of *Endecott* for loose tetrameters, but he uses the same sonic effects—rhyme, alliteration, assonance, repetition. Again Lowell makes the flag his central image; the Union Jack is emblematic of British authority, and the Rattlesnake of the Boston rebellion.

As Endecott is linked and opposed to the Red Cross of England in Lowell's first play, Major Molineux is linked to the Union Jack and opposed to the Rattlesnake flag of rebellion. By the middle of the play, Robin comes to understand: "The Rattlesnake/ means Major Molineux is out./ A British flag means he's at home." A Clergyman (invented by Lowell) prudently carries both flags, along with a whirligig to tell him which way the wind is blowing. Just before the mob brings Major Molineux on stage, the Clergyman tosses away the whirligig and hands the Rattlesnake rebels' flag to Robin, who holds it "unconsciously." When the unfortunate Major is wheeled onstage, Robin cries out: "Oh my poor kinsman, you are hurt!" But even as he speaks, he *"unconsciously wav[es] the flag in his grief."* The Major turns to Robin with the accusation of the dying Caesar, *"Et tu, Brute!"* Heroically, the Major *"grinds the Rattlesnake underfoot."* This arouses the fury of the mob; the Major pleads that the Ferryman row him across the river to safety, but the Ferryman deals the Major's death blow, intoning piously: "all tyrants must die as this man died." Each of the other characters steps up to the Major's corpse and echoes self-righteously: "all tyrants must die as this man died." As the Red Cross of England had to be cut down to prepare the way for The Old Glory, the Boston Rattlesnake had to be subsumed in it. Elegant Molineux and sensuous Morton had to be destroyed for the Old Glory to be realized. And Lowell finds the appropriate dialogue.

Lowell emphasizes the impact of events upon Robin by giving him a younger brother, who is both innocent and childishly belligerent. Whereas Robin comes to Boston to seek his fortune, the boy wants merely a flintlock. Whereas Robin learns quickly to act with prudence, the boy calls consistently for impulsive action. Whereas Robin learns to mistrust alcohol and women, the boy is oblivious to both. And yet the mob corrupts the boy

as it does Robin. When Robin "unthinking" waves the Rattlesnake flag in Major Molineux' face, *"The Boy, unconsciously, too
mingles among the* CROWD *without thinking. Someone asks him to give
some dirt to throw at the* MAJOR *and he unthinkingly picks up some from
a basket."* In the mob, the Boy also finds a gun. Like Robin, the
Boy joins the lynch mob. At the last, the Boy plays happily with
his gun, declaring: "Major Molineux is dead." Robin leads his
younger brother toward tainted freedom in the city, as he
echoes: "Yes, Major Molineux is dead." There is no longer mention of a kinsman.

Though Lowell delineates the insurrection more clearly than
Hawthorne, he bases its infernal character on the latter's hint.
Midway in the story, Hawthorne describes a stranger with
red and black face: "The effect was as if two individual devils,
a fiend of fire and a fiend of darkness, had united themselves to
form this infernal visage." Later that night, Robin sees this
stranger leading the mob of fiends that mock Major Molineux.
Hawthorne's unnamed city becomes Hell through the diabolical
actions of its inhabitants.

In Lowell's play, Hell is a *donnée*. Before a word is spoken, the
Ferryman appears, *"his dress . . . half suggest[ing] that he is Charon."*
Though this may be difficult to suggest on stage, his remark to
Robin recalls Dante: "Legs go round in circles here./ This is the
city of the dead." But Lowell's Dante has no Virgil; the Boy
exclaims: "We've lost our guide." And *we* seem to lose *our* guide
as the characters crowd on scene in swift succession, rather than
in Hawthorne's more decorous procession. Robin at the tavern
and Robin at the brothel are based on Hawthorne, but Lowell
intersperses these scenes with others. Characters appear and
reappear in an infernal phantasmagoria. Hawthorne's mysterious stranger with the two-colored face becomes Colonel Greenough, whose mask changes from gray pocked to pocked-
and-red to "red as blood," marking the progress of the insurrection. Colonel Greenough compares Robin to the man who had
no garments for a wedding; he remarks that the last shall be first
and the first last. When Robin observes that he sounds like
Christ, we recall the ability of the devil to quote Scripture for
his own purpose, and this devil's purpose is revolution: "Whip-
ping-posts, gibbets, bastinadoes/and the rack! I must be mov-

ing." When the Boy asks Robin about the man in the two-colored mask, the answer is: "He is someone out of 'Revelations' —/ Hell revolting on its jailers." In that revolt, the two-flagged Clergyman also draws on Scripture to harangue the crowd:

> How long, how long now, Men of Boston!
> You've faced the furious tyrant's trident,
> you've borne the blandishments of Sodom.
> The day of Judgment is at hand,
> now we'll strip the scarlet whore,
> King George will swim in scarlet blood,
> Now Nebuchadnezzar shall eat grass and die.
> How long! How long! O Men of Boston,
> behave like men, if you are men!

The Clergymen might be a rhetoric student of the Endecott who first revolted against British power.

Pitiable rather than tyrannical, Major Molineux is wheeled on stage. In the final scene, Lowell's two main devils—the Colonel and the Ferryman—combine to kill the Major. The Ferryman who is dressed like Charon "*hits* [the Major] *on the head with his oar.*" Apocalyptic Colonel Greenough "*plung*[es] *his sword in the MAJOR.*" Slowly, the crowd disperses, crying: "Long live the Republic! Long live the Republic!" For the first and only time in the play, Robin and his brother are alone on stage; their lack of self-recognition is meant to trigger ours—we are accomplices in the death of our kinsman.

In *Benito Cereno*, Lowell again uses the past to appeal to our present conscience. Following the events of the Melville novella, his play subverts its intention. Melville based his story on a chapter of the *Voyages and Travels* of Captain Amasa Delano, published in 1817, converting "facts" into metaphors of good and evil, of appearance and reality.[20] Lowell in turn converts Melville's fiction into an ironic commentary upon the symbiosis of oppressor and oppressed, observer and observed. And he does this by joining verbal to theatrical imagery, in an extremely concentrated drama.[21]

Benito Cereno is the only play of the trilogy in which the Old Glory actually appears. It is the standard of Captain Delano's ship, whose name Lowell changes from *Bachelor's Delight* to *Presi-*

dent Adams (of New England, like her captain). The play opens with a *"machinelike"* salute to the American flag, which Delano first compares to a woman, then to a home: "We are home. America is wherever her flag flies." The flag disappears for the rest of the play, and Captain Delano begins to feel less at home after he boards the Spanish *San Domingo* (changed from *San Dominick*). On that ship, the Blacks treat the Spanish flag with contempt. King Atufal is said to be imprisoned for using the Spanish flag as toilet paper, and he is to ask pardon by kissing the flag. As in Melville, Babu uses the Spanish flag for Benito Cereno's shaving towel.

As Lowell used the Rattlesnake flag of the rebellious Bostonians to theatricalize *My Kinsman Major Molineux*, so he introduces a pirate flag of "a black skull and crossbones on white silk." Rebellion's bite is as poisonous as that of the rattlesnake, and a slave society is sick to death. The rebel Blacks carry the *white* bone of Don Aranda as their figurehead, and they adopt a *black* skull and crossbones as their emblem. At the end of the play, the Blacks raise the skull and crossbones as "the flag of freedom," and they order Don Benito to walk across the Spanish flag as his "road to freedom." After Don Benito, Boatswain Perkins walks across the Spanish flag to kiss the mouth of the real skull. When Captain Delano is ordered to take the same road to freedom, his sailors come to his rescue. Defeated, Babu raises a white handkerchief above his head, but declares: "The future is with us." Captain Delano shoots him dead: "This is your future." The Old Glory is not visible, but its presence is felt. We have learned the price of Delano's smoking pistol.

In order to shift our sympathy gradually away from Captain Delano, Lowell adopts a strategy similar to the one he used in *My Kinsman Major Molineux*. As the invention of Robin's younger brother decreased the innocence of the protagonist, so the invention of a New England Boatswain Perkins increases the smug blindness of Captain Delano. Together, the two New Englanders compose an insular American who, ironically, is proud of his cosmopolitan sophistication, and they both utter contemporary clichés that damn them for us: "When a man's in office, Sir, we all pull behind him!" "Buck up. Each day is a new beginning." "We don't beat a man when he's down." "That's why we're strong:/ everybody trusts us." "A little diversion improves their efficiency,/ a little regulated corruption." "We prefer merit to birth, *boy.*" (my italics) "They think America is Santa Claus."

Melville's Delano is a man of good will with severely limited perceptions. Lowell's Delano is a man whose good will is eroded by his severely limited perceptions. With characteristic irony, Lowell uses imagery of vision to emphasize the Captain's lack of vision. Early in the play, when Perkins first reports the "strange sail," Delano calls for his telescope and waxes lyrical about what he sees, but the undercurrent of his lyricism is that "everyone disbelieves in slavery and wants slaves." Once aboard the Spanish ship, Delano orders Perkins to "see if you can find me a Spaniard who can talk." Then the imagery of vision shifts from Delano to Babu. When Delano objects to Cereno's "oversight" in his ship's emergency, Babu explains that his master has a hundred eyes and is incapable of oversight. Babu's double repetition of his master's hundred eyes makes us aware of the total lack of privacy in the master-slave relationship. Benito Cereno hints at Delano's limited vision: "if we only see with our eyes/ sometimes we cannot see at all." And Babu puns: "The Yankee master is at sea on our ship." But it is Delano who keeps repeating "I see . . ." as he continues not to see the true state of affairs on the *San Domingo.*

Less lyrical than Delano, Perkins uses his naked eyes rather than telescope or metaphor. He sees the whaleboat full of American sailors, and he sees the falsity of the black servile front. In the final unveiling, Delano asks Benito accusingly: "Do you see that man-shaped thing covered with black cloth, Don Benito?" "I always see it," the haunted captain replies, confessing his guilt with his punishment. Other repetitions of the verb "see" echo like screams in the war of black against white. Babu about the skeleton: "Let them see it! Let them see it!" Babu to the whites: "Do you see this whip?" Babu to Delano: "You can see that Don Aranda was a white man like you,/ because his bones are white." Atufal to the whites: "Do you see that ribbon?/ It says, 'Follow the leader.'/ We wrote it in his blood." Delano to Babu, *"lifting his pocket and pointing the pistol*): Do you see what I have in my hand?" But as Don Benito implies in his final line, physical vision does not mean moral understanding: "My God how little these people understand!" Spectators and even participants in the action, the stage Americans have been blind to its meaning, in order that the real contemporary American audience may see the more clearly.

Since Lowell's imagination functions visually as well as verbally, he theatricalizes several fictional hints. In *Endecott and the Red Cross*, he dwelt lovingly upon the Maypole masques as a sensuous ceremony. In *My Kinsman Major Molineux*, he enlarged the barber scene and the tavern scene into virtual rites of ablution before the fatal immersion of Major Molineux. In *Benito Cereno*, Lowell makes mock rituals of Atufal's pardon, of the High Mass, of Benito's noon shave, and of Francesco's formal dinner service. He introduces five scenes of gratuitous but pointed entertainment that seems inspired by Genet's *Blacks:* "This evening we shall perform for you. But, in order that you may remain comfortably settled in your seats in the presence of the drama that is already unfolding here, in order that you be assured that there is no danger of such a drama's worming its way into your precious lives, we shall even have the decency— a decency learned from you—to make communication impossible. . . . The tragedy will lie in the color black! It's *that* that you'll cherish, *that* that you'll attain, and deserve. It's *that* that must be earned." And *that* that Delano neither earns nor learns. His patronizing reaction to the entertainment is: "Well, that wasn't much!/ I suppose Shakespeare started that way."

And yet the entertainments trigger the opposing dreams of Delano and Cereno. Both Captains dream of their childhood, the one in harmony with his natural surroundings in New England and the other oppressed by an oppressive social structure. As even Delano recognizes: "We are like two dreams meeting head-on." And neither dream can accommodate Babu, a slave in his own country and a king only by insurrection.

In Gerald Weales' acute and succinct summary: "*The Old Glory* is about revolution—Endecott initiates one, Robin joins one, Delano puts one down. . . . The movement in time from play to play, with its suggestion that there is always a revolution in process, underlines the basic theme of the play—that, under whatever flag, power demands action and that the action is inevitably violent and tyrannical."[22] Lowell's dramatic examination of revolution is less subtle than his lyric poetry, and the plays are less subtle than the fiction at their base. But subtlety may be undramatic, and Lowell's plays are intended for the theater. Without pandering to easy popularity, he has accommodated his elusive imagery to the exigencies of spoken dialogue. Highly rhythmed, it is eminently speakable. The language varies with the play—alternately discursive and abrupt in *Endecott,* conversational but vivid in *Molyneux,* and in *Benito Cereno* a counterpoint of lush Latinisms or African phrasings against Yankee cliché. Within each play, however, the dialogue style is consistent. And though each play contains a conflict—Endecott versus Morton, Robin versus Molineux, Delano versus Babu—the dialogue enriches polarity with poetic nuance. Themes are realized in imagery as much as in characters, who share a nervous intensity rather than a credible roundness. After seeing his plays, we remember the meaning rather than the feeling, the theatricalism rather than the people. But in this time of short memory, we do remember the plays— perhaps more than those of any other American poet.

Howard Nemerov

As Lowell's plays reflect upon American existence viewed through fiction, the two plays of Howard Nemerov reflect upon human existence viewed through the Bible. *Cain* (1959) and *Endor* (1961) are both written in what Frost called "loose iambic." They resemble Frost's masques in their conversational yet formal language. Like his masques, too, their focus is on ideas rather than people. *Cain* depicts the titular hero as a modern existentialist, and *Endor* presents man's inability to act upon foreknowledge.

In *Cain,* Abel is the favorite not only of God, but of Adam as well. Since "Our God/ Is an eater of meat, meat, meat," Cain's vegetable offerings are unacceptable to Him. With contemporary anguish, Cain inquires into the human situation of a man who is rejected by God, but Cain's family shrinks from such inquiries. In a dialogue between Cain and God, the latter answers none of Cain's questions, and Cain realizes that he alone is responsible for his acts. Cain therefore slays Abel to "change the way things are." Instead of punishing him, God sets His mark on Cain's forehead: "You are one/ Of my holy ones, discoverer of limits." And God confesses to Cain that He was the serpent in Eden. Cain then rejects God, declaring that man must rely upon man alone, in the manner of the French existentialists. Like Sartre's Orestes of *The Flies,* Cain leaves his home to act in freedom. But Nemerov's Adam and Eve, fearful and loving, prepare to start life again, without children.

The piece is a dramatic dialogue rather than a drama. Lines are spoken in meditation, with little passion or imagery. Even the murder springs from philosophy rather than emotion. Eric Bentley has called Sartre's plays "philosophic melodramas," but one appreciates melodrama as opposed to pure philosophy on the stage.

In *Endor,* Nemerov seems to have the theater in mind, since there is more cross talk and scenic direction. Basing his play on *Samuel* 1:28, Nemerov expands on Saul's military momentum, even after he learns that he will die in battle against the Philistines. As in the Bible, a disguised Saul, with two companions, asks for a prophecy from the Witch of Endor, though he himself has outlawed witches. As in the Bible, the Witch questions the dead prophet Samuel, who predicts Saul's death and David's kingship. As in the Bible, Saul falls unconscious, and while he is being revived off stage, the Witch predicts that Saul's Minister will desert him for the Philistines. Saul's military Commander then learns by prophesy that he will slay the defeated Saul at his own request, and then he will serve David, the new king. (Nemerov's Commander eclipses into one character the biblical armor-bearer and the Amalekite.)

Each with his separate knowledge accepts the hospitality of the Witch of Endor, and, as they drink, each reveals what he has seen. Each one pities himself and taunts the others. Drunk by morning, Saul and the Commander go forth to fight, while the Minister exclaims: "They have forgotten! And they are going forth/ As blind men, fateless." But it is the Witch who pronounces the play's final words, which seem to summarize Nemerov's viewpoint: "The fire dies in daylight now, and men/ Wake from their dreams into the mercy of time." Finally, the sophisticated knowledge of the men resolves into simple fatalism: What will be will be, and fortunately men can't know what that is.

Except for the Witch's prophesies, the play is psycho-philosophical at the expense of the dramatic. Nemerov himself seems to take an ironic attitude toward the Witch's powers. The scenic directions state that her divinations by fire *"should not look awesome, or even very impressive; after all, it is only a sort of cookery."* This would seem to imply that Endor is only a pretext for verbalizing men's dreams. If their theatricalism is reduced, the dialogue becomes largely discussion of psychologically realistic characters—intellectually interesting but unevocative.

TWENTIETH CENTURY AMERICAN POETS HAVE TENDED to approach their plays as poets; that is to say, they have translated their poetic concerns into dialogue form, often using the characters as mere catalysts. Thus, it is not difficult to situate these dramatic dialogues within the respective oeuvres of the poets, but it *is* difficult to make claims for the dialogues as dramas. Williams, Miller, and Albee may be insignificant poets, but their works carry dramatic force, whereas the plays of significant poets are usually insignificant as drama. Lacking in that "negative capability" for which Keats praised Shakespeare, American poets too often foist upon their characters an imitation of their own idiom. This is a generalization, of course, and exceptions spring to mind—the virtuoso satire of Cummings' *him*, the rhythmic variety of Williams' *Many Loves*, the colloquial vigor of the frame play of MacLeish's *JB*, the marriage of rhythm to image in Lowell's *Old Glory*. But a single play does not make a dramatist of a poet.

In contrast, more recent poets have almost exploded into theater. Freer in their images and rhythms, these poets seem to need the direct confrontation that only dramatic form provides. The most gifted and the most influential of these poets is LeRoi Jones.

LeRoi Jones

In *New Plays from the Black Theatre*, PUBLISHED IN 1969, LeRoi Jones is described as "a Black Nationalist artist and spiritual leader ('imamu') of the Cultural Nationalist Movement." Jones has deliberately assumed this identity, and his writings—poems, essays, dramas—trace the growth of his black nationalism. His *System of Dante's Hell*, conceived in 1960–1961, is the record of a spiritual voyage through the black ghetto. Patterned on the nine circles of Dante's *Inferno*, Jones' epic announces his theme of blackness, his vision of violence, and his intention to shock, which are consistent throughout his prolific production of the 1960's.

In *The System of Dante's Hell*, the eighth Ditch of the eighth Circle—the Fraudulent Counsellors—is written in dialogue form. Set in a "tent among tents," the scene shows a black homosexual rape. #64 attacks #46, a ghetto Black attacks a middle-class black intellectual "so you can narrate the sorrow of my life." As the scene grows increasingly violent, the lyricism of the dialogue gives way to naturalistic obscenities: "Oh, yeh, I came. I came in you. Yeh." Other numbered characters demand that #46 satisfy their lust, and the dialogue ends with #46 asking #64, whom he personalizes as Herman: "But what kinds [of blues], Herman. What kinds?" #64 closes the play with obscene suggestion: "ooh, baby, just keep throwin' it up like that. Just keep thrown it up." Difficult to interpret, the scene may mean that homosexual initiation into the ghetto is fraudulent counsel for the black writer. Or that the black intellectual is a fraudulent counsellor to ghetto blacks. What is unmistakable is a distinctively violent language.

And it is that language which Jones uses in what may be his first formal play, *The Toilet* (1963).[23] As the title indicates, the action takes place in the *"impersonal ugliness of a school toilet."* Exhaling obscenities into the fetid air, a group of high school Blacks force a white schoolmate down to the basement toilet to fight Foots, the smallest and brightest of them. (Foots has an erotic connotation in several Jones' poems.) Ora, a natural bully, breaks the white boy's jaw, and there is some protest about staging a fight under that handicap. But the white boy, Jimmy Karolis, who has sent Foots a love letter, insists upon fighting him. Jimmy shows surprising strength, so that the group of Blacks attack him and beat him unconscious. They then depart, leaving Karolis' inert body on the toilet floor. Stealthily, Foots returns, *"kneels before the body, weeping and cradling the head in his arms."*

Robert Brustein's unfavorable review of the play calls it "a psychodrama, designed for the acting out of sado-masochistic racial fantasies."[24] But now that such sado-masochistic fantasies have become our daily news, it is possible to appreciate Jones' prescience and dramatic intensity. *The Toilet* is a parable beneath its grimy realistic surface. The dirty white urinals are a symbol of our civilization, and whatever Jones' intention may have been, his accurate idiom delineates the way in which sadistic bullies are able to manipulate both white and black to carnage. As I write this (September, 1969), a comparable event has happened in a San Francisco high school; the white boy is dead, and the black boy severely wounded. But headlines alone could not give impact to Jones' play without a dialogue that drives the action to its murderous near-conclusion. Only the final tender gesture is unconvincing.

The Baptism (1964) is written in a different tone, satirizing black revivalist religion. A handsome black adolescent, after first masturbating and then posing as Christ, asks for baptism; his activity puns on the traditional Second *Coming.* A congregation of sleek, "village type" women first embrace the adolescent and then want to crucify him, but the Boy saves himself and slays his molestors. A Minister exudes piety for his own profit. A Homosexual in a red leotard comments sardonically on the proceedings. Finally, a Motorcycle Messenger from The Man summons the Boy to leave before the world is destroyed at the hour the bars close. But the new Savior (ridiculously named Percy) insists upon remaining with humanity, so that the Messenger knocks him out: "This kid's always been a drag." And he drags the kid away. The play ends with the Homosexual alone on stage, heading for the bars and murmuring: "Wonder what happened to that cute little religious fanatic? *(Does his ballet step. Starts to sing his song.)* God, Go-od, God, etc." The "etc" has

already defined God as "The thug of creation. Our holy dilet-
tante."

Within the narrow limits of caricature, Jones shows a deft
hand. The revivalist hysteria of the Minister and Women are
comic; the Homosexual and the Messenger are suitably cynical
in their different ways; only the Boy is earnest. Though the
religious satire is facile, Jones' language is lively, and the play's
brevity sharpens its point. It is Jones' last play in which color
is not the *main* point.

The Slave (1964) is Jones' longest play, consisting of a Prologue
and two acts. In the Prologue, an old Negro slave delineates his
position as "an old man, full of filed rhythms." Denigrating the
intellectual heritage of the West, he announces a poem before an
ominous event, which he does not specify. That poem is the play
proper, in which the old slave plays the role of Walker Vessels.
It is not clear whether that poem is his past, his future, or a work
of his imagination.

The "poem" takes place during a war of black against white.
Walker Vessels, a black fighter, enters the home of his white
ex-wife, Grace, now married to a white professor, Bradford
Easley, who was once Walker's literature teacher. At first they
talk of the past, but Walker grows more virulent, slaps the
professor, and is in turn racially insulted by the white couple.
Most of the first act consists of Walker's explanation of how he
changed from an esthete to a black terrorist. Despite its contemporary relevance, this rationalization slows the dramatic action.
But Act II moves swiftly. Easley attacks Walker, who shoots
him. The professor dies, straining for his last words as Walker
mocks him.

WALKER: Grace! Tell Bradford that he can say, "I only regret that
I have but one life to lose for my country." You can say that,
Easley, but that's all.
EASLEY: (*Straining to talk*) Ritual drama. Like I said, ritual drama
. . . (*He dies.*)

Over the corpse of the professor, Walker and Grace try to hurt
each other—the continuation of their own ritual drama. They
are interrupted by a series of explosions in which Walker is
wounded, Grace fatally wounded. Her dying request is that

Walker go upstairs to see about their children, but he informs her that they are dead, implying that he has killed them. As Grace asks insistently: "How do you know they're dead, Walker?" she dies. After Walker crawls out, again the old man of the Prologue, a child cries very loudly, but the play ends on the sound of explosions—a continuing civil war, in which children are used as weapons.

Though the dramatic pace is uneven, Jones' dialogue is incisive. Walker Vessels is the virtuoso character, from the blues rhythms and sophisticated ideas of the Prologue, through the intellectual taunts and rationale of Act I, to the refined cruelty of Act II. Bradford and Grace serve mainly as his targets, for their own insulting efforts lack point. In Jones' racial triangle, Grace and Bradford must be destroyed by Walker Vessels, walker towards his goal and vessel of his faith—black nationalism. The Slave wishes to destroy both the ideas and the persons of his oppression, and Jones' Walker destroys with the rhetoric of his rage.

The Slave was followed by *The Dutchman* (1964), Jones' deservedly celebrated drama of a subway encounter between a black man and a white woman. The scenic directions suggest the symbolic intent of the play: *"In the flying underbelly of the city. Steaming hot, and summer on top, outside. Underground. The subway heaped in modern myth."* Endless flight is implied in the play's title. The mythical Dutchman was condemned to round the Cape of Good Hope for all eternity, and so perhaps is Clay, the black man at ease in white (Dutch?) society. As in *The System of Dante's Hell,* Jones uses another work—the myth of the Flying Dutchman—for suggestion rather than exact parallel.

The symbolic situation is established in the opening scenic direction: *"The man looks idly up, until he sees a woman's face staring at him through the window; when it realizes that the man has noticed the face, it begins very premeditatedly to smile."* The smile of the "it" will prove the man's undoing; sex is the weapon that destroys this black Clay.

Even before she speaks, Lula resonates danger by the apple she is eating. Like Eve, she uses sex to corrupt Adam, but the corruption lies in her whiteness. Lula's come-on is breezy until her first insult—"God, you're dull." As the flirtation continues,

Clay tries to pigeon-hole Lula into some recognizable category, until her more sustained insult: "What've you got that jacket and tie on in all this heat for? And why're you wearing a jacket and tie like that? Did your people ever burn witches or start revolutions over the price of tea? Boy, those narrow-shoulder clothes come from a tradition you ought to feel oppressed by. A three-button suit. What right do you have to be wearing a three-button suit and striped tie? Your grandfather was a slave, he didn't go to Harvard." In spite of these taunts, however, Scene II finds Clay and Lula in each other's arms—visibly integrated.

Audibly, however, they strain apart, as Lula's insults become more manic and savage. Other people enter the subway car. Lula flings about her the objects in her net bag. When she gets up to dance, she breaks into a paroxysm of vituperation, climaxed by "There is Uncle Tom . . . I mean, Uncle Thomas Woolly-Head. With old white matted mane. He hobbles on his wooden cane. Old Tom. Old Tom. Let the white man hump his ol' mama, and he jus' shuffle off in the woods and hide his gentle gray head. Ol' Thomas Woolly-Head." This moves the other subway-riders to laughter, and it inspires a drunk to dance with Lula. Clay tries to drag Lula toward the seat, and he clubs the drunk. After another insult, Clay slaps Lula and launches into his own manic monologue.

Referring to the great black masters of jazz and blues, Clay recites a rhapsody of black hatred for whites, punctuating it with murderous threats, and concluding: "They'll cut your throats, and drag you to the edge of your cities so the flesh can fall away from your bones, in sanitary isolation." But his fury subsides. He gathers up his belongings to leave the *"subway heaped in modern myth."* As though by prearrangement, Lula remarks: "All right." to the other passengers, who "respond." She stabs Clay, then commands the other subway-riders to "throw his body out" and "get off at the next stop." After she gathers up her belongings, another handsome young Negro enters, and she looks at him pointedly. We may expect a repetition of the action, and yet the play closes on an exchange of greetings between the young black man and the black train conductor. In the first version of the play, black brotherhood sounds the final note, but in keeping with Jones' own increasingly militant position, a revision eliminates the Conductor.[25] *The Dutchman* ends on the repeated confrontation of black versus his white potential murderer. This is the ironic Cape of Good Hope of all black Dutchmen.

Dramatically, the play is daring in that Lula is given vivid dialogue (and actions) throughout the play, whereas Clay reveals himself in a single long monologue. This demands extraordinary acting from Lula and a virtual tour de force from Clay. In his monologue of rage, Clay reveals himself so explicitly that he drains us of emotional response. Lula, in contrast, is seductive and sadistic; it is her very variety that makes her so dangerous. In this *"subway heaped in modern myth,"* Clay, who is clay in her hands, is the flying Dutchman. Imitating Western man, he is cursed to round the Cape of Good Hope forever. In Romantic variants on this theme, the love of a good woman could end the curse of the Flying Dutchman, but in Jones' variant the hatred of a white woman ends the curse by killing the man.

After *The Dutchman*, Jones' plays become candidly agit-prop in the cause of black nationalism and white destruction. A man of great charisma and energy, he is the leading intellectual for today's young Blacks, and yet his drama evokes different reactions from them. In the *Black Theatre* issue of *The Drama Review*, one black theater worker wrote: "Not to produce LeRoi Jones at this time in our history stops any theatre from being a truly black theatre."[26] But another: "LeRoi Jones should belong here [in a group of playwrights who address their work to Negro audiences], but despite his brilliance, he is still trying to do something with whites, either flagellating them verbally, or parading them as beasts. The results are often vivid but shallow abstractions."[27]

In Jones' own introduction to his *Four Black Revolutionary Plays*, he writes: "i am prophesying the death of white people in this land/ i am prophesying the triumph of black life in this land, and over all the world." And his drama-prophesies tend to be as bald as this statement. In *Experimental Death Unit #1* (1964), black revolutionaries kill two white dudes and a black woman who has been socializing with them; they cut the white men's heads off and display them on pikes—as in *Macbeth*. *Black Mass* (1965) dramatizes the black Muslim myth in which Jacoub, a black magician, creates a raving white beast, who is evil incarnate, and who slays Blacks screaming "White! . . . White! Me . . . Me . . . Me . . . White!" *Great Goodness of Life* (1965), subtitled "A coon show," traces the making of a modern Uncle Tom; to partake of the wealth of white consumer America, Court Royal is compelled to fire a gun into the mouth of a black boy, who dies uttering the word "Papa." *Madheart* (1966) dramatizes a confrontation between old and new Blacks; on the one side are Mother and Sister, who are tempted by white culture, and on the other, Black Man and Woman, who are dedicated to its destruction; the Black Man judges Mother and Sister: "They'll die or help us, be black or white and dead. I'll save them or kill them." A fifth play, *Jello*, was evidently censored by the publisher, but it deals with the liberation of Jack Benny's Rochester.

The *Black Theatre* issue of *The Drama Review* (1968) published two short plays by Jones, *Home on the Range* and *Police*. In the former, a Black Criminal enters the home of a Family who watch television and speak nonsense-words. When the Criminal frightens them into a catatonic state, a Crowd of Black People enter to hold a wild party on stage, which the Criminal describes: "This is the tone of America. My country 'tis of thee." He shoots into the midst of the audience, proclaiming "the new the beautiful the black change of the earth." At the last, three Black Men and a Black Girl emerge from the pile of bodies on stage. They greet the morning, as the Criminal forces the Father of the Family to confess that they are "evil ghosts without substance."

In *Police*, a Black Cop is scorned alike by White Cops and Black People. The latter try to report the murder they know the Black Cop will commit. Then, with phallic taunts, the Black People force the Black Cop to shoot himself. After the Blacks leave—"Goodbye Savages"—"WHITE COPS . . . *are all assembled around the dead nigger cop doing pixie steps, or slobbering on his flesh, a few are even eating chunks of flesh they tear off in their weird banquet.*"

Two subsequent Jones plays almost dispense with dialogue. *Slave Ship* (1968), a Theater of Cruelty piece, is a series of tableaux depicting black history from the first slaves to the present national consciousness. As Larry Neal notes, the pageant is "a continuous rush of sound, groans, screams, and souls wailing for freedom and relief from suffering. . . . It is a play which almost totally eliminates the need for a text. It functions on the basis of movement and energy—the dramatic equivalent of the New Music."[28]

The Death of Malcolm X (1969) makes such extensive use of cinematic techniques that the published script could serve either stage or screen. Jones presents the murder of the black leader as a plot of a Klansman, conspiring with the coöperation of the United States Army. Against shots of Klansman, army scenes, street violence, Malcolm X is shown with his family and his people. As the killers move toward him, he pleads: "Oh, O.K., cool it brothers . . . everything's gonna be O.K." After he is shot, the television newscaster announces: "Today black extremist Malcolm X was killed by his own violence." In the last scene, the whites hold a ritualistic celebration.

After *The Dutchman*, Jones' plays devalue dialogue in favor of film, ritual, and incantation. The rich images and controlled rhythms of the earlier plays give way to exclamations, blows, shots, montage effects. Conceived to carry a simple message— usually of hatred against whites—to black audiences, these plays ruthlessly smother Jones' verbal gifts. And following him in this anti-dialogue dramaturgy full of stage violence are several of the young playwrights of the black theater.

RECENT WHITE AND NON-POLITICAL POETS HAVE ALSO turned their backs on distinctive dialogue. Though this is not true of Rochelle Owens, she minimizes the effect of dialogue by lavish gesture and staging. Lawrence Ferlinghetti has published a book of dramatic *Routines*, which are scenarios with little dialogue. Kenneth Koch, a satiric poet, has written six so-called Improvisation Plays with little or no dialogue. Paradoxically, then, poets are abandoning their traditional mastery of language for the primacy of incantation and/or gesture.

ROCHELLE OWENS

ROCHELLE OWENS' SIX PLAYS ARE NOMINALLY SET IN SIX WIDELY different locales. Nominally because there is no pretense of realism for these regions: American farm, Greenland igloo, African field, fifteenth-century Constantinople, nineteenth-century Asia, mythical Greece—all seethe with sex drives, power drives, passion, and farce. This reads like a description of Euripides or Jacobean tragedy, or certain plays of Buechner, Wedekind, Strindberg, or Genet. But the combination is rare in American drama.

Futz (1960), her first play, is by far the best known.[29] The title (and name of the protagonist) suggests *fuck* and *fart*—both recalling man's animality. But Cyrus Futz is the gentlest of animals; in love with his pig, Miranda, he invites the lubricious Majorie Satz to join the man-animal couple in a little orgy. Majorie is so shocked by their activities that she vows vengeance against Futz. Parallel with this all too human reaction is the puritanical murder of Oscar Loop. Inflamed by the amorous acts of Cyrus and his pig, Oscar thinks he kills sin in killing Ann Fox (whose last name sounds like Futz). Oscar Loop becomes his surname when he is hanged for his crime; his mother then announces his respectability: "He's gonna look like a minister high on the pulpit above the congregation." Like the quotation from *Corinthians* that precedes the play—"Now concerning the things whereof ye wrote unto me: It is good for a man not to touch a woman."—Christian society condemns free sensuality. Thus, Oscar kills and is killed. Majorie, for all her sexual freedom, persuades her two lovers to kill the sexually cherished pig. The Narrator comments sardonically: "Hell hath no fury like a woman scorned by a man—for a pig." In prison, Futz protests his martyrdom: "I wasn't near people. They came to me and looked under my trousers all the way up to their dirty hearts." And the brother of Majorie Satz, whom all men call "pig," avenges her honor by stabbing Futz.

From Euripides' *Bacchae* to Pinter's *Homecoming*, playwrights have warned us of man's animal nature; Rochelle Owens dramatizes its grotesque humor as well as its underlying terror. An animal renders Futz tender, Majorie vengeful, her brother evil, and Loop dangerous; the on-lookers are self-righteous and judgmental. In dramatizing this aspect of man's sexual nature, Rochelle Owens uses an artifically simple language, with subtle and pointed repetitions; formal phrases and understatement are counterpointed against the central violence. The economy of the final dialogue shows her control.

Cy [Futz]: Now why Ned why do you want to kill the animal?
Brother Ned (Seething): You make my brains red!
(He stabs Cy.)
Narrator (Ironical): Amanda—there's someone here he needs you.
    Yes.

No other Owens play is as taut as *Futz*, perhaps because of its seemingly homogeneous culture. In Owens' subsequent plays, the action arises not only from a conflict between man's animal nature and his "civilized" drives, but from the antagonism between different cultures. In *The String Game* (1963), an Italian priest and a German half-breed try to "civilize" Greenland Eskimos. During the winter storms, the Eskimos play the string game, exercising their lively imaginations which dwell largely on sex. Though Father Bontempo admonishes them puritanically, he himself has voluptuous dreams of pasta, tomato sauce and olive oil, anchovies and Genoese sausage. Half-breed Cecil bribes Father Bontempo with these goodies, to help him convince the Eskimos to enter his shoe business: "Still playing the string games, fools! No wonder you never get ahead. I read the Finances. I will get ahead. (Flourishing a copy of The Wall Street Journal) I will one day wear a hat and cloth coat . . . and, and . . . marry a bleach blonde!"

Completely lacking in enterprise, the Eskimos agree to business, only to please "Fada." Cecil then pays the promised meal to the priest, but his German soul is disgusted by the latter's insistence on chewing with open mouth. Disciplining the priest as his German father had disciplined him, Cecil slaps the priest, who chokes and dies. The disapproving Eskimos make Cecil go out to wash his mouth in the snow. They grieve briefly for the priest, but then continue to live in their string games, which free their imaginations. Natural virtue endures in this Owens play.

The String Game dwells lovingly on sex to establish the warmth of the Eskimos, whose community is composed of men of good will. Evil enters with Christian puritanism and Western enterprise; neither Bontempo nor Cecil is capable of the lyricism of the string-game artists: "[String games] are alive, like the bodies of the animals our grandparents hunted." Humorous and vulgar, the Eskimos relish their life, their memories, and their voluptuous imaginations. They shrink from constraint.

In her two subsequent short plays, Owen again mixes humor and horror, but the tenderness disappears. *Istamboul* and *Homo* (both 1965) dramatize a clash of cultures; the former is set in Constantinople during the crusades, and the latter somewhere in Asia during the commercial crusades of the nineteenth century. In both plays, European women are fascinated by non-Europeans, and in both plays European men are ready to contribute their women to a larger cause. Istamboul is the meeting place of Eastern and Western Christians shortly before the Saracen invasion. Norman Godfrigh—the spelling combines piety with lust—desires the hairy St. Mary of Egypt, and yet he also thinks of using her saintliness commercially. For that modern attitude, the saint kills him. Godfrigh's wife Alice is fascinated by Byzantine Leo, who is excited by her smooth skin. After Godfrigh's death, Alice and Leo share a voluptuous hour before the arrival of the Saracens and, presumably, of the end of the world.

Homo, whose very title indicates the ubiquitous quality of Owens' geography, dramatizes the myth of the blonde white goddess in the dark cultures of Asia. Thus, a blonde goddess Bernice arouses erotic longing through her cruelties to Asians. White fleshy Elizabeth, however, accepts humiliation at the hands of Asian workers as her white fleshy husband accepts it at the hands of Asian officials (played by the same actors) so long as they remain economically dominant.

Stage lust is at once farcical and familiar, for all the exotic setting; the Normans are aroused by dark hair, and the Asians lick the fingers of the white woman. Though violent actions occur, it is mainly through language that Owens builds her strange familiar empires. In bed with Byzantine Leo, Alice intones: "Godfrigh drooled for the woman . . . one day I'll be toothless and I'll drool—and then I'll remember how Godfrigh

drooled for a woman—not me—an Eastern woman—a saint
... perhaps then, without my teeth ... I will be sweeter and
gentler."

In *Homo* the Asian workers scream for the white goddess
Bernice, but fat Elizabeth sticks her fingers in their mouths and
intones: "Five five five five five when I scream a new race will
emerge from between my thighs—the bones will be big and the
heads long and thin—o for that day we wait and we will have
all wokened at the same time—five five five five five five five five
..." Elizabeth summarizes the white myth that their women are
the most desirable, and that through the women all other races
will be paled and purified. With the violence of farce, Owens
explodes this myth in *Homo*.

Owens' cruellest and longest play is *Beclch* (1966). The title
suggests beak, belch, cluck, lick—all resonant of animals, but
animal innocence has given way to sophisticated animality and
a conscious return to lust and cruelty. Four whites "go native"
in Africa, but what is natural for the natives is exaggeratedly
relished by the whites, especially Beclch. In the opening scene,
Beclch tortures an old woman and kills an adolescent, as she
tries to separate two mother-son couples. In the second scene,
at a cock-fight, Beclch falls in love with Jose, who is half her age
and full of gentleness; she initiates him into cruelty and the
awareness that he enjoys it. In the third scene, she persuades
Yago to accept elephantiasis for power; as Shakespeare's Iago
revelled in the suffering of Othello, she will cause her Yago to
suffer at the hands of the natives. But it is she and not the natives
who commands the death agonies of the deformed King Yago.
Whites and blacks unite in mockery of the king who strangles
himself—except for Jose, who leaves shortly afterward. With
the departure of Jose, Beclch's own position is undermined; the
queen who loses a man must be beheaded, and Beclch looks
forward to her own torture as voluptuously as she tortured man
and animal.

Though Beclch maims and kills on stage, she renders her
cruelty mainly through language. Early in the play, she remarks
scornfully to Yago: "You speak language hollowly!" She herself
relishes images; as she speaks of sanctifying Jose, she rubs a
persimmon over her lips and remarks: "Mmmmm, a persimmon

is like flesh—you can hear it scream when you bite it." Mocking the diseased Yago, she chants: "We bungle in the jungle." After Jose leaves her, Beclch realizes that she has been parasitic of his feelings because she herself is no longer capable of feeling: "I want to cook flesh in fat and throw the gristle at the fire—to hear the sputtering! I wish like hell it could yell! I wish like hell it could yell! I'm a poet!" Who writes her verses to the accompaniment of screams and blood. Her last wish is to "drool like an animal . . . I want to drool without making a sound."

Owens intends Beclch to be a fascinating horror; for civilized man (and woman) there is no simple return to animality because we have too much imagination. Owens' Beclch is so consistently and determinedly cruel that she often emerges as Grand Guignol, and it is difficult to know how much this is intended. The horror of *Futz* is estranged by a Narrator, and it is sustained through swift short scenes. But it is hard to sustain horror, and Owens does not succeed in doing so in this, her longest play.

LAWRENCE FERLINGHETTI

FERLINGHETTI'S PLAYS ARE BRIEF SARDONIC COMMENTS ON OUR CONtemporary life-style. But brevity is not always the soul of wit, and for all their brevity, Ferlinghetti's plays manage to be diffuse. His own view of the seven plays of *Unfair Arguments with Existence* is that they are "variations on similar themes, meant to be played *together*, moving progressively from the representational toward a purely non-objective theatre—with still a long way to go." The themes may perhaps be resolved into a single theme—the unfairness of industrial, consumer-oriented, establishment-dominated existence—and the plays are arguments against submission to such existence.

Though the plays do not move "progressively from representational toward a purely non-objective theatre," they do vary in idiom. *The Soldiers of No Country* is the longest of the plays—perhaps half an hour on stage. In a grotesque lovers' triangle, Toledano, a sixty-year old priest, and Denny, a stuttering deserter of twenty, vie for the favors of Erma, a plain thirty-five year old, love-starved woman. Their rivalry is enacted in a womb-like cave, full of silent people. Erma makes the stage symbolism explicit: "In the womb we are in no country, we are the soldiers of no country, the great unborn of no country, and lead a blind life of our own, a blind life that knows no evil or hate, knows only a blind urge to love, to be born and to love and to love and to give birth again—" The priest Toledano sneers: "Very poetic!" and a character named Payroll keeps intoning his name. One by one, the mute figures on stage topple to the ground; after Toledano's conquest, Erma stumbles out of the cave. The deserter threatens the priest with his gun, and the play seems to end on a universal vision of death, but *"somewhere in the interior of the cave of the theatre a baby is crying."* It grows louder, to end the play on the hope of rebirth.

Ferlinghetti describes *Three Thousand Red Ants* as "a little parable of the crack in anybody's egg or universe," and its dialogue is an experiment in short, abrupt, associational phrases. The exchanges of the married couple, Fat and Moth, who look out of their bed with binoculars, occasionally recall the Hamm-Clov exchanges of Beckett's *Endgame*, but neither the dialogue nor the business is so functional. The play's end recapitulates its rhythms:

> FAT: *(Swings glasses excitedly in all directions, eyes glued to them.)* What a—what a real—what a breakthrough if—a real breakthrough —yes—*(excitedly focusing on audience)* Yes, yes, there it is, there it is, there it still is, by God—no mistaking it—no matter where I look there's that same little crack, that same little crack—"

To which his wife replies, from under the covers: "Your own! Humpty Dumpty!"

In *The Alligation* (defined by Ferlinghetti as "any connexion, situation, relationship, obsession, habit or other hang-up which is almost impossible to break . . .") a heroine named Ladybird is fixated upon her pet alligator, Shooky. A blind Indian warns of the dangers of obsessive possession, but Ladybird bills and coos to her pet in the manner of Tennessee Williams' more grotesque heroines. When she stretches full length on Shooky, he rolls over on top of her, and the Blind Indian calls to the audience for help. But no one can help her.

The Victims of Amnesia is set in the lobby of a seedy hotel, like

O'Neill's *Hughie.* And like O'Neill's *Hughie*, the play contains an existential dialogue between a Night Clerk and a guest. But in Ferlinghetti's play, the guest is named Mazda, and she goes through four stages of diminishing age—Marie, Young Woman, Girl, Baby. Instead of the finally sympathetic response of O'Neill's Hughie, Ferlinghetti's Night Clerk has no sympathy for the flickering human lights: "Out, out! All—all of you! Drop dead! Drop—dead!" At the end of the play, however, after all human life has crashed with the light bulbs of various sizes, *"a very small light bulb is lowered very slowly and hesitantly down the stairwell. It grows brighter and brighter as the houselights come up."* Absurdly, in a play that uses the disjunctive but suggestive scenes of the French Theater of the Absurd.

In contrast *Motherlode* is a metaphor for the human condition as seen through an optimistic vision. Almost a monologue of a miner who spends his life looking for gold, the play traces the triumph of the Schmucks with their commercial non-values. As the epigram phrases it: "that crotch was once a vision of love," and the miner never loses his vision, expressed in the inarticulacy of the movie Western: "Guess this proves once and for all, by Gad, that—you don't—that underground ain't the only way, by Gad—ain't the only way to get where you ain't, in this here—claim I staked." As the Little Schmuck inherits the land, he dies intoning: "Still-runs—after—Damn—I still—I'm still—still coming—still—now—I'll find—"

Like the sexual pun that closes the *Motherlode*, the monologue of the titular Customs Collector in *The Customs Collector in Baggy Pants* is loaded with sexual suggestion, addressed to invisible ladies in pay toilets aboard an ocean liner. The metaphoric meaning, as in Jones' *Toilet*, is explicitly enunciated earlier in his monologue: "This lifeboat full of flush-toilets which we call civilization." Among the double meanings are "a real woman's home companion," "balls and knockers," " 'Thar she blows!' cries Ahab afloat upon his Moby Dick," "I cannot for the wife of me find it," "me without my gun," "my investigation reaches its climax," "a hardened criminal," "my roamin' candle." As the ladies' flushing toilets drown out the Customs Collector, he screams: "But I won't drown! Not I! I won't drown, I won't go down! Hear me? I—I'll—I—I won't *die.* I won't capitulate! I absolutely refuse to die!" Outside the storm continues, and it is difficult to accept the customary Ferlinghetti final note of hope, so salaciously sly has he been in coming to it.

The Nose of Sisyphus, the last of the *Unfair Arguments*, is a scenario in which a Big Baboon seems to get the best of Sisyphus (who pushes a globe with a fake nose) by beating him, stripping him of false nose, and tossing the nose to the audience. There someone else may take up the task of Sisyphus. Ferlinghetti reprints the play as one of his thirteen *Routines*. He defines a routine as "a song & dance, a little rout, a routing-out, a run-around, a 'round of business or amusement.'" On stage, he tends to take the rounds literally in these symbolic scenarios of various aspects of the human condition. Only *Servants of the People* uses dialogue, and, significantly, the dialogue is the weapon of a totalitarian state. Since theatrical translation of *Routines* is almost entirely gestural, we have, finally, the paradox of a theater poet who writes mime.

KENNETH KOCH

WRITTEN OVER THE DECADE 1953–1962, THE BRIEF PLAYS OF KENNETH Koch burlesque the occasional pageants of academic or patriotic tradition. The blurb on the cover of his *Bertha and Other Plays* claims that the plays "use and parody a wide variety of theatrical models and traditions." Rather than parody, however, which is mockery of a specific work or author, Koch's plays are bur-lesque, containing a wider mockery of a genre or style.

At the time of publication (1966) five plays had been produced, and the others are too slight for anything but a collective exer-cise. Even *Pericles*, the first to be written, lasts only a few min-utes, but a series of imaged non sequiturs manage to mock the quest of the Greek tyrant for an ideal polis. Slightly more sus-tained, *Bertha* presents a Wagnerian queen of Norway *"clothed in a ring of white eagles."* In a swift series of pointless battles, she reaps glory for her country, then dies on the throne, whereupon her citizens declare: "She was a great queen! . . . She conquered her own country many times! . . . Norway was happy under her rule!" Even Shakespeare does not escape from this reflection on royal glory, but the tone is far lighter than Brecht's anti-Shakespearean "Between Scenes," which also mock dramatic royalty.

George Washington Crossing the Delaware annihilates the patriotic American historical play, as it has been practised in generations of primary schools. Cornwallis and Washington are in conflict, but Cornwallis declares that Washington will surely join him when he realizes his error: "What is more unnatural than that this man, Washington, who is one of God's gentlemen, should so defy the laws of right and wrong as to raise his hand against the breast that gave him suck, against the tender maternal care of England?" Washington, in contrast, is a rough and ready American: "Friends, soldiers, and Americans, lend me your ears! *(Laughter.)* I have seen the British general, Cornwallis —/ Brightly he shines in regal uniform,/ And brightly shines his sword—but she will cut/ No better, boys, than ours!" There is little to choose between the movie-soldier dialogue of Americans or British, but Washington outsmarts Cornwallis after dreaming a version of the cherry tree story. At the age of six, Washington confesses that he chopped the tree down, but he runs away from his irate father: "I cannot tell a lie, but I can run!" He can also swim, for that is how he escapes a beating. And the dream inspires his military strategy: Washington orders the American army to swim the Delaware, and they too escape a beating.

The Construction of Boston (like *The Building of Florence* and the opera *Angelica*) burlesque another genre—the pageant of the founding of a city. The Boston burlesque is particularly witty in its *trouvailles*, since three contemporary artists are characters in the play: "*Rauschenberg chose to bring people and weather to Boston; Tinguely, architecture; and Niki de Saint-Phalle, art. The people Rauschenberg brought to Boston were a young man and woman who set up housekeeping on the right side of the stage. For weather, Rauschenberg furnished a rain machine. Tinguely rented a ton of gray sandstone bricks for the play, and from the time of his first appearance he was occupied with the task of wheeling in bricks and building a wall with them, across the proscenium. . . . Niki de Saint-Phalle brought art to Boston as follows: she entered, with three soldiers, from the audience, and once on stage shot a rifle at a white plaster copy of the Venus de Milo which caused it to bleed paint of different colors.*" Contrasting with the visual Happening quality of the burlesque are blank verse lines which scan as heavily and grayly as the sandstone bricks; they are interspersed with witty rhymes, or with fairy tale diction in this urban environment. Tinguely addresses Boston's Back Bay: "Back Bay, you're lucky. You and Mill Pond are./ I am going to put/ Sumptuous buildings on you that/ Will make you lovely as a star." As in patriotic pageants, *The Construction of Boston* closes with the three artists heaping praise on one another.

Koch is an able mocker, but his targets are limited—history, legend, patriotic and contemporary clichés. His wit is of cabaret quality, depending on brevity and expert timing. So far, none of his plays has the sustained drive of a *Knight of the Burning Pestle* or *Critic*. As in his equally witty and more imaginative volumes of poetry, Koch runs the danger of repeating his own facility.

THE STATEMENT HAS OFTEN BEEN MADE, DURING THE course of this long and sometimes tedious chapter, that American poets exhibit intermittent or inadequate commitment to theater. This is, of course, a sweeping and circular judgment, since we recognize inadequacy only by the inadequacy of the specific plays, and this survey has yielded no mute inglorious Miltons, no unapplauded *Agonistes*. Generally more reflective than the novelists who flirted intermittently with drama, the poets found difficulty in expressing their vision *dramatically*.

As a group, they approach drama self-consciously, and we find them appropriating exotic forms—the Japanese Noh, the medieval Morality or Miracle. Several poets try to use their self-consciousness by incorporating it into the form of the play within the play—Cummings' *him*, Williams' *Many Loves*, MacLeish's *JB*, Schevill's *Bloody Tenet*, and all Eberhart's plays; the tension between frame and inner play does sometimes provide a substitute for the more conventional conflicts of drama. Though they may contain incidental subtleties, most poetic plays are lacking in sustained tension. All too often, the dialogue is built around ideas, but modern poets show no gift comparable to Plato's dialectical thrust and counter-thrust.

Plays of poets are weakly plotted, but collectively they display a wide variety of rhythms—from the mannered prose of Stevens, through Frost's strict iambics, MacLeish's dactyllics and trochaics, Williams' free short lines, Jeffers' free long lines, the mixtures of *him, JB, Many Loves.* Though the poets often wrote prose plays, their prose tends to be more heavily and more regularly accented than the general run of American dramatic dialogue.

One might expect the dialogue of poets to exhibit a richness of imagery comparable to the rhythmic diversity. But this is only sporadically true—from Stevens in the early years of the century to Jones and Owens in the 1960's. Williams and Lowell have deliberately muted their images in an effort to imbue their dialogue with greater dramatic drive. Only rarely do the poets achieve theatricalization of their imagery—like the flag in Lowell's *Old Glory.* In contrast, birth remains verbal in Cummings' *him* (despite backdrop) and Williams' *Many Loves.* Nor are poets, for all their metaphoric gift, free of abstraction. Somewhat surprisingly, the poets are most concrete when most pointed— through satire and parody.

What seems regrettable is the relative failure of American poets to inject great rhythmic variation or image innovation through example or influence. By far the large bulk of twentieth century American drama is colloquial—simple in syntax and vocabulary, monosyllabic and repetitive in rhythm, narrowly referential in range. By contrast, the plays of the poets, in spite of the dull way they have had to be summarized in this chapter, provide diversity. But what they rarely provide is insight into people and into the dramatic tensions of experience.

8 / The Rest May Be Silence

A CONCLUDING CHAPTER, HOWEVER TENTATIVE, MIGHT MOVE IN several directions. I might sum up traditionally, underlining what I have written at some length—that only four American playwrights have produced distinctive dialogue, and that their most distinguished dialogue is often the least eloquent; that America's major writers have been poor playwrights perhaps because they do not realize that dramatic dialogue has to be acted by actors for the perception of an audience. Most American poets and novelists—so meaningfully concrete in their own genres—lack a physical sense of the living bodies of actors. Though writers' words may move in time and move a plot through time, they often fail to move actors through stage space. Professional playwrights do this knowledgeably, and sometimes they do little more. At their best, however, the dialogue of O'Neill, Miller, Williams, and Albee moves actors through space and plots through time to provide us with insights into human experience. Their best plays are few, and they are imperfect. I have discovered no hidden American masterpieces, and I do not believe that the best American plays approach *Peer Gynt* for scope, *The Ghost Sonata* for suggestivity, *The Cherry Orchard* for wisdom, *Mother Courage* for compassion, *Endgame* for concentration, or *The Blacks* for passion. The best modern American dramas fall short of the best European, and I believe that I have shown that the shortcomings are in the dialogue.

Perhaps I should conclude this book by turning from the past to the present. Since various American playwrights of the 1960's have already produced a corpus of works—Ed Bullins, Rosalind Drexler, Paul Foster, Irene Fornes, Israel Horovitz, John Guare, Sam Shepard, Ronald Tavel, Megan Terry, Jean-Claude van Itallie—their dialogue might be examined, play by play, in the manner of the last two chapters. But critics—including myself—have written too much too soon about playwrights still learning their craft—whatever that craft may evolve to be. Instead, I shall swiftly indicate some of the uses of dialogue by these playwrights. Ed Bullins has created a new and original idiom of the black underworld, but he uses that idiom in Aristotelian fashion—to further plot and delineate character. In contrast, several of these playwrights deliberately spurn coherent plot and consistent character, and their dialogue tends to be self-indulgent with whimsy, obscenity, and meandering monologues. Several contemporary playwrights seek to elevate repetition to incantation, and they pay more attention to sound than to the intelligible meaning of words. A few playwrights have tried to mould their dialogue to the needs of a particular theater group. And since improvisation has loomed so large in actors' training, this has sometimes been built into the text, as in Foster's *Tom Paine*, where Scenes I and VIII of Part One and Scenes I and XI of Part Two are specifically titled "Improvisational." An improvisational technique called transformation—in which the actor *abruptly* transforms identity or situation—has been incorporated into plays of Fornes, Terry, and van Itallie.

Still another conclusion for this book would be a transformation of my own—to shift my subject abruptly from drama to theater, which is generating a new excitement among youth, where the future lies. In New York alone, after indiscriminate publicity to the phrase Theater of Cruelty—invoked with and more often without knowledge of Artaud—we have had Action Theater, Black Theater, Guerilla Theater, Happening, Improvisational Theater, Nude Theater, Radical Theater, Street Theater, Theater Events, Theater Games, Theater of the Ridiculous. And all assign a shrunken role to dialogue.

As I conclude this book—August, 1970—Peter Brook is working with an international company of actors, each to play in his own language. Jerzy Grotowski's *Apocalypsis cum Figuria* is acted in Polish, but the text is a composite of the Bible, Dostoyevsky,

T. S. Eliot, and Simone Weil. In Eugenio Barba's Odin Teatret productions, each of the actors speaks his own Scandinavian language. The now splintered Living Theater, an international company of American origin, shouted its dialogue in the language of the country in which it was playing.

Whether cause or result of the de-emphasis on dialogue, productions of the New Theater bear an international stamp. In the past, theater enthusiasts often attended theater in a language they did not understand, but today one loses less in such attendance. Theoretically, the actor's instrument has always been his body, but practically the actor's body moved us through his mannerisms and another's words. Today, the words are slighted while the actor is enjoined to use his *whole* body. Artaud was inspired, not by a poet, but by the Balinese *dancers.* Grotowski turned to Kathakali and Yoga for his arduous actors' training. Comparable exercises are being performed in this country in lofts and cellars, cafes and churches.

For the distinguishing feature of the New Theater is its disinterested commitment. Throughout this century, America has had dedicated theater groups, and a few of them have had tangible rewards in spite of their dedication. The Provincetown Players became the Theater Guild; the Group Theater died, but Clurman, Crawford, Odets, and especially Strasberg knew personal success that influenced the course of Broadway and Hollywood performance. The Living Theater, the Open Theater, and the Cafe La Mamma Repertory Company have had foundation grants or international invitations. Their attitude toward dialogue travels with them, and even before them. In a recent trip around the shrinking world, I was struck by the formal similarity of New Theater productions: stress on actor-to-audience impact, opportunity for improvisation in performance, emphasis upon movement in space rather than time. Whereas Aristotle implied a distinction between dramaturgy and performance, the New Theater seeks to blend the two. Since each performance is an event, the dramatic text—if one exists—becomes a score or scenario to be orchestrated and choreographed.

The academic critic—I—will suggest that this too is not new. The Commedia dell'arte worked from scenarios, not texts.

Shakespeare has been rewritten in every century and in every country. Other texts have been altered by actors or directors. During the course of this study, we have noted how Elia Kazan "suggested" a shift in emphasis at the end of MacLeish's *JB* and a different ending for Tennessee Williams' *Cat on a Hot Tin Roof.* What is new today is the widespread and matter-of-fact manipulation of texts and scenarios, after decades of relative fidelity to written dialogue.

More important than such manipulation to the future of dramatic dialogue is a divergence of attitudes in the New Theater, polarized around Grotowski on the one hand and Beck on the other. Like their mentor Artaud, both directors view theater as THE instrument of cultural reorientation. Neither director has any sympathy for classical rationalism—to instruct while delighting. Rather, the spectator is to be shocked by the Theater of Cruelty into a new self-awareness that may commit him to a new way of life. But Grotowski rigidly limits the number of spectators and casts them in a specific role with respect to the actors, while Beck's performances absorb his spectators and sometimes spill over into the streets. Grotowski's actors go from the theater to separate homes, while those of Beck lived communally.

What is the relevance to dialogue? Just this. Grotowski works with a *dramaturg* who helps him fix a text, for words are as discriminately chosen as costume, prop, and gesture. In America the Open Theater and Theater Genesis are somewhat similar; the former group has worked with Megan Terry and Jean-Claude van Itallie, the latter with Murray Mednick, so as to arrive at a text for performance, and the texts have subsequently been printed. Other American theater groups have been hospitable to embryonic playwrights, and we may expect printed texts in which the dialogue will reflect the training and orientation of the group.

As nearly as I can tell, however, the path of the Living Theater is more usual among young people with a theatrical urge. Judith Malina is rumored to be responsible for most of the dialogue of the last four Living Theater productions, but no credit is given her in the programs, and no text has been published. This indicates a desire to do away with the dialogue of playwrights; the words must spring from actors and audience—at least theoretically. "No more masterpieces," cried Artaud. The anarchic New Theater adds: "No more masters. Actors and audience intermingle. Theater is life." The dialogue of such theater will die with its immediacy.

The theater has survived several periods of debased dialogue. Can it do so once again?

Notes

1. *Artaud versus Aristotle in America*

1. My translation differs slightly from that of Mary Caroline Richards, in Antonin Artaud, *The Theater and its Double* (New York, 1958).

2. I have neither the competence nor the temperament to establish theoretical boundaries for drama, but see the brilliant attempt by Darko Suvin, "Reflections on Happenings," *The Drama Review* #47 (125–144).

2. *The Wet Sponge of* EUGENE O'NEILL

1. For convenient reference, I refer to quotations as reprinted in Oscar Cargill, N. Bryllion Fagin and William J. Fisher, eds., *O'Neill and His Plays: Four Decades of Criticism* (New York, 1961), 236.

2. Cargill, 272.

3. "The Retreat from the Word," *Kenyon Review* (Spring, 1961), 211.

4. Cargill, 143.

5. Joseph Wood Krutch, ed., *Nine Plays by Eugene O'Neill*, xxi.

6. Cargill, 14.

7. Cargill, 464.

8. John Henry Raleigh, ed., *The Plays of Eugene O'Neill* (Carbondale, Ill., 1965), 220.

9. Cargill, 250, 251, 255. I am indebted to Horst Frenz for the information about Hofmannsthal's reading in English.

10. Cargill, 125.

11. Dates are those of completion, insofar as I could ascertain them. Otherwise, date is publication or performance, whichever is earlier.

12. Cf. Signi Falk, "Dialogue in the Plays of Eugene O'Neill," *Modern Drama* (December, 1960), 317–318.

13. Neither memory nor lighting is used mechanically, however: the chain-gang incident is the most recent memory, but O'Neill places it after the vision of Jeff, whose murder sends Jones to the chain gang. The slave ship, a racial memory, is dimly lit.

14. Cargill, 146.

15. Arthur and Barbard Gelb, *O'Neill* (New York, 1962), 439.

16. Barrett H. Clark, *Eugene O'Neill: The Man and His Plays* (New York, 1947), 83.

17. Ibid.

18. Quoted by Edmund Wilson, in Cargill, 465.

19. Cargill, 161.

20. Cargill, 111

21. Gelb, 499.

22. Clark, 83, and Mardi Valgemae, "O'Neill and German Expressionism," *Modern Drama* (September, 1967), 111–123.

23. O'Neill saw the Abbey Theatre on their New York visit in 1911, and he read Synge in the tuberculosis sanatorium.

24. Cargill, 108–9.

25. Clark, 97.

26. Raleigh, 215.

27. Cargill, 342.

28. For disagreement, see Y.M. Biese, *Aspects of Expression I* (Helsinki, 1963), 28. Biese refers to Eric Linklater's parody of *Strange Interlude* in his *Juan in America*: "*Black Bread* was the story of the woman Kathleen and her three lovers, Sidney Bush, Walter Hood, and Gerald Tomkins. There was not very much action in the play. Every half-hour the scene shifted. Kathleen was introduced on the verandah of her home in the Adirondacks. She was talking to Sidney and Gerald. Then she was shown in bed, talking to Walter. Then in the living room, the dining room, on board a train, in an art gallery (some enlightened observations were offered here), a corridor, a garden, and a bath-room. But wherever she was she talked, and Walter, Gerald and Sidney very often replied to her. But more often they wrote in their diaries. For this was the revolutionary device invented by Mr. Knut Blennem for discovering to the audience the true and secret thoughts of his *dramatis personae.*"

29. Edwin A. Engel, *The Haunted Heroes of Eugene O'Neill* (Cambridge, 1953), 200.

30. Gelb, 659.

31. Lee Simonson, *The Stage is Set* (New York, 1946), 435.

32. Gelb, 661.

33. Gelb, 648.

34. Gelb, 649–50.

35. Cargill, 187.

36. Reprinted in Horst Frenz, ed., *American Playwrights on Drama* (New York, 1965).

37. Gelb, 698.

38. For a contrast of the Greek and American plays, see Angela Belli, *Ancient*

Greek Myths and Modern Drama (New York, 1969); Hugh Dickinson, *Myths on the Modern Stage* (Urbana, 1969); and especially Thomas E. Porter, *Myth and Modern American Drama* (Detroit, 1969).

39. A melodramatic scene that Lillian Hellman imitated in *The Little Foxes.*

40. Arthur H. Quinn, *A History of the American Drama from the Civil War to the Present Day* (New York, 1945), 258. Letter is dated February 10, 1932.

41. *Nine Plays by Eugene O'Neill* (New York, 1954), xxi.

42. Cargill, 67.

43. Clifford Leech, *O'Neill* (New York, 1963), 95.

44. Donald Gallup, Preface to *More Stately Mansions*, vii.

45. Doris Alexander, "Eugene O'Neill and Charles Lever," *Modern Drama* (February, 1963), 419–20.

46. Gelb, 871.

47. Ibid.

48. Robert Brustein, *Theatre of Revolt* (New York, 1965), 341.

49. Eric Bentley, *In Search of Theater* (New York, 1954), 229.

50. O'Neill first wrote the Jimmy Tomorrow story as a short story, "Tomorrow," published in *Seven Arts* (June, 1917), but that Jimmy, spurned in love and unable to succeed in sobriety, commits Parritt's suicide.

51. Timo Tiusanan, *O'Neill's Scenic Images* (Princeton, 1968), 273–77, provides illuminating comment on the chorus.

52. Gelb, 835.

53. Gelb, 841.

54. Cf. Doris Alexander, "The Missing Half of Hughie," *Tulane Drama Review* (Summer, 1967), 125–6.

55. Eric Bentley, *The Dramatic Event* (Boston, 1957), 33.

56. Ibid.

57. Cargill, 46.

3. *The Articulate Victims of* ARTHUR MILLER

1. Harold Clurman, *The Fervent Years* (New York, 1957), 140.

2. Cf. Bentley in *The Dramatic Event*, 32: "Assignment for a linguist: how much of O'Neill's dialect and slang comes from life, how much from stage tradition and personal hunch?"

3. Clurman, 107.

4. Mary McCarthy, *Sights and Spectacles* (New York, 1956), xxiv–xxv, and Leslie Fiedler, *Waiting for the End* (New York, 1964), 91. Miller has denied this, since his family did not speak Jewish, but Jewish inflections in English nevertheless permeate his plays. See Robert A. Martin, "The Creative Experience of Arthur Miller: An Interview," *Educational Theatre Journal* (October, 1969), 315.

5. Cf. Introduction to the *Collected Plays* (New York, 1957), and Martin interview.

6. George Steiner, "The Retreat from the Word," *Kenyon Review* (Spring, 1961), 211.

7. Leonard Moss, "Arthur Miller and the Common Man's Language," *Modern Drama* (May, 1964), 52–59.

8. Dennis Welland, *Arthur Miller* (New York, 1961), 64–65.

9. Introduction to the *Collected Plays*, 39.

10. Cf. Arthur Ganz, "The Silence of Arthur Miller," *Drama Survey* (Fall, 1963), 224–237 for a critique of Willy's dream and an analysis of his likeability.

11. Henry Popkin, "Arthur Miller: The Strange Encounter" in Alan Downer, ed., *American Drama and Its Critics* (Chicago, 1965), 234.

12. Biff and Happy, respectively, speak such flawed lines as: "It's a measly manner of existence." and "That's what I long for."

13. Philip Gelb, "Morality and Modern Drama: Arthur Miller," *Educational Theatre Journal* (October, 1958), 199.

14. Moss, 56–57.

15. Introduction to Bantam edition of *A View from the Bridge*, x.

16. Cf. Allen J. Koppenhauer, "*The Fall* and After: Albert Camus and Arthur Miller," *Modern Drama* (September, 1966), 206–209.

17. Moss, loc. cit.

18. "Arthur Miller" in *Writers at Work: The Paris Review and Interviews*, Third Series (New York, 1967), 223–224.

19. Ibid, 198.

4. *The Garrulous Grotesques of* TENNESSEE WILLIAMS

1. Kenneth Tynan *Tynan on Theatre*. (Baltimore, 1961), 141.

2. "Talk with the Playwright," *Newsweek* (March 23, 1959), 75.

3. Lester A. Beaurline, "*The Glass Menagerie*: from Story to Play," *Modern Drama* (September, 1965), 142–149. Mr. Beaurline kindly allowed me to examine his xerox of the Williams manuscript in the University of Virginia Library.

4. Williams' Introduction to New Directions edition, vii.

5. Cf. Thomas E. Porter, "The Passing of the Old South," in *Myth and Modern American Drama* (Detroit, 1969).

6. Jessica Tandy was chosen to play the role of Blanche in the New York production of *Streetcar* because she had played Miss Lucretia in the Los Angeles Actors' Laboratory production of *Portrait of a Madonna*.

7. Program for the Los Angeles Mark Taper Forum Theater production of *El Camino Real*, n.p.

8. Published in Toby Cole and Helen Chinoy, eds, *Directors on Directing* (New York, 1963). See, too, Harold Clurman, *Lies Like Truth* (New York, 1958), 72–80, for a view that Brando was acting "against" Kowalski as written.

9. Bernard Dukore, "The Cat Has Nine Lives," *Tulane Drama Review* (Fall, 1963), 95–100.

10. Cf. William Sacksteder, "The Three Cats," *Drama Survey* (Winter, 1966–67), 252–266, for a different viewpoint.

11. "Five Fiery Ladies," *Life* (February 3, 1961), 86.

12. Benjamin Nelson, *Tennessee Williams: The Man and His Work* (New York, 1961), 221.

13. Cf. Paul J. Hurley, "*Suddenly Last Summer* as a Morality Play," *Modern Drama* (February, 1966), 392–402.

14. Program for the Los Angeles Mark Taper Forum Theater production of *El Camino Real*, n.p.

5. *The Verbal Murders of* EDWARD ALBEE

1. Albee consistently uses . . . to indicate actors' pauses; in this chapter, therefore, such punctuation is his.

2. Gilbert Debusscher, *Edward Albee: Tradition and Renewal* (Brussels, 1967), 19–20.

3. Cf. Rose A. Zimbardo, "Symbolism and Naturalism in Edward Albee's *The Zoo Story,*" *Twentieth Century Literature* (April, 1962), 10–17.

4. Paul Witherington, "Language of Movement in Albee's *The Death of Bessie Smith,*" *Twentieth Century Literature* (July, 1967), 84–88.

5. Preface to Signet edition of *The American Dream*, 9.

6. *Writers at Work, Third Series* (New York, 1967), 331, gives Albee's account of the origin of his title—soap-writing on the mirror of a Greenwich Village bar—but he nevertheless exploits the resonances of the English novelist's name.

7. Ibid. for Albee's denial that the play was conceived with four men in mind. Though George calls Nick "toots," "love," and "baby"; though Martha says George is a "floozie," this is irrelevant to the sado-masochistic interdependence of George and Martha.

8. Ibid., 337.

9. A comparable *Walpurgisnacht* atmosphere is evoked in Book III of St. Augustine's *Confessions*, which describes his domicile in Carthage from his seventeenth to his nineteenth year. Not only lust, but play-acting and illusion are central to Augustine's experiences in Carthage.

10. Michael E. Rutenberg, *Edward Albee: Playwright in Protest* (New York, 1969), 232.

11. Thomas Porter, "Fun and Games in Suburbia," in *Myth in Modern American Drama* (Detroit, 1969), 225–47, presents an excellent critique of the play in this light.

12. Cf. Lee Baxandall, "The Theatre of Edward Albee," *Tulane Drama Review* (Summer, 1965), 19–40.

13. *New York Times* (December 27, 1964). Section 2, p. 1.

14. In the movie *All About Eve*, Marilyn Monroe remarks that it would be funny if the butler were named Butler.

15. Tiny Alice evidently means "tight anus" in homosexual argot, though Albee has denied having this "arcane information." In any case, *Tiny Alice* does not depend upon knowing the argot, as *Virginia Woolf* does not depend upon knowing St. Augustine's *Confessions*.

16. Rutenberg, 250.

17. Rutenberg, 214: "Instead of writing out the speeches one after the other, Albee has said he 'wrote each speech for each character' on a different page."

6. Less Than Novel

1. See Mary Otis Hivnor, "Adaptations and Adaptors," *Kenyon Review* (#2, 1968), 265–270, for an account of mid-century dramatizations of fiction.

2. B. R. McElderry Jr., "Thomas Wolfe: Dramatist," *Modern Drama* (May, 1963), 1–11.

3. Doris Abramson, *Negro Playwrights in the American Theatre, 1925–1959* (New York, 1969), 269.

4. Richard Schechner, "White on Black," *The Drama Review* #40, 27.

5. Parts of a first draft, called *Humanitas*, were published in *Partisan Review* (Summer, 1962), 313–349.

6. The specific historical events correspond to the infancy, not of 60-year-old Bummy, but of Bellow himself, who was 50 at the time of the play's completion.

7. *Lectures in America* (New York, 1935), p. 93.

8. Ibid., pp. 121–2.

9. Donald Sutherland, *Gertrude Stein* (New Haven, 1951), 104.

10. *Lectures in America*, p. 122.

11. Sutherland, 104.

12. In his introduction to *Last Operas and Plays*, Carl Van Vechten enumerates Stein's plays in other volumes: *A Play Without Roses: Portrait of Eugene Jolas* (1932) and *A Play A Lion for Max Jacob* (1932) in *Portraits and Prayers*; plays beginning with page 63 of *The Geographical History of America* (1936); *Daniel Webster: Eighteen in America: A Play* in *New Directions*, 1937; *In a Garden, Three Sisters Who Are Not Sisters*, and *Look and Long* in *First Reader* (1947). These are plays of slight importance. The 1970 *Selected Operas and Plays*, ed. John Malcolm Brinnin, contains nothing new.

13. *Last Operas and Plays* (New York, 1949), p. xviii.

14. Ibid., xv.

15. Preface to *Three Plays* (New York, 1958), xii.

16. Ibid., xi.

17. Ibid., ix.

18. "Some Thoughts on Playwriting" in Frenz, 60.

19. Francis Fergusson, *The Human Image in Dramatic Literature* (Garden City, 1957), 55–6.

20. Joseph Campbell and H. M. Robinson, "The Skin of Whose Teeth?"

Saturday Review of Literature (December 19, 1942), 3–4; (February 13, 1943), 16–18.

21. Frenz, 58.

22. "The Drunken Sisters," *Atlantic Monthly* (November, 1957), 92–5.

23. Travis Bogard, "The Comedy of Thornton Wilder" in *Modern Drama: Essays in Criticism*, ed. Travis Bogard and William Oliver (New York, 1965), 355–73; Robert Corrigan, "Thornton Wilder and the Tragic Sense of Life" in *Essays in the Modern Drama*, ed. Morris Freedman (Boston, 1964) 311–19; John Gassner, *Form and Idea in Modern Theater*, (New York, 1956), 142–43; Malcolm Goldstein, *The Art of Thornton Wilder* (Lincoln, 1965); Bernard Hewitt, "Thornton Wilder Says 'Yes'," *Tulane Drama Review* (December, 1959), 110–20.

24. *Atlantic Monthly* (July, 1952), 34.

25. Gelb, 870.

26. Preface, x.

7. Poets at Play

1. In spite of the accident of birth in St. Louis, Eliot wrote *English* verse drama; the pallor of his dramatic dialogue is an *English* drawing-room pallor. I do not wish to harp on English as Ionesco does in the opening scenic direction to his *Bald Soprano*, but I can find no reason to treat Eliot as an *American* poet dramatist.

2. For other accounts of American poets in the theater, see Donna Gerstenberger, "Verse Drama in America: 1916–1939," *Modern Drama* (December, 1963), 309–22; and Katherine Worth, "The Poets in the American Theatre" in John Russell Brown and Bernard Harris, eds., *American Theatre*, (London, 1967), 87–107.

3. Wallace Stevens, *Opus Posthumous* (New York, 1957), xxviii.

4. Frenz, 95.

5. "Preface to 'Judas,'" *New York Times* Drama Section, October 5, 1947.

6. *From the Modern Repertoire*, ed. Eric Bentley, Series Two (Bloomington, 1952), p. 487.

7. Denis Donoghue, *The Third Voice* (Princeton, 1959), 71. See Francis Fergusson in Cargill, 281–82, for praise of its avant-gardism.

8. Donoghue, 74.

9. MacLeish also wrote ten radio scripts, broadcast and published in 1944 as *The American Story*. They are not plays.

10. "The Three Voices of Poetry" in *On Poetry and Poets* (London, 1957), 89.

11. Cleanth Brooks, *Modern Poetry and the Tradition* (Chapel Hill, 1939), 120.

12. For a detailed critique, see Randall Jarrell, "The Fall of the City," *Sewanee Review* (April, 1943), 267–80.

13. *The Third Voice*, 203.

14. Ibid., 200.

15. Cf. MacLeish and Kazan, "The Staging of a Play," *Esquire* (May, 1959), 144–58.

16. Cf. Ralph E. Hone, ed., *Voice out of the Whirlwind* (San Francisco, 1960), 275–310.

17. "The Men Behind 'J.B.'," *Theatre Arts* (April, 1959), 62.

18. *The Classic Theatre*, ed. Eric Bentley (New York, 1961), 473. See Gerald Weales, *The Jumping-Off Place* (New York, 1969), 154–57, for a comparison of Racine and Lowell. Weales also writes admirably on *The Old Glory*, but my emphasis is different.

19. Note on the revised edition (1968).

20. Sidney Kaplan, "Herman Melville and the American National Sin" in *Images of the Negro in American Literature*, ed. Gross and Hardy (Chicago, 1966).

21. Of an eighteen-page combination of "Maypole" and "Endecott" came a play of fifty-odd pages; of "My Kinsman's" fifteen pages came a play of fifty-odd. Of the hundred or so pages of "Benito Cereno," Lowell made a play of a little over seventy pages.

22. Weales, 159.

23. Jones' plays are difficult to date, since many of them were written and performed several years before publication. I use the earliest dates available to me.

24. Robert Brustein, *Seasons of Discontent* (New York, 1967), 306.

25. Cf. Weales, 139.

26. Woodie King Jr., "Black Theatres: Present Condition," *The Drama Review* (Summer, 1968), 119.

27. Adam David Miller, It's a Long Way to St. Louis," *The Drama Review* (Summer, 1968), 150.

28. Larry Neal, "The Black Arts Movement," *The Drama Review* (Summer, 1968), 36–7.

29. Dates kindly supplied me by the author.

Selected Bibliography

American Drama

Abramson, Doris. *Negro Playwrights in the American Theatre, 1925–1959.* New York, 1969.

Belli, Angela. *Ancient Greek Myths and Modern Drama.* New York, 1969.

Bentley, Eric. *The Dramatic Event.* Boston, 1957.

———. *The Playwright as Thinker.* New York, 1946.

———. *In Search of a Theater.* New York, 1953.

Bigsby, C.W.E. *Confrontation and Commitment: A Study of Contemporary American Drama.* London, 1967.

Bogard, Travis and William Oliver, eds. *Modern Drama: Essays in Criticism.* New York, 1965.

Broussard, Louis. *American Drama: Contemporary Allegory from Eugene O'Neill to Tennessee Williams.* Norman, 1962.

Brown, John Russell and Bernard Harris, eds. *American Theatre.* Stratford-Upon-Avon Studies 10. London, 1967.

Brustein, Robert. *Seasons of Discontent: Dramatic Opinions 1959–1965.* New York, 1965.

Clurman, Harold. *The Fervent Years.* New York, 1957.

Cole, Toby and Helen Chinoy, eds. *Directors on Directing.* New York, 1963.

Dickinson, Hugh. *Myth on the Modern Stage.* Urbana, 1969.

Downer, Alan, ed. *American Drama and Its Critics: A Collection of Critical Essays.* Chicago, 1965.

———. ed. *The American Theater.* Washington, 1967.

———. *Fifty Years of American Drama.* Chicago, 1951.

———. *Recent American Drama.* Minneapolis, 1961.

Dusenbury, Winifred L. *The Theme of Loneliness in Modern American Drama.* Gainesville, 1960.

Fergusson, Francis. *The Human Image in Dramatic Literature.* Garden City, 1957.

Fiedler, Leslie. *Waiting For the End.* New York, 1964.

Freedman, Morris, ed. *Essays in Modern Drama.* Boston, 1964.

Frenz, Horst, ed. *American Playwrights on Drama.* New York, 1965.

Gagey, Edmond M. *Revolution in American Drama.* New York, 1947.

Gassner, John, ed. *Form and Idea in the Modern Theatre.* New York, 1956.

Gould, Jean. *Modern American Playwrights.* New York, 1966.

Hewitt, Barnard. *Theatre U.S.A., 1688 to 1957.* New York, 1959.

Hughes, Glenn. *A History of the American Theatre, 1700–1950.* New York, 1951.

Kernan, Alvin B., ed. *The Modern American Theater: A Collection of Critical Essays.* Englewood Cliffs, N.J., 1967.

Kinne, Wisner P. *George Pierce Baker and the American Theatre.* Cambridge, 1954.

Kourilsky, Françoise. *Le Théâtre aux Etats-Unis.* Paris, 1967.

Krutch, Joseph Wood. *The American Drama Since 1918: An Informal History,* rev. ed. New York, 1957.

Lewis, Allan. *American Plays and Playwrights of the Contemporary Theatre.* New York, 1965.

McCarthy, Mary. *Sights and Spectacles, 1937–1956.* New York, 1956.

Meserve, Walter, ed. *Discussions of American Drama.* Boston, 1965.

Porter, Thomas E. *Myth and Modern American Drama.* Detroit, 1969.

Quinn, Arthur H. *A History of the American Drama from the Civil War to the Present Day,* second ed. New York, 1945.

Simonson, Lee. *The Stage is Set.* New York, 1946.

Tynan, Kenneth. *Tynan on Theatre.* Baltimore, 1961.

Weales, Gerald. *American Drama Since World War II.* New York, 1962.

———. *The Jumping-Off Place: American Drama in the 1960's.* New York, 1969.

Eugene O'Neill

WORKS

The Plays of Eugene O'Neill, three volumes. New York, 1941.

Nine Plays. New York, 1932.

Hughie. New Haven, 1959.

Long Day's Journey Into Night. New Haven, 1956.

A Moon for the Misbegotten. New York, 1952.

More Stately Mansions. New Haven, 1964.

A Touch of the Poet. New Haven, 1957.

CRITICISM

Alexander, Doris. "Eugene O'Neill and Charles Lever." *Modern Drama* (Spring, 1963).

———. "The Missing Half of *Hughie.*" *Tulane Drama Review* (Summer, 1967).

———. "*Strange Interlude* and Schopenhauer." *American Literature* (May, 1953).

———. *The Tempering of Eugene O'Neill.* New York, 1962.

Biese, Y.M. *Aspects of Expression I: Eugene O'Neill's "Strange Interlude" and the Linguistic Presentation of the Interior Monologue.* Helsinki, 1963.

Blackburn, Clara. "Continental Influences on Eugene O'Neill's Expressionistic Dramas." *American Literature* (May, 1941).

Braem, Helmut M. *Eugene O'Neill.* Velber bei Hannover, 1965.

Brustein, Robert. *The Theatre of Revolt.* New York, 1965.

Cargill, Oscar, N. Bryllion Fagin and William J. Fisher, eds. *O'Neill and His Plays: Four Decades of Criticism.* New York, 1961.

Carpenter, Frederic Ives. *Eugene O'Neill.* New Haven, 1964.

Clark, Barrett H. *Eugene O'Neill: The Man and His Plays.* New York, 1947.

Clark, Marden J. "The Tragic Effect in *The Hairy Ape.*" *Modern Drama* (February, 1968).

Dorn, Knut. *Die Erlosungsthematik bei Eugene O'Neill: Eine Analyse der Strukturen im Spatwerk.* Heidelberg, 1968.

Driver, Tom F. "On the Last Plays of Eugene O'Neill." *Tulane Drama Review* (December, 1958).

Engel, Edwin A. *The Haunted Heroes of Eugene O'Neill.* Cambridge, 1953.

Falk, Doris V. *Eugene O'Neill and the Tragic Tension: An Interpretive Study of the Plays.* New Brunswick, 1958.

Falk, Signi. "Dialogue in the Plays of Eugene O'Neill." *Modern Drama* (December, 1960).

Fitzgerald, John J. "The Bitter Harvest of O'Neill's Projected Cycle." *The New England Quarterly* (September, 1967).

Gassner, John. *Eugene O'Neill.* Minneapolis, 1965.

———, ed. *O'Neill: A Collection of Critical Essays.* Englewood Cliffs, N.J., 1964.

Gelb, Arthur and Barbara. *O'Neill.* New York, 1962.

Kaucher, Dorothy J. *Modern Dramatic Structure.* The University of Missouri Studies, October, 1928.

Leech, Clifford. *O'Neill.* New York, 1963.

Long, Chester C. *The Role of Nemesis in the Structure of Selected Plays by Eugene O'Neill.* The Hague, 1968.

Miller, Jordan Y., ed. *Playwright's Progress: O'Neill and the Critics.* Chicago, 1965.

Pallette, Drew B. "O'Neill and the Comic Spirit." *Modern Drama* (December, 1960).

Raleigh, John Henry. *The Plays of Eugene O'Neill.* Carbondale, Ill., 1965.

———, ed. *Twentieth Century Interpretations of "The Iceman Cometh."* Englewood Cliffs, N.J., 1968.

Sheaffer, Louis. *O'Neill, Son and Playwright.* Boston, 1968.

Shawcross, John T. "The Road to Ruin: The Beginning of O'Neill's *Long Day's Journey.*" *Modern Drama* (December, 1960).

Stamm, Rudolf. " 'Faithful Realism': Eugene O'Neill and the Problem of Style." *English Studies* (August, 1959).

Tiusanen, Timo. *O'Neill's Scenic Images.* Princeton, 1968.

Valgemae, Mardi. "O'Neill and German Expressionism." *Modern Drama* (September, 1967).

Whitman, Robert F. "O'Neill's Search for a 'Language of the Theatre.' " *The Quarterly Journal of Speech* (April, 1960).

329

Winther, Sophus K. *Eugene O'Neill: A Critical Study.* New York, 1961.
Zeraffa, Michel. *O'Neill dramaturge.* Paris, 1956.

ARTHUR MILLER

WORKS

After the Fall. New York, 1964.
All My Sons. New York, 1947.
Collected Plays. New York, 1957.
The Crucible. New York, 1953.
Death of a Salesman. New York, 1949.
Incident at Vichy. New York, 1965.
The Misfits. Viking, 1961.
The Price. New York, 1968.
A View from the Bridge and *A Memory of Two Mondays; Two One-Act Plays.* New York, 1955.

CRITICISM

Corrigan, Robert W., ed. *Arthur Miller.* Englewood Cliffs, 1969.
Ganz, Arthur. "The Silence of Arthur Miller." *Drama Survey* (Fall, 1963).
————. "Arthur Miller: After the Silence." *Drama Survey* (Fall, 1964).
Hogan, Robert. *Arthur Miller.* Minneapolis, 1964.
Koppenhauer, Allen J. "*The Fall* and After: Albert Camus and Arthur Miller." *Modern Drama* (September, 1966).
Huftel, Sheila. *Arthur Miller: The Burning Glass.* New York, 1965.
Martin, Robert A. "The Creative Experience of Arthur Miller: An Interview." *Educational Theatre Journal* (October, 1969).
Moss, Leonard. *Arthur Miller.* New York, 1967.
————. "Arthur Miller and the Common Man's Language." *Modern Drama* (May, 1964).
Murray, Edward. *Arthur Miller, Dramatist.* New York, 1967.
Weales, Gerald, ed. *Death of a Salesman: Text and Criticism.* New York, 1967.
Welland, Dennis. *Arthur Miller.* New York, 1961.

TENNESSEE WILLIAMS

WORKS

Camino Real. New York, 1953.
Cat on a Hot Tin Roof. New York, 1955.
Dragon Country. New York, 1970.
The Eccentricities of a Nightingale and *Summer and Smoke.* New York, 1964.
The Glass Menagerie. New York, 1945. (Acting version published by Dramatists Play Service, 1945).

I Rise in Flames, Cried the Phoenix: A Play in One Act about D.H. Lawrence. New York, 1951.

Kingdom of Earth: The Seven Descents of Myrtle. New York, 1968.

The Milk Train Doesn't Stop Here Anymore. New York, 1964.

The Night of the Iguana. New York, 1961.

Orpheus Descending and *Battle of Angels.* New York, 1958.

Period of Adjustment. New York, 1960.

The Rose Tattoo. New York, 1951.

A Streetcar Named Desire. New York, 1947.

Suddenly Last Summer. New York, 1958.

Summer and Smoke. New York, 1948.

Sweet Bird of Youth. New York, 1957.

27 Wagons Full of Cotton. Norfolk, 1946.

CRITICISM

Anon. "A Talk with the Playwright." *Newsweek* (March 23, 1959).

Anon. "Five Fiery Ladies." *Life* (February 3, 1961).

Beaurline, Lester A. *"The Glass Menagerie:* From Story to Play." *Modern Drama* (September, 1965).

Donahue, Francis. *The Dramatic World of Tennessee Williams.* New York, 1964.

Dukore, Bernard. "The Cat Has Nine Lives." *Tulane Drama Review* (Fall, 1963).

Falk, Signi. *Tennessee Williams.* New York, 1962.

Fedder, Norman J. *The Influence of D.H. Lawrence on Tennessee Williams.* The Hague, 1966.

Hurley, Paul J. *"Suddenly Last Summer* as a Morality Play." *Modern Drama* (February, 1966).

Jackson, Esther M. *The Broken World of Tennessee Williams. Madison, 1965.*

Kazin, Alfred, ed. *Writers at Work: The Paris Review Interviews,* Third Series. New York, 1967.

Maxwell, Gilbert. *Tennessee Williams and Friends.* Cleveland, 1965.

Nelson, Benjamin. *Tennessee Williams: The Man and His Work.* New York, 1961.

Sacksteder, William. "The Three Cats." *Drama Survey* (Winter, 1966–7).

Tischler, Nancy Marie. *Tennessee Williams: Rebellious Puritan.* New York, 1961.

EDWARD ALBEE

WORKS

The American Dream. New York, 1960.

The Ballad of the Sad Cafe. New York, 1963. (Adaptation of Carson McCullers' novel.)

Bartleby. 1961. (Unpublished libretto adaptation of Herman Melville's short story.)

Box and *Quotations from Chairman Mao Tse-Tung.* New York, 1969.

The Death of Bessie Smith. New York, 1959.

A Delicate Balance. New York, 1966.
Everything in the Garden. New York, 1967. (Adaptation of Giles Cooper's play.)
Fam and Yam. New York, 1960.
Malcolm. New York, 1965.
The Sandbox. New York, 1959.
Tiny Alice. New York, 1965.
Who's Afraid of Virginia Woolf? New York, 1963.
The Zoo Story. New York, 1959.

CRITICISM

Amacher, Richard E. *Edward Albee.* New York, 1969.
Baxandall, Lee. "The Theatre of Edward Albee." *Tulane Drama Review* (Summer, 1965).
Debusscher, Gilbert. *Edward Albee: Tradition and Renewal.* Brussels, 1967.
Downer, Alan S., ed. "An Interview with Edward Albee," in *The American Theater.* Washington, 1967.
Flasch, Mrs. Harold A. "Games People Play in *Who's Afraid of Virginia Woolf?*" *Modern Drama* (December, 1967).
Gussow, Mel. "Albee: Odd Man In on Broadway." *Newsweek* (February 4, 1963).
Hilfer, Anthony Channell. "George and Martha: Sad, Sad, Sad," in *Seven Contemporary Authors,* edited by T.B. Whitbread. Austin, 1966.
Lyons, Charles R. "Two Projections of the Isolation of the Human Soul: Brecht's *Im Dickicht der Staedte* and Albee's *The Zoo Story.*" *Drama Survey* (Summer, 1965).
Miller, Jordan Y. "Myth and the American Dream: O'Neill to Albee." *Modern Drama* (September, 1964).
Oberg, Arthur K. "Edward Albee: His Language and Imagination." *Prairie Schooner* (Summer, 1966).
Rule, Margaret W. "An Edward Albee Bibliography." *Twentieth Century Literature* (April, 1968).
Rutenberg, Michael E. *Edward Albee: Playwright in Protest.* New York, 1969.
Witherington, Paul. "Language of Movement in Albee's *The Death of Bessie Smith.*" *Twentieth Century Literature* (July, 1967).
Zimbardo, Rose A. "Symbolism and Naturalism in Edward Albee's *The Zoo Story.*" *Twentieth Century Literature* (April, 1962).

NOVELISTS

WORKS

Baldwin, James. *Amen Corner.* New York, 1968.
———. *Blues for Mr. Charlie.* New York, 1964.
Barnes, Djuna. *A Book.* New York, 1923.
———. *Antiphon.* New York, 1958.

Bellow, Saul. *The Last Analysis.* New York, 1966.

————. *The Wrecker,* in *Seize The Day, with Three Short Stories and a Play.* New York, 1956.

Dos Passos, John. *Three Plays: The Garbage Man, Airways, Inc., and Fortune.* New York, 1934.

Dreiser, Theodore. *The Hand of the Potter.* New York, 1918.

————. *Plays of the Natural and Supernatural.* New York, 1916.

Fitzgerald, F. Scott. *The Vegetable: or, From President to Postman.* New York, 1923.

Harris, Mark. *Friedman and Son.* New York, 1963.

Hawkes, John. *The Innocent Party.* New York, 1966.

Hughes, Langston. *Five Plays.* Bloomington, 1968.

Stein, Gertrude. *Geography and Plays.* Boston, 1922.

————. *Operas and Plays.* Paris, 1932.

————. *Last Operas and Plays.* New York, 1949.

Wilder, Thornton. *The Angel That Troubled the Waters, and Other Plays.* New York, 1928.

————. *The Long Christmas Dinner, and Other Plays in One Act.* New York, 1931.

————. *The Merchant of Yonkers.* New York, 1939.

————. *The Skin of Our Teeth.* New York, 1942.

————. *Three Plays: Our Town, the Skin of Our Teeth, and The Matchmaker.* New York, 1961.

————. *Our Town.* New York, 1938.

Wolfe, Thomas. *Mannerhouse.* New York, 1948.

————. *Welcome to Our City. Esquire* (October, 1957).

CRITICISM

Campbell, Joseph and H.M. Robinson. "The Skin of Whose Teeth?" *Saturday Review of Literature* (December 19, 1942 and February 13, 1943).

Fergusson, Francis. *The Human Image in Dramatic Literature.* Garden City, 1957.

Goldstein, Malcolm. *The Art of Thornton Wilder.* Lincoln, 1965.

Hewitt, Barnard. "Thornton Wilder Says 'Yes.'" *Tulane Drama Review* (December, 1959).

Hivnor, Mary Otis. "Adaptation and Adaption." *Kenyon Review 2,* 1968.

McElderry, B.R., Jr. "Thomas Wolfe: Dramatist." *Modern Drama* (May, 1963).

Sutherland, Donald. *Gertrude Stein: A Biography of her Work.* New Haven, 1951.

POETS

WORKS

Cummings, E.E. *Three Plays and a Ballet.* New York, 1967.

Eberhart, Richard, *Collected Verse Plays.* Chapel Hill, 1962.

Ferlinghetti, Lawrence. *Routines.* New York, 1964.

————. *Unfair Arguments with Existence.* New York, 1963.

Frost, Robert. *A Masque of Reason* and *A Masque of Mercy*, in *Complete Poems of Robert Frost*. New York, 1949.
Goodman, Paul. *Stop-Light: Five Dance Poems and an Essay on the Noh*. Harrington Park, N.J., 1941.
———. *Three Plays: The Young Disciple, Faustina, and Jonah*. New York, 1965.
Koch, Kenneth. *Bertha and Other Plays*. New York, 1966.
Jeffers, Robinson. *At the Birth of an Age*, in *Solstice and Other Poems*. New York, 1935.
———. *At the Fall of an Age*, in *Give Your Heart to the Hawks and Other Poems*. New York, 1933.
———. *The Cretan Woman*, in *From the Modern Repertoire*, Series III, edited by Eric Bentley. Bloomington, 1956.
———. *Dear Judas*, in *Dear Judas and Other Poems*. New York, 1929.
———. *Medea*. New York, 1946.
———. *The Tower Beyond Tragedy*, in *The Roan Stallion, Tamar, and Other Poems*. New York, 1925.
Jones, LeRoi. *The Baptism* and *The Toilet*. New York, 1966.
———. *The Death of Malcolm X*, in *New Plays from the Black Theatre*. New York, 1969.
———. *Dutchman* and *The Slave*. New York, 1964.
———. *Four Black Revolutionary Plays*. New York, 1969.
———. *Home on the Range* and *Police*, in *The Drama Review*, No. 40.
Lowell, Robert. *The Old Glory*. New York, 1965.
MacLeish, Archibald. *Air-Raid: A Verse Play for Radio*. New York, 1938.
———. *The Fall of the City*. New York, 1937.
———. *Herakles*. Boston, 1967.
———. *JB*. Boston, 1958. [Acting version published in *Theatre Arts* (February, 1960)].
———. *The Music Crept by Me Upon the Waters*. Cambridge, 1953.
———. *Nobodaddy*. Cambridge, 1926.
———. *Panic: A Play in Verse*. Boston, 1935.
———. *The Trojan Horse*. Boston, 1952.
Nemerov, Howard. *Endor—A Drama in One Act*. New York, 1961.
———. *The Next Room of the Dream: Poems and Two Plays*. Chicago, 1962.
Owens, Rochelle. *Futz, and What Came After*. New York, 1968.
Rexroth, Kenneth. *Beyond the Mountains*. San Francisco, 1951.
Schevill, James. *The Black President and Other Plays*. Denver, 1965.
Stevens, Wallace. *Carlos of the Candles* and *Three Travelers Watch a Sunrise*, in *Opus Posthumous* edited by Samuel French Morse. New York, 1957.
Williams, William Carlos. *Many Loves and Other Plays*. New York, 1961.

CRITICISM
Anon. "The Men Behind *J.B.*" *Theatre Arts* (April, 1959).
Bentley, Eric. *him* in *From the Modern Repertoire*, Series II. Bloomington, 1949.
"Black Theatre"—special issue on Black theatre. *The Drama Review*, No. 40.
Brooks, Cleanth. *Modern Poetry and the Tradition*. Chapel Hill, 1939.

Donoghue, Denis. *The Third Voice: Modern British and American Verse Drama.* Princeton, 1959.

Eliot, T.S. *The Three Voices of Poetry.* London, 1953.

Gerstenberger, Donna. "Verse Drama in America: 1916—1939." *Modern Drama* (December, 1963).

Hone, Ralph E., ed. *The Voice Out of the Whirlwind: The Book of Job.* San Francisco, 1960.

Jarrell, Randall. *"The Fall of the City." Sewanee Review* (April, 1943).

Jeffers, Robinson. "Preface to *Judas."* *New York Times* drama section (October 5, 1947).

Kaplan, Sidney. "Herman Melville and the American National Sin," in *Images of the Negro in American Literature,* edited by Seymour L. Gross and John Edward Hardy. Chicago, 1966.

MacLeish, Archibald and Elia Kazan. "The Staging of a Play." *Esquire* (May, 1959).

Index

337